Troubleshooting Your Macintosh

· ·

THE COMPLETE, HANDS-ON GUIDE
TO UPGRADING AND MAINTAINING
YOUR MACINTOSH.

· ·

Douglass High

First published in 1992 in North America by M&T Publishing, Inc., 411 Borel Avenue, Suite 100, San Mateo, CA 94402, U.S.A., and co-published for sale outside North America by Prentice Hall International (UK) Limited, 66 Wood Lane End, Hemel Hempstead, Hertfordshire, HP2 4RG, England, a division of Simon & Schuster International Group.

© 1992 by M&T Publishing

British Library Cataloging-in-Publication Data and Library of Congress Cataloging-in-Publication Data are available from Prentice Hall International, (UK), Ltd.

High, Douglass

ISBN 0-13-928706-X

95 94 93 92   4 3 2 1

Developmental Editor: Tom Maremaa   **Cover Design:** Lauren Smith Design
Copy Editor: Barbara Conway   **Layout:** Stacy L. Evans

Troubleshooting Your Macintosh

To Laura, the woman I love, the woman I married,
the woman I want to spend the rest of my life with. This one's for you!

Contents

Acknowledgements

I would like to take this opportunity to thank the following individuals who have unselfishly given me their time, talent, and support in making this project a success.

To Tom Maremaa whom I owe a very special thanks. He went above and beyond the call of duty and he kept me on the right track, which is not so easy to do.

To Brenda McLaughlin, Sherri Morningstar, Tova Fliegel, and all of the other wonderful people at M&T books whom I've stressed out. Thank you for giving me this oppportunity to share my knowledge with others.

To my Mom and Dad for getting me my first computer, for always believing in me, and for being such good teachers. I love you both!

To my sisters Pam and Kay and the rest of my family, friends, and neighbors for being so encouraging and supportive.

Another special thanks my wife for proof reading the manuscript, over and over again, and for getting on my case whenever I deserved it.

To Edward "Bud" and Barbara Skudrna of Bay Area Services for their support and assistance.

To Dillon and Bodie Llamas, Robert Yount of MIT and his family for the reverse engineering talent.

To John Norman Huffington for the many hours he spent drafting work on our original Mac schematics.

To Tom Thompson of *Byte* magazine for the tech edit.

To my attorney and good friend John O. McManus and his lovely wife Rosemary.

To Johnathon and Iaan of Arrow Graphics.

To the thousands of students that have attended my hands-on training seminars. I hope you have learned as much from me as I have learned from you.

To the dedicated and hard working staff at High Tech Training International.

To my bassett hound Myrtle, who's always there to greet me when I get home.

And finally, I'd like to say one last thing to my mother. Hey Mom, I think you and that nun at Saint Edwards Elementary School might have been right about me after all.

Why This Book Is for You

Troubleshooting, upgrading, and maintaining your Macintosh computer is essential for the broad range of Macintosh professionals who work with their computers on a day-to-day basis and demand maximum performance from their systems. To achieve this performance and handle the job effectively requires an array of tools and techniques, along with a solid understanding of Macintosh fundamentals.

Troubleshooting Your Macintosh, written in a clear, easy-to-understand style, contains a wealth of valuable information on these tools and techniques. It takes you through the Macintosh operating system and teaches you how to diagnose and solve the most common hardware and software problems on your system. The approach is straightforward and hands-on, with a compendium of tips and problem-solving strategies. You don't, however, have to be a Macintosh technician to take advantage of the book's practical advice and tips.

This book covers a range of important topics, including how to decipher the various problem icons and error codes; adding memory (SIMMs); troubleshooting networks, SCSI, video, keyboard, and printing problems; tranferring data from your Mac to DOS and back; and finally, the issues of preventive maintenance and warranty services.

- If you're a *Macintosh service technician*, consultant, or support provider, you can use the troubleshooting sections to enhance your knowledge base and raise your level of expertise in isolating and fixing Macintosh problems.

- If you're a *Macintosh MIS manager* or *small business professional*, you'll find useful advice on how to maintain and extend the life your system.

1

- If you're *an everyday Macintosh user*, you'll find, in the question-and-answer format at the end of each chapter, solutions to the most frequently encountered problems with the compact, modular, and portable families of Macintosh computers.

Preface

On October 23, 1992, major newspaper headlines around the world read "Apple Computer Seizes IBM's PC Crown," signaling a shift in the balance of power between the two personal computer giants. After a decade-long reign atop the personal computer industry, IBM surrendered its throne to the industry pioneer Apple Computer, Inc., which shipped more than 2 million personal computers during the first three quarters of 1992—100,000 more than IBM shipped.

It's amazing when you think about it. There are millions of Macintosh computers around the world and not a single book (until this one) that adequately addresses the important hardware and software troubleshooting issues that the average Mac user confronts on a day-to-day basis. I should know: I've been troubleshooting computers for more than two-thirds of my life and have been teaching hands-on, component-level, troubleshooting, and repair seminars on a variety of computer platforms for over 10 years all over the world.

In 1987, I pioneered this type of training for Macintosh computers. The folks that come to these seminars are real people. The questions and problems that they have are very real. My job and duty to them is simply to answer their questions and to train them in all aspects of Macintosh troubleshooting and repair strategies. This training is further reinforced in our intensive hands-on labs and in our question and answer sessions.

My expertise and ability to answer their questions comes from three main sources.

First, from my own experience with problems that I've encountered working on the Mac. Additionally, I have a very heavy educational and practical background in electronic and systems engineering as well as computer science and information systems management. Second, from my experience as the former owner of a component-level repair facility that averaged over $1,250,000 each year in repair volume. We worked on every kind of computer and printer imaginable as well as toaster ovens. Since Apple would not sell us schematics to repair the Macs, we reverse engineered most of them, and made our own. I learned an incredible amount about the Macintosh during that project. I finally gained expertise from working and listening to people. Every year, thousands of people come to my company's training seminars. It doesn't matter which of our classes they come to–they all come with the objective of getting some of or all of the following questions answered:

> How does this thing work? What frequently goes wrong? What are the symptoms? Why does this happen? Can I fix this problem myself or should I send it out? How do I fix it? What hardware and software tools do I need and where do I get them? Where can I get spare parts? And finally, where can I turn for help?

I can't tell you how much I have learned by watching, listening to, and interacting with these people. There is one thing that I say to all of my classes: I may not know the answer to every one of your questions. But I can answer about 99% of them and if I run into one I don't know, I will tell you that I don't know, and I will make damn sure that I find out and get back to you with an answer. I don't know the answer to every Mac question nor do I claim to. That would be impossible.

The idea for this book came from real people with real problems. It is not a book on reverse engineering and schematic interpretation, digital circuit analysis, or surface mount component replacement on the Macintosh. That will be another book for me to write. However, it is a comprehensive troubleshooting guide for almost all of the Macintosh computer models. It is meant for both the average Mac user and the techie alike. It has been written so that it answers questions that I have heard thousands of these people ask. It has been written for you.

Here is a brief overview of each chapter.

Chapter 1 addresses the art and science of Mac troubleshooting and troubleshooting basics.

Chapter 2 focuses on troubleshooting the Macintosh operating system, operating system components, undesireable problems, and how to fix them.

Chapter 3 has two sections. The first section discusses the hardware and software "tools of the trade" which you need to work on your Mac. The second part of the chapter focuses on how to troubleshoot your Macintosh safely.

Chapter 4 is devoted to the Macintosh Power-on Self Test (P.O.S.T.), Startup Sequence, and how to decipher the various problem icons and error codes.

Chapter 5 addresses memory, upgrading and adding SIMMs, and common problems.

Chapter 6 focuses on the power supply, the Achilles' heel of the Macintosh. It also discusses specific testing and adjustment procedures that can be performed.

Chapter 7 covers floppy disk drives and common problems associated with them.

Chapter 8 discusses the Apple Desktop Bus (ADB) and problems with keyboards, trackballs, and mice.

Chapter 9 is a very technical chapter on video. It primarily focuses on color monitors, the different monitor types, sync input methods, resolution, scanning methods, RGB background, and drive controls. My favorite part of the chapter is the RGB color mixing chart. I use it all of the time when performing adjustments on my color monitor. This chapter also includes information on the compact Macs that use the built-in black and white video circuitry.

Chapter 10 is devoted to the common problems associated with SCSI and hard disk drives.

Chapter 11 focuses directly on networking issues and troubleshooting strategies.

Chapter 12 discusses file transfers and how to avoid and resolve problems that arise when going from Mac to DOS and back.

Chapter 13 is the big daddy of them all. It is a collection of common Macintosh problems and solutions to those problems. We have covered every model of the Macintosh from the Plus, SE, and Mac II right through the PowerBook models 100, 140, 145, and 170. This information is based on actual failure histories and proven repair strategies. It is designed to give you a place to start looking for the problem and includes a process-of-elimination method for resolving the problem down to module level. In some cases I have gone to component level, but for the most part I have tried to avoid it for two reasons. First, I could spend all day telling you about each and every chip on the logic board and how and why they fail. But the reality is that a large percentage of these chips are proprietary and are next to impossible to find.

Second, most of the logic boards utilize surface mount technology, which requires some serious soldering equipment and talent to master. It's not my style to give information that people really don't care about or can't actually use.

Chapter 14 addresses printers, printing problems, and sound troubleshooting strategies. Both dot-matrix and laser printers are discussed.

Chapter 15 discusses preventive maintenance and warranty services. Finally, the appendix section of the book has a listing of the names, addresses, and phone numbers of excellent vendors that you can turn to for services, parts, supplies, information, and help.

I would like to thank you for purchasing this book. I am sure that it will prove to be a wise investment in ensuring a long and happy life for your Macintosh. I hope you enjoy reading this book as much as I did writing it.

Douglass G. High, Jr.
October 1992

CHAPTER 1

The Art and Science of Troubleshooting Your Macintosh

Understanding how and why things go wrong can be child's play, or it can be painful. It all hinges on your ability to recognize, isolate, and correct problems. This book focuses on how to recognize and isolate common Macintosh problems as they apply to various models—from the compact Macintosh computers (Mac Plus, SE, SE/30, Classic, and Classic II) to the modular family (Mac II, IIx, IIcx, IIci, IIsi, LC, LC II, IIfx, Quadra 700, 900, and 950) and the PowerBook family (PowerBook 100, 140, 145, and 170). Each chapter gives you detailed information on problems and fixes.

Troubleshooting Basics

Macintosh troubleshooting is best described as an organized, methodical approach to resolving problems and failures that occur in Macintosh computers. Troubleshooting typically falls into two categories: hardware and software. The majority of problems in the Macintosh are related to software or the Macintosh operating system. The Mac, however, does have its fair share of hardware failures.

The first question you have to address is, How can you tell if the problem you have with your Macintosh computer is related to hardware or software? The answer is simple enough: You look for clues and use a process of elimination, just like a detective. In many cases your Macintosh will try to tell you what went wrong. It may give you some error chords, an "ID=" message, or maybe a Sad Mac face with a numeric error code. Sometimes your Mac may just blow up or do nothing at all.

Every situation in troubleshooting is unique. No two troubleshooting problems are exactly alike every time, but there is a pattern to various problems, and there are things you can get in the habit of looking for. What you'll have to do is rely on your senses of sight, sound, touch, and smell to answer questions like the following:

1. Do you see anything unusual about your Macintosh? For example, is the green light on at the front of your machine?
2. Do you hear any unusual noises, such as grinding, screeching, or popping? Do you hear nothing at all? Do you hear the fan inside the power supply spinning or the sound of the hard drive turning?
3. Does your machine feel excessively hot or cold? Is the humidity level high in the room? Environmental factors are frequently overlooked. Is anything loose to the touch?
4. Do you smell anything abnormal, such as smoke or burning? Obviously any smoke and burning aren't good signs.

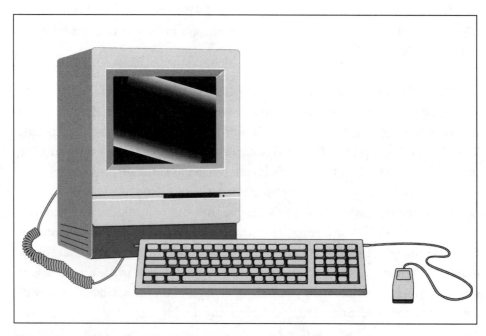

Figure 1-1. A video display problem in the compact Macintosh family

After you've let your senses feed you information, you may want to ask the following questions, just as you would if you were a detective on a case:

1. Rule out the obvious: Is the machine plugged in? Is the power on? Are all the cables properly connected? Is the brightness turned down on the monitor? Is the software corrupt?

2. Document the symptoms of the problem. What is your machine doing or not doing? When did the error occur and what were you doing prior to this? Were you upgrading the machine, and if so, what did you remove or install? Were you just working on the machine before it died?

3. Check if your computer has passed the power-on self test (P.O.S.T.). In other words, did it make a bong noise (which is good), or did it sound the death march (which is bad)? Did it make no noise at all? (That's not good either.) Did you get a happy Mac (which is good)? Did you get some other startup icon or error code? Or did you get nothing at all? (For the most part, this is not good either.) Once these determinations are made, you can begin to eliminate certain things.

Figure 1-2. A video display problem in the PowerBook family

For example, let's apply these rules to the following hypothetical situations:

1. Your machine passes P.O.S.T. (and makes the bong noise), then crashes with a question mark icon (?). This indicates the problem is most likely one of the following (listed in order of likelihood):

    a. External SCSI devices not turned on prior to Mac.
    b. Improper SCSI configuration (loose or bad cable, improper termination, SCSI ID, and so on).
    c. Bad or missing System Folder, Finder, or boot blocks, or hard disk driver. It could also be caused by a disk crash or a nasty virus.
    d. Hard disk drive unit failure.
    e. SCSI circuit failure on the logic board, for example, a bad fuse, or integrated circuit (IC) failure.

In this example the machine bonged, so you know that it passed P.O.S.T. This indicates a low probability of a major failure on the logic board or power supply. Obviously you have power. You documented a ? icon, which is defined as the inability of the Macintosh to locate the disk-based portion of the operating system. This is necessary to start up your Macintosh computer. Since you have a picture, it's not the video. So you begin by ruling out the obvious: cables and software.

As luck would have it, you discover it's a loose SCSI cable. Mission accomplished, problem resolved. This is an example of a nonfatal error, most of which are caused by a bad or improper configuration or by software.

If your machine hasn't passed P.O.S.T., you could have a serious problem. Let's say the machine does nothing at all. Again, you always rule out the obvious first: Is it plugged in? Is the power turned on? Are the cables properly attached? Is anything loose?

Let's say there is nothing obviously wrong. Do you smell anything burning? No. Do you hear any error chords or tones? No. Do you hear the fan running in the back? Yes. Is there anything displayed on the screen? Yes, zebra stripes or jail bars.

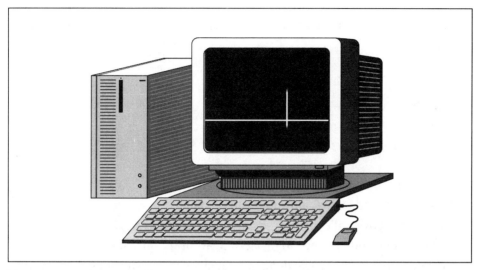

Figure 1-3. A video display problem in the modular Macintosh family

In this fatal situation the problem is most likely one of the following (in order of likelihood):

1. Malfunctioning power supply. Most Macs are woefully underpowered. (Chapter 6 discusses power supply problems in detail.) If the power supply doesn't deliver adequate levels of DC voltage to the logic board, this type of an error could result.
2. Severe SIMM (single inline memory module) failure on the logic board. This is not your average memory failure. This failure is so severe that P.O.S.T. was not properly executed, and it happens, for example, all of the time on the Mac SE. (See Chapter 5 on SIMMs and Memory Upgrades for more details.)
3. Some other severe problem on the logic board, such as a ROM or other critical circuit failure. This generally is not an easy, or chcap, problem to fix.

Fatal situations such as this can be analyzed by reading the appropriate chapters in this book for detailed and precise troubleshooting methodology.

The highest percentage of fatal Macintosh problems occur in the following components:

1. Power supply
2. SIMMs
3. Logic board
4. Other hardware

The highest-failure item is the first in the list, the next highest is second, and so on. As mentioned earlier, most Macintosh computers are underpowered, and if you don't have power, it's difficult for anything else to work properly.

It takes time and patience to master the art of troubleshooting. It would be impossible to list every possible thing that could go wrong with your Mac. The bottom line is that problems are going to be either hardware, software, or user error. Typically software and user error are the most common problems. Software is the easiest to remedy, while user error and hardware are the most difficult. You may need some hardware and software tools to help you in your troubleshooting quest (which is the focus of the Chapter 3).

Macintosh problems and failures are like getting a flat tire on your car or motorcycle. Nobody really wants to go through the hassle, but if it does happen, you want the problem fixed as quickly and inexpensively as possible. You might even learn something from the experience.

CHAPTER 2

Troubleshooting the Macintosh Operating System

When your Macintosh computer is powered up, several things happen. As electricity pours into the circuits like blood, the central processor starts running and begins executing startup routines in the ROMs. These startup routines first perform a series of hardware tests, and a brief memory test. If everything passes these tests, the Mac makes a single bong or chime noise that indicates successful completion of the hardware check. Next, the hardware is initialized and basic system management routines take over. These load the remainder of the Mac operating system code from your disk drive. This additional code is loaded into memory from a special file common to all Macintosh startup drives, which is called a System file. This System file resides in a special area on the disk called the System Folder. The System Folder also contains various application programs used to manage the computer. For example, there are applications used to set the time and date, set your mouse click rate, and select your network connection (that is, LocalTalk, which is a built-in network service, or Ethernet, or token ring connections if they are available).

The Mac's operating system (OS) is commonly referred to by its version number (System 6.0.x or System 7). For the Mac OS, many of its basic functions (in fact, hundreds of them) reside in ROM. The main advantage to having a significant portion of the Mac OS in ROM is that the code in ROM executes quickly. It doesn't have to be loaded from a hard drive into memory. Second, it lets Apple maintain complete control of the Mac OS because there are very specific laws against copying the ROM code. This eliminates clones of the Mac computer, since much of what makes the Mac a Mac resides in these ROMs. Finally, because these ROMs provide a rich set of graphic interface functions (such as creating windows or pull-down menus), programmers adhere to Apple's development guidelines, rather than a "roll their own" non-standard interface.

Desktop

The Desktop is the gray area of the screen (it can be in color, if you have a color system) where the icons rest. These icons correspond to hard disks, application programs, or data files. The Trash icon is a special icon, in that any file you place in is marked for elimination from your computer. As a desk in your home is a place where you can work, so is a Mac Desktop a place you can work on your Mac. This Desktop is maintained by a special, invisible file called the Desktop file. (With System 7, several invisible files are used to maintain a Desktop database, that performs the same function.) This Desktop file can easily be damaged by turning the Macintosh off either in the middle of an application program or by powering down the Macintosh before letting it perform necessary housekeeping through use of the Shut Down command. Since the Mac relies heavily on information in this file to draw

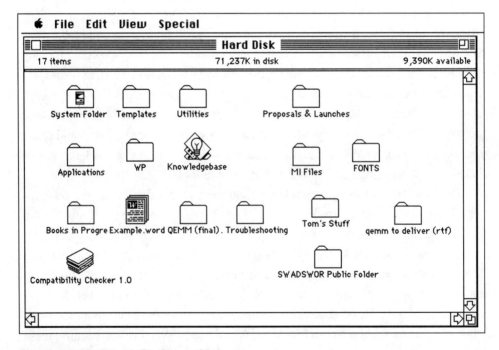

Figure 2-1. Macintosh Desktop with icons

the Desktop you see on the screen, a damaged Desktop file often confuses the OS to no end. This results in poor system performance or the failure of the machine to boot at all. For this reason, the Desktop file is also a favorite target of unscrupulous individuals that write virus programs.

Minor Desktop file damage can be repaired easily by holding down the Command and Option keys while the Mac is booting up or by using good utility software such as the Norton Utilities for the Macintosh from Symantec Corp. It is also a good idea to have a quality virus utility program, like SAM, Virex, or Disinfectant, loaded as well.

Finder

The Finder is a special application program that is started (or "launched," in Mac parlance) automatically when the computer starts. It acts as the Mac's disk and file management system. Don't confuse the Finder with the Mac OS: the Finder is a shell that displays the Desktop and its files and hard drives. It uses the Mac OS to do this, and it helps you visually manage your Mac's files and resources. To view general information about your computer, it's only necessary to enter the Apple menu and choose About the Finder (About this Macintosh, under System 7). The machine will display something like this:

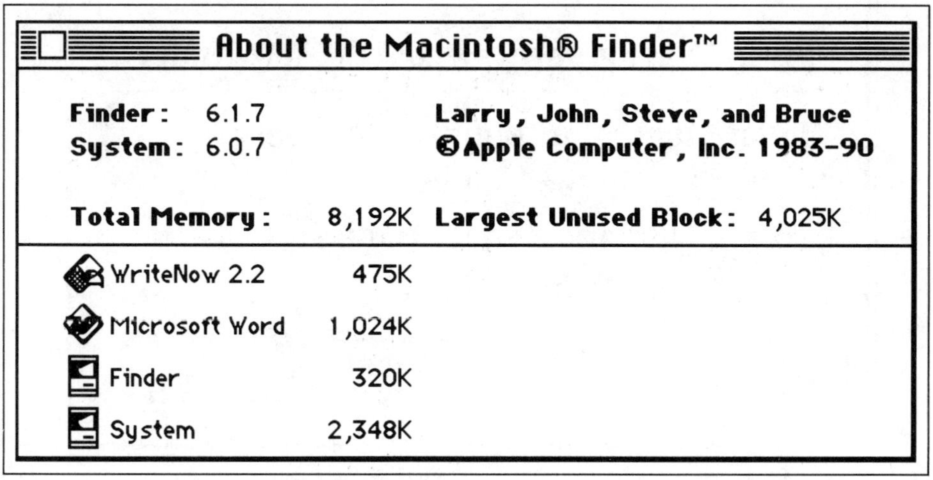

```
≣▯▭▭▭▭▭ About the Macintosh® Finder™ ▭▭▭▭▭

  Finder:  6.1.7              Larry, John, Steve, and Bruce
  System:  6.0.7              ®Apple Computer, Inc. 1983-90

  Total Memory:    8,192K  Largest Unused Block:  4,025K

  ◈ WriteNow 2.2         475K
  ◈ Microsoft Word     1,024K
  ▣ Finder               320K
  ▣ System             2,348K
```

Figure 2-2. About the Macintosh Finder

Note that this Finder screen displays a great deal of valuable information, such as OS version, Finder version, total installed memory, and how this memory is divided between the operating system and the Finder. This can be useful when upgrading the memory or OS in a Mac and can serve as a valuable aid in troubleshooting your Mac.

MultiFinder or Process Manager

MultiFinder is a sophisticated application program that enhances the Finder by permitting multiple applications to run. In this mode, MultiFinder serves as a task switcher, transferring the thread of execution among the various applications loaded in memory. Many people erroneously believe that the MultiFinder is a Finder substitute, but in fact the Finder still continues to serve as the file manager, and still maintains the Desktop display. Under System 6.0.x, you have your choice of operating the Mac with or without MultiFinder. In 7.x or greater, this MultiFinder environment is no longer an option but a permanent feature. Now called the Process Manager, it has been improved to be about as close to true multitasking as one can

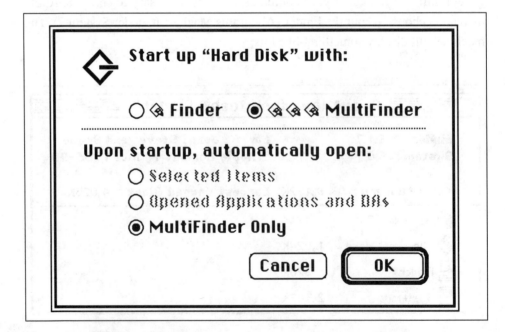

Figure 2-3. MultiFinder and Finder option box

get without a time-sliced OS kernel. It's important to note that although the MultiFinder/Process Manager is a powerful feature of the Mac OS, there are many problems and traps users can fall into with it. I will address these and other issues later on in this book.

> **Note:** People erroneously believe that the MultiFinder is a Finder replace-ment, because the Mac Set Startup Screen, confuses some users.

Chooser

The Chooser is a special program that lets you choose (hence the name) vari-ous peripheral devices with which to work. The most common of these devices are printers. Before the Chooser can recognize these devices, a driver program (some-times called a device driver) that communicates with the devices must be present in the System Folder. If this driver isn't present, then you can't select a device. Once the device drivers are properly loaded into the System Folder, they appear as

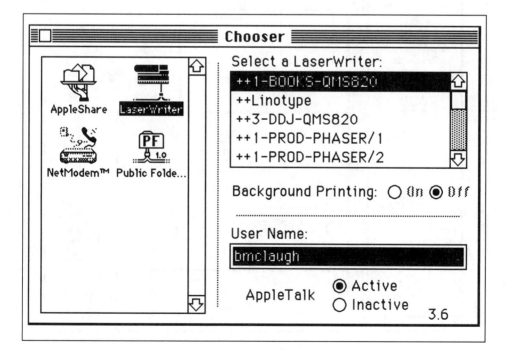

Figure 2-4. Chooser

icons in the Chooser's window. These drivers usually come from the factory with the device. If not, contact whoever you bought it from, or the customer service department of the product manufacturer. Under System 6.0.x, the Chooser is a Desk Accessory (DA); under System 7, like other DAs, it now is a small, stand-alone application located in the Apple Menu Items folder.

The general control panel lets you control several system settings, such as time and date, speaker volume, color selections, mouse speed, RAM cache, Desktop pattern, blinking rates, keyboard, and special sound effects. Some of these settings are stored on the startup disk while many others are stored in a specific area of memory called Parameter RAM (PRAM). A special chip on the main logic board called the Real Time Clock chip contains typically 256 bytes of memory (the amount depends upon the type of Macintosh) specifically reserved for PRAM. The values

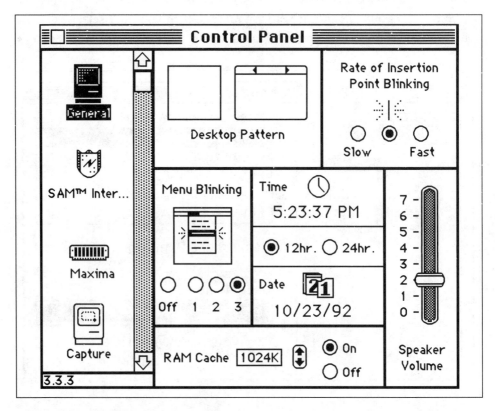

Figure 2-5. Typical control panel screen

and settings stored here are continuously powered by a battery when the machine is off, so that these settings are not lost. Under System 6.0.x, the general control panel and other control panels are special modules that are activated and managed by a DA called the control panel. With System 7, these modules behave as small stand-alone applications and reside in a folder called control panels.

We have not covered all of the control panels or DAs provided by the Mac OS, nor the army of third-party versions available. However, for our purposes, I have restricted attention to those that will directly impact your trouble-shooting efforts.

In summary, the Mac OS is a unique and powerful operating system that maintains user friendliness through the use of a graphic user interface (GUI). Unlike DOS or other literal OS's (such as UNIX), a good portion of the Mac OS resides in ROM while the remainder is disk resident. Both pieces work together to form this graphical operating system. The Mac OS is enhanced by several specialized application programs, especially the Finder.

The real beauty of all this is that Apple Computer, Inc. maintains complete control over the Mac OS. This forces developers to adhere to Macintosh standards. For this reason, most Macintosh applications look and feel alike. Therefore, if you have used one such application, you have a head start on learning another. That's why the Macintosh is a computer that most people can not only use easily, but also like to use.

This operating system is both very powerful and complex. It's a master control program that basically acts as a traffic cop, overseeing such functions as data and task management.

Data and Task Management

The Data Management function tracks where data resides on the disk. This is necessary because application programs (software) such as Microsoft Word, Excel, and PageMaker really don't know where the data is stored or how to retrieve it. This intelligence is an integral part of the OS and device driver routines (access method). When an application program needs data, a request is sent to the OS. The OS will then find and deliver the required data to the program. When the program is prepared to generate output, the OS will move the data from the application program to either storage (typically disk) or to an output device such as a monitor or printer.

The Task Management function permits the concurrent operation (multitasking) of one or more application programs or tasks. In the OS version 6.x, this is achieved by activating the MultiFinder, which gives the illusion of multitasking through a technique called task switching. Task switching permits several applications to be opened or launched, but the machine can typically only work with one at any given time. The user has to switch between the tasks. Under System 7.x the MultiFinder has been improved (among other things) and task switching has been replaced by cooperative multitasking (CMT).

This environment is about as close to true multitasking as Apple has ever gotten. Under CMT each application program takes its turn with the CPU, then passes control to the next one, rather than forcing the user to switch back and forth, like passing bread at the table. This technique permits the user to have many applications running in the background (behind the scenes), while they are working on something else, which increases overall productivity. The only problem with CMT is that each application decides when it's going to "pass the bread basket," which means some programs may be hogs while others are more gracious.

The relationship between the OS, hardware, applications software and user productivity is an important one. This is a common boundary where these elements come together. When there is a problem in this environment, one or more of the elements is adversely affected, which typically results in undesirable problems such as:

A. Question Mark Icons
B. Sad Mac Icons with an 0F exception code
C. System bombs and crashes
D. Dialog boxes with "Id=" error codes
E. Machine freezing or locking up
F. User beating the machine to death

It would be impossible for anyone to document the causes, symptoms, and remedies of all Macintosh system errors—for many reasons. First, the Macintosh has a very limited internal error reporting capability. The sheer complexity of this machine often overwhelms this mechanism, rendering many of the generated error codes and messages useless. Second, many of the error codes and definitions aren't very descriptive, which makes problem isolation difficult. Finally, there are millions of things that can go wrong in this environment: hardware failures, software incompatibilities, user error, improper OS configuration and installation, corrupt or missing OS files, bugs in the OS, incorrect OS revision level, virus attacks, INIT and heap problems.

This chapter explains how to recognize, remedy, and prevent many of the most common and annoying OS-related failures.

Where the Trouble Begins

Remember the old saying, "A chain is only as strong as its weakest link?" This can be applied to almost anything in life, especially computers. We've seen how important the OS is to the Mac's relationship with hardware, software, and, of course, the user. With this in mind, it's not surprising that the overwhelming majority of Mac-related troubles, such as system crashes, lock-ups, bombs, and error message codes are OS-related. But where should you begin?

OS-related problems take many shapes and forms. They can look like hardware error messages such as Sad Mac startup icons with hex codes, "Id=01, Bus Error," or "Id=25, Out of Memory" to name just a few. OS errors can also produce what would seem to be software (program) errors such as: "Id=41, cannot load the Finder," "Id=-37, Bad file name," "System bombs," and even the question mark startup icon. Then again, the computer might just lock up without any warning or error message.

To the novice (and even the expert) some of these errors, such as the "Id=01, Bus error," are common and frightening, especially when you call an Apple authorized dealer and are told, "Oh, you should never get that error." But you did get this error. On the flip side, your serious techie types get excited and say, "Alright we have a bus error. Let's get out the soldering gear and remove our Nubus slots." Tempting but not necessary. In this case an "Id=01, Bus error" simply means that the computer has tried to access memory that does not exist. In other words, the machine was looking for memory address references beyond what is actually installed in it. These references are indeed out of bounds, and in theory if you attempt to access one byte beyond the end of memory, you are really accessing the first byte in memory. This is a roll-over effect. Theoretically, you really should not get this error, which means that the Mac is probably reporting the wrong system problem.

Most of the time this error and many other "Id=" errors are either OS file or application program malfunctions. For example, I recently got this particular error—"Id=01, Bus error"—after finding several fonts in my System Folder that had become corrupt. In addition to the error, I also got a "Math co-processor not found" error. I was having a really bad day. How did I get rid this problem? I followed the Five Step Fix.

The Five Step Fix

This procedure is a useful first strike against some of the most common and annoying system problems mentioned in this chapter. It's also a good place to start when you don't have a clue as to what's going on. You may want to document (write down) any symptoms, error messages, everything that you tried, and the results. Technical support hotlines love it when users are prepared to discuss the problem and possible solutions intelligently. The Five Step Fix can actually be done in any order you like. However, I prefer the methodical approach (that is, the process of elimination) to troubleshooting. The Five Step Fix involves the following:

1. Check the Mac for viruses
2. Check the System software revision levels
3. Check the application software revision levels
4. Reload the application software
5. Reload the System software

Let's take a closer look!

Step 1: Check the Mac for viruses

First boot (startup) your Mac with a known good copy of the Macintosh operating system (systems diskette) in the floppy disk drive. Make sure that the write-protect feature is enabled. This ensures that if a virus is present, your good disk won't be infected.

If the machine wasn't booting previously and it boots from this diskette, you have evidence that the problem is most likely System related and that you may need to reload the System software. However, before you do this make certain that you check the machine for viruses with virus eradication software, such as SAM, Virex, or Disinfectant.

Many viruses search out, damage, and/or destroy important System related files such as the Desktop, Finder, and others, which can cause the Mac to misbehave. If you find a virus, it's a good idea to trash your old OS (System) and rein-stall the System from scratch. You can also use the Norton Utilities or Mac Tools to repair the damage. I prefer to start from scratch and lay a good foundation. Pre-tend that you are building a house. If the foundation that your house rests on is weak, who knows what will happen to it as the years go by? It may fall down. So it is with the Mac. If your operating system foundation is weak or questionable, the machine will be prone to crashes.

Step 2: Check the system software revision levels

As a rule of thumb, it's a good idea to use the more current releases of the Macintosh operating system that Apple deems suitable for the Mac that you own. From time to time, Apple makes fixes and feature enhancements or additions to the System software that you might need or would like to use. When in doubt, call Apple directly or an authorized Apple dealer and just ask. Apple is pretty good at disseminating System revision and compatibility information. For instance, I have recently upgraded one of my Mac SEs from version 6.04 to 6.08. Now, because of this upgrade, my machine is able to share printers on a network with users of System 7.x.

Unless there is some life-saving fix involved, don't run out and get the latest, greatest, and hot-off-the-presses operating system release. It may have bugs or com-patibility problems with your particular machine. These quirks might not surface for weeks after the release of that version and every version of System software does not necessarily work on all Macintosh computers. Case in point: System 7.x. If you try to install System 7.x on a 512KE Mac or a Mac Plus, it won't work, since these machines work best with System 3.x through 6.x. (However, I wouldn't use anything less than 6.0.5 these days, even on these older Macs.)

You can install System 7.x on a Mac SE or a Mac Classic and it will work, but you won't be able to take advantage of its many powerful features, including vir-tual memory and 32-bit addressing. System 7.x is also a memory hog and needs 2 to 2.5 MB to do its thing. The Mac SE and Classic have ROM limitations that restrict them to 4 MB of addressable memory. Four MB total addressable memory (assuming that you have this much physically installed in the machine), minus the 2 to 2.5 MB needed by System 7.x, leaves you with about 1.5 to 2 MB or so for your application programs, which isn't a lot. And you would like to run some appli-

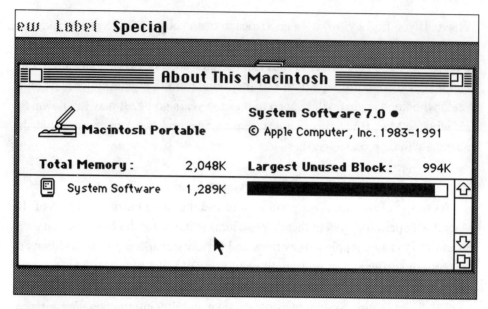

Figure 2-6. About the Finder

cation programs with your operating system, wouldn't you? In this example, you would be better off staying on 6.0.5 or 6.0.8. and not going to System 7.x.

On the other side of the coin, System 7.x is a decent upgrade path for the the 32-bit Macs, such as the Mac SE/30 and Mac II family, except the original Mac II model, which needs a PMMU (paged memory management unit) chip upgrade. With most new operating system releases, there are serious compatibility issues (both hardware, software, and networking) that you should be aware of. That's why you need to keep informed of new problems and fixes (like the System 7.x Tune-Up) by watching what is being written in trade publications such as *Byte, MacUser, Macworld,* and *MacWeek.*

Newer machines like the IIsi, Macintosh Quadra 700, 900, and 950, are now shipping with 7.x from the factory. If you can't or just don't want to use System 7.x with these machines, you should use nothing less than 6.0.7 or 6.0.8. Failure to adhere to this rule results in unpredictable machine behavior, which is not what you want or need.

Let's suppose that you have a Mac Plus running System 3.0, or a Mac SE running 4.2, or perhaps a Mac II running 6.04. How do you really know which revision of the system software is right for you? Well, there is a very easy rule to follow:

There is no life before six (System software revision 6.0.x). More specifically, on any unit from the Mac Plus on up: There is no life before 6.0.5. I am not saying that all earlier versions are bad; they are just outdated and don't have all the nice features of the newer releases, such as enhanced color capability for Mac IIs, printing improvements, and other new accessory and utility programs. The three versions that I prefer are 6.0.5, 6.0.8, System 7, and the System 7 Tune-Up. I don't care for anything prior to 6.0.5 (especially 6.0.4), and I have had some real strange printing problems with 6.0.7. When in doubt, go for version 6.0.5 on the older models and 6.0.8 on the newer machines.

What version do I have?

So far, we've reviewed the importance of the Macintosh operating system software. We've also seen that there are many versions of this software available. It's natural for one to wonder, "How do I know which version I have?" There are at least three ways to determine this. First, you can utilize the About the Finder function from the Apple menu (located in the upper left-hand of your Mac screen) when either Finder or MultiFinder are active. A window will appear that lists your version number.

This figure displays the following information:

A. Finder version *
B. System version *
C. Total installed memory recognized by the machine
D. Available memory
E. Application heap (area of memory)
F. System heap (area of memory)

Note: In version 6.x, the first number or Finder and System must agree. For instance, Finder 6.1.7 and System 6.0.7 both begin with six. This is good. What would not be good would be Finder 5.4 and System 6.0.7. This type of situation happens when you have a whole bunch of older copies of software floating around and one of the disks has an older version of either the System or Finder. When you copied this version to your startup disk (usually a hard disk) the correct version of either the System, Finder, or both were overwritten.

The second way to display either the System or Finder revisions is also very easy. Go into your System Folder, select (click) the file called System and choose the Get Info option from the File menu. The following information will be displayed:

    A. Size of the System file
    B. The disk where this file resides
    C. Creation date
    D. Modification date
    E. OS version

Repeat this process for the Finder file and the following information should be displayed:

    A. Size of the Finder
    B. The disk where this file resides
    C. Creation date
    D. Modification date
    E. OS version
    F. Suggested memory size*
    G. Application memory size*

*These items tell you the size of the memory partition that will be allocated for this file. If you are going to work with the MultiFinder, it is a good idea to increase the Application memory size or the Finder memory partition to 256K. You can also increase the Application Memory Size of any application program the same way, but you will have to experiment with how much to increase it. I have remedied many "Out of Memory errors" under MultiFinder through this technique.

The final and most accurate way to determine which version of the System Software is installed on your machine is accomplished by using a special program called ResEdit. This method will positively identify the version with which you are working. The procedure is as follows:

    1. Launch ResEdit
    2. Open the System file

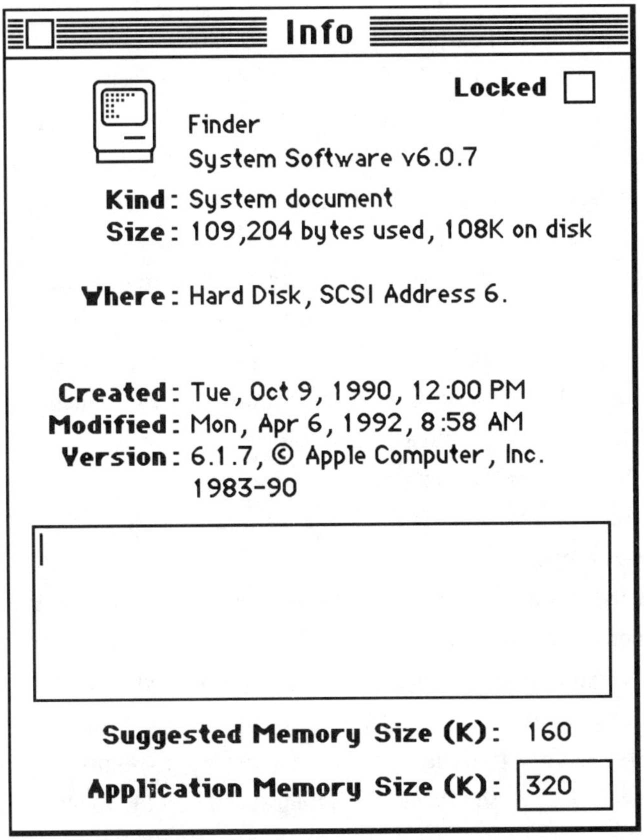

```
┌─────────────────────────────────────────────────────────┐
│  ┌───────────────────────────────────────────────────┐  │
│  │ ≡□≡════════════════ Info ════════════════         │  │
│  │                                    Locked  □       │  │
│  │    ┌─────┐                                          │  │
│  │    │ ▓▓▓ │   Finder                                 │  │
│  │    │     │   System Software v6.0.7                 │  │
│  │    └─────┘                                          │  │
│  │     Kind : System document                         │  │
│  │     Size : 109,204 bytes used, 108K on disk        │  │
│  │                                                    │  │
│  │   Where : Hard Disk, SCSI Address 6.               │  │
│  │                                                    │  │
│  │                                                    │  │
│  │   Created : Tue, Oct 9, 1990, 12:00 PM             │  │
│  │  Modified : Mon, Apr 6, 1992, 8:58 AM              │  │
│  │   Version : 6.1.7, © Apple Computer, Inc.          │  │
│  │             1983–90                                │  │
│  │  ┌──────────────────────────────────────────────┐ │  │
│  │  │ |                                            │ │  │
│  │  │                                              │ │  │
│  │  │                                              │ │  │
│  │  └──────────────────────────────────────────────┘ │  │
│  │     Suggested Memory Size (K) :  160               │  │
│  │    Application Memory Size (K) : ┌─────┐           │  │
│  │                                  │ 320 │           │  │
│  │                                  └─────┘           │  │
│  └───────────────────────────────────────────────────┘  │
└─────────────────────────────────────────────────────────┘
```

Figure 2-7. Finder using Get Info

3. Open the item called STR(s) from System
4. Open STR Id=0

When you open STR Id=0 it will contain the correct version number. This approach is more accurate than the Get Info approach because the creation date of a file is not changed when the System is updated by the Installer program. This means that you can not be certain whether or not the System has been updated, unless you use ResEdit.

Steps 3 and 4: Check revisions and reload application software

If you're still having trouble at this point, especially when trying to launch a particular program, you may have a corrupt or incompatible application program. The latter is quite simple to determine. If the application has been working fine for a long time, and then it bombs, it's probably corrupt, not incompatible. If you recently upgraded your operating system (that is, to 7.x) and the program bombed, the application is most likely incompatible with the version of the System that you've just installed. The keys to good troubleshooting are deductive reasoning and the process of elimination. Has anything in the System been updated or changed recently, such as the operating system or memory configuration? Have you added or removed any files (new application programs or INITs) recently? When did this problem occur? Can you duplicate this problem again on the suspect machine? Can you duplicate this problem on a different machine? Does this problem only happen when you run a particular file? Is anything missing? (The Mac sometimes makes things go bye-bye.)

Getting the version of an application is very easy, assuming that it will load and run. When most applications are launched (for example, Microsoft Word), they display the version of the program that is being loaded. You can also look at the label on the original program disks to make absolutely sure. If the application won't launch (run), you have to punt! That is, trash the original application and reload it. Be sure that you follow the installation instructions in the manual (I hope that you kept it). After you have completed this process, check to see if it works. If it does, good show! If not, proceed to step 5.

Step 5: Reload the system software

More than likely, you've arrived at this point because all else has failed. Reloading the system software is a very simple thing to do, but you would be very surprised how important this simple thing gets overlooked. In fact, most Mac-related problems that people call me about are operating system/System Folder (where the System resides) related. Most of the time the solution is very simple—punt! (That is, reload the operating system.)

Reloading System 6.0.x

Before you reload your operating system (6.0.x), you should backup (copy) the contents of your System Folder to a diskette. The reason for this is simple; many of our system folders are polluted with oodles and oodles of neat little programs and fonts that we love and will want back. However, to do this properly you'll need to gather the following operating system diskettes:

1. Macintosh System Tools
2. Macintosh Printing Tools
3. Macintosh Utilities Disk 1
4. Macintosh Utilities Disk 2

Then follow these procedures:

1. Boot your Macintosh as you normally would.
2. Backup your old System Folder files to a diskette.
3. Select the Finder's Find File command under the Apple menu (upper left-hand corner of the screen). This utility program will ask you what you wish to search for. Type: System Folder <then hit the RETURN key>. The machine will then display all of the System Folders on your Mac. You should have only one. If more than your main System Folder is displayed, you'll have to search out and trash each of these additional folders. Find File will tell you where they are hiding, just click on each System Folder in the window (one at a time) and write down the location. Please keep in mind that more than one System Folder is unacceptable. The Mac might not know which one to use, get confused, and that could be the underlying cause of all of your problems. How do you get more than one System Folder on your hard drive? Very easily, you or one of your friends or kids might have inadvertently copied a diskette (like a game or some shareware) onto the hard drive that had its own System Folder. It may have even been a real old version that doesn't work right with your machine.
4. Next run the Finder's Shutdown command and turn the Mac off.
5. Locate the Macintosh System Tools diskette and insert it into the floppy disk drive.

6. Turn the Macintosh on and let it boot from the System Tools diskette.

7. Open your hard drive icon. Locate your old System Folder and trash everything inside it that you can, especially the old standard Apple system software files. Or simply rename the folder something other than System Folder (like Old Sys). The standard Apple software system files for Version 6.0x are:

Access Privileges	Keyboard
Appletalk	Laser Prep
Appletalk Imagewriter	Laserwriter
Appleshare	LQ Appletalk Imagewriter
Backgrounder	LQ Imagewriter
Battery	MacroMaker
Brightness	Monitors
Clipboard File	Map
CloseView	Mouse
Color	MultiFinder
DA Handler	Personal Laserwriter
Easy Access	PrintMonitor
Finder	Responder
Finder Startup	Scrapboard File
Font/DA Mover	Sound
General	Startup Device
ImageWriter	System
Key Layout	32-bit QuickDraw

8. Select and open the System Tools Diskette icon.

9. Select and open the Setup Folder.

10. Select and open the Installer. Follow the instructions as Installer will walk you through the process. If you get confused, this process is explained in greater detail in the Macintosh System Software User's Guide that came with your unit.

11. After Installing the System Software, quit from the Installer and shut-down your machine.

12. Restart your machine to verify that the install worked. If not go back to step 5.

13. If everything is OK so far, you can start putting your old stuff (INITs, for example, that you backed up, not the old operating system files) back into your System Folder. I recommend putting them in one at a time, each time verifying whether or not the original problem came back. It's possible that one of your programs hammered the System.

14. If the problem still hasn't disappeared, it may be necessary for you to use a powerful software utility like Norton or MacTools Deluxe (See Chapter 3). If these still don't help, you may need to back up your data and run a hardware diagnostic (like Mac Ekg or Disk Manager Mac) on your hard drive. It's possible that you have to reformat the disk drive and reload everything from scratch.

Reloading System 7.0.x

Reinstalling System 7.0.x is as simple as reinstalling System 6.0.x. The same considerations apply. You'll need to gather the disks (seven or eight of them depending on which release of System 7 you have), back up your good stuff and trash the suspect System Folder. Then restart the Macintosh with the Install 1 Diskette in your floppy drive and follow the installation instructions. It's a very simple and automated process. If you get lost, consult your System 7.0.x User's Guide.

This completes the Five Step Fix. In nine out of 10 cases, these procedures will remedy the problem. If you've followed the Five Step Fix and are still having trouble, you may be experiencing one or more of the following situations:

1. Intermittent hardware failure (Cause: power, memory, SCSI logic, or a bad/picky hard disk drive).

2. A hard disk that has corrupt volume or other drive information. (Solution: Norton Utilities or Mac Tools Deluxe may be required.)

3. Your drive may need to be reformatted and partitioned. You can use the Apple HD setup, Disk Manager Mac, Silver Lining, or some other drive utility to do this.

4. Bad cabling or termination with your SCSI devices (if applicable).
5. You might just be having a bad day.

Many of these situations are potential hardware problems and will be discussed in their respective chapters in this book. The next topic related to operating system troubleshooting will be INITs and the System heap.

Application Heap, System Heap, and INITs

INITs, startup documents, system extensions, cdevs, and control panels are all technical buzzwords for the same thing: Low-level programs that are written to load automatically when the Macintosh first starts. These are the programs that must lurk in your System Folder in order to be loaded. Although there are slight differences between these four types of programs, I'll refer to them here collectively as INITs.

INITs are very common programs such as screen savers, virus checkers, neat utility programs, sounds and, of course, Oscar the Grouch that Mac users seem to treasure. You'll usually see some sort of representative icon displayed (one for each INIT) quickly across the bottom of your Macintosh screen during the startup process. The more icons that pop up, the more INITs you have. Sometimes INITs can cause problems.

First of all, it's a proven fact that INITs are notorious for causing nasty system problems, such as crashes, lock-ups, and other kinds of System misbehavior. Typically, when an INIT problem is suspected (which is all the time), it's natural for many users to immediately adjust their System heap. What's a heap? Why should I adjust it? How much and how do I adjust it? These are all excellent questions. However, before we can troubleshoot these problems, you must first be familiar with the Application and System heaps and their relationship with INITs.

Application and System heaps

All working Macs have a fixed amount of memory installed internally that acts as workspace for the things like programs and documents. Programs and documents are stored on floppy, hard, removable disk drives, or some other medium that acts like a big storage closet. When you want to work on a particular program, file, or document, the item is taken out of the closet (storage) and placed into an area where the computer can work with it; this area is called memory.

Application heap

The amount of memory inside your computer is a limited resource. Memory must be rationed to each of the programs that you run. Actually, every program that you run will take (reserve) a fixed amount of memory when it executes. The program does not relinquish this memory until it has been terminated. This occupied area is an example of a heap, or simply, an area of memory. In this example, the application had an area of memory (application heap) set aside for its own exclusive use. Since this is a reserved area, each application may use some or all of its application heap memory. The default size of the application heap is called the recommended size.

From time to time a specific application heap may need to be adjusted (increased or decreased) to alleviate problems (for example, out of memory) while operating under the MultiFinder or System 7.0.x. In these environments it's possible to have several applications open at once with each establishing a memory partition or heap. The MultiFinder and System 7.0.x manage the applications and the memory that they use. In theory, when you quit out of an application the MultiFinder is supposed to reallocate (make available) the previously occupied memory. Occasionally, it does not reallocate properly and you end up getting an "out of memory error" or a system crash or lock-up. When you increase a specific application's heap, more memory is reserved for that application only when it's launched. Keep in mind, it's easier to grow into the extra reserved amount of memory than out of a small initial allocation.

When you grow out of your recommended allocation, the MultiFinder "steals" memory for you, which occasionally results in system crashes, lock-ups, or "out of memory" errors. I always allocate more than I need, so that MultiFinder reserves this extra for that application only, and nothing can "steal" it. When working under MultiFinder or System 7.0.x many of your programs need more memory than the recommended size.

I frequently increase the application heap size of the Finder, PageMaker, QuarkXPress, and Adobe Photoshop. It has practically eliminated those problematic "out of memory errors" that I used to get under MultiFinder. If you aren't working under System 7.0.x or MultiFinder mode of other versions, you're only working in Finder mode (single task). Under the standard Finder environment only one application can run at a time, so adjusting the application heap really doesn't matter. The program will use all of the memory that's available.

Adjusting an application's heap is very simple. Select (click on) the application that you wish to adjust. Choose Get Info from the FILE menu option. You will see the recommended size and can change the current setting to your liking. Even though the recommended settings are usually conservative, I would not increase it too much (more than 100K) at a time. You might have to play with this. For instance, I typically increase the memory allocated to the Finder from 160K to 256K: It really seems to help out. You can also choose to leave the settings the way they are. If you do change the settings, they'll be used the next time that the application is launched.

System heap

There is another smaller yet important area of your computer memory (RAM) that is set aside and called the System heap. The System heap is a reserved area of memory that is around even when you aren't running all of your applications. This area is used by the operating system software and other low-level (system level) programs that let your Mac operate properly. ROM patches (fixes) and device drivers are examples of programs that reside in the System heap. The System heap exists because it's not always possible for programmers to develop software that works in the Application heap. Some programs such as INITs need to reside in the System heap instead.

To display your system, select About the Finder from the Apple Menu. Your System heap is the System memory bar. There should be at least 10 to 15 percent free (white) space at the end of the memory bar. If the memory bar is pegged black, you might have a problem loading INITs and other low-level programs. Perhaps this is why your System has been crashing, locking up, or experiencing some other conflicts.

INITs

INITs are low-level initialization programs that are hooks, or extensions, of the OS and occupy a portion of the System heap when they are loaded. INITs are loaded automatically when the computer is started. In order for an INIT to be loaded, it must reside in the System Folder (System Extensions and/or control panels folders if you're using System 7.0.x). To turn INITs off, simply move them out of these areas. You might have to do this when you suspect an INIT conflict. When your Macintosh first starts, the System heap has a fixed size. As INITs are loaded, the

System heap grows to load any INIT that requires more memory. This memory is stolen from your Application heap, which means after a boatload of INITs are loaded, you might not have enough memory to launch all your applications.

The System mechanism that loads INITs and lets the System Heap expand is called Init-31. Most INITs also utilize another system function called Sys-Z, or System Expansion Zone. Sys-Z, when implemented, informs Init-31 how much memory an INIT needs to load. Accordingly, the System heap increases to at least this value. (Keep in mind that the System heap is an area shared by INITs and the System Software.) The INIT will be loaded and executed then. INITs that are written properly work with Init-31 and Sys-Z and do not cause system conflicts. Unfortunately, not all INITs are written properly. Bad programming technique and improperly written INITs are the leading causes of INIT problems and conflicts.

When people suspect an INIT conflict, the first words out of their mouths are Did you increase your System heap? This can be accomplished by using special utility programs, such as Heap Tool, Heap Fixer, and Bootman. The problem here is that this isn't a solution to the all INIT problems. However, increasing your System heap about 25K to 30K doesn't hurt anything and can be beneficial in some instances.

Common INIT-related problems

1. Some INITs are poorly written and/or don't get along with other INITs. With poorly written INITs, you can try increasing your System Heap 25K to 30K, but this may only be a temporary fix. When INITs don't get along with other INITs, you may have to either remove the suspect INIT or update it to a newer version that doesn't conflict with others. INITs are loaded alphabetically. Occasionally, a particular INIT might have to be loaded before other INITs, which means you might have to put the letter A in front of an INIT's name to get it to load first or a Z to get it to load toward the end.

2. Some INITs don't implement Sys-Z. In this situation Init-31 has no means of determining how much memory to give to the INIT. In this situation, increasing the System heap (no more than 50K to 60K) will really help. Any INITs that don't implement Sys-Z were poorly thought out and I recommend avoiding them.

3. The System heap is a shared area of memory. If an INIT requests more memory (let's say 40K) then it actually uses during startup, the unused

portion (let's say 30K) is returned to the System heap, and can be used by something else. The problem here is that the INIT may still think that it has the requested memory available (that is, the 40K), when in reality it only has 40 minus 30K, or 10k. The end result, the INIT tries to use memory it doesn't have and the System crashes. There is not much that you can do in this situation. Increasing the System heap will only have a very limited benefit. Only the person who wrote this INIT can truly fix it.

MultiFinder, System 7.0.x, and INITs

If you're working under the MultiFinder, increasing your System heap is not a big concern. (But a little increase of around 20 to 30K still wouldn't hurt.) In this type of environment the System heap can grow after startup to accommodate an INIT's request for more memory than is currently available. The heap simply gets bigger. Unfortunately, it doesn't always go back to its original size. This means the additional memory is not given back to your Application heap. Another problem is that on some rare occasions the MultiFinder can not expand the System heap, and the machine locks-up. Using a decent release of the Macintosh operating system (6.05, 6.07, 6.08, and so on) and current versions of INITs is a good way to avoid these problems.

System 7.0.x

Macintosh operating system 7.0.x has implemented a new and improved version of MultiFinder. The System heap can grow and/or shrink to accommodate any INIT requests for memory. This has eliminated almost all of those chronic INIT-memory related problems and the need to increase the System heap. However, I still increase it 20 to 30K out of habit.

This new operating environment is not compatible with most of the older INITs out there. This means that you will have to upgrade most of your INITs to a 7.0.x compatible version if you plan to use them.

Finally, keep these last three things in mind.

1. Make sure that you have at least 10 to 15 percent free space on your system memory bar (located under About the Finder). If not, then you will need to adjust your heap.

2. Keep your INITs to a minimum, only use what you need. INITs use up System heap space (memory) and some INITs don't get along with others. Better safe than sorry. Also, try not to use several of the same type of INITs. For example, don't run three different screen savers: Pyro, After Dark, and Screen Blank all at the same time. You might laugh at this, but a lot of people do it.

3. Only use INITs from a reputable source that has some sort of update or upgrade program and decent technical support behind the products.

Things to consider when upgrading to System 7

Although System 7 offers many significant new features, they aren't without a price. If you're planning to upgrade and make the switch as painlessly as possible, you need an accurate understanding of what System 7 requires and what's necessary before you attempt to install it.

First, plan on adding more memory (RAM). Apple has finally given up on stating that you can use System 7 with only 2 MB of RAM. In reality, you need a minimum of 4 MB (2 MB RAM to boot, plus another 2 MB to run small applications like MacWrite II or WriteNow). With the exception of some low-cost models, most Macs nowadays come equipped with 4 MB of RAM standard. To use System 7 effectively—that is, having several Extensions loaded while running numerous small applications or running two large ones simultaneously—requires 8 MB of RAM. Save yourself some grief and plan on a minimum of 8 MB RAM, plus more if you can afford it.

After memory comes hardware-specific software problems caused by drivers. Some drivers require an upgrade to run with System 7. For example, I waited several months for a System 7-compatible video driver for Apple's 8•24 GC display board. Also, the driver for a SyQuest cartridge drive or an Ethernet board you use might need new software when you switch to System 7.

Finally, don't get hammered by software incompatibilities. When System 7 was first released, it came with a software compatibility checker. Although the accuracy of this checker was poor, its existence alone made an important point: There are fundamental differences between System 6.0.x and System 7. These are common enough to break some applications. Now that System 7 has been out for over a year, many vendors have rewritten their applications to be System 7-compatible. If you haven't upgraded your software in the last year or so, consider it suspect.

How can you tell if your software requires upgrading? Most garden variety applications, such as word processors, terminal emulators, and spreadsheets, don't exploit certain operating system features. These should operate under System 7 without problems. High-end applications such as drawing or page-layout programs that make heavy use of the text formatting capabilities supplied by Adobe Type Manager are likely to break because of conflicts with TrueType. Also, utility programs such as disk repair utilities or disk defragmenters that rely on specific operating system features will likely "break," or not work properly.

Budget some money for upgrading applications and drivers. If you've been putting off upgrading your software either because of the cost, or you had no need of the version's extras, now might be the time to bite the bullet and upgrade your software all at once. Apple's future plans hinge on people using System 7. Once your software is compatible, you may avoid another round of upgrades for a year or two.

Will all your INITs or cdevs work with System 7? That's a question that crops up often. First, let's get the nomenclature issue out of the way here. With System 7, Apple calls a cdev file a control panel, and an INIT file an extension. Nothing has changed but the names. The new names describe accurately the files that cdev and INIT code belong. The terms are also easier on the nonrocket scientist Mac user.

As for compatibility issues, that depends on what traps these files patch, and how much those traps have changed. You'll just have to try them and see. Some control panels and extensions will work, but they get confused by the new System Folder organization under System 7. Under System 6.0.x, the System Folder was just one big compartment where all the files hung out. With System 7, there are subfolders for control panels, extensions, and desk accessories. This could—and did—confuse a lot of software. Here's an example using Adobe Type Manager (ATM). ATM is composed of two files: the control panel, and a satellite driver file. In older versions of ATM, the control panel simply searched the current folder for the driver file. This was fine for a 6.0.x System Folder layout, but under System 7 the control panel winds up in the different folder from the driver. The end result was that ATM couldn't locate its auxiliary code file, and so it crashed and burned. You can occasionally fix problems such as these by moving the satellite files to the same subfolder as the control panel/extension, or vice versa. Again, most software written within the last year knows how to deal with this.

If your Mac is acting erratically, you might have a control panel/extension that has conflicts with the operating system or other control panels/extensions. Use the Extension Manager, written by Ricardo Batista and distributed by Apple, to selectively deactivate and activate these files to determine the guilty party.

System 7 networking and printing problems

System 7 uses AppleTalk Phase 2, a slightly revised version of the original AppleTalk protocol. It's designed to work with large networks. If you're upgrading all your Macs to System 7, the AppleTalk version issue is irrelevant, since they'll all use the same protocol. However, if you're upgrading your Mac network in a piecemeal fashion, you need those Macs running System 6.0.x to talk the same protocol as those running System 7. Simply put, upgrade all System 6.0.x networked Mac board drivers to AppleTalk Phase 2, or wall them off with their Phase 1 traffic behind a hardware router such as a Cayman GatorBox or Shiva's FastPath 5.

Printing is another problem with an office full of Macs running a mix of System 6.0.x and 7. The PostScript dictionary that the System 7 LaserWriter driver downloads to a printer differs from the 6.0.x driver's dictionary. A PostScript printer must reboot to accept a new PostScript dictionary—a common situation in an office of mixed Mac operating systems. To prevent the PostScript printer from rebooting every few minutes and delaying printing jobs, upgrade the System 6.0.x Macs with System 7.0's LaserWriter driver. This driver was written to be compatible with both operating systems. With every Mac running the same version of the LaserWriter driver, the printer uses the same PostScript dictionary, and no dictionary conflict occurs.

One big plus when using System 7 on networked Macs is that the site license CD-ROM for System 7 comes with an Installer application that operates over networks. You can copy the installation software to your file server and access the Installer on the server from the target Mac when it's time to upgrade that particular computer.

Disappearing files and folders in System 7

If you have files and folders that have disappeared, you've just got bit by a System 7.0 bug. It hasn't helped that it took Apple three attempts to distribute a System 7 Tune-Up file—an extension file that patches out the bug—that didn't introduce more problems of its own. Luckily, this bug only prevents the Finder from displaying the files. They're still there, just hidden from view.

Now comes the classic catch-22: To fix this problem, you have to reformat the hard disk, but first you must rescue those invisible files created by the problem in the first place. If you happen to have an application launched, select Open from the File menu. In the Standard File dialog that appears, you'll discover many of the missing files and folders: The files are still there. There's a couple of ways out of this dilemma, but they both involve relocating the files to a temporary safe haven. This can be either an external SCSI drive or a folder on a remote server that can hold all of the contents of the affected hard drive.

If you have a disk utility handy, it becomes a matter of selecting the hidden files and copying them to the other drive. If you don't have a disk utility, you can still recover the missing files. First, select Find from the Finder's File menu. If you know the name of a missing file or folder, type the name in the dialog that appears. Voilà! The file or folder reappears, but only for several seconds. While it's visible, quickly drag it to the other drive to be copied. If you're not sure of the names, an approximation will do. Work your way through the alphabet until you've copied all the files to the other drive. Since you're going to reformat the drive anyway, drag the remaining folders to the other drive. Now, reformat the affected drive, reinstall System 7 (don't forget to install Tune-Up 1.1.1!), and copy your files back to your Mac.

Addressing more than 8 MB of memory in System 7

If you've got 16 MB of RAM installed in your Mac running System 7, and you bring up the About This Macintosh... dialog box, you may see that most of the memory is allocated to the System rather than to your applications. With System 7, you are theoretically supposed to be able to address more than 8 MB of memory.

If this is the case—that is, you see that most of the memory is allocated to the System rather than your applications—open the Memory control panel and examine the settings. Is the disk cache size reasonable? With 16 MB of RAM, by default it should be about several hundred kilobytes in size, or if the computer has a slow hard disk, you might want it as large as a megabyte or two. If the cache size is bloated beyond reason, it's the culprit. The disk cache is swallowing up all the available RAM.

If the disk cache size is reasonable, then check the addressing mode section of this control panel. See if the addressing mode is set to 24 bits. If it is, this explains where the memory is going. The explanation itself requires a history lesson. The Mac operating system was designed around the 68000 processor, which could only handle 24-bit addresses. Therefore, the Mac operating system was designed using only 24-bit addressing. This results in a memory space of a maximum of 16 MB in size. Even then, the OS didn't give you access to all of that memory. For example, in the Mac II, this memory is partitioned such that 8 MB of RAM is available for applications, 6 MB for the slots (1 MB per slot, for six slots) 1 MB for the ROM addresses, and 1 MB for IO addresses. While System 7 is a 32-bit operating system, it also supports this 24-bit addressing mode for software compatibility. When in this mode, the memory map resembles the Mac II's layout just described, even on a Mac like the Quadra 950. Therefore, System 7 only makes 8 MB of memory available for your use, as described in your situation. To get the rest of your memory, switch the memory mode to 32 bits in the Memory control panel and reboot. What if the Memory control panel won't let you to switch to the 32-bit addressing mode? In this case, there are three possible causes of this problem: (1) your machine isn't 32-bit capable; (2) your machine needs a hardware modification to be 32-bit capable, such as the addition of a PMMU chip for the Mac II; or (3) "dirty" ROMs, that is, code written using the old 24-bit addressing scheme. What you're missing is MODE32, a control panel made by Connectix and licensed by Apple. It patches the ROM code of these computers to be 32-bit clean. Check to see if this file is located somewhere on the computer other than the System Folder. If you can't find it, contact Apple for the file.

Techniques for Troubleshooting Software Problems:
A Quick Reference Guide

Just to recap some of the troubleshooting techniques that you'll find in this book—you might want to keep this list handy at all times:

1. Document the error and try to repeat it on the questionable machine. If possible, try to duplicate it on a known good machine. If you have a problem on both machines, the problem might be the application software.
2. Write all error codes down, so that you can look them up for reference and explanation.
3. Turn the machine on as you normally would and let it warm up.
4. Run diagnostic software tools such as Mac Ekg, Norton Utilities, or Mac Tools Deluxe. (See the next chapter on tools of the trade.)
5. Use the Five Step Fix:
   - Check for viruses
   - Verify your System revision levels
   - Verify your application software revision levels
   - Reinstall any corrupt, missing, or incompatible versions of the applications
   - Reinstall the system software
6. Make darn sure that you don't have more than one System Folder. It's also equally important to be sure that you're using an appropriate version of the operating system. Remember, there is no life before 6.0.5.
7. Increase the Finder's memory partition from 160K to 256K, so that it has room to breathe, especially under MultiFinder. Select Finder in the System Folder then Get Info to change Finder memory allotment. (Under MultiFinder you may also have to do this for applications that you use frequently like PageMaker, QuarkXPress, Photoshop, and others.)
8. Try to keep your System Folder clutter free. Keep the INITs and other add-in programs to a minimum. INITs have the extension startup document under 6.0.x and system extension under 7.0.x. When in doubt, take them all out and then put them back one at a time. INITs can be almost anything from screen savers, virus checkers, and utility programs to Oscar the Grouch, and they sometimes fight with each other (INIT conflicts).

INITs also take up memory that would otherwise be available to the system. INITs are loaded alphabetically and some need to be loaded before others. You really need documentation or an INIT management program, such as INIT manager or INIT Picker to handle potential conflicts.

9. Unless you have some application program that absolutely needs it, turn the RAM cache in the control panel off. Many people go overboard on this setting when there is no need to. (Check your documentation.)

10. Rebuild your Desktop periodically. The Desktop file is an important operating system structure. It can be easily damaged by, turning the Mac off without running shutdown, virus attacks, and even by using your Mac often. To rebuild your Desktop, hold down the <COMMAND> and <OPTION> keys while the machine is booting. You will be prompted by the machine.

11. If you're using System 6.0.x, check your System heap. There should be at least 10 to 15 percent free space available extra. If not, you'll have to use programs such as Heap Tool, Heap Fixer, or Bootman to remedy the problem. (But don't allocate any more than 50K additional heap space). System 7.0.x automatically adjusts the heap for you, so this isn't a concern for these systems.

12. If you are experiencing system errors while operating under the Multi-Finder go to Set "Start-up" under the Finder's Special menu and switch to the Finder environment. Restart the machine under Finder only and see if you have the problem. Some programs, for whatever reason, don't like the MultiFinder. Likewise, there are some applications that can only work with the MultiFinder. It's important for you to discover these.

CHAPTER 3

Tools of the Trade & Troubleshooting Safely

Undertaking the repair of your Macintosh computer without proper tools is as foolish as a doctor performing major surgery in a garage without a scalpel, clamps, or sutures. That surgeon's patient would be very much at risk. So will your Macintosh if you're unprepared. In other words, if you aren't prepared to do the repair, don't start it. Good preparation requires thought, organization, a safe place to work, and of course, a decent set of tools. Good tools and skill are important ingredients in doing good work.

Tools and techniques used to repair your Macintosh can be broken down into two basic categories: software and hardware. Software tools are programs and utilities that help you get the machine up and running. Hardware tools are the screwdrivers, pliers, and test equipment that you use as well. This chapter covers each of these categories in detail.

Software Tools

Many of the problems that can plague your Macintosh aren't hardware-related. A significant percentage of these failures are operating system or software-related problems, such as corrupt or missing files, software that's incompatible with your hardware, conflicting programs, virus attacks, or poorly written program code. Since it's not practical to combat these problems with a soldering iron, voltmeter, or other conventional tool (but wouldn't that be nice!), it's necessary to take a software approach to troubleshooting. This approach uses software tools to resolve specific problems and requires that you be familiar with several of the available software tools (utility programs). Literally thousands of good programs have been written for the Macintosh, but it would be impossible to cover each and every one of them in this century. Therefore, I will cover only those items that I keep nearby and use on a regular basis.

A Known Good Copy of the Operating System

A great deal of Macintosh problems are related to the operating system. Sometimes important files become corrupt or get deleted and cause system failures, lockups, and worst of all, bombs. One of the most important software tools that you should have around is a known good copy of the operating system version that you use most frequently (that is, version 6.0.5, 6.0.7, 7.0.1, and so on). In fact, there is no excuse not to have it. The operating system diskettes and manuals come standard with all Macintosh computers. However, if you misplaced these items or just want to keep current, a free copy of the system software usually can be obtained from an authorized Apple dealer or through most Macintosh user groups (if you bring your own blank diskettes).

I am not certain whether Apple "officially" encourages this practice. However, I can tell you that I've never had a problem getting free copies from an authorized dealer or Macintosh user group (contrary to what the Apple License Agreement says). But keep in mind they are under no obligation to furnish you with the documentation or diskettes.

If you need a complete set of both the Macintosh operating system and documentation, but your originals are nowhere to be found, I suggest that you bite the bullet and purchase it. The cost is usually under $100 and can be purchased from your local dealer. If you don't have a dealer nearby (or dislike the one you have), I am certain that someone at Apple or APDA can point you in the right direction. In any case, don't leave home without it!

Norton Utilities for the Macintosh

Occasionally you'll encounter problems that can't be resolved by using the standard operating system resources and utilities. Disk crashes, file structure problems, deleted files, virus attacks, and corrupt data are examples of such problems. That is why you should always make backups of your data. The reality is a lot of people don't, and they end up getting burned. That's why Peter Norton devised Norton Utilities for the Macintosh from Symantec Corp. These utilities pick up where the operating system leaves off. At less than $150 (retail), Norton Utilities is pound-for-pound one of the best utilities for the buck.

Installation of this package is very easy and can be done in just a few minutes. Any Macintosh user, from novice to guru, will truly appreciate the power and user-friendliness that's built into this package. One particularly handy feature is the

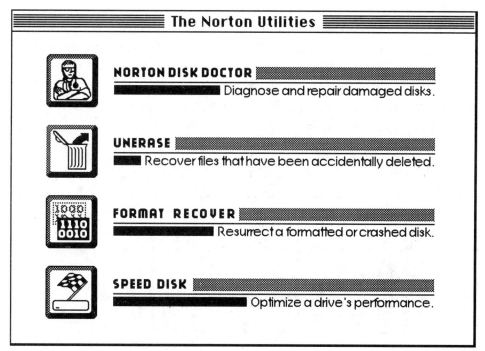

Figure 3-1.

bootable Emergency Disk, which can help you attempt resurrection of a floppy diskette or hard disk drive that won't boot. Noteworthy utilities in this package include Norton Disk Doctor, Unerase, Format Recover, and Speed Disk.

Norton Disk Doctor (NDD) is an excellent utility for repairing damaged files and disk structure (elements used to locate and store data) such as the directory and volume information, disk hierarchy, and block allocation. Damage to these areas is common and can be caused by turning off your Macintosh without running the Shut Down command, by nasty viruses, or by problems with the operating system and other software. The best feature of NDD is that it not only reports on the actual problem found, but also tells you in layman's terms which files have been affected and suggests a course of action.

Unerase is another fine Norton utility that can be a lifesaver (actually a data saver). Certainly almost everyone has experienced the horror of accidently deleting valuable data. You know, the day that big report is due, you're in a hurry, and instead of trashing the rough drafts, you inadvertently delete the final copy. Well,

Unerase does just that, it unerases things that have been deleted. However, there is some limit to its power. You can't really expect to go back and retrieve data from years gone by. The trail gets stale and the data itself eventually is overwritten. When you delete a file, directory entries and references to the file are zeroed out of the map of your disk that the operating system keeps. These references let the computer know which locations on the disk are reserved to store the specific allocation units (data) that comprise each file. They also tell the machine the size of the file and where it begins and ends.

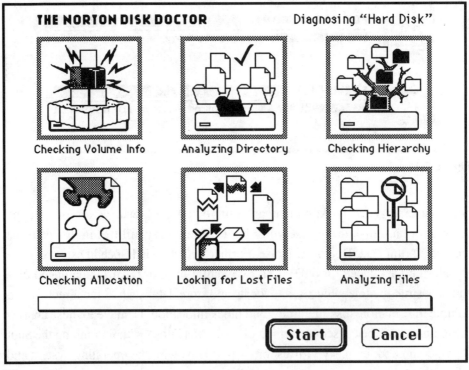

Figure 3-2.

When a deletion occurs, the map is affected while the allocation units or actual data itself are left intact. Even though the data is left intact, this area is now available for use and is no longer reserved for any specific file. This area could be wiped out by simply copying something to the disk. Unerase works its magic by reestablishing references and directory entries to the deleted information (assuming that it hasn't been overwritten). For this reason it is imperative that you use Unerase as soon as you are aware that you've deleted something important.

Format Recover (FR) is a Norton utility that specializes in recovering drives that have been accidently reformatted or have experienced minor crashes. When a hard disk is reformatted, everything on the disk is not erased. Typically during this process the disk itself is verified—checked for areas that are defective and unusable. Not much is actually destroyed during this process. When the verification is completed, the old road map of the disk drive is discarded, and a new blank map showing marked defective areas is created. The data area is left untouched. This road map points to the locations where all of your folders and files are stored. Since the old map is gone and the new map and Desktop are now bare, it looks like the data has been destroyed. However, just because you can't see it doesn't mean that it's not out there. FR works very much like Unerase (but on a much larger scale) because it rebuilds the links to the data and attempts to recreate your old road map and Desktop. Once again, this is assuming that you get to it right away!

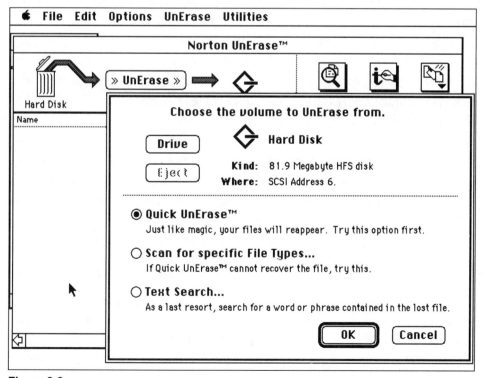

Figure 3-3.

The last program in the Norton Utilities that we'll evaluate is called Speed Disk (SD). Speed Disk is a type of disk maintenance program that's sometimes referred to as an optimizer program. Optimizers keep your hard disk drive running at peak performance by unfragmenting files stored on the drive. File fragmentation occurs with use over time. Files are stored in pieces. These pieces contain the file data and are often referred to as allocation units, blocks, or clusters. A file is nothing more than a group of allocation units (blocks or clusters) with a particular name.

The pieces comprising the file don't necessarily have to reside in a contiguous (sequential) order. They literally can be strewn all over the disk. The operating system keeps track of which pieces are associated with a particular file and in what order they go. When all the pieces of a file are stored in exact order, the file is called contiguous. When files aren't contiguous, they are called fragmented. It's common to have both types of files on your hard drive. However, contiguous files are more desirable because they're easier for your machine to handle. Fragmented files make your machine work a bit harder and can cause a decrease in performance.

Since fragmentation is a natural occurrence and happens over time, you can do very little that to prevent it. But you can use optimizers like SD to correct the situation. SD starts by locating fragmented files and their pieces. The program then attempts to put the strewn pieces of the file into a nice, contiguous order. It tries to accomplish this by moving other files and their pieces around until it can find a clear spot to fit the newly formed contiguous chain. The process is then repeated to unfragment the remaining files.

Warning: Think of this as a big jigsaw puzzle. But be careful! These programs move a great deal of your data around, and this can be dangerous. You should always have a complete backup of your hard disk before using optimization programs, just in case. Furthermore, since many areas of the hard disk will get overwritten, it's unlikely that you'll be able to recover any data that was deleted prior to optimization.

Without doubt the Norton Utilities are a very powerful set of software tools. You can use these tools to combat data recovery situations as well as file and disk structure-related problems. With the Emergency Disk you can often repair a non-bootable disk drive (assuming it's not a hardware problem). Additionally, the Norton Utilities are now compatible up through System 7.x. Whether you support one Mac or a thousand, you should at least consider getting the Norton Utilities.

Mac Tools Deluxe

I realize that most of us are working within a budget here, but Mac Tools Deluxe by Central Point Software, Inc., is another excellent set of disk utilities. In fact, if asked to choose between Norton or Mac Tools, I would have to pick them both. There have been too many strange instances where one of the packages could partially remedy the situation and the other was needed to finish the job. I use them both. These packages are very powerful and complement each other well. They are the one-two punch of utility programs.

Figure 3-4.

Mac Tools Deluxe installs very easily with the help of the Mac Tools Installer utility. The most noteworthy of the Mac Tools utilities are the five primary programs: Mirror, Rescue, Secure, Backup, and Optimize. Rescue, Optimize, and Backup are three of my favorites. Rescue is similar to Norton Disk Doctor, Unerase, and Format Recover—all rolled into one neat package. Rescue repairs damaged files, recovers deleted files, and allows you to recover from an accidental format, just like the Norton programs. Optimize is another example of a hard disk optimization program. Optimize corrects file fragmentation problems, just like Norton Speed Disk, but personally I like Optimize better because it's more stable. My colleagues and I have experienced sporadic data loss and some other very strange quirks with Speed Disk and have since switched to Optimize. Backup is a simple file backup program that works well. It doesn't have the fancy bells and whistles that some other backup utilities have, but it's reliable and gets the job done. Incidentally, backing up your files is an essential precautionary measure to avoid total data loss in the event of a disaster. If everybody backed up his or her files, there would be no need for data recovery. But the reality is that many people don't, and that's what keeps packages like Norton Utilities and Mac Tools Deluxe selling like hotcakes.

Mac Tools Deluxe retails for about the same price as Norton and other good disk utilities. Like Norton, it can be purchased at your local software dealer or through many mail order companies. Do yourself and your Macintosh a big favor: Buy them both!

Mac Ekg

Mac Ekg from Micromat Computer Systems is a one-of-a-kind Macintosh hardware diagnostic program. It doesn't do file recovery or fix corrupt data like Norton Utilities and Mac Tools. It's a true hardware diagnostic in that it really puts your Macintosh through its paces. As the name implies, Mac Ekg is an electrocardiogram for your Mac—that is, a thorough battery of component-level testing and recording of your Macs' internal activity, "pulse," and other "vital signs" (or lack thereof). The information that Ekg reports to you can easily be used to assess the condition of your machine.

This program is loaded automatically during the startup process and executes over 35 intensive diagnostic routines. Each test and its result are displayed on your screen for you to view. Upon completion of these routines, Mac Ekg assigns a numeric benchmark or performance rating to the machine tested. This number is

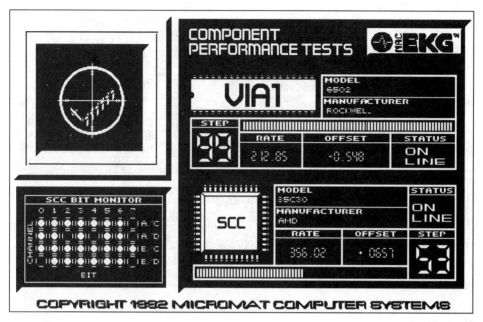

Figure 3-5.

based on how the unit scored on the diagnostic routines. The program then stores this rating in a log file, where it's compared to the score achieved during the program's "maiden launch" (when the program was first installed). If any significant deviation from the original score that could affect your computer's performance occurs, Mac Ekg gives you an audible alert message: "Warning: System performance has degenerated." This serves as an early warning and allows you to detect and correct the problems that may be lurking before they clobber your system. If the tests are within an acceptable range, Mac Ekg says in a very HAL-like voice, "All systems nominal."

Mac Ekg helps both you and the Macintosh technician isolate pesky problems related to hardware failure and/or software problems. By learning and displaying each system's performance and alerting you of any deviation, Mac Ekg provides the gauges to analyze how alterations such as the installation of INITs, CDEVs, and other modifications affect your computer's overall system performance. It could be said that Mac Ekg was designed to augment the Macintosh P.O.S.T.

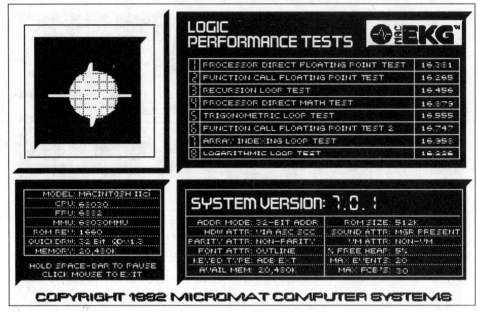

Figure 3-6.

The following are the primary Mac Ekg tests used to calculate overall system performance. They are divided into five categories:

- **Logic Tests**
  Processor direct floating point
  Function call floating point
  Recursive loop
  Processor direct math
  Trigonometric loop
  Function call FP/dual step
  Array indexing loop
  Logarithmic loop
  MPR (performance) calculation

- **Quickdraw Tests**
  Off-screen bit map retrieval
  Quickdraw latency
  Quickdraw speed
  Bit depth alteration

- **Media Tests**
  Open sector block read stability
  Open sector block write stability
  Open sector block read latency
  Open sector block write latency
  Drive performance differential
  Driver declaration integrity
  Volume status verification
  Logical ID conflict
  Mount results

- **Parameter Tests**
  System heap to minimum
  Maximum open files to minimum
  Maximum SYS events to minimum
  Maximum memory to heap
  ROM check-sum verification
  Maximum RAM to heap calculation
  Maximum O/S events to init queue
  Processor to model
  RAM to model
  ROM to model

- **Fatality Tests**
  Forward-record fatality capture

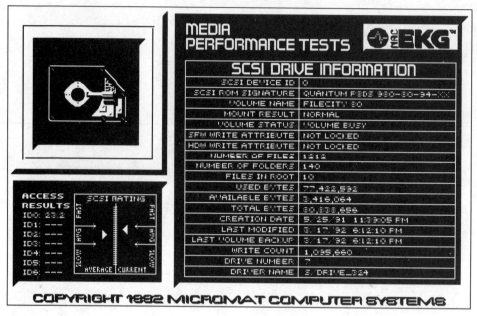

Figure 3-7.

In addition to performing and displaying the results of these tests, Mac Ekg displays a wealth of other information about the system, such as

> Macintosh model
> Main processor type
> Operating system version
> Type of math co-processor (fpu)
> Quickdraw revision
> ROM version
> Free heap
> SCSI device IDs

and much, much more.

The Ekg Reactivator is a special option used for concentrated testing, or burn in, of the unit.

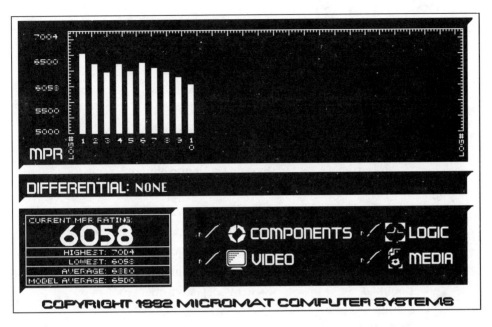

Figure 3-8.

It's important to mention here that no software can diagnose or fix a machine that is truly dead (that is, with a blown power supply or toasted CPU chip). That's why we have voltmeters, logic probes, oscilloscopes, soldering irons, and the like. However, programs such as Mac Ekg let you know when and where the machine is showing signs of illness. You can then remedy the situation before it turns into a real nightmare.

The latest release of Mac Ekg is compatible up through System 7.x. This program is the best Macintosh hardware diagnostic package that is commercially available. Two thumbs up!

Honor Roll

We have examined three topnotch software packages that are very effective troubleshooting tools. There are literally thousands of others out there. It's just not feasible to review all of them here (that could be a whole other book). However, I use several other programs that deserve to be mentioned:

Utility	Specialty
Mac Sleuth	Hardware info
Mac Envy **	Hardware info
Mug Shot	Hardware info
Disinfectant **	Virus protection
SAM	Virus protection
Virex	Virus protection
Crash Barrier	System crash prevention
Help!	System problem dolver
Silver Lining	Hard drive formatter/diagnostic tool
Disk Manager Mac	Hard drive formatter/diagnostic tool
Heap Fixer **	System heap adjustment tool
Heap Tool **	System heap adjustment tool
Bootman **	System heap adjustment tool
Startup Manager	INIT conflict resolution
INIT Picker	INIT conflict resolution

Note: As of this printing, all items marked with ** are shareware (send a donation to them if you liked it). All other utilities are commercial software products that are sold through stores, magazine ads, and so on.

In the end you may not need or want all of the programs mentioned in this section. That's a decision that you'll have to make on your own. I would most definitely take the shareware programs for a "free" test drive and get some propaganda on the others. The names and addresses of these folks are listed in the Appendix section of this book. No matter which software you do eventually get, please make sure that you have virus protection installed on your Macintosh. There are just too many of those mutant programs out there waiting to trash your disks.

Please keep in mind that I can't predict whether you'll like or find useful the programs mentioned in this section (I am not Kreskin). I can tell you that I have had good experiences with them. Additionally, all of these programs have been acclaimed by very reputable trade publications and books such as: *Byte Magazine, Macworld, MacWeek, The Macintosh Bible*, and so on. By the way, if you have a favorite diagnostic utility, please write and let me know about it. If enough people are talking about it, or if it is really good, I might be able to mention it in future revisions of this book.

Hardware Tools

Software tools and the software approach are excellent in combatting many chronic Macintosh ailments. However, they are no match for serious hardware problems. The way I see it, if the machine is as dead as a doornail, how could you possibly load a diagnostic program? Without divine intervention, you can't! You have to bring in the heavy artillery: tools and test equipment. This is also referred to as the hardware approach. Now tools are a very personal thing to you hard-core techie types. Most techies have amassed a great collection of standard, odd-ball, and specialized tools that are irreplaceable to them. They typically cringe and/or go into fits when people want to borrow their stuff (especially when it's not returned). So, if you're new to computer repair, it's advised that you get at least a basic tool kit to call your own. This is the focus of this section.

The Basic Tool Kit

A basic tool kit is typically an inexpensive set of tools that you can use to perform fundamental computer work, such as basic upgrades and preventative maintenance. In other words, it's the bare minimum you can get by with. What tools that you require also depends on the Macintosh model you need to maintain or support. For instance, if you have a Macintosh II-class machine (a II, IIx or IIsi), you can get by with a couple of screwdrivers. These units are modular in design and very easy to take apart and put back together. The Mac Plus, SE, SE/30, Classic, and Classic II aren't quite so easy. A basic tool kit for one of these models requires, at a minimum,

- a Torx #15 long-handle driver
- a Mac Cracker (to pop it apart)
- a CRT discharge tool (see "Troubleshooting Safely" later in this chapter)
- antistatic video adjustment tweakers and the screwdrivers

Several companies can sell you basic computer service tool kits. Curtis Tools, Jensen Tool, and Techni Tool are examples of three mail-order companies that sell reliable tools. You may even have a hardware or electronic store in your neighborhood that would give you as good a deal or better. Shop around for a good buy and make sure that you pick up an antistatic wrist strap to keep in your tool kit (see "Troubleshooting Safely" later in this chapter).

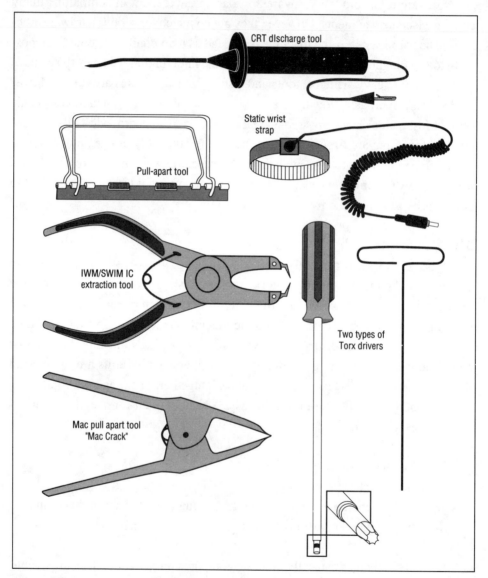

CRT discharge tool

Static wrist strap

Pull-apart tool

IWM/SWIM IC extraction tool

Two types of Torx drivers

Mac pull apart tool "Mac Crack"

Figure 3-9.

Keep in mind the basic tools can only get you into the machine. If you're doing upgrades or just looking around, this is really all you should need. But if you want to do some serious troubleshooting, you'll need some sophisticated tools and test equipment, as we discuss next.

Test equipment

Test equipment consists of specialized tools and devices that are useful in the troubleshooting and repair process. These devices can be used to perform module and component-level testing. Tests performed at this level vary from the very simple to the extremely complex. Test equipment used to perform these tests varies as well. Generally speaking, test equipment can be divided into two categories: standard and advanced.

Standard test equipment

Standard test equipment can be used to help troubleshoot basic Macintosh hardware related problems such as power, memory, basic logic and hard disk drive failures. This class of test equipment is usually moderately priced and easy to come by. Multimeters, SIMM testers, logic probes, and the Blinky are examples of test equipment that fall into this category.

Multimeters

Multimeters (meters) are one of the most important electronic test instruments you can own. They can be used to test electronic devices and components, such as batteries, fuses, switches, cables, and resistors. Meters are also used to measure AC/DC voltage as well as electrical current. They range in price from $9 to $900, depending on type, model, features, and of course, quality. The two most popular types of meters are analog and digital.

Analog meters (sometimes referred to as moving coil meters) are inexpensive multimeters that use the motion of a magnetic compass needle in a magnetic field to measure current flow. To some extent these meters are not as precise as digital meters. However, they are by far the best meters for observing the trends of changing current, resistance, and voltage. Triplett Corp. and Simpson are two excellent manufacturers of high-grade analog meters. These meters can be purchased from mail-order or local electronic supply companies. Inexpensive meters can always be purchased at a Radio Shack near you.

Digital multimeters are high-precision meters that are easy to use. Their digital readout also makes them easy to read. These meters typically have high input impedances (input resistance) that usually does not draw or load down a digital circuit. This feature, as well as the increased accuracy, make the digital multimeter ideally suited for computer circuit testing. The John Fluke Manufacturing Corp. (Fluke) and Beckman Industrial are two of the best digital meters in the business. These meters range in price from $70 to over $900 (retail), depending on the model and features you choose. High-end meters can be found in your better electronics stores and through specialty tool companies such as Jensen Tool and Techni Tool.

There are many average meters out there as well. They're sold through typical retail channels, such as department stores, local electronics stores, and mail order. When in doubt, take a trip to Radio Shack.

SIMM tester

If you maintain or support several Macintosh computer systems, it behooves you to purchase a SIMM tester. A SIMM tester tests SIMMs (single inline memory modules), which are used frequently in Macintosh RAM (random access memory) configurations. SIMMs were first introduced into the Macintosh product line starting with the Mac Plus. A SIMM is really nothing more than a small PCB (printed circuit board) with memory ICs (integrated circuits, or chips) affixed to it. These modules are then placed into SIMM sockets, which are typically located on the motherboard. SIMMs are very easy to install but not so easy to troubleshoot. True, if the SIMM is dead, you should be able to isolate the failure quickly by using the Easter Egg Approach, that is, one-at-a-time removal and replacement. However, intermittent failures are very common and not so easy to detect. The absence of a RAM parity check (error detection) in the Macintosh doesn't make the troubleshooting process any easier. (See Chapter 5, "Memory, Upgrading, and Adding SIMMs," for more information.)

The SIMM tester is a self-contained unit designed to put each SIMM module through its paces. You may elect to do either single or multiple pass testing. This device verifies the integrity of each chip on the SIMM and allows you to analyze their true access times as well. These features make the SIMM tester a valuable troubleshooting tool, especially when dealing with dead SIMMs, questionable SIMMs, and intermittently failing SIMMs.

The SIMM testers range in price from $250 to over $1000, depending on which model you purchase. I purchased the Mactronics Quick SIMM tester for around $250. This particular unit tests both IBM and Macintosh SIMMs, specifically 256K, 1MB, and 4MB modules. It tests all of these very well, and I am fairly certain that Mactronics will offer some future upgrade to this product that will allow this device to test the 16MB SIMMs as they become more popular and affordable.

I have only one minor complaint against SIMM testers: These devices come with a crummy plastic test socket. This is where the SIMM is inserted while it is being tested. These sockets are identical to those that Apple uses on the Macintosh motherboard. The problem is that the plastic tabs that hold the SIMM in place always seem to break off after a couple of insertions. This can be annoying when testing a box full of SIMMs. For an extra $100 and change, Mactronics sold me a quasi-ZIF (zero insertion force) adapter for my SIMM tester. The ZIF is a high-quality production-grade socket that is very strong, with 24-karat gold contacts for extra reliability, and no plastic tabs to break. It is definitely worth having!

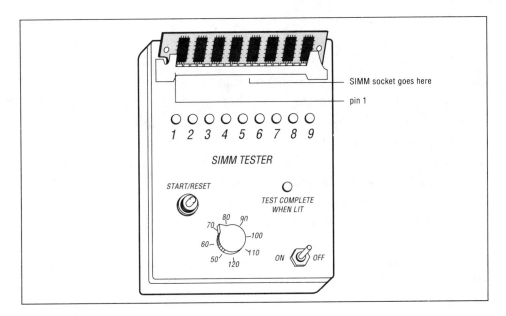

Figure 3-10.

In summary, the SIMM tester is a very handy piece of test equipment to keep around. Most models are moderately priced and easily pay for themselves in the reduction in downtime and unnecessary service calls. If you support or plan on upgrading a fair amount of Macintosh units that use SIMMs, the SIMM tester is a must have. If you only support a couple of Macs, the expense may be overkill.

Blinky

Blinky is a SCSI port tester. SCSI (pronounced skuzzy) is the acronym for the Small Computer Systems Interface, which now comes standard on all Macintosh models. The SCSI port on the Macintosh is the DB-25 pin female port located in the rear of the unit. This is where you can attach a variety of devices, such as laser printers, CD-ROMs, scanners, external hard drives, and tape backups. Occasionally, the SCSI port or devices fail.

The following are the most frequent SCSI failures that Mac users encounter:

1. Improper SCSI configuration (bad or conflicting ID number, improper termination, and so on).
2. Bad or incorrect cable(s).
3. Macintosh fails to initialize SCSI circuit during power up (usually because you forgot to turn external SCSI devices on prior to the Mac itself).
4. Bad device driver software.
5. Device that is bad or does not respond.
6. SCSI port does not respond (usually caused by a blown fuse on the motherboard that protects SCSI circuit on newer Macintosh models SE/30, II, IIx, IIci, IIsi, and IIfx. A fuse blows because of a short created when you either plugged a bad cable into the port or tried to attach a SCSI device to the Mac while it was on and the port was powered.)
7. Bad SCSI controller chip.
8. Any combination of the above.

Without Blinky these problems could be troublesome and annoying to conquer. Blinky is a small, specialized test device used to monitor SCSI activities. It plugs directly into your SCSI port, and then your external SCSI devices plug into Blinky.

Blinky has eight status LEDs that monitor activity (or lack of activity) on all valid device ID numbers (0 to 7, targets and initiator) that can exist on the SCSI bus of the Macintosh. This visual information is valuable in many ways. For example, when Blinky "lights up," you can "see" the Macintosh initialize the SCSI bus during the power-on sequence. This is useful in the sense that it tells you that both the port and the SCSI circuit of the Macintosh are functioning properly.

Blinky also visually monitors which SCSI devices are communicating and when they are finished talking, as well as the ID number for which they are set. This type of information is excellent in helping you to answer the following questions:

- Which devices are communicating?
- How long did it take for a device to finish a file access or transfer?
- What are the SCSI ID numbers of the attached devices?
- Which devices are not responding?

This can help you remedy conflicting device ID number problems. Device conflicts usually result when two or more devices share the same SCSI ID number. Each device must have a unique ID number from 0 through 6. Blinky tells you which ID numbers are assigned and which ones are available.

This simple device can save you a great deal of time and frustration when you are trying to resolve all kinds of SCSI problems. Blinky is distributed by Mactronics. The retail price is about $150. The unit is very small and fits well into a tool kit.

The logic probe

The logic probe is a very popular and inexpensive tool used for troubleshooting problems in electronic circuits. It's especially useful in helping the Mac technician locate high percentage failure components, such as integrated circuits (chips) and oscillating crystals. The logic probe is very simple to use and easy to understand.

The logic probe looks like a very large pen with a sharp needlelike tip. The probe is powered by attaching two alligator clips (power and ground) directly to the + and - points on the unit under repair. Once powered, the probe is used to test questionable components by placing its metal tip against a pin or test point within the circuit. Indicator lamps on the probe report the logic state (high, low, pulse, and so on) at that point. These readings can then be compared against a schematic diagram or known good values. Gate failures and brief, low-frequency pulses are typical conditions that you can detect using the logic probe.

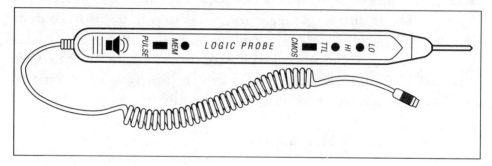

Figure 3-11.

When using this tool, it's important that you're careful where you probe. Circuit boards can easily be damaged if you put the probe in the wrong place (that is, between two pins on a chip). It's also important to use the right probe for the job. Probes vary in price and quality. If you are planning to troubleshoot Macintosh computers up through the Mac IIfx and Macintosh Quadra family, you should purchase a probe rated between 80 and 100 MHz that can test both CMOS and TTl components. If you're only going to test Macs below the faster units, you can settle for a probe rated at 50 MHz or better. Beckman Industrial manufactures several excellent probes that are ideal for Mac troubleshooting. Radio Shack sells logic probes as well, but these are typically lower-end models.

The Golden Paper Clip

No tool kit would be complete without the inclusion of a paper clip. Yes, as many of you are aware, the paper clip is the magic tool of the Macintosh. With it you can eject floppy diskettes that don't want to come out of the drive. You can also unbend it into a long piece of wire, which then can be used as a probe extension of sorts for when you want to take voltage readings with your meter in hard-to-reach places. On one desperate occasion, I reluctantly used a paper clip as a temporary substitute for a motherboard fuse (definitely not recommended, but it worked).

Advanced test equipment

Previously we discussed basic tools and standard test equipment. These are the tools that most of us have or will use in our troubleshooting endeavors. However, there are repair depots and others out there that use advanced test and repair equipment. Equipment such as oscilloscopes, capacitor and transistor testers, break-out boxes, EPROM and PAL programmers, logic and signature analyzers, and multi-layerboard-safe soldering equipment fall into this category.

Some of these devices are easier to use than others and can range in price from $25 to over $10,000. Most of this equipment is priced out of the average person's budget. Additionally, most of this equipment requires expertise in electronics and circuit analysis or other specialized training. This type of equipment is best left to the professional. I remember when techies used to live by the motto "No scope (oscilloscope), no hope!" That really isn't the case these days. Time is a very precious commodity to most of us. Why spend hours on a machine with an oscilloscope or logic analyzer that you can swap out with a board shop for $100 to $200? Your time and mental well-being are worth a lot more than the technical show. Work smarter, not harder!

In summary, many repairs and tests can be easily done using the basic tools and test equipment mentioned in this chapter. What you choose to put in your tool kit is a personal choice based on questions that only you can answer. What do I already have and what do I really need? How many and which Macs will I be working on? How much can I afford to spend, and how deep do I really want to get into troubleshooting and repair? In any case you should, at a minimum, have most of the software tools that we discussed and a multimeter. While you're at it, throw in a cheap Weller pencil tip soldering iron, some 60/40 or 67/33 solder, and a desoldering tool, for repairing basic stuff like keyboards and mice. If you plan to do soldering work on Mac motherboards, keep in mind that all of them are multilayer (typically six or more) and some use SMD (surface mount devices).

These boards are easy to butcher and require specialized solder equipment for most repairs. Pace, Ungar, and Weller make this type of equipment, which starts at around $500 for the basics and goes way up from there. Shop around for all of your tools. Most of the reputable mail-order tool companies, such as Jensen Tool, Techni Tool, and Specialized Tools, sell the better soldering equipment and tools, at pretty good prices, and typically with a 30-day satisfaction guarantee.

Tools to Upgrade, Repair, and Keep Your Macintosh Happy

Beginner to intermediate

If your level of expertise is beginner to intermediate, you need

1. Digital multimeter (Radio Shack or other): from $20 and up
2. Antistatic wrist strap (Radio Shack or 3M): from $5 to $35
3. Standard tool kit with basic hand tools (mail order): from $10 and up
4. One paper clip (get from work or home): exact price of one clip unknown
5. Mouse cleaning pad (mail order): less than $25
6. Floppy disk drive cleaning kit (mail order): less than $25
7. Known good copy of the Macintosh operating system (comes with your machine): $0
8. MAC Ekg (Mactronics or Micromat): around $100
9. Norton Utilities and Mac Tools (mail order): from $150 to $250 for both
10. Some of the shareware utilities mentioned earlier: cost varies
11. Torx #15 driver and a Mac Cracker (Curtis/mail order): $10 to $20 ***
12. CRT discharge tool (see next section) ***
13. Cheap soldering iron and desoldering tool (Radio Shack): $5 to $25 each
14. One small roll 60/40 or 67/33 solder (Radio Shack): $2 to $10

***These items are required only for the compact Macintosh models, such as the Plus, SE, SE/30, and Classic.

If your level of expertise is intermediate to advanced, you require most of the items listed above, except the Radio Shack meter and the standard tool kit. Substitute either a Fluke, Beckman, or Simpson volt meter for the Radio Shack. In addition, delete the standard tool kit with basic hand tools and go with Jensen, Xcelite, or other high-grade tools. In addition the following is recommended:

1. Blinky (Mactronics): less than $125
2. SIMM tester (Mactronics): around $250
3. ZIF adapter for SIMM tester (Mactronics): between $100 and $150
4. Logic probe (Beckman Industrial): from $75 and up

5. Advanced ESD-safe soldering and desoldering stations (Pace, Ungar, Weller): range from $100 to $2000 or more depending on the type of soldering you want to do
6. 3M antistatic work mat (mail order): from $50 and up
7. Safety glasses (mail order): from $10 and up

Advanced to expert

These levels of expertises require very expensive equipment and extensive electronics training. The equipment varies depending on which and how many Macintosh units are to be supported by the expert and at what level of repair they intend to go. This type of repair would be done by a board depot, third-party maintenance organization, or a very technical support department. I doubt if any Apple authorized dealers are even equipped at this level. At a minimum, the expert should have the aforementioned items in both categories plus some advanced test gear. This gear could include, but is not limited to oscilloscopes, transistor testers, EPROM and PAL programmers, monitor testers, signature analyzers, and multilayer board soldering gear. The minimum investment for these items could be thousands of dollars.

Troubleshooting Safely

Owning a Macintosh computer is an experience that can be both rewarding and frustrating at the same time. The hardware and software involved represent a considerable financial investment. The time spent selecting, purchasing, configuring and learning the machine represent a significant personal investment. The reward occurs when you finally get the machine up and running and are able to do something productive with it. Each of us has a different perception of what is productive. You may want to write letters, prepare a home budget, do desktop publishing, play games, or all of the above. Whatever makes you happy. The frustration occurs when things don't go as they should. Contrary to what some believe, computers, manufacturers, and people in general are not perfect. No matter how lucky we are or how hard we try, mistakes sometimes happen, and our machines sometimes do not work properly. Many computer problems require simple fixes, such as reloading software, plugging the machine in, or connecting a loose cable. Other failures are more serious and may require you to open up your Macintosh. This is where things can get dangerous, for both you and the computer.

I cannot begin to tell you how many expensive computers (and some cheap ones too) have been destroyed or how many users have been unnecessarily injured by simply poking around in places they shouldn't have been. When computers break down, otherwise sane and normal people suddenly are transformed into weekend warriors armed with screwdrivers. People have this perception that since the Mac is so cute and user friendly it must be harmless. Some people call it an expensive toy. If the Macintosh is a toy, then it's a toy that could hurt or even kill you. Yes, I said it could even kill you.

This section focuses on three topics. We begin with safety precautions, discussing the danger zones and how to protect you from getting injured while troubleshooting or upgrading your Macintosh. Second, were view ESD (electrostatic discharge) precautions that protect your Macintosh from getting injured by you. Finally, we review basic troubleshooting techniques that can help you resolve common Macintosh problems. More detailed troubleshooting techniques for specific hardware problems (such as SIMMs and memory, power supplies, and so on) are located in their respective chapters.

Safety

Safety is more than a six-letter word. It's the development of good habits and the use of common sense to prevent personal injury. When working inside the Macintosh or other electronic equipment, safety should be more than a primary consideration. It should be second nature.

General Hazards

Serious injuries such as cuts, scrapes, puncture wounds, burns (heat and chemical), facial and eye damage, respiratory problems (due to chemical and particle inhalation), and, of course, electrocution may occur when working around repair equipment and computers.

Solder burns, cuts, scrapes, puncture wounds, and minor electrocutions are among the most common injuries that happen to students in my technical seminars. Most injuries can be avoided through the use of three simple rules:

1. Pay attention to what you are doing.
2. Go slowly and concentrate on your work.
3. Use common sense.

For instance, soldering equipment gets very hot. The average tip temperature can range from 300 to 1000 degrees Fahrenheit or 149 to 538 degrees Celsius. This is hot enough to cause severe burns or to start a fire. When soldering use extreme caution and good common sense. Furthermore, keep this equipment unplugged and out of the way when not in use.

Cuts, scrapes, punctures, and other injuries can be avoided by taking your time, being careful, and handling tools and equipment properly. Some of the worst injuries I have seen in my classes have occurred when people mishandle tools, such as screwdrivers and logic probes. These tools have sharp tips that can easily puncture skin or put out an eye. In one incident a young man was trying to remove a small screw that had become completely stripped. With the module in one hand and a flat-blade screwdriver in the other he held the unit in the air, quite close to his head. He then proceeded to try to force the screw out while looking at it. The tip of the screwdriver slipped off the screw head and struck this man in the forehead. He was lucky! Just one more inch and he may have been blinded in an eye. Take safety precautions eriously. The "It won't happen to me attitude" has no place in the computer-repair field.

High-Voltage Hazards

Many people don't know, care, or believe that they can be seriously injured while working inside computers. They're wrong! Computers and monitors are powered by electricity. Electricity is dangerous and must be treated with care and respect.

The human heart operates by electrical impulses. It can be started or stopped by powerful electric shocks. Hospitals use a device called a defibrillator to stimulate and control the heartbeat of heart attack victims. This device delivers a brief electrical shock through electrodes attached to the chest. If used incorrectly, this device can stop a working heart. In the movie *Flatliners* a group of misguided medical students used this device to stop and start their own hearts. The plot was a bit far-fetched but technically correct. Electricity can stop and start your heart. IT CAN KILL YOU! Please keep this in mind when you work on monitors, power supplies, and any Macintosh or other computer with a built-in CRT (monitor) and video circuitry. These units have high-voltage areas that should be avoided.

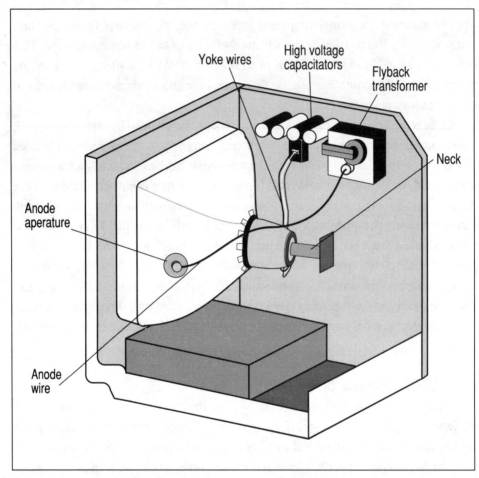

Figure 3-12. High-voltage areas that should be avoided

As a rule of thumb, video equipment (especially displays) and power supplies should be serviced only by persons experienced in those areas. However, when performing repairs and upgrades on the Mac Plus, SE, SE/30, Classic, Classic II, or any Macintosh with a built-in CRT, it's necessary to open the unit.

Naturally these units require more caution than units without built-in CRTs, such as the Mac II and others, for three reasons:

1. Built-in video circuitry can produce voltage levels between 9 and 12,000 volts. These levels are quite dangerous.

2. The CRTs are made of glass and are quite fragile, especially the neck area. Never handle the CRT by the neck — it may break and cut you. If you do get cut on a broken CRT, the wound probably will need medical attention. The glass is embedded with lead and phosphor, which splinters and can get trapped under the skin. There also is a remote chance that a cracked CRT could implode and strew glass everywhere.

3. The CRTs have capacitive properties, like a big, old battery. They can retain relatively high electrical charges even when they are off and unplugged. It's necessary to perform a CRT discharge (removal of charge) procedure to be sure the machine is safe to work on.

Hazardous Areas

The CRT discharge is an important procedure that should be performed prior to any internal repair or upgrade on Macintosh computers with built-in CRTs. Before we get into the actual procedure, now would be a good time to point out some hot spots (very dangerous areas). These areas are (but are not limited to) the anode well, anode wire and connector, yoke wires, flyback transformer, high voltage capacitors, and the on/off switch. Don't touch these areas when working on a hot (live) Mac. A high-voltage hazard is present until the Macintosh is off and fully discharged. You must become familiar with all of these areas before you perform the discharge procedure.

> **Warning**: If you are pregnant or have a cardiac condition (any heart problem), it's not a good idea to work around high-voltage equipment!

CRT Discharge Tool

To properly discharge a CRT, you need a special discharge tool. The discharge tool is basically a large (8 to 12 inches), flat-blade screwdriver or test probe with a heavily insulated handle, a long piece of heavy duty wire, an alligator clip, and a resistor (1/4 to 1/2 watt, 10 to 100 meg ohm) attached to it.

The official Apple tool, not available to most of us, looks like a large hypodermic needle with a fancy handle. Since the official tool is difficult to get, you must either build one yourself or find an electronics store in the area that stocks them. For my seminars I buy these tools from a company named Mactronics, Inc.

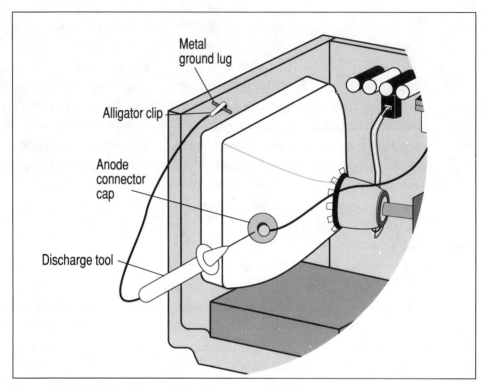

Metal
ground lug

Alligator clip

Anode
connector
cap

Discharge tool

Figure 3-13. CRT discharge tool

(see Appendix A for the phone number). The retail price is around $30. For my own personal use, I build them myself for about $5 to $10; however, assembly is required. If you're new to electronics, a word of caution: You're better off purchasing this tool. This tool performs a very serious and vital function; better safe than sorry.

CRT Discharge Precautions and Procedures

The CRT discharge procedure is necessary only when working on the compact Macintosh computers, such as the Macintosh Plus and earlier, Macintosh SE, SE/30, Classic, and Classic II.

The following is a list of discharge precautions:

1. Prepare the work area. Move unnecessary equipment and objects out of the way. Remove liquids—coffee, soda, and water, etc.—out of the area. Electricity and liquids don't mix.

2. Remove all jewelry, including wedding rings and watches. These items are good conductors and pose a potential shock hazard if they come in contact with certain electronic components.

3. Remove all antistatic wrist straps, heel straps, and so on when working on high-voltage equipment. Put those conductive work mats aside for now. These items are not to be used on live (powered) equipment.

4. Whenever possible work with another person nearby, in case something goes wrong. Also it's a good idea to take a CPR course for those who work with electronics frequently. You never know when it may be needed.

5. Protect your eyes. There is always the chance that a CRT may implode (blow in on itself) and strew glass fragments. Protective eye wear such as safety goggles or prescriptive lenses are a good idea.

6. Run the Macintosh Shutdown command before turning the machine off. This command performs housekeeping features that prepare the Mac for a graceful power down. It's a feature available in all Macintosh computers. In Macintosh II-family computers (II, IIx, IIcx, IIsi, IIci, IIfx, and so on), this command also shuts off the machine for you. Failure to run Shutdown prior to turning off the machine can sometimes result in damage to files on your disk drive.

The following are discharge procedures:

1. Disconnect power from the Macintosh unit—not only turning off the unit but also unplugging it from its power source. With the power disconnected turn the power switch on and off two or three times. This discharges any dangerous stored electrical charge inside the power supply.

2. Carefully open the Macintosh unit. If necessary, refer to the disassembly procedures specific to the model you are working on.

3. Locate the ground lug on the inside of the Macintosh unit. It's located in the upper-left corner of the chassis. It has a black wire attached to it. Attach your discharge tool to this lug.

4. Place one hand behind your back or in your pocket (left hand for right handers, right hand for lefties). This prevents stray current from accidently passing directly through your heart.

5. Slip the tip of the discharge tool under the anode cap until it touches the metal anode clips. Hold it in place for several seconds. The high voltage, if any, dissipates through the attached discharge tool. On older Mac units you may hear a crackling sound and/or see a blue spark. Newer Macintosh units are equipped with a bleeder resistor that usually prevents this. The discharge procedure ensures that the charge is gone, just in case the bleeder resistor fails.

6. Gently, peel up the anode cap and pinch in the anode clips. Remove them from the anode well.

7. Sometimes a residual charge develops in the anode well area. Immediately after discharging the tube, take an alligator wire and attach one end to the anode well area, the other to the ground lug. This eliminates any residual charges. The unit is now discharged of high voltage, and it's safe to begin work.

Summary

In this section we've reviewed many safety-related issues and hazardous situations. Each must be considered when working on Macintosh computers.

Injuries are painful, as anyone who has been hit by high voltage can attest to. Most injuries can be avoided by being patient and careful, and by using common sense.

Thanks for taking the time to read this section. It was rather lengthy and involved. I hope novices will learn from my experiences and experts will be reminded of some things they may take for granted. Remember: Safety is no accident!

Static Electricity and ESD Precautions

No hardware book would be complete without a discussion of static electricity and ESD (electrostatic discharge) precautions.

Most internal Macintosh upgrades require physically opening the machine and handling very expensive circuit boards and related components. These circuit boards and ICs (integrated circuits, or chips) are very sensitive and easily susceptible to a condition known as electrostatic discharge (ESD) or static electricity. Since this phenomenon can irreparably destroy many types of electronic components and cause the permanent loss of data, it's of utmost importance that you not only understand

ESD but also develop the skills, practices, and procedures to minimize its threat. Such is the focus of this section.

Causes of static electricity

ESD is caused by friction. Specifically it involves the separation of dry noncon-ductors. When dry nonconductors separate they each take an opposite charge. The charges remain until contact is made with a conductor. When such contact is made, the charge is then discharged to that conductor (think about the television ads that refer to static cling). For example, when you walk across a typical carpeted room, your shoes separate from the floor, generating a charge through induction. Your shoes then charge your feet, and the sweat layer of your skin conducts the charge across your body. The charge then remains on your body until you come in contact with a conductor, such as a doorknob, light switch, or motherboard. That was the zap you felt last winter when you ran across the room to turn on the television.

ESD problems are worse when the relative humidity level is low. In colder climates this problem is magnified during the winter when forced-air heaters dry the humidity from the air. The result: more dry conductors that cause more static problems.

Effects of Static Electricity

A small static charge can be generated simply by moving around in your chair. In many instances this charge is powerful enough to damage many of today's VLSI (very large scale integrated) and SLSI (super large scale integrated) circuits found in high-end electronic devices. These circuits can house millions of tiny transistors, which may be damaged by charges as low as 20 volts. You cannot feel a 20-volt charge, but a chip sure can. When you feel a zap or can feel the charge, then you are carrying over 3500 volts! Under an electron microscope, the resulting damage looks something like a moon crater or small trench dug into the circuit. Frequently the chip is not killed but wounded. It is possible that the chip can still pass basic functional tests and appear to be fine. However, the latent defect may still be there. Then in a few hours, weeks , or months the chip may die or exhibit erratic behavior.

This type of failure is referred to as an intermittent failure. In my opinion these type of failures are the worst! They are frustrating, sporadic problems that usually don't sit still long enough for you to identify or cure. However, not all intermittent problems are static related. A dead chip, on the other hand, is much easier to diagnose; dead is dead! Neither a dead chip nor an intermittent problem is desirable. Both cost you time, money, and maybe your sanity. Why not avoid these problems with a little effort?

ESD precautions

Contrary to popular belief, most people cannot attain a 100% static free environment, due to the very nature of static and ESD. It is possible to reduce the ESD threat to reasonable levels. This reduction is accomplished through the application of some good handling techniques.

For instance, whenever you handle electronic components (with a few exceptions), it's advisable to wear a static wrist strap, also called a ground strap. The strap can be purchased at your local electronics store and ranges in price from $2 to $30. My personal favorite is 3M, but any brand will do fine. Ground straps dissipate the ESD charge to the ground. The best ground to use is normally the earth ground, which can be found in the AC (alternating current) outlet of most homes and offices. If you don't have convenient access to an earth ground, attach your wrist strap to a metallic area on the Macintosh chassis (like the metal part of the frame on the Mac II). This is called a chassis ground. Remember, a chassis ground isn't as good as an earth ground, but it's better than no ground at all.

> **Warning:** Under no circumstances attach your wrist strap inside a monitor or any Macintosh with a built-in screen (such as Mac Plus). These units are very dangerous due to the presence of many high-voltage components. In these cases, for your own safety, put the ground strap away!

If you don't use a ground strap on your wrist because it restricts movement too much, consider using heel straps on your footwear and a conductive floor mat.

Wrist Strap Warning

Many people don't believe in ground straps. They believe ESD problems can be eliminated simply by touching the metal casing of the power supply or those "touch me first" pads. In theory this does discharge the individual, but only momentarily, which is better than nothing. Remember, ESD is caused by friction.

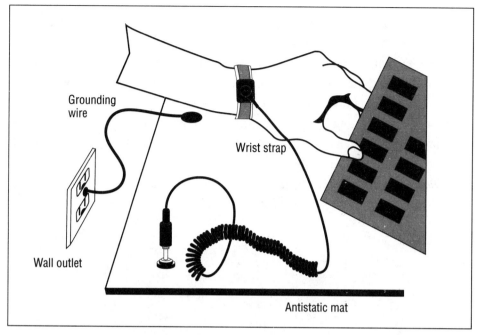

Figure 3-14. Grounding the wrist strap

Movement causes friction. Combing your hair, walking, standing up, waving to someone, even moving air molecules, all generate some charge. Is it enough to kill a chip, motherboard, or other component? Quite possibly. It depends on the component and the amount of charge.

For example, CMOS (complementary metallic oxide semiconductors) and TTL (transistor-to-transistor logic) components commonly are used in computers. CMOS-type components typically are more sensitive then TTL components. Who has the time to stop and evaluate each chip in the Macintosh to determine in which group it belongs? For your own sake, treat all components as if they are very sensitive. Better safe than sorry!

Tips to Reduce Static-Related Failure

- When handling electronic components, wear static straps attached to an earth ground, if possible, except when near a high-voltage hazard.
- Handle circuit boards by the outside edges—like a hot tray, not a baseball.

- Try to store and transport circuit boards and chips in static-proof bags and containers. 3M makes very good ones.
- Carpeted areas are not ideal work places to repair and upgrade computers. Try to avoid them when possible, or treat areas with antistatic spray. ACL of Elk Grove, Illinois, sells some of the best.
- Consider investing in antistatic work, keyboard, and CPU mats. When used properly they really do help. 3M has a great antistatic mat, and several mail-order companies sell them.
- Keep plastic, Styrofoam, silk, wool, and hair away from the components. They are excellent sources of static electricity.

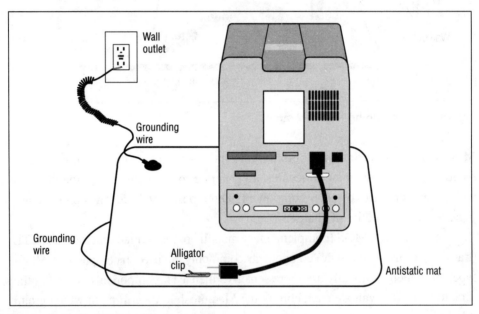

Figure 3-15. Grounding the computer

Summary

This section has discussed the causes and effects of static electricity. I have offered methods of controlling ESD and static electricity.

Computer manufacturers understand the reality of ESD. Many are developing techniques for testing field components for ESD damage. In the future I wouldn't be surprised to see Apple Computer looking for this type of damage on high-end machines such as the Macintosh IIfx and Macintosh Quadra 900 and Quadra 950. These machines use a great deal of expensive surface-mount VLSI circuits that are very sensitive. These boards are costly to manufacture and repair. Profit is lost when a manufacturer has to replace a board or machine under warranty. If they could quickly and inexpensively isolate the cause of the failure to a user-related ESD problem, they could void your warranty. By the way, opening your Macintosh technically voids your warranty. If Apple were prepared to enforce this, they legally could and probably would.

With everyone being bottom-line conscious, manufacturers are less willing to absorb ESD-related problems. Someone else must pay, maybe in overall higher prices for everyone or as a direct repair expense to the individual.

By forming good habits and using common sense, you can reduce the rate of ESD failures. Ultimately this saves you time, money, and lots of aggravation. Apply the principles in this section, and keep your Macintosh happy and healthy!

The Macintosh Power-on Self Test (P.O.S.T.) and Startup Sequence

Every time you power up or reset your Macintosh, something special takes place. In the blink of an eye, electricity pours into the machine, breathing life into thousands of intricate circuits. In a matter of seconds (sometimes an eternity in older Macs) the Mac is up and running, awaiting your command.

You've just experienced P.O.S.T. (power-on self test), a battery of ROM-based diagnostic routines that were performed during those first brief moments. Many users aren't aware (or don't really care) that anything has happened at all.

What's being overlooked by some is a valuable diagnostic tool that is built into every Macintosh computer. It's not difficult to use these tests to help troubleshoot and isolate many (but not all) bothersome and common Macintosh ailments. If your Macintosh is healthy, you have nothing to worry about. However, you should still be aware of what's really going on inside your machine. Just in case!

Macintosh Versus Other P.O.S.T.s

It's important to point out that ROM-based P.O.S.T. routines aren't exclusive to the Macintosh. While the actual tests are machine specific, this concept is used by most (if not all) computer manufacturers. For instance, IBM (yes, I said IBM) has a very intensive P.O.S.T., with an extensive listing of visual and audible error codes. These codes are generated by a failure during P.O.S.T. They can be easily deciphered to reveal the items that have failed.

Table 4-1. Examples of IBM P.O.S.T. error codes

Visual

1XX	System board failure
2XX	Memory failure
3XX	Keyboard failure
4XX	Monochrome errors
5XX	Color errors
6XX	Floppy drive errors
7XX	8087, 80287, and 80387 math coprocessor errors

Audible

No beep	Power
1 long 1 short beep	Motherboard
1 long 2 short beeps	Video adapter card
1 short beep & faulty display	Video cable or display
1 short beep & no boot	Disk cable, drive, or adapter

The Macintosh P.O.S.T. and startup procedure is similar to that of IBM and other manufacturers. It verifies the internal condition of the machine. Like IBM, the Macintosh has its own audible and visual error codes that are generated when a problem exists. The visual codes are called startup icons; the audible codes referred to as startup tones or chords. These icons and tones can be used to assess the condition of your Mac. However, unlike other manufacturers' extensive error code listings, your Macintosh has only four basic startup icons: Happy Mac, Sad Mac, ?, X, and some very interesting diagnostic chords. These are discussed in this chapter.

To the average user, these icons and tones seem helpful. Unfortunately, when a major problem occurs, you're then made aware of how vague they really are. For instance, let's suppose you're working on your Macintosh IIfx, doing your income tax return. Suddenly, your system locks up right in the middle of your work. You attempt to perform CPR (computer program resuscitation) to no avail, and the tax return is lost. No big deal, right? You can start over again. Wrong! Now your Macintosh won't boot, and you're greeted with these horrible sounding chords: Doo

Doo Dee Doo (the infamous death march—in D Flat?). Frantically you look through your owner's manual searching for answers and are told to call your authorized Apple dealer. You call the dealer only to be told that you should never get that error or perhaps the motherboard needs to be replaced. Frustrated, you call Apple Computer directly, get put on eternal hold, and then you're referred back to the dealer! Sound familiar? Maybe, but this is only a hypothetical example (or is it?). The real problem in this case is a bad batch of SIMMs that Apple got from NEC. The SIMMs produce intermittent and very strange errors. Apple has known about them for some time, yet I don't ever remember getting any sort of recall notice, like those that car manufacturers send out. I know that a computer isn't the same as a car. My car only cost about $7000 while my computer cost $11,800 loaded.

In this section we're going to take a more detailed look at P.O.S.T., the startup icons, and the chords and tones that are generated and why. This information will provide you with a valuable reference when you need help.

Detailed Startup Sequence

Between the time you apply power to your Macintosh and the Desktop appears, a carefully orchestrated and detailed series of events takes place. These events can be referred to as the startup sequence and is composed of three stages: hardware initialization, power-on self test (P.O.S.T.), and the actual operating system startup (boot/load) process.

Hardware initialization

A typical Macintosh hardware initialization consists of the following events:

1. Power is applied to the system.
2. The power supply establishes the appropriate voltage levels required by the system.
3. These voltage levels typically are monitored by one of the Sony sound integrated circuits on the logic board. If the levels are acceptable, a reset signal is then generated by this IC.
4. This reset signal forces the central processing unit (CPU), math coprocessor (FPU), primary logic ICs, expansion cards, and other internal devices to come to a known state.

5. The reset signal is withdrawn.

6. The CPU obtains the reset vector (typically four eight-bit words), which begins at memory address 0000 0000 (hexadecimal). A ROM overlay address map then is used by the memory decode and control circuitry to map the standard memory locations to a ROM address. The CPU goes to the reset vector memory address, which is now mapped to ROM.

7. Special program code called the Macintosh reset handler (MRH) is executed. The MRH remaps ROM and RAM to their respective locations.

8. The MRH initiates the P.O.S.T. sequence.

If your Macintosh fails any portion of the initialization, it appears to be dead. Refer to the general troubleshooting portion of this book for possible remedies.

Detailed P.O.S.T.

As I mentioned, the MRH initiates the P.O.S.T. stage of the startup sequence. This is done in conjunction with a special low-level routine called the Start Manager. The P.O.S.T. begins by testing ROM and other critical circuitry on the logic board. If all is well, the machine emits a medium-pitched (soft) startup chord that sounds like Bong! If an error is encountered at this point, the machine appears to be dead or emits a short, harsh error cord. This may be followed by a four-tone test cord. The harsh cord is most important because it indicates a serious hardware problem, such as an IC failure on the logic board.

It could also be a stuck programmer switch on a Macintosh II-family computer.

Next, the system memory is tested, which can take a considerable amount of time in older Macintosh computers with upgraded memory configurations. You can bypass this test by holding down the mouse button when you turn your computer on.

If the machine fails the memory test, you are greeted with either a medium-pitched error chord, with or without the four-tone test chord, or a medium- and/or high-pitched error chord, with or without the four-tone test chord.

Typical error chord sequence (the Death March)

When an error occurs during P.O.S.T. startup, the typical sequence of chords produced is as follows:

1. Normal, medium-pitched soft chord.
2. One of three error chords: short and harsh, medium, or medium followed by high. These chords are the most critical.
3. A four-tone test chord (from low to high).

It's important to note that older Macintosh computers won't give you an audible error chord when an error occurs. For instance, if a Mac Plus or Macintosh SE has a RAM failure, it would be unusual to get audible tones. Instead you typically face the infamous Sad Mac, one of four startup icons that we discuss next.

Operating system startup sequence

Now that the hardware has been initialized and tested, we come to the final stage: the Macintosh operating system startup sequence. At this time the operating system software is loaded. Here's how it works: Your Macintosh computer searches all floppy drives for a diskette that contains a file called System File. It usually ejects any diskette not containing such a file. If the System File is present and valid (that is, not damaged), the machine proceeds to boot—load the disk-based portion of the operating system from the diskette. If no such diskette is found, the machine looks for a valid startup drive attached to the SCSI port, starting with SCSI ID number 6, then 5, 4, 3, 2, 1, and 0. The drivers (control programs) are then loaded for the first device that contains valid boot blocks (allocation units of data). If all is well up to this point, a Happy Mac startup icon is displayed on your screen.

As the operating system begins to load into memory, one of the first commands executed is to display any special file in the System Folder that has the name Startup Screen. The default startup screen, also referred to as the System Startup Alert, on the Macintosh simply states "Welcome to Macintosh."

After the startup screen is displayed, the system looks for and loads a special debugging program called Macsbug, if it's present in your System Folder. The system has now been loaded into memory. As a final gesture the Macintosh loads any INITs (initialization programs) or other special programs located in your System Folder. Now the machine is ready to go to work!

If you encounter a problem during this process, you'll most likely get one of the following icons or messages displayed on your screen:

1. A startup icon other than the Happy Mac, such as the Sad Mac, ?, or the X icon. We discuss these next.
2. A familiar message, "Sorry, A system error has occurred," which is usually accompanied with a very nice "ID= error code." This usually is some Macintosh operating system or application-related problem (that is, a corrupt system file or device driver, bad Finder, wrong heap size, or bug in your program). This error is generated by the Macintosh System Error Manager, also known as the Bomb Manager.
3. A Happy Mac icon and "Welcome to Macintosh" message, but following these messages, the unit hangs or freezes up. Once again this problem could be operating-system-related. It could also be a corrupt driver, a bad INIT, or conflicting INITs. Another possibility is a defective power supply or memory chip on the main logic board. Before you tear your machine apart, refer back to Chapter 2 in this book, which discusses operating system problems, and rule that stuff out first. You would be surprised how many problems are miraculously cured by simply reinstalling a new copy of your Macintosh operating system.

Startup Icons

"Where do they come from and what do they really mean?" That's a question I hear a lot. There are four basic startup icons: Happy Mac, Sad Mac, ?, and X, three of which are associated with problems. Each startup icon is unique (also a bit vague) and can be used to give you a starting point when diagnosing a sick Mac. They are also kind of cute. Let's examine each one in greater detail.

The Happy Mac icon

The Happy Mac icon is self-explanatory: The Mac hardware is happy (working). The unit has passed the initialization and P.O.S.T. phases and has found a valid startup disk as well. The machine should then say "Welcome to Macintosh," your Desktop should appear, and you're ready to go. If you're lucky, this is the most common startup icon that you'll encounter.

The Sad Mac icon

Just as the Happy Mac icon means all is well, the Sad Mac icon indicates that the Macintosh has seen better days. There is definitely something wrong. Where is the problem and what can it be? Well, it could be any number of things: bad boot blocks on your disk drive, a real bad cable, device driver, or corrupt Desktop file or Finder. It could also be a serious hardware problem, such as insufficient power or a memory failure and configuration problem, or maybe just a stuck programmer switch. It all depends on which Macintosh you have and what accompanied your Sad Mac icon. You see, the Sad Mac icon typically is accompanied with a hexadecimal error code. It can be a single string of six characters, two strings of eight characters, or a bunch of unintelligible characters. Deciphering this code is the key to revealing where the real problem lies. It's important at this time to note that there are times when the Sad Mac codes are garbled and not legible. If this is the case, with the garbled message on the screen, depress the reset switch on your Macintosh. Look very closely. The real code may appear for an instant. You may have to do this several times. If the code is still illegible, chances are you have a serious memory- or power-related problem. If your error is legible, you'll have to decipher and then decode it.

Deciphering Sad Mac Error Codes

Sad Mac hex error codes fall into two basic categories: Those that begin with 0F,00F, or 0000000F in the first positions of the error code and those that don't.

0F0065 is an example of a 0F-type error code (first position). This error is defined as a bad Finder (software) in a Mac Plus.

000000## is an example of a non-0F type error. This exact error indicates a memory failure in SIMM #1 of an older SE or SIMM #3 of a newer one. The ## means any number other than zero. We talk about this later.

Generally the 0F errors indicate that the problem occurred after the startup device (your floppy or hard drive from which you tried to boot) was spinning. This typically is a software problem. It could also be a problem with your SCSI cable or configuration or even a stuck programmer switch.

Possible 0F error problems and solutions

- *Stuck programmer switch:* Locate the switch to make sure nothing is pushing it in and that it is not stuck.

- *Corrupt desktop:* The desktop structure may have been damaged. Restart the machine while holding down the <Command> and <Option> keys. If you were booting from a floppy disk and this does not work, try a different known good disk. If booting from a hard disk, you may need the help of a good utility program such as Norton Utilities or Mac Tools to attack this problem.

- *Bad boot blocks/device driver on the hard drive:* Boot blocks are the first two logical blocks (storage units) on a hard disk. This is where important system startup information resides. If these blocks are damaged, the 0F error may be generated. To remedy this situation, you must reboot the computer with a disk that contains a setup program for your hard disk to update or reinstall the hard disk drivers. If you're using an Apple-issued hard disk drive, you must use the HDSC program that is part of the Macintosh System Utilities disk. (This disk should have been included when you bought the computer.) If you have a third-party disk drive, you must use the installation disk that usually comes with the purchase. If you lost your disk, you have to either call the manufacturer for another copy or use a specialty program such as Disk Manager Mac or Silver Lining. They're available through many dealers and mail-order companies.

- *Corrupt operating-system-related file:* This is a very common problem. It can be caused by a corrupt or missing Finder, System File, or some other operating-system-related file. They are typically caused by write errors to the disk. The solution is very simple: Punt!

  What I am referring to is the deletion of the existing System Folder and reinstallation of the system software. The procedure is very simple: Backup any fonts or desk accessories that you may want to keep, then trash (delete) the existing System Folder on your hard disk (there should only be one), and reboot the machine with the System Tools disk. Run the Installer to reload the appropriate files. After the process is complete, reboot the machine to see if the problem has been cured.

- *SCSI drive or configuration problem:* On some rare instances the 0F Sad Mac errors can be generated by bizarre SCSI problems, such as a hard disk drive (usually a stepper motor class drive) that is experiencing a temperature-related problem (that is, it got real cold in the basement where the machine was last night). The problem could also be configuration-related. A bad SCSI cable or completely fouled up cabling of SCSI devices may be the culprit here. Even a very sick hard drive can produce this error. Rule out the external SCSI devices and cables by disconnecting them from the system. You also can disconnect your internal hard disk drive and cable to rule them out as well. However, you should try the suggestions previously mentioned in this chapter first before opening up your Macintosh. Realistically, the SCSI-related problems typically manifest themselves in the form of the question mark startup icon (?), which we'll soon examine.

In summary, the 0F Sad Mac error codes can be very frustrating to solve. They are frequently software-related and can strike any Mac at any time. The aforementioned suggestions can be used to combat the most common Sad Mac problems. Try to keep your hard disk virus free, occasionally rebuild your desktop, and always run the Shut Down command before turning off your Macintosh. Keep Norton Utilities and Mac Tools as well as a good working copy of your operating system around. You'll be surprised at how easily these problems can be resolved.

Non-0F Sad Mac error codes

The non-0F Sad Mac error codes indicate that a very serious problem has been encountered, which is usually hardware related. These Sad Mac errors are very common in the Mac Plus and the Mac SE. The Plus codes usually consist of a single string of six characters (hex). The SE codes typically are two rows of eight characters. They're not very common in the Mac II family and the newer Macintosh computers, such as the Macintosh Quadras. These computers typically default to a series of error chords (the death march) instead. On rare occasions I've seen these errors in a Mac II-family machine. The last one I saw was on a IIci with a flaky

RAM cache card. The machine produced the Sad Mac with the dual hex codes along with the death march. The death march is common in Mac IIs, while the Sad Mac with the non-0F hex codes is not.

The overwhelming majority of Sad Mac non-0F errors are found in the Mac Plus and Mac SE. These errors typically are ROM failure (Mac Plus), RAM failure, incorrect RAM configuration (both Plus and SE), or inadequate power being provided by the power supply (both Plus and SE).

These codes indicate a specific failure. For instance, if you're greeted by a Sad Mac with 01_ _ _ _ , that would indicate a ROM failure in a Mac Plus. An 02_ _ _ _ indicates one of four possible RAM errors in a Plus. The (_ _ _ _) indicates which chip went bad. A typical RAM error in an SE was discussed earlier in this section. However, since most Mac units do not have a parity bit for RAM error detection, these Sad Mac chip locations can be false. You may have to replace each SIMM one at a time until the problem goes away.

Also, the Mac Plus and SE have chronic problems with inadequate DC (direct current) output from their power supplies that may require adjustment. Keep in mind that memory chips are power hogs (that is, they're high-consumption items), and if they aren't powered properly, they can't work properly, which can cause the Sad Mac to be generated.

Occasionally the Sad Mac codes aren't legible. As previously mentioned, you can press the reset switch and see if you can catch a glimpse of the actual codes. If you're really unlucky, they may look like gibberish or you may have jail bars or zebra stripes going through the Sad Mac. These cases are almost always power or memory related. Rule out the power first, and then go for the SIMMs.

Summary of Sad Mac error codes

If you were to press the NMI interrupt button on the side of your Macintosh when booting, you would get a Sad Mac icon with 0F000D and some bits cycling under the icon indicating it's performing a memory test, which would be normal. The code 0F000D indicates that the NMI button has been depressed.

This numeric code is in two parts: the first two characters are the class code and the second four are the subclass code. The class code tells what part of the diagnostic program found the error, and the subclass code tells what the error was. In the case of a bad RAM chip, the subclass code indicates the bad chip(s).

Table 4-2.

Class Code	Subclass Code
1 ROM test failed	Has no meaning
2 Memory test (bus subtest)	Indicates failed chip(s)
3 Memory test (byte write)	Indicates failed chip(s)
4 Memory test (Mod-3 test)	Indicates failed chip(s)
5 Memory test (address uniqueness)	Indicates failed chip(s)

Single chip identification (subclass code locations)

Data Bit	Location	Subclass Code Bits
0	F5	0001
1	F6	0002
2	F7	0004
3	F8	0008
4	F9	0010
5	F10	0020
6	F11	0040
7	F12	0080
8	G5	0100
9	G6	0200
10	G7	0400
11	G8	0800
12	G9	1000
13	G10	2000
14	G11	4000
15	G12	8000

Class Code	Subclass Code
F – Exception	
0001	Bus error
0002	Address error
0003	Illegal instruction
0004	Zero divide
0005	Check instruction

Class Code	Subclass Code
0006	Traps instruction
0007	Privilege violation
0008	Trace
0009	Line 1010
000A	Line 1111
000B	Other exception
000C	Nothing
000D	NMI (normal NMI switch)
0064	Couldn't Read System File into Memory

Macintosh SE and Macintosh II ROMs

The Sad Mac error codes have been changed to incorporate additional power for testing and to support the 32-bit world. Generally, the same codes are used for 68000 exceptions as the Macintosh, however they are displayed differently.

The traditional Macintosh error codes are displayed like this:

0F0003

where F indicates that an exception has occurred, and 3 indicates an illegal instruction occurred. On the Macintosh SE and II, the display would appear:

0000000F
00000003

Please note that 00000003 is a hexadecimal number. The new power on error codes have the following format:

XXXXYYYY
ZZZZZZZZ

where XXXX is internal test manager state information (ignore this), YYYY contains codes that indicate either an exception code or the test number for a power on test failure. The ZZZZZZZZ code contains additional failure information to help track down the problem.

YYYY error codes

$0001 ......The ROM checksum test failed. Ignore the Z field.

$0002 ......The first small chunk of RAM to be tested failed. The Z field indicates which RAM Bit(s) failed. This small chunk of RAM is always in Bank B.

> *For example:* $AABBCCDD
> AA=8-bit mask for bits 31-24
> BB=8-bit mask for bits 23-16
> CC=8-bit mask for bits 15-8
> DD=8-bit mask for bits 7-0

$0003 ....The RAM test failed while testing Bank B, after passing the chunk tested for code $0002. The Z field indicates which bits failed, as in code $0002.

$0004 ....The RAM test failed while testing Bank A. The Z field indicates which bits failed, as in code $0002.

$0005 ....The RAM external addressing test failed. The Z field indicates a failed address line.

$0006 ....Unable to properly address the VIA1 chip. The Z field is not applicable.

$0007 ....Unable to properly address the VIA2 chip (Macintosh II only). The Z field is not applicable.

$0008 ....Unable to properly access the front desk bus. The Z field is not applicable.

$0009 ....Unable to properly access the MMU. The Z field is not applicable.

$000A.......Unable to properly access NuBus. The Z field is not applicable.

$000B .....Unable to properly access the SCSI chip. The Z field is not applicable.

$000C .....Unable to properly access the IWM chip. The Z field is not applicable.

$000D ....Unable to properly access the SCC chip. The Z field is not applicable.

$000E ......Failed data bus test. The Z field indicates the bad bit(s) as a 32-bit mask for bits 0-31. This may indicate either a bad SIMM or data bus failure.

$000F ....Reserved for Macintosh compatibility.

$FFxx ....A 680xx exception occurred during power on testing, where xx indicates the specific exception:

$01............Bus error

$02............Address error

$03............Illegal Instruction error

$04............Zero divide

$05............Check instruction

$06............cpTrapCC, Trap CC, Trap V

$07............Privilege violation

$08............Trace

$09............Line A

$0A...........Line F

$0B ....Unassigned

$0C...........CP protocol violation

$0D...........Format exception

$0E ....Spurious interrupt

$0F ....Trap 0–15 exception

$10............Interrupt Level 1

$11............Interrupt Level 2

$12............Interrupt Level 3

$13............Interrupt Level 4

$14............Interrupt Level 5

$15............Interrupt Level 6

$16............Interrupt Level 7

$17............FPCP unordered condition

$18............FPCP inexact result

$19............FPCP divide by zero

$1A ....FPCP underflow
$1B...........FPCP operand error
$1C...........FPCP overflow
$1D...........FPCP signalling NAN
$1E...........PMMU configuration
$1F ....PMMU illegal operation
$20............PMMU access level violation

Macintosh Portable ROMs

The ROM code in the Macintosh Portable contains a series of P.O.S.T. tests that ensure the machine is working properly. If any of those tests fail, a Sad Mac icon appears on the screen with a code below that describes what failure occurred. Here's a typical example of a Sad Mac display with an error code below it:

The two codes are actually the contents of the two CPU data registers D6 and D7. The upper word (upper four hex digits, in this case 0546) of D7 contains miscellaneous flags that are used by the start-up test routines and are unimportant to just about everybody except a few test engineers within Apple. The lower word of D7 is the major error code. The major error code identifies the general area the test routines were in when a failure occurred. D6 is the minor error and usually contains additional information about the failure, something like a failed bit mask.

The major error is further broken into the upper byte that contains the number of any 68000 exception that occurred ($00 meaning that no exception occurred), and the lower byte that usually contains the test that was being run at the time of failure. If an unexpected exception occurred during a particular test, then the exception number is logically ORed into the major error code. This way both the exception that occurred as well as the test that was running can be decoded from the major error code.

In this example the code says that an address error exception ($0200) occurred during the RAM test for Bank A ($03); $0200 0Red with $03 = $0203.

Major Error Codes

Below are brief descriptions of the various test codes that might appear in the major error code. (Note: Some of these codes may mean slightly different things in Mac models other than the Macintosh Portable.)

These description describe specifically how they are implemented in the Macintosh Portable.

$01 ....ROM test failed. Minor error code is $FFFF, means nothing.

$02 ....RAM test failed. Minor error code indicates which RAM bits failed.

$05 ....RAM external addressing test failed. Minor error code indicates a failed address line.

$06 ....Unable to properly access the VIA1 chip during VIA initialization. Minor error code is not applicable.

$08 ....Data bus test at location eight bytes off of top of memory failed. Minor error code indicates the bad bits as a 16-bit mask for bits 15-00. This may indicate either a bad RAM chip or data bus failure.

$0B ....Unable to properly access the SCSI chip. Minor error code not applicable.

$0C ....Unable to properly access the IWM (or SWIM) chip. Minor error code not applicable.

$0D ....Not applicable to Macintosh Portable. Unable to properly access the SCC chip. Minor error code is not applicable.

$0E ....Data bus test at location $0 failed. Minor error code indicates the bad bits as a 16-bit mask for bits 15-00. This may indicate either a bad RAM chip or data bus failure.

$10 ....Video RAM test failed. Minor error code indicates which RAM bits failed.

$11 ....Video RAM addressing test failed. Minor error code contains the
following:

        Upper word= Failed address (16-bit)

        Msb of lower word = Data written

        Lsb of lower word = Data read

        Data value written also indicates which address line is being
actively tested.

$12 ....N/A

$13 ....N/A

$14 ....Power Manager processor was unable to turn on all the power to
the board. This may have been due to a communication problem
with the Power Manager. If so, the minor error code contains a
Power Manager error code explained in the next section.

$15 ....Power Manager failed its self test. Minor error code contains the
following:

        Msw = Error status of transmission to power manager

        Lsw = Power Manager self test results (0 means it passed,
non-zero means it failed)

$16 ....A failure occurred while trying to size and configure the RAM.
Minor error code not applicable.

Minor Error Codes

If a problem occurs during communication with the Power Manager, the following error codes will appear somewhere in the minor error code (usually in the
lower half of the code, but not always):

$CD38......Power Manager not ready to start a handshake

$CD37......Time out waiting for a reply to the initial a handshake

$CD36......During a send, the Power Manager did not start a handshake

$CD35......During a send, the Power Manager did not complete a handshake

$CD34......During a receive, the Power Manager did not start a handshake

$CD33......During a receive, the Power Manager did not finish a handshake

Diagnostic Code Summary

Below is a summarized version of the Sad Mac error codes.

Test codes

$01 ....ROM checksum test
$02 ....RAM test
$05 ....RAM addressing test
$06 ....VIA1 chip access
$08 ....Data bus test at top of memory
$0B ....SCSI chip access
$0C...........IWM (or SWIM) chip access
$0D ....N/A to Macintosh Portable; SCC chip access
$0E...........Data bus test at location $0
$10 ....Video RAM test
$11 ....Video RAM addressing test
$14 ....Power Manager board power on
$15 ....Power Manager self test
$16 ....RAM sizing

Power Manager communication error codes

$CD38......Initial a handshake
$CD37......No reply to initial a handshake
$CD36......During send, no start of a handshake
$CD35......During a send, no finish of a handshake
$CD34......During a receive, no start of a handshake
$CD33......During a receive, no finish of a handshake

CPU exception codes (as used by P.O.S.T.)

$0100 ....Bus error exception code
$0200 ......Address error exception code
$0300 ....Illegal error exception code
$0400 ....Zero divide error exception code
$0500 ....Check inst error exception code
$0600 ......cpTrapcc, Trapcc, TrapV exception code

$0700 ....Privilege violation exception code
$0800 ......Trace exception code
$0900 ......Line A exception code
$0A00 .....Line F exception code
$0B00 ......Unassigned exception code
$0C00 ......CP protocol violation
$0D00 .....Format exception
$0E00 ......Spurious interrupt exception code
$0F00 ......Trap inst exception code
$1000 ......Interrupt level 1
$1100 ......Interrupt level 2
$1200 ......Interrupt level 3
$1300 ....Interrupt level 4
$1400 ....Interrupt level 5
$1500 ....Interrupt level 6
$1600 ....Interrupt level 7

The question mark (?) startup icon

The question mark startup icon is the most common icon associated with a startup problem. It simply means that your machine has passed the P.O.S.T. and wants to load the disk-based portion of the operating system, but for some reason it can't. In other words, no startup disk has been found. This error can be hardware- or software-related and sometimes a little bit tricky. For instance, if you're booting from a floppy drive that is very dirty, and the drive can't read the startup diskette properly, you'll get an instant question mark icon. This is a hardware problem which you can solve by cleaning the disk drive. However, it's possible that the drive itself may be defective, which would also be hardware-related. If this is the case, repair or replace the disk drive. If the floppy diskette is missing a valid System Folder file, the same error appears and you should try a known good diskette. This would be a software problem.

Now, suppose you're attempting to boot from a hard disk drive and you get the ? icon. The drive or cables could be bad or misconfigured. These are typical hardware problems that require you to verify your hardware and configuration (ID number, termination, cables, and so on).

101

If a virus or some unknown force were to corrupt your operating system, boot blocks, or device drivers, these are other forms of software problems. You should punt! Trash your old System Folder, reinstall your hard disk drivers, search and destroy the virus (if one was present), and then reinstall the system.

However, the most common cause of the ? icon is forgetting to turn on your external SCSI devices before your turn on their Macintosh. This is important because part of the Macintosh startup sequence is to poll the SCSI bus starting with ID number 6, then 5, 4, 3, 2, 1, 0, searching for a valid startup disk. If the external devices are not on before the Mac is powered up, the Mac will blow right by them. End result: You get the ? startup icon.

Other common hardware problems can be improper or bad SCSI configurations, conflicting ID numbers, improper termination, bad cable, bad drive, temperature problem (that is, your drive is too cold—let it warm up first), faulty SCSI controller IC, or a blown fuse on the drive or logic board. Apple also had a large batch of bad Quantum 40 and 80MB hard disk drives. Most dealers got a recall notice (the average Joe/Jane did not). It makes you wonder how many people bought new ones versus how many got them fixed free under warranty. They also have some real nasty problems with some older Sony 40MB drives. These drives occasionally fail to boot or just stop spinning. Any one of these things could generate the ? icon. Rule this stuff out first.

Things to try

1. Were the external SCSI devices (drives and so on) powered up before your Mac was? If not, start over.
2. Did you recently change your SCSI configuration? If so, perhaps you have a configuration problem. Verify ID numbers, cables, connections, and termination. If not, verify them anyway.
3. If you were booting from a floppy drive, does the drive itself look dirty? If so, clean it with a drive/head cleaning kit. If the floppy drive isn't spinning or is acting up, it may need to be repaired or replaced.
4. If you're booting from a hard disk drive, can you hear it it spinning? If not, you may have a defective drive with a stiction or some other serious problem. Apple has a bunch of these defective drives floating around. It's possible that your drive was one of these. There was a quiet recall notice issued. Most Mac users are not aware of this, so a call to Apple may be in order.

It's also possible that the drive is dead. You may want to test the drive with a program such as Disk Manager Mac or Silver Lining, both of which are excellent hard disk utility programs. Some fine shareware programs are out there as well. You might also want to check whether your drive has a blown fuse on its little circuit board. A fuse is typically marked with an "F" (as in F1).

In addition to this fuse, almost all newer Macintosh computers typically have a 1-amp pico fuse on the logic board directly behind the SCSI port. It's usually marked with an "F" and is there to protect the SCSI circuit. When this fuse blows, no external SCSI devices can work, but the internal device (if any) typically can.

These fuses frequently go bad due to users plugging in SCSI cables while the unit is on. This is a no-no! Fuses are tested by performing a continuity test. By the way, if your 25-cent fuse is bad, don't count on Apple replacing it. The technical procedures manual their technicians have doesn't mention it. It simply states: Replace logic board and of course collect all of that money. Ouch!

5. You could have a software problem, such as a missing or corrupt system, bad boot blocks, missing driver, real bad Desktop, or other problems related to the data structure. The way to recover from these situations is simple. Follow the exact procedures previously mentioned in this chapter (except the stuck programmers switch) used to combat the 0F software-related Sad Mac startup icon. Just make sure you have that known good copy of the operating system software around.

As we've seen, there are many things that can cause the question mark (?) icon. Through a methodical process of elimination, you can eventually have a good idea whether the problem was due to the software or the hardware. Most are easily corrected and typically your Apple dealer need not evaluate the problem. Save your money for a vacation or for more computer goodies.

The X startup icon

Last but not least we come to the X startup icon. This icon is a piece of cake compared to the other icons that we've reviewed. It appears on the Macintosh screen when the Mac attempts to execute the operating system startup process from an uninitialized (unformatted) or non-Macintosh floppy diskette. The Mac ejects the diskette (usually) and then displays the X icon. This error is most common in Macs without hard disk drives or in any Macintosh configuration where the user is booting up from a floppy diskette. On some rare occasions the X icon is generated because the diskette ejected during startup. If you hold down the mouse button during startup, it could cause the disk to eject. The solution in this case is very simple. Locate a known good startup diskette and insert it into your floppy drive. The machine does the rest. That's all there is to it!

Summary

This chapter has covered the Macintosh power-on self test and startup process in great detail. Startup chords, the four basic startup icons—Happy Mac, Sad Mac, ?, and X—where they come from, and what they really mean have been discussed as well. When trying to troubleshoot a sick Mac, these startup icons may seem vague compared to other manufacturers' P.O.S.T.s. However, they do give you a place to start. Whether the problem is hardware- or software-related, a methodical approach to the problem is always the best. While everyone usually has his or her own way of doing things, this chapter offers some suggestions you may not have thought of trying before. It's impossible to say that this information will cure all Mac ailments, but you better believe it can make most of them go away.

CHAPTER 5

Memory, Upgrading, and Adding SIMMs

Memory in a computer refers to any integrated circuit (IC) capable of storing information that will be used by your computer at a later time. In some ways this is similar to the way human memory works, in that we store and retain memories of events, people, places, and things for future use. Like human memory, which consists of many specialized brain cells, a computer's working memory—or RAM (random access memory)—is also made up of many specialized circuits, which are defined as memory chips. Most Macintosh computers use DRAM (dynamic random access memory) chips. Dynamic, as used in this context, refers to something that is constantly changing. Because of their design, DRAM chips need to have their contents continuously refreshed by the computer. This makes them constantly changing, or dynamic.

System RAM

System RAM is the working memory of your computer's system. The amount of RAM available and the memory addresses it occupies are different, however, on various models in the Macintosh family. The main reason for these differences is the use of different microprocessors and their different-sized address buses: the MC68000, with 24-bit addresses; and the MC68020, MC68030, and MC68040, with 32-bit addresses.

System RAM contains the system heap, a copy of parameter RAM, global variables, application heaps, the stack, and other information used by applications.

In the Macintosh Classic and earlier Macintosh computers, the following hardware devices share the use of system RAM with the MC68000:

- The video display, which reads the information for the display from one of two screen buffers in RAM
- The sound generator, which reads its information from one of two sound buffers in earlier Macintosh computers, or from one sound buffer in the Macintosh Classic
- The disk-speed controller, which shares its data space with the sound buffers

System RAM in the Classic II, SE/30, and modular Macintosh II-family computers contains the system heap, a copy of parameter RAM, various global variables and trap handlers, application heaps, the stack, and other information used by applications. The video display and sound generator in the Classic II, SE/30, and modular Macintosh II family have their own dedicated memory buffers and do not use system RAM. In the Macintosh IIsi and IIci, the built-in video generator uses system RAM for its screen buffer.

Access Time

The time needed to refresh, read, or write to the computer's memory chip is known as access time. All chips have an access time rating. This rating isn't a speed rating, such as 100 mph, but rather a rating in time, specifically nanoseconds (billionths of a second). A chip with a rating of 150 nanoseconds can be accessed every 150 billionth of a second. A chip with a rating of 120 nanoseconds can be accessed every 120 billionth of a second. This is 30 nanoseconds better (or 20%) than the 150-nanosecond chip. When describing memory chips, a lower access time equals better performance (just like golf).

Memory can come in single-chip or multiple-chip configurations. Newer Macintosh computers use a multiple-chip package known as a SIMM (single inline memory module). A SIMM module is nothing more than several memory chips mounted on a small printed circuit board. These circuit boards are then installed into special SIMM sockets located on your computer's logic board. This approach has the following advantages over single-chip configurations found in, for example, the older IBM PC-XT machines.

- It's impossible to bend the metal legs of the chip during installation. SIMMS already have the chips soldered into place.
- Since the chips are soldered into place, it's impossible for them to "walk" or work themselves loose.

The SIMM configuration also has some disadvantages:

- If a single chip of the SIMM fails, the entire SIMM module must be replaced. This wastes the remaining good chips. Repairing SIMM modules is not yet cost effective.
- It's rather easy to break the plastic SIMM sockets on the logic board.

The following SIMM speed ratings are recommended for the particular Macintosh models:

Mac Plus	150 nanoseconds or better
Mac SE	150 nanoseconds or better
Mac SE/30	120 nanoseconds or better
Mac Classic & Classic II	120 nanoseconds or better

You can use SIMMs that are rated better (that is, have lower access times) than the recommended access times. These modules work well because they can be used only at the system's predetermined memory refresh rate, no faster. Thus you won't hurt anything by using modules with a better rating, except your wallet since you'll be paying for speed you can't use.

Never use SIMMs with higher access times (that is, slower) than the recommended rating. These SIMMs won't be able to keep up with the refresh cycle and will fail.

SIMMs and Why They Are Used

Basically a SIMM is a small PCB (printed circuit board) that has two, three, eight, or nine chips affixed to it, depending on the density and capacity of the SIMM. The SIMM easily fits into a special socket located on the main logic board. In the

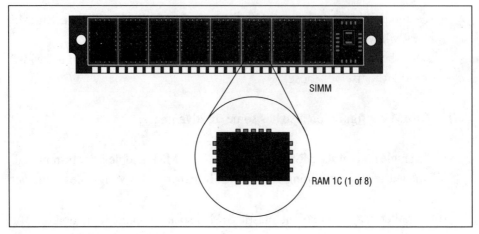

SIMM

RAM 1C (1 of 8)

Figure 5-1. RAM ICs in a SIMM

past, memory upgrades and repairs were made by removing single ICs (chips). These chips were either socketed or soldered. The soldered chips were extremely difficult to remove properly without high-grade soldering equipment. The logic boards are multilayered and easily damaged by cheap soldering irons and inexperienced troubleshooters. The advantage to the soldered chips is that when mounted (soldered) to the board, they do not pop out of their sockets, a phenomenon known as chip walking, which is common with the socketed chips.

Users hate soldered memory chips because they cannot upgrade or repair their systems easily. Manufacturers love them because the chips stay put, which keeps the failure rates lower. Users love socketed chip designs because they can use a chip puller or butter knife to pop them out and replace them in a few minutes. The major drawbacks to this type of design are the chip walking effect and the ease with which the legs can be accidentally bent on the individual chips when they are being replaced. The SIMM is the best of both worlds: the chips are soldered to a small PCB board, making them permanent, but the whole module plugs into a socket, making it easily replaceable.

Why do memory chips walk, and is this a problem on any particular Macintosh computer? Well, chip walking isn't confined just to memory chips: it can occur in any computer or electronic device that utilizes single-dip socketed (dual inline package) ICs. The reason that the chips walk is simple—the legs of the socketed ICs are made of metal. Whenever you heat and cool metal, it expands and contracts. When the computer is off, it's cool; when it's on, it heats up, as do all of your computers components.

Over a period of time the chips will work themselves partially out of the socket, which will cause either an immediate or an intermittent failure. When a chip walks it may not be visually noticeable. However, if you were to reseat all of your socketed ICs by gently pushing down on them, you would probably feel several of them move back down into the socket, making proper contact. Reseating should be an integral part of any preventative maintenance program. Also, when reseating make sure that you don't forget about static electricity precautions.

As far as the Macintosh is concerned, any Mac that uses socketed chips of any kind can experience this problem. Since there are so many different models and revisions of Macintosh computers, it's hard to give you an exact listing. I can tell you that the older Macs such as the Plus, the SE, and the original Mac II have more socketed ICs (and problems with walking) than, for example, a Mac SE/30, Mac IIcx, IIci, or IIfx. You'll never have this problem, however, with the PowerBooks or the original Macintosh Portable because almost all of the ICs in those computers utilize a heavily soldered surface-mount design. These units use expensive, custom, memory upgrade boards—not conventional chip or SIMM packages. Even though it's expensive, you get what you pay for. In this case, you are paying for the advanced technology and reduced design.

Disadvantages of using SIMMs

The obvious disadvantage of using SIMMs is that you have several chips mounted on the little baby PCB that functions as a module or unit. If one or more of the chips on the SIMM fail, the entire module has to be replaced, even though the module may still have several good chips on it. This is a quick and convenient way to fix a machine.

Despite its convenience I still have a problem throwing away the good chips on a SIMM, so I don't. I save them and sell them in quantity to companies that recycle memory modules. These companies typically advertise in magazines such as *Service News* and pay or barter with you for your dead SIMMs. You aren't going to get rich doing this, but it if you have a bunch of them, you can often get enough to buy some more Mac goodies. The SIMMs are not hard to repair if you have a SIMM tester, surface-mount soldering equipment, and the time. But I personally would not waste my time or money unless I had a box of dead 16MB SIMMs, which at this time are very expensive, as opposed to the 256K, cheapie SIMMs. Then, I might make the time or send them out. It's a lot easier to call MacWarehouse, Mac-Connection, MacZone, or whoever and order new ones.

The second problem with SIMMs are the SIMM sockets on the motherboards themselves. This is where the SIMMs are physically installed. The real problem is that most of these sockets are made of cheap plastic and can break easily if the user uses Hulk Hogan-like force when installing the SIMMs and tears off the two little tabs. Newer sockets are coming with high-grade metal tabs that usually don't break.

On the socket are two of these tabs that hold the SIMM in place. If you do break them, you might get lucky and only break one of the tabs. The other can still hold the SIMM in place if you seat it carefully and securely. Under no circumstances should you put anything conductive in the machine to hold it in place. I have found paper clips and balls of tin foil wedged between SIMMs inside clients' machines. No wonder they had problems.

Incidentally, the SIMM sockets are almost impossible for the average user to replace without expertise and proper equipment. There are third-party maintenance organizations such Mactronics, Micromat, and GTE that service Macintoshes and can do this repair at a reasonable price. Apple dealers don't provide this service. However, they will sell you a new motherboard.

Although a new replacement is more convenient than a repair job, it's not more cost effective. Recently an "authorized Apple dealer" gave me a quote of $372 for a replacement SE motherboard, plus $175 for labor to install it, making the grand total $547. And that was with my old board in exchange.

I can buy an entire used Mac SE listed in the back of *MacWeek* magazine for between $595 to $695. Mactronics and Micromat will repair this for less than $200 with a complete warranty, and I can install the board myself and save the labor money. Turnaround time for the repair can be within 48 and 72 hours, if you are willing to spend about $25 more for Federal Express overnight delivery.

Apple doesn't endorse this practice, and third-party repair voids your Apple warranty. But then again, so does busting your SIMM sockets. Apple technicians are trained to look for this stuff. If your warranty has expired, do what you have to do within your budget. If it's under warranty, never work on that machine: take it back to Apple for service.

Keep in mind I have waited from three days to three weeks for Apple dealers to get my repair parts. If you are going to use an authorized dealer for repair, call around and see if they have parts for your model in stock or on order. The mega-dealers, like Falcon Micro in Maryland, have enormous quantities of repair parts in stock and are good places to go for service.

Other problems with SIMMs

Debris build-up in the sockets can make connection with the SIMM contacts poor. In addition, the wires in the SIMM socket that make contact can also easily be bent, making a poor connection or no contact.

Over a period of time the contacts on a SIMM can become corroded. You must clean the contacts with a nonconductive contact cleaning solution such as Blue Shower or Tech Wipe. If you're in a crunch, use a pencil eraser every now and then to remove the corrosion, but I wouldn't make a habit of it. If you use the eraser too much, you can actually erode away the contacts.

Adding Memory

You can expand or modify the RAM of your computer by adding SIMM modules or upgrading to ones that have chips with greater storage capacity. (Another option that increases system RAM is installing a NuBus memory card.) Be careful when performing any of the SIMM upgrades because if you damage your computer Apple may void your equipment warranty.

But regardless of how you choose to expand your computer's memory, make certain that the chips or SIMMs you use are suited for your specific Macintosh model, as shown in the following chart. The SIMMs shown are those sold by Apple. You can also buy third-party SIMMs that may have different chip configurations but work fine. The amount and configuration of RAM you can add to a Macintosh varies. Each model can accommodate only certain configurations.

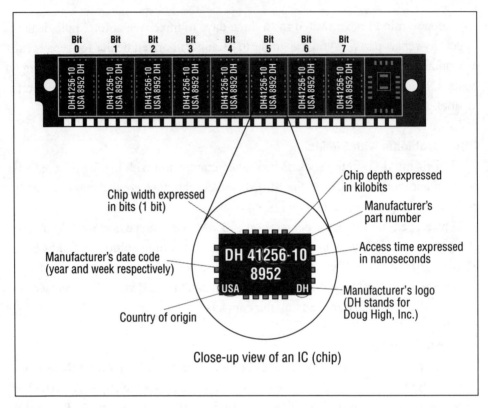

Figure 5-2. Typical 8-bit 256K SIMM rated at 100 nanoseconds access time

Macintosh Plus and SE

The Mac Plus and Mac SE have the same upgrade potential.

Table 5-1.

Desired RAM	Mac SIMMs
512K	Two 256 Kbit SIMMs
1 MB	Four 256 Kbit SIMMs
2 MB	Two 1 Mbit SIMMs
2.5 MB	Two 1 Mbit SIMMs and two 256 Kbit SIMMs
4 MB	Four 1 Mbit SIMMs

Although the possible configurations are identical, memory does not reside in the same place on a Mac Plus and a Mac SE motherboard. SIMMs must be placed in the correct location when you are using combinations of SIMM sizes, and the correct resistors must be cut. Two-SIMM configurations use slots 1 and 2 in a Mac Plus and an SE with the original motherboard. They use slots 3 and 4, however, on an SE with a revised motherboard.

Macintosh Classic

The Mac Classic comes with 1MB of RAM soldered on the motherboard. To expand the system, you must buy an expansion card. This card will have another 1MB of RAM soldered in place, and two SIMM sockets. This gives you the following options:

Table 5-2.

Desired RAM	Mac SIMMs
1 MB	Eight 128 Kbit DRAMs soldered to the main logic board
2 MB	The memory expansion card and the jumper set to "SIMM NOT INSTALLED"
2.5 MB	Two 256 Kbit SIMMs on the memory expansion card and the jumper set to "SIMM INSTALLED"
4 MB	Two 1 Mbit SIMMs on the memory expansion card and the jumper set to "SIMM INSTALLED"

If you choose to fill the SIMM socket on the expansion card, Apple recommends that you use either two 256 Kbit or two 1 Mbit parts rated at 120 ns or better.

Macintosh Classic II

The Classic II comes with 2MB of RAM soldered on the logic board and two SIMM sockets. Each socket can hold 1, 2, or 4MB SIMMS, running at 100 ns or better SIMMs. Configure your system at 2, 4, 6, or 10MB, as the following table shows.

Table 5-3.

Built-in	+	SIMM size	x2	=	Total RAM (MB)
2		0			2
2		1			4
2		2			6
2		4			10

Macintosh SE/30, II, IIx, and IIcx

The Macintosh SE/30, II, IIx, and IIcx computers use a 32-bit data bus with eight-bit SIMMs. You must, therefore, upgrade in four-SIMM chunks. The SIMM slots were organized with this in mind: there are two banks of four SIMM slots on each motherboard. All you have to do is install the SIMMs in the correct banks.

Table 5-4.

Macintosh model	Bank A	Bank B
Macintosh SE/30	Located next to the ROM SIMM	Located next to the 68882 coprocessor
Macintosh II and IIx	The bank located closest to the edge of the board	Directly behind Bank A
Macintosh IIcx	Located closest to the disk drives and power supply	Directly behind Bank A

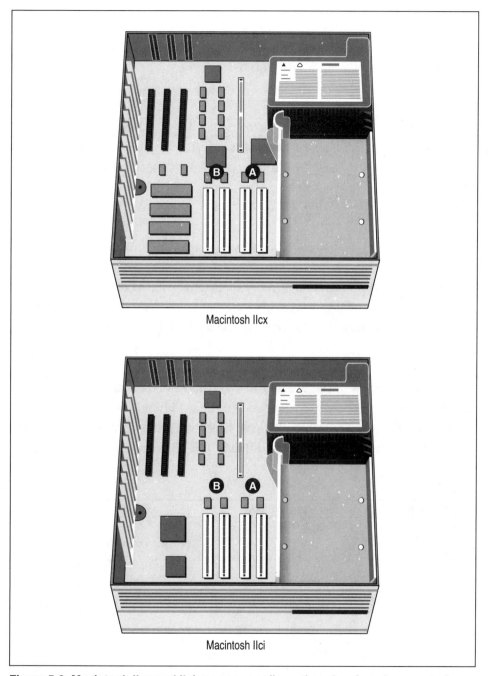

Macintosh IIcx

Macintosh IIci

Figure 5-3. Macintosh IIcx and IIci memory configuration showing placement of Banks A and B

Apple calls these banks Bank A and Bank B. You may also hear them referred to as Bank 0 and Bank 1, respectively. I will follow Apple's nomenclature. An example of bank placement is shown in Table 5-3.

Table 5-3.

Desired RAM	Necessary SIMMs	SIMM location
1 MB	Four 256 Kbit SIMMs	Bank A
2 MB	Eight 256 Kbit SIMMs	Banks A and B
4 MB	Four 1 Mbit SIMMs	Bank A
5 MB	Four 1 Mbit SIMMs	Bank A and four 256 Kbit SIMMs in Bank B
8 MB	Eight 1 Mbit SIMMs	Banks A and B

Theoretically, the maximum memory supported by the models will be 128 MB when using 16 MB SIMMs. Make sure the SIMMs are in the appropriate Bank. If you're using a combination of SIMMs, the larger SIMMs must be in Bank A.

Macintosh LC

The Mac LC comes with 2MB of RAM soldered to the main logic board and two SIMM connectors used as a single additional RAM bank. Memory can be added by installing SIMM pairs in this additional bank. You must, however, upgrade two SIMMs at a time, using 100 ns or faster SIMMs. This gives you the following options:

Table 5-4.

Desired RAM	Necessary SIMMs	SIMM location
2 MB	Four 1 Mbit x 4 DRAMs	Soldered to the motherboard
4 MB	Two 1 Mbit SIMMs	In the SIMM connectors
6 MB	Two 2 Mbit SIMMs	In the SIMM connectors
10 MB	Two 4 Mbit SIMMs	In the SIMM connectors

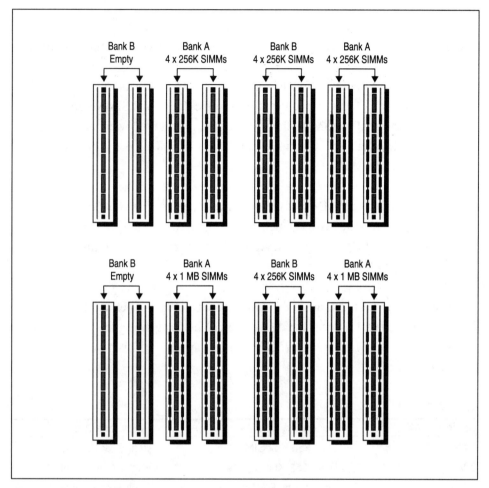

Figure 5-4. Typical Macintosh SE/30, II, and IIx memory configuration

Macintosh IIsi

Similar to the SE/30, II, IIx, and IIcx, memory in the Macintosh IIsi must be upgraded in four SIMM chunks. The IIsi, however, only has one SIMM bank. Also, the IIsi can only use 100 ns or better SIMMs.

Macintosh IIci

Installing SIMMs on the IIci can be very tricky. Physically, the IIci has two SIMM banks, A and B. Like the other 32-bit Macintosh computers, one bank consists of four, 8-bit SIMMs. However, because the IIci has special built-in video circuitry that "steals" from system memory, you must observe two important rules.

- If you are installing two banks of memory (8 SIMMs total) and the SIMMs are of two different capacities (for example, four 1MB SIMMs and four 256 SIMMs equalling 5MB), then you should install the lower capacity SIMM in Bank A, and the higher capacity in Bank B. This is the oppostie of the other 32-bit Macs.

- When ordering SIMMs for the IIci, always specify that you require dynamic, fast-page mode SIMMs, which are optimum for this unit. You may use conventional SIMMs; however, Apple does not reccommend this, and it may slightly decrease performance.

The IIci's SIMM banks are in the same location on the motherboard as the IIcx's. Bank A, for example, is near the disk drives. When upgrading the IIci, you must use 80 ns or better SIMMs with 256K or 1MB capacities. This gives you the following options:

Table 5-7.

Desired RAM	Necessary SIMMs	SIMM location
1 MB	Four 256 Kbit SIMMs	Bank A or Bank B
2 MB	Eight 256 Kbit SIMMs	Banks A and Bank B
4 MB	Four 1 Mbit SIMMs	Bank A or in Bank B
5 MB	Four 256 Kbit SIMMs	Bank A and four 1 Mbit SIMMs in Bank B
5 MB	Four 1 MBit SIMMs	Bank A and four 256 Kbit SIMMs in Bank A
8 MB	Eight 1 Mbit SIMMs	Banks A and Bank B

If you have one of the special Macintosh IIci models that includes parity error detection you will need to upgrade using parity RAM chips. These SIMMs are nine bits wide rather than eight, but installation is the same as on other IIci computers.

Macintosh IIfx

Like the Mac IIx, the IIfx has two banks of SIMM slots. These banks are located in about the same place on the motherboard as the IIx banks, but they are in slightly different positions: Bank A is near the back of the machine while Bank B is near the 68030.

The IIfx will accommodate 1 and 4MB, 80 ns or better SIMMs. Do not use SIMMs with a lower access time. If you are mixing SIMMs of differing capacities, larger SIMMs (those adding more megabytes) should go into Bank A. And finally, if you're only adding 4 SIMMs, add them to Bank A. Following these rules gives you the options in Table 5-8.

Table 5-8.

Desired RAM	Necessary SIMMs	SIMM location
4 MB	Four 1 Mbit SIMMs	Bank A
8 MB	Eight 1 Mbit SIMMs	Banks A and Bank B
16 MB	Four 4 Mbit SIMMs	Bank A
20 MB	Four 4 Mbit SIMMs	Banks A and four 1 Mbit SIMMs in Bank B
32 MB	Eight 4 Mbit SIMMs	Banks A and B

Macintosh Quadra 700

There are two banks of dynamic RAM on the Quadra 700 that are controlled by an Apple custom IC, the memory control unit (MCU) chip. The first bank contains 4MB of dynamic RAM soldered down, and therefore permanently placed. The second bank can support 1 or 4MB, 80 ns SIMMs. Although the Quadra 700 can theoretically support 16MB SIMMs, this has not been tested. The Quadra 700 can use 60 ns SIMMs. There is no reason to use these more expensive SIMMs, however, since the memory circuitry is timed to work at 80 ns.

If you do use 60 ns SIMMs, you must fill the entire bank with them. You should never mix SIMMs of varying speeds in a single Quadra 700 bank. It is also important to avoid partially filling a memory bank. A bank should either be empty or completely populated.

Macintosh Portable

Like the newer PowerBook computers, the Macintosh Portable uses memory expansion cards rather than SIMMs. The Portable ships with 1MB of RAM on the main logic board and one slot for a RAM expansion card. Since there is only one slot, upgrade possibilities are limited by the size of available, compatible expansion cards. Currently, there is only one official expansion card available: Apple's 1MB memory expansion kit. However, third-party expansions are available.

PowerBook 100

The PowerBook 100 comes with 2MB of PSRAM (pseudo-static RAM) of four 4 Mbit chips of 512 by 8 bits each. These are 100 ns chips with no processor wait states, except when the pseudo-static RAM itself is being refreshed.

As with the other PowerBooks, the 100 has a 70-pin RAM expansion connector that can accommodate 2, 4, or 6MB expansions cards.

Like the Macintosh Portable, the PowerBook 100 has batteries that power the System RAM even when the computer is off. This protects your RAM disks, saving their contents even after the System is shut down.

PowerBooks 140, 145, and 170

The PowerBook 140, 145, and 170 have 2MB of PSRAM, made up of four 4 Mbit chips of 512K x 8-bits each. There is one expansion slot, which you can use to expand the systems to 8MB of RAM. All three PowerBooks use 100 ns PSRAM. They also all have a 70-pin RAM expansion connector that supports a 2, 4, and 6MB RAM expansion card.

Frequently Asked Questions on SIMM Upgrades

Q. **I plan on upgrading my SE and SE/30s to System 7. Do I need to upgrade my memory, and if so how much do I really need?**

A. First of all, I personally wouldn't upgrade any Macintosh to System 7 that didn't utilize true 32-bit data path and processor architecture. Macintosh computers that utilize the MC68030 or MC 68040 processors are your best bet (SE/30, IIcx, IIsi, IIci, IIfx, Quadras, and PowerBook 140, 145, and 170).

Table 5-9. RAM configuration summary

	Permanent RAM	No. of SIMM slots	Allowable SIMM sizes	Physical RAM Totals	Req. Speed
Compact Family					
Plus	0	4	256K,1	512K,1,2,2.5,4	150 ns
SE	0	4	256K,1	512K,1,2,2.5,4	150 ns
Classic	1	2	256K,1	1,2,2.5,4	150 ns
Classic II	2	2	1,2,4	2,4,6,10	100 ns
SE/30	0	8	256K,1,4,16	1,2,4,5,8...128	120 ns
Modular Family					
II	0	8	256K,1,4,16	1,2,4,5,8...68	120 ns
IIx	0	8	256K,1,4,16	1,2,4,5,8...128	120 ns
IIcx	0	8	256K,1,4,16	1,2,4,5,8...128	120 ns
LC	2	2	1,2,4,16	2,4,6,10	100 ns
IIsi	1	4	256K,512K,1,2,4,16	1,2,3,5,9,17...65	100 ns
IIci	0	8	256K,1,4,16	1,2,4,5,8,16, 10,17,20,32...128	80 ns
Quadra 700	4	4	1,4,16	4,8,20...68	80 ns
Quadra 900	0	16	1,4,16	4,8,12,16,20, 24,28,32,36, 40,48,52,64...256	80 ns

Portable Family

You add RAM to Macintosh Portable and the PowerBook computers via expansion cards. Memory of these cards can range from 1MB to 4MB for the Portable, 1MB to 3MB for the backlit Portable, and 2, 4, or 6MB for the PowerBook.

	Permanent RAM	No. of SIMM slots	Allowable SIMM sizes	Physical RAM Totals	Req. Speed
Portable	1	0	n/a	1,2,3,4,5,6,7,8,9	100 ns
Portable (backlit)	1	0	n/a	1,2,3,4,5,6,7,8	100 ns
IIfx	0	8	1,4,16	4,8,16,20,32...128	80 ns
PowerBook 100	2	0	n/a	2,4,6,8	n/a
PowerBook 140/145	2	0	n/a	2,4,6,8	n/a
PowerBook 170	2	0	n/a	2,4,6,8	n/a

Your Macintosh SE/30 uses a 68030 and will be a good candidate for System 7. Most people either go with 4 or go with 8MB of RAM. On the SE/30 I personally would go 8MB and 8, 16, or higher megabytes on the IIfx and Quadra-class machines. With System 7, the more the merrier.

The Macintosh Plus and Macintosh Classic use a 68000 processor, which can run System 7 (but not well); however, due to a ROM limitation, these models can only be upgraded to 4MB maximum, which is not a lot. Additionally, these units are not nearly as powerful as their 68030 and 68040-based counterparts.

Q. **I properly upgraded several IIx, IIcx, IIci, and IIfx machines to 8MB or greater, but I can't see all of the memory. What's going on here?**

A. Oops, some of the higher-end Macs have a compatibility problem addressing above the 8MB barrier. The fix for this is called Mode 32, a program developed by Connectix. You used to have to buy this program from Connectix; now Apple offers it free to fix this glitch. APDA or your local dealer should be able to help you get it.

Q. **I recently upgraded several Mac II and IIx's to 5MB using four 1MB SIMMs and four 256K SIMMs, but the Finder says I only have 2MB present. I have previously seen this type of error before on a Mac SE, but I really don't know why it happened or what's going on now.**

A. First make sure that all of the SIMMs are seated properly in their sockets. If they are properly seated, verify that the SIMMs are in the correct sockets. Yes, I said the correct sockets. In most Macintosh computers (except some SE models and the IIci), you must fill Bank A first. (Bank A should be stenciled on your motherboard.) If you are using two different capacity SIMMs (that is, 256K and 1MB), you must put the higher capacity SIMMs in Bank A and the lower capacity in Bank B. You must follow this rule in this situation, or a great deal of your memory won't be recognized.

There are exceptions to this rule. For instance, in the Mac IIci, the lower density go in Bank A the higher in Bank B. This is because the IIci has built-in video but no built-in video RAM. The unit therefore "steals" memory from Bank A. The nice thing about any of the SE/30, Mac II, IIx, IIcx, IIci, IIsi, IIfx computers is that these machines autoconfigure when the memory is added or removed. You don't have to move any jumpers or switches, and you don't have to cut any resistors.

The SE is another strange exception. There are two flavors of the Mac SE motherboard. The banks are reversed and you have to either move a jumper or cut a resistor to achieve certain memory configurations, which is a real pain (this is discussed later in this section). But, if you don't get it right, the machine will not know how much memory is in there.

Q. My SIMMs have all kinds of numbers on them. Are they important? If so, what do they tell me?

A. The numbers on a SIMM are important can tell you the capacity and access time of the SIMM, which is important information for you to know. Let's look at an example of a typical SIMM part number:

MC41256-120 9052

This part number can be broken down as follows: MC tells you that Motorola Corporation is the manufacturer.

The number 1 is the width of each chip as expressed in bits, which is pretty useless to most people. As an unofficial rule, you can sometimes take this number and divide it into the number 8 to arrive at how many chips usually will be mounted on the SIMM. For instance, almost all Macintosh SIMMs have a data bit count of 8 bits. If the width of each chip is 1 bit, as in the example above, there will be 8 chips mounted on the SIMM. If you had a 42256-120, you would have four chips on that SIMM and so on. Not all manufacturers do things this way; there are always exceptions. Anyway, it's easier to visually count the chips than it is to do the math.

The 256 is the depth of each chip in kilobits, which is 262,144 bits x 8 chips total in this example, which is 2,097,152 total bits. Since there are 8 bits in a byte, the byte total of this SIMM is also 262,144 (2,097,152 / 8). Simplified, 262,144 bytes is 256K (1K=1024 bytes; 262,144 /1024=256K) total capacity of this SIMM. In other words this is a 256K SIMM.

The 120 is the access time of the SIMM as rated in nanoseconds (ns), or billionths of a second. Since this is a rating in time, the lower the number the better the access time. For instance, a 100-ns rating is a better rating than 120-ns. Even though 120 is a bigger number than 100, the 100 is still a better rating. This is a rating in time, not miles per hour. The lower the number the better. Think of it this way: if I jog to the 7-Eleven in 200 minutes and you run there in 100 minutes, you got there much quicker than I did. One hundred minutes is less time than 200 minutes, and I probably would have a heart attack running that long. The manufacturer always determines which access times are acceptable for a particular computer. If they say that you require 100-ns or better, they mean 100, 80, or 75, not 120 or 150. A -10 or a -1 on the end of a SIMM is an abbreviation for 100-ns, a -12 for a 120-ns, and a -8 for an 80-ns. You get the idea. Always try to work within the manu-facturer's recommendations.

The 9052 is a manufacturer's date code. This date code means that this SIMM was produced during the 52nd week of 1990. The date code can be helpful in iden-tifying SIMMs that Apple or other manufacturers may have recalled, such as NEC. NEC had a major problem with SIMMs date coded 9052 or earlier when installed in the Macintosh IIfx. That means any NEC SIMM prior to 1991 doesn't belong in your IIfx.

It was nice of Apple not to tell any of you IIfx users out there about the prob-lem and subsequent recall notice. Especially since the lovely symptoms were machine crashes, boot problems, error chords, system errors, and a strange ghosting effect on your screen! I found out by accident when I replaced all of the SIMMs in my IIfx two years ago—at my expense. My Apple dealer should have advised me of the recall and fixed it at no charge, but he didn't. Incidentally, many other people have been having problems with the older NEC brand SIMMs in other Macs.

It's important to note at this time that the SIMM in the IIfx is physically dif-ferent from the standard Mac SIMM. It will appear larger with a V-like indentation on the contacts located at the bottom of the SIMM.

Q. **Why must SE upgrades be done two SIMMs at a time while SE/30 and Mac II-family machines are done four at a time.**

A. The Macintosh SE has a 16-bit electrical path to the microprocessor. Since each SIMM represents 8 bits, it takes two of them to complete a 16-bit path. Tech-nically, each SIMM is a row, and the 16-bit completed path is a bank. A bank in a Mac with a 16-bit data path would be two 8-bit SIMMS. The SE has 4 SIMM sock-ets (2 banks) on the motherboard.

The SE/30, Mac II, IIcx, and most other 32-bit Macs have 32-bit data paths. Upgrades in these models must be done in increments of four 8-bit SIMMs at a time.

$Q_\bullet$ **Can I mix different capacity SIMMs on my Macintosh?**

A. You can use different capacity SIMMs on a Macintosh provided that you follow certain rules.

1. The SIMM capacity must be the same within a given bank, and each bank must be complete. For instance, a Mac SE has four SIMM sockets. You could put two 1MB SIMMs in Bank A and two 256K SIMMs in Bank B. You could not put one 256K, one 1MB, and one 4MB SIMM. In this example you don't have a complete bank, nor have you matched the SIMMs within any bank. Finally, a Mac SE doesn't support a 4MB SIMM. Now a Mac IIci could support a 4MB SIMM, but since it's a 32-bit machine, you would have to put four of them in the machine to complete the bank. This would give you 16MB of total memory (4 x 4=16), which might be more than you really want or can afford. If you want 4MB, then go with four 1MB SIMMs. Under no circumstances could you get away with just one 4MB SIMM, but I've seen people try it.

$Q_\bullet$ **I have all kinds of different brands of SIMMs. When installing them in my Macintosh, should I install all of the same kind whenever possible? Can I mix them around, or is there a problem with doing this?**

A. This question has several answers. Yes, you can mix SIMMs of different brands and access times, provided you have followed all of the rules that we have previously discussed in this section (that is, same-capacity SIMMs within a given bank, they meet or exceed the manufacturers' minimum specification for SIMM access times, and so on). However, I would like to qualify this statement by saying that on a few occasions I have had problems mixing SIMMs of different origin. For instance, I had a situation where my Mac would not function when Goldstar SIMMs were mixed with Hitachi SIMMs. Yet when I switched to all Hitachi or all Goldstar, the problem went away. Both sets of SIMMs passed 100% on my SIMM tester. It could have something to do with quality control and tolerance. Even so, I still try to keep like brands together whenever possible.

$Q_\bullet$ **Some computer books say that you shouldn't mix SIMMs with different access times, while other books say that you can. Which position is correct and why?**

A. There is no problem mixing SIMMs with different speeds as long as you follow one simple rule: You must use SIMMs that at a minimum meet or exceed Apple's recommended access time for your Macintosh.

Apple is very good about providing you with this information in its systems documentation. For example, let's say that you have a Mac Plus or an SE. Apple says that the recommended access time for these models is 150 nanoseconds. The access time of RAM is an indicator of how long it takes for a character to be transferred to or from the microprocessor, and is represented in nanoseconds, or billionths of a second. The lower the rating, the better the access time.

Now back to your Mac Plus and SE. Apple says that you should use a SIMM with an access time of 150 ns. You could use a 120-, 100-, 80-, or 75-ns SIMM in this example. These access times meet or exceed the requirement of 150 ns. In fact, these SIMMs are better than what the machine calls for. They can handle much faster transfers if they have to—therefore, the 120-, 100-, 80-, and 75-ns SIMMs will work fine, but a 200-ns SIMM won't. It simply can't keep up. This is important to understand. The next time one of your 150- or 120-ns SIMMs goes out and the dealer only has an 80-ns SIMM, go ahead and get it. You'll find it's well worth the extra cost.

If you own or support several of the older model Macs, such as the Plus, SE, SE/30, Mac II, IIx, or IIcx, rather than mixing and matching SIMMs, you might want to consider standardizing all of your memory upgrades around the 80-ns SIMM. This SIMM works in all of these models with no problem. One SIMM in this case fits all, which will save you time money and aggravation. There is nothing worse than having a box full of SIMMS and saying, "Well, I have one 150-ns, two 200-ns, and one 75-ns, and I need to upgrade my Mac SE/30 and IIcx, which both require at least 120-ns access times." Had you standardized on 80-ns SIMMS, you would have had no problem. Standardization makes upgrades and repairs a snap.

There are several reasons that people have trouble mixing SIMMs with different access times. The main reason is that they are usually installing SIMMs of inferior quality, such as the NEC 9052 batch and Korean or Taiwanese brands. The quality control on many of these brands is poor, as is the overall quality of the SIMM. As a result, you may have a problem mixing high-grade SIMMs, like Hitachi, Siemans, TI, and Micron, with a SIMM of lesser quality, such as Goldstar, Samsung, or Hyundai. A second reason for problems could be that you're not using a brand that Apple has certified to be fully compatible, or perhaps you just got SIMMs from a bad batch.

Q. I have a Macintosh LC with 4MB of memory. My SIMMs are rated at 100 nanoseconds. This machine is very slow. Could I replace the 100-nanosecond memory in this machine with 40- or 50-nanosecond memory to improve the LC's performance. I know it would cost me some money, but would it be worth it?

A. Save your money. Many users are under the impression that by putting the fastest memory on the market in their machine that they are increasing their machine's speed. Nothing could be farther from the truth. If you're using SIMMs that are the correct rating for the machine, replacing them with SIMMs with a better rating will do absolutely nothing for you. You will spend more money for nothing. Although the 50-nanosecond SIMM will work in the LC, it won't speed anything up. The memory access algorithm has already been engineered into the machine. In other words, if the system requires 100-nanosecond RAM, then 100 nanoseconds is the best that the LC's memory access circuit will do. Putting a 50-ns SIMM in there won't change this circuit. The point here is the 50-ns SIMM can easily support the 100-ns access time of the LC.

You can't seriously expect the LC's memory access time to double by simply adding new SIMMs. Someone swore to me once that his machine was running twice as fast with 50-ns SIMMs as it was with the 100's. It really wasn't, he just thought it was. He spent a lot of money and wanted and expected it to run faster. However, it's important that if you install a SIMM that does not at least meet or exceed the manufacturer's recommended specifications, you could have a problem on your hands.

One final note: We have demonstrated that you can install SIMMs that have a better rating than required. However it's possible to go overboard when trying to standardize on a SIMM. There is actually an unofficial way of determining the range of SIMMs that should be used in your Mac. The formula is very simple:

1. The highest access time you should consider is the manufacturer's recommended rating.
2. The lowest access time you should consider is 1/2 of the manufacturer's recommended rating.

Therefore, if you have a Macintosh SE, which requires 150-ns SIMMs, the correct range of SIMMs that you should consider using would be from 150 nanoseconds (recommended) to 75 nanoseconds (one half of the recommended). You could use a 150-, 120-, 100-, 80-, or 75-ns SIMM in this application. You could not use a 50- or 60-ns SIMM in this example. If you were to find and use a 40-, 50-, or 60-ns SIMM, it may or may not work. It has been my experience that when you go below one half of the recommended access time, timing problems increase exponentially.

Q. **I have several Mac SEs at work and have been having trouble understanding how to perform a memory upgrade. Several of the logic boards look different and I just can't seem to figure it out. What could I be doing wrong?**

A. Well, you are absolutely right. There are two different types of SE logic boards. The first is a solder type resistor board that requires you to either cut or install a small component called a resistor to properly perform certain memory configurations. These resistors are marked R35 and R36 on the logic board and are located in an area marked RAM SIZE in white lettering behind the rear row of SIMMs (SIMM slot 1) located on the front left side of the logic board (if you are looking at the board from front to back). Below is a chart of how to perform the various memory configurations.

Table 5-10. SE resistor type board chart

Total Memory (Cut or Installed)	Resistor Status (cut or uncut)	SIMM Size Desired (Installed)
1MB	Make sure R35 is installed and R36 is removed	Use four 256K SIMMs
2MB	Make sure R35 is removed and R36 is installed	Use two 1MB SIMMs
2.5MB	No resistors installed	Use two 1MB + two 256K SIMMs
4MB	No resistors installed	Use four 1MB SIMMs

If you follow this chart and the other rules that I have discussed, you won't have any problem. I do have one suggestion: Don't remove the resistor completely. Just cut one side and bend it up so it does not make contact. This is just in case you cut the wrong one, you can easily spot-solder it in place. If you remove the entire resistor and it's the wrong one, you have to resolder the whole thing back in, which is time consuming and increases the likelihood that you will damage the SE's multi-layered logic board.

The second type of Macintosh SE logic board is called a jumper type board. Instead of cutting a resistor to configure RAM size, you simply move a jumper, which is located in the same place the resistors would have been (RAM SIZE location) There are three possible positions of the jumper: 2/4MB, 1MB, or removed. When configuring memory in a Macintosh SE with this type of board, please use the following chart:

Table 5-11. SE jumper type board chart

Total Memory Desired	Jumper Position	SIMM Size
1MB	1M Position	Use four 256K SIMMs
2MB	2/4M Position	Use two 1MB SIMMS
2.5MB	No Jumper installed	Use two 1MB +two 256K
4MB	No Jumper installed	Use four 1MB SIMMS

Q. Do I have to cut a resistor or move a jumper to configure the memory on my Macintosh SE/30?

A. No. The Macintosh SE/30 utilizes an advanced design that will automatically configure and recognize your memory upgrades, provided you properly installed the correct SIMMs. The Mac II family and other advanced Mac's do the same thing. This is a lot better than cutting resistors and moving jumpers.

Q. I have a Macintosh Classic with 1MB of memory. I want to upgrade this unit, but I don't know where to put the SIMMs on my logic board.

A. The Macintosh Classic doesn't have SIMMs installed directly on the logic board. The 1MB that you currently have consists of eight ICs soldered directly to your logic board. If you want to expand the memory of your Classic to 2, 2.5, or 4MB of total memory, you must purchase a Classic Memory Expansion Board from Apple or another vendor. This expansion board installs vertically into a special connector on the logic board.

Q. How much memory will the Classic Memory Expansion Board accommodate?

A. The Classic Memory Expansion Board comes standard with 1MB of memory soldered directly on board (just like the logic board), plus it has two SIMM sockets for expansion. You can fill these SIMM sockets with either two 256K SIMMs or two 1MB SIMMs.

Table 5-12. Classic memory chart

Total Memory Desired	Is Classic Memory Expansion Board Required ?	Are SIMMS Required?
1MB	No, not used	No
2MB	Yes	No
2.5MB	Yes	Yes, two 256K **
4MB	Yes	Yes, two 1MB **

** When SIMMs are used on the Classic Memory Expansion Board, it's necessary to move the jumper from the second and third pins to the first and second pins (from the outside edge). If you fail to put the jumper in the correct position, the upgrade won't work properly.

Q. I have a standard Macintosh LC. What are my upgrade options?

A. The LC comes with 2MB of memory soldered directly to the main logic board, plus it has two SIMM sockets** available for additional upgrades. The maximum memory that the LC will support is 10MB total RAM.

Table 5-13. LC memory chart

Total Memory Desired	SIMM Size Installed
2MB	None (standard on-board memory)
2.5MB	This configuration is not supported
2MB	This configuration is not supported
4MB	Two 1MB SIMMs
6MB	Two 2MB SIMMs
10MB	Two 4MB SIMMs

Note You should not use 256K SIMMs in an LC, as they won't be properly supported.

Q. How much memory can I add to my Macintosh IIsi?

A. The Macintosh IIsi comes standard with 1MB of RAM soldered directly to the motherboard. There are four SIMM sockets that permit the unit to be expanded to 17MB of total RAM. At present the Mac IIsi will support 256K, 1-, 2-, and 4-MB (100-ns) SIMMs in these sockets.

Q. I have a Macintosh IIci. I want to upgrade my memory. Someone told me I can use regular SIMMs. Is this true?

A. I've gotten away with using standard dynamic RAM SIMMs in a Macintosh IIci. However, you really should be using dynamic fast page mode SIMMs with access time ratings of at least 80 nanoseconds. Sometimes regular old 100-ns SIMMs will work for a while, but most machines will exhibit serious timing problems.

Q. Can I use the large SIMMs from an Apple LaserWriter printer in my Macintosh IIfx?

A. No. It's true that the IIfx uses a physically larger SIMM than your traditional Macs, such as the SE, IIcx, and IIci. It's also true that these SIMMs resemble the LaserWriter SIMMs, but they won't work in the IIfx.

Q. Can I take a SIMM out of an IBM computer and use it in my Macintosh II or IIx?

A. You can't use a SIMM from an IBM PS/2, as they are model-specific and of a proprietary design. However, many IBM PC clone 286 and 386 machines utilize a standard 9-bit SIMM that will work in your Mac II or IIx, provided that they are at least 100 nanoseconds. You could even use the standard IBM SIMMs in any of the lower-end Macs up to and including the IIcx and IIsi, but not the IIci, IIfx, and so on.

Q. Wait a minute. The Mac SIMMs are 8-bit and the IBM's are 9-bit. How can the 9-bit SIMMs work where an 8-bit is called for?

A. Easily. When you put a 9-bit IBM SIMM in place of an 8-bit Macintosh SIMM, the ninth bit is ignored and the SIMM works fine. This is done all of the time by people that own both IBM's and Macintoshes. The one thing that you can't do is put an 8-bit SIMM in the IBM machine. The IBM machines need the ninth bit for parity (error reporting). Since parity is optional in Mac Land (and only on a few select models), it is fine to use the 8-bit SIMMs.

Q. Is parity a very expensive option? Should I spend the money to get it for my IIfx.

A. At this time the parity option is a very expensive option that requires that you exchange your standard IIfx logic board for a parity board. I was quoted over $1000 for this option last year. It may however come down in time. Do you really need it ? Well, it certainly would be nice, considering even the cheapest IBM $200 clone has it. Parity (error checking/reporting) is important. It lets you know when a memory problem occurs so that you don't put valuable data into a black hole in memory and lose it. However, despite its importance, it's still too pricey for me. The government purchases a lot of Macintoshes loaded with the parity option for important projects to ensure data integrity. Aside from the government, and a few other individuals, I don't know of too many people who have purchased this option. This option also requires that you replace all of your SIMMs with parity SIMMs, which is another additional expense.

Q. Do any of the Macintosh PowerBooks use SIMMs ?

A. No. The Macintosh PowerBook 100, 140, 145, and 170 all come with at least 2MB of memory that is soldered directly to the motherboard. In addition, the Power-Book 170 has another 2MB of memory installed on a secondary logic board for a total of 4MB standard.

Q. What are my upgrade options for the Macintosh PowerBooks?

A. The PowerBook 100, 140, 145, and 170 all support RAM expansion via a 70-pin RAM expansion connector. In the PowerBook 100 and 140, this connector is located to the rear left of the unit, in front of the batteries. In the PowerBook 170, this expansion connector is located on the secondary logic board, which is also located to the rear left.

The RAM expansion connector will support an optional memory expansion card. These cards usually come in capacities of either 2, 4, or 6MB.

Q. Can I take a memory expansion card out of my PowerBook 100 and use it in a PowerBook 140, 145, or 170. If not, why?

A. You can't take a standard PowerBook 100 memory card and put it in a Power-Book 140, 145, or 170. The reason is the PowerBook 100 has a 16-bit data path, while the PowerBook 140, 145, and 170 utilize a 32-bit data path. This means that the PowerBook 140 and 170 have more signal lines; therefore, the PowerBook 100 board would not be upwardly compatible. However, I have seen a few cleverly designed memory cards for the PowerBook 140 and 170 that are downwardly compatible with the PowerBook 100. The board is 32-bit, but the PowerBook 100 only uses part of the circuitry to function.

Q. Can I take my memory expansion card out of my old, original Mac portable and install it into my PowerBook 170.

A. No. None of the memory expansion cards are compatible between the original Portable and the new PowerBooks.

Q. How can I get System 7's virtual memory feature to work properly on my PowerBook 100? Do I need more memory?

A. While more memory always is helpful when running under System 7, you really can't do virtu

al on this machine. Virtual memory should be run on a 32-bit processor. I recommend at least a 68030-based machine. Your PowerBook 100 only has a Motorola 68HC00 processor, which is like a turbo Macintosh Plus, SE or Macintosh Classic. If you really need all the features of System 7 on your PowerBook (like virtual memory), you really need to step up to a PowerBook 140, 145, or 170. These three models all utilize a 68030 microprocessor.

Q. I want to upgrade my PowerBook 170 to 8MB of memory. However, I am concerned that if I do this, my battery will drain much quicker. Should I be concerned?

A. Go ahead and upgrade your PowerBook 170 to 8MB of RAM. You'll find that the added memory makes System 7 and the unit run a whole lot smoother. As far as power drain is concerned, it will be more than if you had 4MB, but it's still negligible. The PowerBooks utilize a 2.5 ampere-hour battery, which is pretty good. I have personally gotten a little more than this out of a fully charged PowerBook 170. Additionally, the PowerBooks utilize a great new feature called Power Cycling. The old Macintosh Portables didn't have this feature.

Power Cycling is a technique that conserves power, replacing the Idle mode from the older Macintosh Portables. Basically, when there is no input activity on your PowerBook for more than 2 seconds, power to the main processor chip sets is reduced. However, the contents of the CPU registers are saved and restored when activity resumes. During this whole process your cursor still blinks and the keyboard is still scanned for input.

Finally, the PowerBooks use a special type of memory called pseudostatic RAM (PSRAM), which has much lower power consumption than traditional dynamic RAM found in the desktop Macs. I would be more worried about excessive hard drive use devouring all of your available power.

CHAPTER 6

Power Supply

Macintosh computers are very sophisticated electronic computing devices. But for any active electronic device to be functional, obviously it requires a source of power. This source is called the power supply. The power supply is as important to the health of your Macintosh computer as the human heart is to the health of your body. In fact, these two "organs" have many similarities. The heart pumps blood through your veins and arteries to your muscles, lungs, brain, and other vital organs. If your heart were to malfunction and not properly supply these areas with blood, one or more of your organs would shut down, causing you to fall ill. If your heart were to stop pumping blood altogether, you would most certainly die.

When you power up your Macintosh, the power supply is supposed to do one thing: deliver and maintain the appropriate levels of electrical voltage (electricity) to the thousands of intricate circuits that comprise the computer. Electricity in this case is equivalent to the blood in a human body. If the power supply does not deliver enough electricity to sustain these levels within a specific tolerance, the computer cannot operate properly. It may work for a while and then die or malfunction, or it may never come to life.

The Achilles' heel of Macintosh computers has always been the power supply. Simply put, Macintosh power supplies are expensive and prone to constant failure. In fact, many Macintosh computers have barely enough power to sustain even a mild upgrade such as additional memory or a hard drive. In this chapter we discuss power supply basics, the theory of operation, and power control circuitry. We also review the various technical aspects of Macintosh power supplies and discuss general troubleshooting techniques for power-related problems.

Power Supply Basics

Computers have one of two basic types of power supplies: linear and switching. Linear power supplies are found in very old computers and electronic devices. These units typically deliver the same amount of power, such as 5 volts or 12 volts DC (direct current) steadily without variation. They are usually large, heavy, and very susceptible to power surges, voltage drops, line noise and fluctuations—none of which is a desirable feature of microcomputer power supplies.

Today's computers use a large variety of sophisticated integrated circuits and electronic components. These machines, therefore, have unique and demanding power requirements. Switching power supplies are specifically designed to meet the more complex demands that modern technology requires. A switching power supply has the following advantages over a linear power supply:

1. Switching power supplies make extensive use of semiconductors instead of the large copper-wound steel coils, making them smaller, lighter, and more reliable than linear power supplies.
2. Switching power supplies are designed to work with a wide range of AC (alternating current) line voltages.

Theory of Operation

The switching power supplies found in microcomputers may come in many shapes and sizes, but they all perform the same basic task. They take the incoming AC line current, which typically is 110/115 volts (US) or 220/230 volts (overseas) and 50 or 60 Hz (cycles), and convert it into something that the computer can use. This is necessary because digital circuits found in computers usually don't work well with fluctuating power like AC (alternating current). Digital circuits need continuous power, or DC (direct current).

Specifically, today's computers use 5 and 12 volts DC, and the Macintosh is no exception. Most of the Mac's integrated circuits and logic (chips and boards) are powered by 5 volts DC, while the fan, floppy, and hard disk drive motors use 12 volts DC. The switching power supply provides and maintains both of these levels by delivering the power in a series of bursts as it is needed. This entire process is accomplished through a sequence of six basic stages, which are described below.

Primary line filter (PLF) stage

The primary line filter stage performs two functions. First, it suppresses surges and spikes that may come across the AC line and damage the computer. Second, it prevents any RF (radio frequency) noise from going back onto the AC line. Radio frequency noise can cause interference to other electronic devices—yours or someone else's. For this reason the RF function is a legal requisite of all approved FCC, Class B, Subpart J computing devices.

Rectification stage

The rectification stage converts the incoming AC line voltage (110/220) to high voltage DC (typically 300 volts). This stage is somewhat complex since most Macs have an autoranging capability that allows them to self-adjust to the incoming AC voltage. This range can be from a minimum of 90 volts to a maximum of 270 volts AC, at 50 or 60 Hz (cycle). These power supplies automatically adjust to work with any power level within these specifications.

Capacitor stage

The capacitor stage stores energy used to power the computer. Switching power supplies are designed to draw and supply current in bursts. To do this, while using varying AC voltages, this stage stores incoming power so that a continuous output supply is always available while the machine is on, regardless of the input voltage variances. This stage allows the machine to tolerate subtle voltage fluctuations which are very common when dealing with AC power from the wall.

Solid-state switch stage

The solid-state switch stage converts the high-voltage DC (typically 300 volts) from stage 2 into high-voltage AC (typically 300 volts). This may get confusing. In stages 1 through 3 we converted the incoming AC (let's say 110 volts) into high-voltage DC (300 volts). Stage 4 then converts 300 volts DC into 300 volts AC.

To recap:

1. The incoming power is "cleaned up" (stage 1).
2. 110 AC is converted to high-voltage DC (stage 2).

3. Some of this energy is then stored (stage 3).

4. High-voltage DC is converted to high-voltage AC (stage 4).

What confuses most people is that we've gone from AC to DC, then back to AC, when the desired output levels that the computer works with are 5 and 12 volts DC, not AC. There are benefits in going back to high voltage AC. First, by converting back to AC you have isolated the power from the original AC line source. This makes for cleaner and more stable power. Second, to achieve the desired outputs of 5 and 12 volts DC from high-voltage AC, transformers are required to step down the voltages. We discuss this benefit next, in stage 5.

Transformer stage

Transformers are electromagnetic devices that simply change the voltage of AC. They consist of two coils of wire; the primary coil on the input side and the secondary coil on the output side. The voltage change is derived from the total windings in each coil. One property of high-voltage AC is that it can be passed through smaller transformers to get the final output levels of 5 and 12 volts. This reduces both the weight and heat buildup in the power supply, which is desirable. During this stage, step-down transformers convert high-voltage AC to 5 and 12 volts (again). This output is then passed through a rectifier, which is used to create direct current. The end result is 5 and 12 volts DC, which are the voltages that the computer can now use.

Final filter stage

The final filter stage eliminates any remaining RF noise on the line. Once in a while you will get noise from stage 4 that needs to be filtered out.

These are the basic stages of a switching power supply. Please keep in mind that this is a simplified model, and that this entire process is very complex, with many substages that would exceed the scope of this book. However, it's important for you to have a good understanding of what's really going on inside your power supply.

Power Control Circuitry

The power control circuitry of the Macintosh coordinates the power-on and power-off processes of the machine. The power-on process is very simple to understand: it turns the machine on. The power-off process turns the machine off. Let's examine these processes in greater detail.

Power-on process

The power-on process is a very straightforward process. It's simply a matter of locating the on/off switch in the rear of the unit and depressing it to the on position. This switch connects and disconnects the AC current to the power supply. All Macintosh units have an on/off switch.

This switch is actually an easily replaceable part of the power supply module in the following units: Plus, SE, SE/30, Classic, and Classic IIs. Other Macs have the on/off switch soldered directly to the motherboard. These models are the LC, LC II, II, IIx, IIcx, IIsi, IIci, IIfx, and Quadra 700, 900, and 950. However, there are two serious disadvantages to having the on/off switch on the motherboard:

1. Switches are mechanical devices. Turning the machine on and off over and over will eventually cause this switch to wear out, which means someday it will need to be replaced.
2. If the switch is soldered to the motherboard, great care must be taken in removing it. The motherboard is a multilayered circuit board that can be easily damaged, making this a tricky operation for the novice. As you've probably guessed by now, Apple won't replace this switch for you. However, they will replace your motherboard at a great expense.

If you have decent soldering skills and equipment, you can purchase this switch for less than $5 (made by C & K) and replace it in 3 to 4 minutes. If you don't feel comfortable doing the work yourself, there are hundreds of repair depots that will do it for you at a fraction of what Apple would charge.

The Mac II, IIx, LC, LC II, IIcx, IIsi, IIci, IIfx, and Quadra 700, 900, and 950 can also be started by pressing the power-on key located on the ADB (Apple Desktop Bus) keyboard. This key is normally located in the upper-right-hand corner of the extended keyboards, which have the function keys (F1, F2, F3, and so on) across

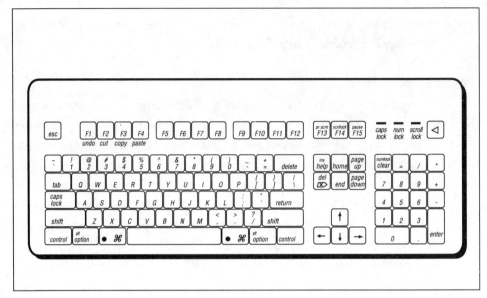

Figure 6-1. The Apple extended keyboard

the top. On standard ADB keyboards, this key is located upper-center. During this keyboard variation of the power-on process, the following events take place:

1. The user presses the power-on key located on the ADB keyboard.
2. When the ADB power-on key is depressed, pins 2 and 4 are shorted together, which causes the power-on line to go to a logic low.
3. When the power-on line is forced low, the power control circuitry releases power (from 3 to 6 volts DC) to the PFW (power failure warning) line, pulling it to a logic high. In the Mac II, IIx, and IIfx, this power is provided by a pair of 3-volt lithium batteries. In the Mac LC, LC II, IIsi, IIcx, IIci, and Quadra 700, 900, and 950, this power comes from a +5-volt DC trickle line inside of the power supply.
4. A charged capacitor on the logic board discharges to the power supply. This signals the power supply to turn on. Basically, the power supply is being "jump started."
5. The power supply then turns on, and the computer comes to life. The machine will remain on as long as the supply can maintain +5 volts to the PFW line.

The keyboard power-on key cannot be used to turn the Mac off. There are other ways of doing this.

Power-off process

The power-off sequence is an equally straightforward process to understand: it shuts your Macintosh off. In the Mac Plus, SE, SE/30, Classic, and Classic II, you should run the Shut Down command prior to power off. This command prepares the machine for a graceful power down. You then place the on/off switch in the off position to complete the job.

In the Mac LC, II, IIx, IIcx, IIsi, IIsi, IIfx, and Quadra 700, 900, and 950, the Shut Down command performs both functions mentioned above. When Shut Down is executed, these machines are prepared for a graceful power down, and a power interrupt is automatically asserted to the general logic circuitry. The general logic circuitry interrupts the CPU (central processing unit) and the power control circuitry then forces the PFW line low. The power supply then shuts itself down.

Technical Overview

Power supplies come in many shapes and sizes. Typically a power supply is a separate, self-contained, boxlike unit located inside the computer case. This unit is easily replaced. The Mac SE, SE/30, LC, II, IIx, IIcx, IIsi, IIci, IIfx, and Quadra 700, 900, and 950 all fall into this category.

The Mac Plus, Classic, and Classic II don't have separate power supplies. Instead, the power supply circuitry has been incorporated directly onto the analog video board, making it a dual-function board. The design of this board is very poor, and it shows. Both the Mac Plus and Classic units are high-failure units, which is directly related to this design. Most of the components are underrated (that is, not quality components), and to make matters worse, Apple didn't even provide a cooling fan in the Plus. Built in obsolescence? Could be.

Interchangeability

Many of the Mac power supplies are interchangeable with other members in the various Mac families. This can be very beneficial to know when trying to locate a replacement power supply for your machine. It's always good to know which power supplies you can and cannot substitute.

For instance, your dealer might not have a power supply for a Quadra 700, but might have one for a IIcx. The IIcx supply is identical to the supply in the Quadra 700, fits perfectly, and works the exact same way. But for some strange reason, dealers sometimes try to charge more money for the Quadra 700 power supply. It's the same part!

The table below is a cross compatibility listing of the various Macintosh power supplies.

Table 6-1. Power supply

Mac Power Supply	Interchange With
PLUS	PLUS or 512, 512KE, etc
SE	SE or SE/30
SE/30	SE/30 or SE
CLASSIC	CLASSIC or CLASSIC II
CLASSIC II	CLASSIC II or CLASSIC
LC	LC ONLY
II	II, IIX or IIFX
IIX	II, IIX or IIFX
CX	CX, CI or QUADRA 700
SI	SI ONLY
CI	CX, CI or QUADRA 700
IIFX	II, IIX or IIFX
QUADRA 700	CX, CI or QUADRA 700
QUADRA 900	QUADRA 900 or QUADRA 950
QUARDA 950	QUADRA 900 or QUADRA 950

Note: The Macintosh IIfx power supply is interchangeable but has a better cooling system than II or IIx power supplies. I suggest that IIfx users not substitute with the lower-grade II/IIx power supplies, except in a pinch

Generally speaking I don't replace Macintosh power supplies with Apple factory replacements. They're hard to get (without paying a dealer to install them), expensive, and don't have a great deal of output. If your original power supply has died after a year or so of use, what can you realistically expect out of another factory-issued unit? Especially, if you have upgraded your system with additional memory or an internal hard disk drive. These things tend to require a great deal of extra power.

For instance, I recently burned up a Mac IIci power supply. At the time this computer was less than two years old. I called the local authorized Apple dealer only to find that they didn't have the part in stock. They invited me to leave my computer with them for two to three weeks and pay them $475, plus $150 for them to install and test the new supply. That's a total of $625 for a 90-watt power supply and installation. The thing is only worth about $150 to $250, and you can remove this supply blindfolded with one hand tied behind your back.

Solution? I scoured my trusty trade magazines searching for vendors selling replacement Macintosh power supplies at reasonable prices. I found three vendors: Quadmation, Power Systems, and Mactronics (see Appendix A). Each of these three companies offered power supplies ranging from 200 to 400 watts for around $250 to $350. And their power supplies were approximately three to five times more powerful than the Apple-issued power supply. The Quadmation model lasted about 15 minutes, and their tech support and general attitude was lousy. They wouldn't even give me a refund. The Power Systems and Mactronic units performed admirably. Both of these units were very high quality and had well-engineered designs that worked the first time. In addition, their customer service and tech support was top notch and I had their units in less than 48 hours.

Output voltage ratings

The output voltage ratings of a power supply are very important. They tell you how much power you have to work with in a given machine. Every board, chip, and disk drive requires power to be functional. The more power they draw, the less you have left to work with. Some Macs, such as the Plus, Classic, and Classic II, come from the factory with very little power remaining for upgrades (such as memory, hard drives, and so on). A typical hard disk drive can draw anywhere from 12 to over 30 watts of power, which is a substantial loss to the Mac Plus, SE, SE/30, Classic, Classic II, LC, and IIsi. These units have less than 100 watts of output.

It's very easy to calculate DC output power. The first thing that you have to do is get a pencil and paper, then look at the lid of your power supply. Most manufacturers provide a decal listing output information. For example, the decal on a power supply in a Mac SE might list the following output information:

+5 volts DC	6.00 amps
+12 volts DC	1.25 amps
+12 volts DC	2.10 amps
-12 volts DC	0.05 amps

To calculate the output power, you'll need to use a formula from Ohm's law: P=V * I. In this example P=power, which is the work that can be performed by an electrical current. The unit of measure for power is the watt. V=Voltage, which is electrical pressure or force. I=current, which is the quantity of electrons passing a given point. The unit of current is the ampere. To get the wattage of this power supply, simply multiply volts times amps, then add up all of the numbers.

According to the formula ((5 * 6 = 30, 12 * 1.25 = 15, 12 * 2.10= 25.2, -12 x .05 = 6)) [ignore the - sign] = (30+15+25.2+6)=76.2 watts. This is how much power the SE and SE/30s have to work with. This formula can be applied to all Macintosh power supplies.

General Troubleshooting Techniques

Whenever you have a problem with your Macintosh that appears to be hardware related, always test the power supply first. The reason is very simple: All Macs are underpowered (except the Quadra 900 and 950), and everything in the machine needs power to function properly. Therefore, power-related problems can look like other hardware problems. You must always ask yourself the question, is that device (hard drive, board, and so on) really defective, or could it be getting too little or no power from the supply? Many a board and hard drive has gone to an early grave when the real culprit was the power supply.

The following are good procedures and techniques with which to begin:

1. Is the machine plugged in and turned on?

2. Do you have at least 90 volts AC going from the wall to the Mac? The ideal levels would be from 110 to 120; however, this unit is resilient. To test power output coming from the wall, you'll need to use a voltmeter. Plug one end of the power cord into the wall, then test the other. If you get acceptable voltage at this point, you know that the wall power and the cord power are both good. If you don't have at least 90 volts AC, you won't have a working Mac. For this reason, keep your computer off of the same circuits that copiers, laser printers, space heaters, wall unit air conditioners, and coffee urns use. These things can cause the power to dip, which may "anger" your machine.

3. Next, test the DC outputs of the power supply. If you have a Mac II, IIx, or Quadra 900 or 950, you'll have to open the machine to test them. You must first ground the black (common) probe, then test pins 1 through 15 on the internal power supply to logic board connector with the red probe. Make sure that the machine is on before and while you test.

Table 6-2. Test points for the II, IIX, and IIFX

Pin	Signal Name	Signal Description
1	+12 volts	+12 volts
2	+5 volts	+5 volts
3	+5 volts	+5 volts
4	+5 volts	+5 volts
5	+5 volts	+5 volts
6	+5 volts	+5 volts
7	GND	Ground
8	GND	Ground
9	GND	Ground
10	GND	Ground
11	GND	Ground
12	GND	Ground
13	N/C	Not used
14	-12 volts	-12 volts
15	PFW	Power fail

Note: *Pin #15 can be used to turn the machine off and on by grounding it.

If you have a Mac Plus, SE, SE/30, Classic, Classic II, LC, LC II, IIcx, IIsi, IIci, or Quadra 700, testing the DC voltages inside the machine can be difficult. These power supplies are harder to get at. However, you don't need to open up these machines to take the voltage readings—you can cheat. These machines are equipped with an external floppy disk drive port. You'll have to locate this port. It's a DB-19 female-type connector located in the rear of the unit (see diagram below). Most external floppy kits that use this port require both 5 and 12 volts DC, making it an ideal place to "tap" the Mac.

The pins that we're most interested in are pins 1 through 8. To perform this test, you need a voltmeter and a small paper clip. Unbend the paper clip into a thin piece of wire. Set your voltmeter to DC. Ground the black probe by placing it inside a screw hole on the back. While the machine is on, place the paper clip in pin 1, touch the paper clip with the red probe, and record your readings. Repeat this procedure for pins 1 through 8.

Acceptable Voltage Levels

When testing the 5, 12, and -12-volt output levels, exactly 5, 12 and -12-volt readings would be best, although not likely. There are acceptable ranges that your readings may fall into. These test points and ranges are listed below.

Table 6-3. Test points for machines with DB-19F connector.

Pin	Signal Name	Signal Description
1	GND	Ground
2	GND	Ground
3	GND	Ground
4	GND	Ground
5	-12 volts	-12 volts
6	+5 volts	+5 volts
7	+12 volts	+12 volts
8	+12 volts	+12 volts

Range would be signal description + or - 5 to 10 percent. For example, let's take 12 volts DC—10 percent either way would be 1.2 volts which would make the range 10.8 to 13.2 volts. I would not go outside these boundaries. Even though a 10 percent tolerance is generally acceptable, my preference is within 5 percent.

I always like my readings to be a little bit on the high side when I test the power supply. If your readings are seriously outside these ranges, you most likely are experiencing a power-related problem. If you got nothing at all, reverify that the machine is plugged in, turned on, and so on. If you still don't get anything, you may have a blown fuse, a bad on/off switch or relay, or a dead power supply. Any one of these things require that you remove the cover and look inside of the power supply. Removal and installation procedures for each Mac model are found in their respective chapters. As far as the fuses go, it has been my experience that nine out of ten times, the $400 power supply will blow and the 6-cent fuse will hang tough and go unscathed.

When switching power supplies really blow up, they generally are not worth fixing. If you don't replace every damaged component during the rebuild process, it will blow up again.

Voltage Adjustments

Let's assume that you got some voltage readings (too little or too much) when you tested the power supply, but they were out of the acceptable range. You can try adjusting the power supply. It's important to note that only a handful of Mac power supplies are adjustable. For instance, several manufacturers make power supplies for Apple. Astec, GE, Taiwan Limited, and Sony are the major players. Typically the Sony and Taiwan Limited supplies that are found in the SE, SE/30, II, IIx, and IIfx can be adjusted. The combo power supply/analog video sweep boards found in the Mac Plus, Classic, and Classic II can be adjusted as well. The adjustment potentiometer is located right on or inside the power supply. In the Mac II, IIx, and IIfx, it's marked RV-171-REGADJ. In the SE and SE/30 it's marked VADJ. On the Plus it simply says "voltage," and on the Classic and Classic II there are no markings. These potentiometers are located almost dead center on the board.

This adjustment is something that you may have to do as your machine ages, or when the machine is upgraded with extra memory, boards, disk drives, and so on. Heavily upgraded machines increase the load on the power supply. The Astec and GE power supplies can automatically adjust to the increased loads, where most Sony and Taiwan Limited supplies must be manually adjusted.

Note: When performing the adjustments, do not attempt to turn the potentiometer 360 degrees. It will break.

Power-Related Problems

The following are common symptoms of power-related problems.

1. The machine fails to turn on via the ADB power-on key.
2. The machine fails to turn on via the on/off switch.
3. The machine fails to turn on via both ADB power-on key or the on/off switch, and appears to be dead.
4. The machine overheats and shuts itself down after it is powered on.
5. A previously working machine unexpectedly freezes or locks up (bad software can do this too).
6. Your disk drives don't respond or spin up.
7. A known good expansion card does not work in an expansion slot.
8. The machine spontaneously reboots.
9. Intermittent and changing Sad Mac error codes occur, often an indicator of a floating memory error.
10. Devices that use the external Macintosh ports (such as keyboards) and external disk drives for power don't respond.

Power for the Macintosh PowerBooks

Power for the PowerBook family of computers is provided by a built-in battery, which is charged by an external battery charger. The PowerBook computers are designed to use components with low power requirements and employ special hardware and firmware to further reduce power consumption when your machine isn't in use. The battery in the PowerBook computers provides power for the main logic board, an internal disk drive (in the PowerBook 140, 145, and 170, but not the PowerBook 100), a flat-panel video display, the keyboard, and a trackball or other pointing device.

The PowerBook family has a battery charger and power transformer in a separate unit connected to the main system unit by a cable. The battery is in a compartment inside the main system unit.

The PowerBook 140, 145, and 170 computers are switched on by the power on/off button. In these computers, the Power Manager IC puts the computer in a low-power-consumption state (the sleep state) when the computer isn't being used.

A/C power adapter

The A/C power adapter in the PowerBook family is designed to typically operate in a constant current and constant voltage mode. This means that the voltage supplied by the power adapter remains relatively constant and fluctuates only slightly (in the range of 7.5 to 7.9 volts) as a result of current supplied by the power adapter. Likewise, the current supplied by the power adapter remains relatively constant and fluctuates only slightly (in the range of 1.8 amps to 2.2 amps) as the result of voltage supplied by the power adapter.

As the computer's battery approaches its fully charged state, the power adapter changes from a constant current mode to a constant voltage mode, at which point the voltage supplied by the power adapter slowly increases until the battery reaches its fully charged state.

The A/C power adapter for the PowerBook 140, 145, and 170 computers, which is limited to 7.9 volts maximum, is different than the A/C power adapter for the PowerBook 100, which is limited to 7.5 volts maximum. The A/C power adapter is designed to draw a maximum of 100 microamps of leakage current at 7 volts when A/C power is not supplied to the adapter (that is, the adapter isn't plugged in). This design prevents excessive draining of the battery by always maintaining the battery voltage at the computer's power adapter terminal, regardless of the state of the A/C power adapter (that is, whether or not the power adapter is plugged in).

Shut down

The PowerBook 140, 145, and PowerBook 170 computers all use a "true" shut-down feature that conserves battery power by allowing you to turn your computer off to the point where only the real-time clock, parameter RAM, and other essential support circuits remain on. This is unlike the original Macintosh Portable, in which the choice provided by the Shut Down menu leaves the Power Manager and other power-consuming devices on.

The main difference between the shutdown and sleep states is the amount of DC current drain. The shutdown state turns off main RAM, all custom integrated circuits, the keyboard processor, the Power Manager, VIA, SWIM, SCC/SCSI, serial driver chips, and many other nonessential devices, resulting in a DC current drain of about 400 µA (or about 4 percent of the DC current drain of the sleep state). By contrast, the sleep state acts about the same on the PowerBook computers as it does on the original Macintosh Portable by leaving these devices on but in a low-power mode, where the total DC current drain is about 5 mA. The result of the shutdown feature is a longer battery storage life (without recharging) compared to the original Macintosh Portable, in which shutdown and sleep modes are approximately the same in terms of power drain on the battery.

Power cycling

Power cycling is a power-saving feature designed specifically for the Power-Book 140, 145, and 170 that replaces the idle mode used in the original Macintosh Portable. When the Macintosh Portable or PowerBook 100 is in the "idle" state, the number of main processor wait states to RAM increases from 1 to 64, saving at best 10 percent of the CPU power (approximately 75 mW for the MC68030). Power cycling in the PowerBook 140, 145, and 170 reduces the processor's power up to 90 percent (450 mW for the 68030 and 150 mW for the 68882) during idle periods.

Power cycling works in the following manner. The registers of the 68030 (and the 68882 of a PowerBook 170) are saved, and power to them is turned off if no input activity is detected for approximately 2 seconds. The remaining system is left on, the cursor continues to blink, and the keyboard is still scanned.

The power cycle consists of driving the processor's address and data lines low, disabling the selects to any chips that are on, and then restoring power to the processor no later than 16 milliseconds after power is turned off. When power is back on, the processor registers are restored and the processor monitors the system for activity. If none is detected, the power cycle repeats.

Battery charger and voltage control circuits

The PowerBook's battery charger rectifies AC line power to DC and transforms it to 7.5 ± 0.1 volts on the PowerBook 100 and to 7.9 ± 0.1 volts, which is input to the main system unit. The battery charger can accept input power of 85 to 270 volts, and limits output current to 1.5 amps. The PowerBook's voltage-control circuits on the logic board generate three voltages: +5, +12 (on the PowerBook 100 and +8 maximum on the PowerBook 140, 145, and 170), and −5.

The PowerBook's battery monitor consists of an operational amplifier, an analog-to-digital converter, and a comparator. The amplifier converts the battery voltage of 5.12 to 7.68 volts, or 5.12 to 8.9 volts on the PowerBook 140, 145, and 170 to a 0-to-5-volt input to the A to D converter. The comparator monitors the output of the A to D converter, and removes power from all circuitry except itself if the battery voltage drops below 5.65 volts. If the battery voltage rises to above 5.65 volts (as, for example, if the battery charger is connected), the comparator restores power to the system.

The input from the battery charger is also monitored by a comparator. If the charger input voltage is higher than the battery voltage—that is, if the battery charger is plugged in and connected to the computer—then the comparator applies voltage to the battery charge controller and asserts a signal that tells the Power Manager IC that the battery is being charged.

The battery charge controller is a voltage regulator with a switchable output. When the charger is initially connected to a Macintosh PowerBook computer with a low battery, the Power Manager IC connects the charger directly to the battery. The battery is therefore charged at the maximum rate (1.5 amps) until battery voltage reaches 7.2 volts. The Power Manager IC measures the time required to raise the battery voltage to this level, and maintains the connection for an equal amount of time to assure that the battery is fully charged. At the end of that time, the Power Manager IC switches the voltage regulator into the circuit.

The voltage regulator maintains the input voltage to the battery at a level that causes the battery to accept just enough charge to replace that lost through self-discharge. The maintenance voltage is 6.94 volts to 7.16 volts at 20° C, and decreases with increasing temperature at the rate of -7.5 ± 1.0 mV per degree C.

Sleep state in the PowerBooks

Whether or not your PowerBook computer enters the sleep state is controlled by a firmware routine known as the BatteryMonitor. The BatteryMonitor routine is called by the interrupt handler each time a one-second interrupt occurs. This routine performs the following functions:

- Checks the battery voltage to see if it is necessary to alert the user that the battery voltage is low.
- Checks to see if you have used the Control Panel desk accessory to change the length of time that your PowerBook must be idle before the Battery-Monitor routine automatically invokes the sleep state. If you've changed this time, the BatteryMonitor routine stores the new time in parameter RAM.
- Turns off the sound circuit when it's not needed. The sound circuit uses a relatively large amount of power.
- Updates the real-time clock function of the Power Manager IC.
- Checks the internal temperature of the PowerBook to see if it's necessary to alert you that a high-temperature condition exists.
- Monitors the amount of time your PowerBook has been idle, and causes the Power Manager IC to put the system into the sleep state if the idle time you've selected has been reached.

To further conserve power and enhance battery life, the operating system software detects if the sound chip is being used. If it hasn't been used, power is disconnected from the sound circuitry. During this process, a click may be heard from the speaker as the speaker coil de-energizes. The electrical discharge and subsequent sound can be stopped by plugging in a mini-jack into the Sound Output port.

The PowerBook computers aren't considered to be idle if any of the following kinds of activity are occurring:

- any ADB routine other than routine monitoring of the bus
- any I/O call to firmware (Read, Write, Control, Format, Status)
- any change in the cursor (for example, the rotation of a hand in the clock icon)

- any post-event call (for example, a call resulting from insertion of a disk)
- any communication through a serial port

The PowerBook 140, 145, and 170 computers do power-cycling after a 2-second delay. In comparison, the PowerBook 100 is considered idle after 15 seconds without activity of any kind. When the BatteryMonitor routine determines that the computer is idle, it causes the CPU to insert 64 wait states into RAM and ROM accesses; this lowers the effective clock rate to approximately 1 MHz. Interrupts continue to be processed at the full speed of the CPU.

After the PowerBooks have been idle for the amount of time you've selected, the BatteryMonitor routine puts the machine into the sleep state. When in sleep state, the PowerBooks maintain full power to system RAM, video RAM, and the Power Manager IC. The Power Manager IC stops the clocks to the SCC, the SWIM, and the ASC. By stopping the clocks to these devices, their power consumption is reduced almost to zero without requiring that they be reset, as would be necessary if all power were switched off. The Power Manager IC switches off power to the serial drivers, ROM, the flat-panel display, the ASC, the Sony sound ICs, the SCSI, and to a variety of pull-up resistors and other components. The Power Manager IC sends a signal to the internal modem (if one is installed) that causes the modem to shut itself down.

After putting the rest of the system in the sleep state, the Power Manager IC does no processing, except to monitor the 60-Hz interrupt signal. Each time the 60-Hz interrupt occurs, the Power Manager IC performs the following functions:

- updates the real-time clock.
- checks the wake-up timer to see if it matches the real-time clock.
- checks for events that should return the machine to the operating state, such as a keystroke or a Ring Detect signal from the modem (when you've enabled the modem feature)

Summary

In conclusion, we've taken an exhaustive look at the Macintosh power supplies. They are very important components that, unfortunately, fail frequently. Many times people overlook the power supply as the culprit. Think about it the next time a hard drive or a memory SIMM appears to be dead. Is it really dead? Could be. It could also be a power fuse on the bottom of the drive or just maybe it's not getting the +12 volts DC that drive motors need to spin up. Perhaps the memory SIMMs didn't get the necessary +5 volts that logic requires. In any case, there's one thing you can be sure of: Power supply problems are like a cancer—if you let them go untreated they'll get progressively worse.

Troubleshooting Power Supply Problems

Q. **Why is the power supply on my Macintosh so critical?**

A. Your power supply is critical because it takes AC (alternating current) from the wall outlet and converts it into the appropriate levels of DC (direct current) that your computer requires. All of the integrated circuits (chips) that comprise your Macintosh must have an adequate source of power to function properly. The power supply serves as this source. Without it, there's no life as we know it in Mac Land

Q. **Why does the power supply convert AC into DC. Wouldn't it be easier to use AC for everything?**

A. Yes, it would be much cheaper and easier to eliminate power supplies altogether and simply run a wire from your wall outlet to the Macintosh motherboard. However, it would not be very practical, nor would it work.

The reason that the Macintosh power supply converts AC to DC is very simple. In order for the Mac to be functional, it has to make this conversion. The chips inside your Mac (CPU, memory chips, and so on) are digital circuits that require a continuous source of power to function properly. These circuits can tolerate very little fluctuation, which makes DC the ideal choice to power these circuits. DC (direct current) is continuous power as opposed to AC. AC (alternating current) is an electrical current that reverses or changes direction (alternates). The frequency that AC alternates or reverses is measured in cycles per second (Hz). In the US, this frequency is 60 Hz, while 50 Hz is common in Europe and many other countries.

Q. **Is it possible for the current coming from my AC outlet to be insufficient to properly power my Mac? If so, what would be the symptoms be?**

A. Yes, it's possible for the AC power source from your wall to be inadequate.

Some symptoms are as follows:

- Your Mac does not respond.
- The Mac reboots for no apparent reason (usually when you are in the middle of something important).
- Your Mac shuts down for no apparent reason (usually when you are in the middle of something important).

If your Mac exhibits this type of behavior, the first thing you should do is check the incoming AC power from the wall with a voltmeter. In the US, you should be looking for a reading of around 100 or 115 volts AC. However, anything between 90 and 137 volts will suffice, with 110 to 115 being ideal. If the power goes below 90 volts AC, the Mac will never come to life.

Q. What would cause my the power to drop below 90 volts AC?

A. Brownouts and blackouts are very common causes of power loss. In addition, plugging many high-power consumption devices into the same outlet or power strip can cause problems, especially in older buildings. Here's a good example of this:

Mr. Peterson works in an office with several Macintosh computers, laser printers, and photocopiers. Unfortunately for Mr. Peterson, there is a shortage of wall outlets to plug this equipment into. As a result, two of his employees have had to resort to using multiple power strips and extension cords in an effort to share the only outlet that is available. For six and a half months this hasn't been a problem. But lately, these two employees have been complaining about their equipment—that they keep tripping their circuit breaker and losing power, an apparent overload condition. After resetting the breaker, they tested their outlet and got a reading of 108 volts AC, which is perfectly acceptable.

Frustrated, they both go back to work and turn on their Macs, laser printers, and space heaters. Only the laser printers and monitors come to life, while the Mac lays dead. What could be the problem? Yes, you guessed it—the space heaters. Recently it's been cold in the office and the space heaters were brought in. Space heaters are giant heating elements with coils that draw large quantities of power. With all of the computer equipment and the space heaters plugged into the lone outlet, it's no wonder there isn't enough left for the Macs. (Remember they need at least 90 volts, preferably 110 to 115.)

This may sound familiar to only some of you. But the reality of this situation is that items such as space heaters, wall unit air conditioners, microwave ovens, photocopiers, and laser printers all draw a great deal of power, which can adversely affect your Macs and other electronic equipment on your circuit. The bottom line is this: If the incoming power isn't good, the machine won't work.

Q. My Macintosh doesn't power up and my incoming power is around 120 volts, which is acceptable. What should I check for next?

A. Rule out the obvious things first. Ask yourself the following questions:

1. Is this machine plugged in?
2. Is this power cord good?
3. Is the power strip or surge suppressor on? Try plugging the machine straight into the wall without the strip/surge protector.
4. Is other electronic equipment in the room working ?
5. Has anything been moved lately?
6. Has anything out of the ordinary happened around here lately (such as a thunderstorm, earthquake, hurricane, blackout, brownout, or lightning strike)?
7. Have I tripped a circuit breaker or blown a fuse for this room?
8. Am I trying to run too much equipment off one outlet? Some people may laugh at you for asking these questions. But I can tell you from experience that many so called "service calls" are nothing more than machines that become unplugged or otherwise disconnected. And, yes, power cords can go bad (typically from people pulling or dogs chewing on them). If your Mac is still dead after ruling out the obvious, there's an excellent chance that your problem is with the power supply.

Q. I have a Macintosh SE/30 that's just dead. It doesn't appear to do anything at all. The incoming power, however, is good. Is it safe to assume that my problem is in the power supply? If so, is there an easy way to test it ?

A. Yes. Based on the information that you've provided, I would say your problem is most likely power related (a bad power supply, dead short, or similar problem).

Furthermore, you're in luck. There's a very simple test that you can perform on your SE/30 and any other Macintosh that has an external floppy disk drive connector (DB-19). To perform this test, you'll need a voltmeter and a paper clip, straightened out. To perform this test, you must follow these steps:

1. Set your voltmeter to DC (direct current).
2. If your voltmeter isn't autoranging, set it to the 20-volt scale.
3. Ground the black probe (ground/common) by inserting the tip into one of the screw holes on the back of your Mac's motherboard (not the external speaker jack). One of the screw holes located on either side of the SCSI port connector will do nicely.
4. Unbend the paper clip until it is a straight, stiff piece of wire.
5. Plug the machine in and try to power it up.
6. Insert the paper clip into the following pin holes on the external floppy disk drive connector: 4, 5, 6, 7, 8.
7. After you insert the paper clip into the pinhole, touch the paper clip with the red (hot) wire of your voltmeter. Look at your voltmeter, and record the voltage reading. Repeat this step for the remaining pins. The voltages that you should get are as follows:

Pin 4	0 volts DC
Pin 5	-12 volts DC
Pin 6	+ 5 volts DC
Pin 7	+12 volts DC
Pin 8	+12 volts DC

If you don't get exactly 5, 12, or -12 volts DC, don't worry. I rarely get these numbers exactly. There is some margin to work with here. As a rule of thumb, I am happy with 5, 12, or -12, plus or minus 5 to 10%. For example, if 12 volts was called on pin 7 and I got 10.9 volts, that would be okay, although it's on the low side. Likewise if I got 13.0 volts on the high side, it's close enough. However, pin 4 should read exactly 0 (ground).

It isn't necessary to test all five of these pins. I only test pins 6, 7, and 8. These are the most critical pins.

Note: Not all Mac's have -12 connected on pin 5. So don't worry if you don't get anything on this pin. Worry about pins 6, 7, and 8.

Q. Which Macs can I perform this test on ?

A. You can perform this test identically on any Macintosh computer that has a DB-19, external floppy disk drive connector. Macintosh computers that fall into this category are Macintosh 128, 512, 512KE, Plus, SE, SE/30, Portable, IIcx, IIci, Classic and Classic II.

Q. Why can I perform this test on the original Macintosh Portable, but not on my PowerBook?

A. The PowerBooks don't have a DB-19 interface. In fact, of the PowerBook 100, 140, 145, and 170 models, only the PowerBook 100 has an external floppy drive interface port. It's a special 20-pin port. You can test pins 6 ,7, 8, and 9 with the paper clip. Each of these pins should read 5 volts.

Q. I performed this test and got very strange readings on all of the pins. What am I doing wrong?

A. Verify that everything is plugged in and that the on/off switch is in the on position. Next, verify that you are using the correct pins on the DB-19 connector. If you're standing behind the Macintosh, the pins are numbered from top right to left:

10 9 8 7 6 5 4 3 2 1

o o o o o o o o o o(Rear View)o o o o o o o o o

19 18 17 16 15 14 13 12 11

Q. I've never heard of this test before. What does it really tell me? How do I interpret the results?

A. Stated simply, this test tells you whether or not your Macintosh's power supply is functioning properly. There is a method to this madness. First, rule out the obvious. Second, check the power coming into the computer. If these two things are good, then the next logical step is to verify that the power coming out of the power supply is good. This is a methodical process of elimination to problem solving. If the power coming out of the power supply is good, the problem isn't in the wall, power cord, or power supply. It's somewhere else. However, if the power coming out is bad, the problem is inside the power supply (assuming that the incoming power is good).

Q. Should this test be performed only when the Mac is dead?

A. No. The techniques and test mentioned in this chapter should be used first when trying to troubleshoot any serious Macintosh failures. Always check the power first. The reason for this is logical. Every board, chip, disk drive, fan, and motor inside your Macintosh requires power to be operative. Think about this. Just because your hard disk drive stops spinning doesn't mean that this disk drive is bad. It could be an absence of power. In fact, I have a client who experienced this very same situation.

Ms. Smith (not her real name) is an experienced computer technician. She had a Mac SE/30 computer with 4MB of RAM, a 20MB hard drive, and one floppy drive. Recently she upgraded to 8MB of RAM. One month later her hard drive stopped spinning. She tried replacing all of the memory chips to no avail. She then called me to order a new hard disk drive. I told her to check the power first. She told me she didn't have the time and to just send her the new drive. (Kind of pushy if you ask me.) I sent her the new drive and an invoice. She installed the new drive and the machine worked. Ms. Smith called me up laughing hysterically, "It worked, it worked. I told you it wasn't the power. Ha,Ha...." Hey, I'm human, I could be wrong, it was just a hunch. I then asked her if I could have her old disk drive as a trade in. I like to try to fix these things. She told me that she had already tossed it in the garbage. Oh well, I tried.

Guess what? Two weeks later I got another call. Guess who? Yup, Ms. Smith. Her new hard drive had conked out and she wanted another one. I was getting a little bit suspicious, so I asked her to please take the voltage readings. Sure enough, her voltage readings were very, very low. It wasn't her hard drive, it was a power problem. Lucky for her, there's an adjustment inside the Sony version of the Mac SE/30-class power supply. We made one five-minute adjustment and the hard drive came to life. Unfortunately, Ms. Smith had thrown out the old hard drive that wasn't defective after all. She also threw out a couple of hundred dollars. Never throw anything away until your absolutely sure it has no significant value. Even dead parts can be cannibalized to aid in the repair of simple problems.

Ms. Smith was confused, and you might be asking yourself the same question that Ms. Smith did. How could a power supply problem cause one hard drive to appear to be dead while the new one worked fine? Easily. Let's examine this issue. The power supply takes AC and converts it into 5 and 12 volts DC. Typically the 5 volts is used by logic (chips), while the 12 volts is used by motors and fans. Most hard drives use both 5 and 12 volts: 5 volts for the chips on the small PCB (printed circuit board) and 12 volts for the motor that turns the platters and so on.

The original drive in Ms. Smith's machine was an older 3.5-inch internal hard drive. The new one was a very small 2.5-inch internal hard drive. The new drive was smaller and used fewer components. A smaller drive usually means a smaller motor that draws less power than the old hard drive. Since the machine drew less power, the machine had barely enough power to function. This gave Ms. Smith the illusion that the problem had been cured. But power supply problems are like poison ivy. They can come right back. This has the potential of adversely affecting any electronic device inside the Macintosh (not just hard drives). Ms. Smith learned a valuable lesson, but it cost her a couple of hundred dollars.

Please keep that in mind whenever you are trying to troubleshoot any Mac—check the power first. There's no excuse for not doing this if you have a Mac with the DB-19. You don't even have to open up the machine.

Q. How would I go about testing the power supply of Mac without the DB-19, such as the Macintosh LC, LC II, Macintosh II, IIx, IIfx, and Quadra 900 and 950?

A. I could take each of these machines on a case-by-case basis. However, it's both easier and more practical to tell you one simple universal rule: Open the machine and locate the power cable that goes to your hard disk drive. (Most Macs as of 1992 have hard drives.) This cable is a four-wire cable. A typical color scheme and the corresponding values would be as follows:

Table 6-4. Four-wire color scheme cable

Internal Hard Drive Wire	Wire Color	Value
Ground	Black (B)	(0 volts)
	Red (R)	+ 5 volts DC
	Orange or Yellow (R)	+ 12 volts DC

```
    o  o  o  o
    |  |  |  |
    |  |  |  |
   O/Y  B  B  R
```

Like the other tests, you're still looking for 5 volts DC, 12 volts DC, and ground, with a nominal tolerance of 5% to 10% on the 5 and 12 volts. You could remove the power cable from the hard drive and test it this way, but I prefer to leave the cable plugged into the drive. This makes the test a little bit trickier. You have to follow each wire into the connector while it's plugged into the drive.

Q. **Why do I have to leave the hard drive power wire in the drive when I use this test ?**

A. You don't have to leave it in, it's just a good idea. The hard drive is an excellent 5- and 12-volt load factor. The power supply requires a good load factor to function properly. I like to keep the hard drive attached and running while I take my power readings. It doesn't make a huge difference; however, I feel that the readings are more accurate when the machine is under full load. Occasionally I even copy files from the floppy drive to the hard drive while I do the test. Since the floppy draws most of its power while it's turning, copying files back and forth really puts a good load on the unit. This is especially useful if you're adjusting the output of the power supply.

Q. **Which power supplies can be adjusted, and when should I adjust it?**

A. The integrated power supply/analog board modules of the Plus, Classic, and Classic II can be adjusted by gently turning a small potentiometer either clockwise or counter clockwise, depending on whether you want to turn the power up or down. On the Plus, the potentiometer is clearly marked: voltage. In the Classic and Classic II, the potentiometer is located toward the center of the analog board and is not marked.

Some models of the SE and SE/30 and the II, IIx, and IIfx use power supplies manufactured by Sony and/or Taiwan Limited that are equipped with a potentiometer marked either VADJ or RV. Voltage can be adjusted by turning the potentiometer either clockwise or counterclockwise. Under no circumstances should the poten tiometer be turned 360 degrees. It is not meant to be turned that much and can break if you go too far.

If you find that your power supply is on the low side and needs adjustment, you may need to adjust and retest the power supply several times before you get it right. Always try to go a little bit higher than the required 5 and 12 volts. Then lock the potentiometer down with nail polish or Elmer's glue to make sure it does not vibrate back out of adjustment. Use something you can get back off, not Super Glue.

Q. Should I adjust the power supply while the machine is off or on?

A. It would be very unwise to stick anything into a power supply while it is on. Adjust it while it is off and unplugged. Better safe than sorry.

Q. I recently tired to adjust the Sony power supply in my Macintosh IIfx. I turned off the unit and unplugged it from the AC power source. I then opened up the power supply and got zapped pretty bad. What caused this?

A. Power supplies make heavy use of electronic components called capacitors. Capacitors do one thing—store energy. Occasionally stored charges stay inside the machine even though the machine is unplugged and off. A good habit before opening up your power supply is this: After you shut down, turn off, and unplug your Mac, depress the on/off switch of your machine two or three times to discharge any charges that may still linger inside your power supply. You'll know if anything significant was in there if you happen to hear the machine try to start up while you're trying to discharge the power supply.

Q. What would cause my power supply to need adjustment?

A. Old age and upgrades, especially upgrades. When you add big, beefy memory and hard disk drive upgrades to the Macintosh, you increase the power demands placed on the power supply. Most IBM and other computers don't have a problem with this. Unfortunately there are several Macintosh power supplies that are pathetic, and heavy upgrades can cause these units to overload and even go up in smoke. The

Plus, SE, SE/30, Classic, LC, and IIsi are models with power supplies that are mediocre at best.

Q. **I have a Macintosh IIcx with a power supply manufactured for Apple by Astec. Is this a better power supply than the Sony?**

A. I am not aware of a Sony power supply used in the IIcx, IIci, or Quadra 700. (There could be one, but I've never seen it). These units use the same model and form factor power supply (Model 699-0392) and are interchangeable. The Astec power supply used in the IIcx, IIci, and Quadra 700 is a well-built unit. Astec makes excellent power supplies. Unfortunately, the specifications that Apple gave Astec and other vendors to work with were pretty bad. The approximate 90 watts of output is on the low side. It should be around 150 watts to accommodate the majority of memory and hard disk drive upgrade paths.

Q. **Is the power supply in the Mac II, IIx, and IIfx the same power supply?**

A. Yes and no. The power supplies in the Mac II and IIx are identical. The IIfx power supply differs only slightly. It has an upgraded fan and cooling mechanism. I have used IIfx supplies in Mac IIs and II supplies in IIfxs without any problem.

Q. **If my original Mac power supply dies, should I replace it with another Apple power supply or with a third-party supply?**

A. That depends. If your Macintosh is still under warranty, you should go to your local dealer for immediate warranty service. Don't open up the power supply. If the machine is under warranty, you may void it.

If the machine is out of warranty, that's a different story. I would never purchase any power supplies that Apple has spec'd out. Their power supplies are mediocre and expensive. In addition, Apple won't sell repair parts to individuals; they go through their service channels only. These service providers aren't supposed to allow end users to do their own repairs. They usually require that you bring your machine to them, wait until they have time to fix it, pay for parts and labor, and give them your old parts that Apple recycles. These costs add up.

Keep in mind that most (if not all) Mac power supplies are marginal. (Could it be built in obsolescence?) Why would you want to pay for and put something marginal back into your machine? If it's your nickel, you should purchase a third-party replacement supply rated at least double what your original supply was.

Q. **Where can I purchase third-party power supplies for the Macintosh?**

A. I know of only two companies that currently manufacture replacement Macintosh power supplies: Quadmation and Power Plus Systems (PPS).

Recently I had an opportunity to evaluate and benchmark power supplies from both companies. Being an expert in electrical engineering and design, I really put these units through their paces. The results were mixed. The Quadmation IIcx power supply I evaluated performed worse than Apple's. My Mac would not come on and stay on. Their technical support was unfriendly and not very helpful. When I inquired how to return this power supply for a refund, I was given a hard time. I would be surprised if the unit they shipped me would pass either UL or FCC certification.

The second company I evaluated was Power Plus Systems in Salt Lake City, Utah. I evaluated their IIcx/IIci/Quadra 700 power supply in the same manner as I did the Quadmation unit. The Power Plus unit was superior in every way to both the Quadmation and the Apple unit. I got at least twice the power of the Apple model at one half the price. When I had questions, they answered them promptly and intelligently. The president, Craig Rosenthal, even got on the line to see how I liked the unit. (He didn't even know me!) They also have a very generous two-year warranty. Double thumbs up to Power Plus Systems. You can contact PPS at 1-800-722-0602.

Q. **I have a brand new full page display plugged into the spare power jack on the back of my Macintosh IIfx. The unit had been working fine for one week. Now my Mac starts up, but my monitor appears to be dead. However, when I plug the monitor directly into the wall, it works fine. Is my power supply going bad? What should I do ?**

A. You did the right thing by plugging the monitor into the wall. It seems as though your monitor is drawing more power than your Mac can handle. The problem that you now have is a blown fuse inside your power supply. Your monitor was plugged into the secondary receptacle, which is schematically referred to as J2, which is protected internally by a fuse (F101). Normally, replacing fuses is a 50-50 proposition. However, this particular fuse has a much better survival rate. The rating of this fuse should be approximately 250 volts and 6.3 amps. When you replace fuses use only those with the proper rating. Make sure that the machine is unplugged before you attempt replacing the fuse. If the fuse keeps blowing, it's possible that capacitor C 101 (250 volts, 0.22 uf) located inside the power supply is defective. If you aren't familiar with electronics, however, this is best left to a professional. If the machine is still functional, simply plug the monitor into the wall, and you'll be on your way.

Q. How hard is it to repair a defective power supply? Is it worth the time and money ?

A. There are very few things that the average user can replace inside the power supply. Typically when one major component blows in a switching power supply, it often has a domino effect that takes out other components. Often you need sophisticated equipment to properly diagnose and remedy the problems. Another major drawback to repairing power supplies is that if you miss one defective part, it will most likely blow up on you again. Time is money. If you can't completely fix it quickly (in less than 30 to 60 minutes), it's not worth your time. Buy a new power supply. It will preserve your mental health and, besides, you get a warranty.

Q. What common failures in Mac power supplies are user-serviceable? What causes these failures?

A. The following is a list of high-failure, user-serviceable items in the power supply:

1. Fuses
2. On/off switches
3. Voltage adjustments (Sony and Taiwan Limited units only)

Since we've already discussed items 1 and 3, let's now move along to item 2.

On/off switches are mechanical switches that get a good bit of use. They eventually wear out. When these switches wear out, the power supply cannot be turned on. These switches cost less than $5 at local electronics stores and can be replaced in less than 10 minutes.

Q. I have heard many people debate the issue of leaving the Mac on while they are out of the office or home. Some people leave it on all day, while others turn their machines off every five minutes to save energy. What should I be concerned with and why?

A. It's a common misconception that energy is saved by turning the computer on and off every five or ten minutes. In fact, turning the machine on and off is very bad for the machine for several reasons. First, every time the machine is powered on, there is an initial surge of power. Second, every time you turn the machine on and off, all of the metal inside the Mac is heated and cooled. When you heat and cool metal too much, it can become fatigued and crack. The areas in the computer that are most prone to cracking are solder joints. When solder joints crack badly, they no longer make contact within their circuit, and the machine dies. Finally, all of this on and off physically wears out the switch. It's actually better to leave your computer on than to keep turning it on and off.

I am not a big fan of leaving the computer on 24 hours a day, 7 days a week. I prefer to come into work in the morning and turn the machine on, and then turn it off when I leave for home.

Q. I have a Mac II that won't boot up. I have ruled out the obvious and replaced my power supply and I still get absolutely nothing. My Apple dealer says that I should replace my motherboard. What should I really do ?

A. The odds are against two power supplies being bad in a row (but it could happen). First, I would remove all of the expansion cards from the six Nubus slots in the Mac II. A dead short in a card could knock out your machine. Second, test the two batteries located on your main logic board. The Mac II, IIx, and IIfx all use a two-battery combination to jump start the power supply. It's a terrible design. If one battery goes bad, that machine isn't coming on. The problem is that most people don't bother to check their batteries. These batteries need to read above 3.0 volts DC each for the II, IIx, and IIfx to turn on. If the batteries are very low, you must replace them. The problem here is that some logic boards have the batteries soldered in place. You'll have to be careful when removing them. The newer boards have a battery holder, which makes life easier.

When replacing batteries it's important to use 3.5- to 4.0-volt lithium batteries, not alkaline batteries. Alkaline batteries tend to leak, and this could damage your logic board.

Q. **I work for a repair shop. We have the equipment and talent to rebuild Mac power supplies. We can easily handle the quick fixes. What are the more serious failures in these power supplies?**

A. Aside from the simple and obvious failures, there are several chronic problem areas in Mac power supplies:

1. Filter capacitor failure: The filter capacitors inside the power supply dry out over time and lose their electrolytic properties. In addition, Apple uses some components that are somewhat under rated. The capacitors could have better temperature and voltage ratings. In many instances, 1/4-watt resistors have been used instead of 1/2-watt resistors, and so on. Simply put, they cut quite a few corners.

2. Relays and thermostats: These items typically function as electrical switch These switches are energized by a small current, which then closes a gate that permits a larger current to flow through. Occasionally the gate gets stuck open and does not close enough to complete the circuit, which means that the relays and thermostats must be replaced or somehow reset. This is a chronic problem on the Sony version of the IIFx power supply (Sony model # CR-45-S) and the IIcx, IIci, and Quadra 700-class power supply (Apple part #699-0392). Thermostats can reset themselves after 10 to 20 minutes. I have actually had to hit the relays with the handle of a screwdriver to free them. The Omron Corporation sells replacement relays for these power supplies.

3. On/off switches on the motherboard: Another thing that I don't like about Apple's power-control circuitry is the fact that they put the on/off switches for most of the Mac II family (II, IIx, IIcx, and IIci) on the motherboard instead of inside the power supply. There are several reasons why this is a big deal. First, it's very easy to replace an on/off switch inside a power supply. Second, it's not easy to replace an on/off switch that is attached to the motherboard. What an absolutely stupid design! They mount a cheap

$5 switch on an expensive, multilayered main logic board that costs over $1000. This switch gets a great deal of use, and it's going to break. When it breaks you're screwed. Apple dealers won't replace it, but they most certainly will sell you a brand new or refurbished motherboard. However, there are people who have the proper soldering equipment to work with multilayered boards who can replace this switch in five minutes.

Q. **Where is the power supply located in my Mac Classic II?**

A. The power supply in the Mac Plus, Classic, and Classic II isn't a separate boxlike unit, as in other Macs. Apple has integrated the power supply into the analog video board. Apple often refers to this module as a power/sweep board.

Q. **Is the power/sweep combination board a better design than having the two units separate? If not, why is it a problem?**

A. I am not a big fan of integrating the power supply on the analog video board. They used this power/sweep design in the older Macs such as the 128, 512, 512KE, and Plus for years. Unfortunately, these modules fail left and right. The problem is the power supply and video circuitry work at very high frequencies and temperatures and are very prone to failure. The older Macs lacked adequate cooling. In fact, they had no real cooling. One of the best upgrades for those older Macs is a cooling fan. They are inexpensive and can prolong the life of your older Mac considerably. My personal favorite is Fanny Mac. The cooling in the Classics is much better and they are using fewer and slightly better components. However, I still don't like the combo design.

Q. **I recently purchased a Macintosh LC and have been experiencing a very strange problem. From time to time, my machine just shuts itself down. I took the machine to my dealer for a warranty check-up and they found no problem. Is it possible that there is an intermittent problem in the power supply that they didn't find? What are my options?**

A. It's always possible that you have an intermittent problem in the power supply. However I believe it's more probable that you have a either a monitor or CPU placement problem. This is a very common problem with the Mac IIs and the LCs. Many users are not aware that there are cooling vents on the top and side covers of the unit. If these vents become obstructed, the thermal shutdown circuitry turns off the Macintosh. Once the thermal shutdown has kicked in, it can take from 15 to 45 minutes to reset.

The irony of this situation is that the cooling vents always seem to be where users put the monitors. I have also seen people inadvertently cover the vents by turning the CPU up on its side and then they put it up against a desk or wall. This also can block the cooling vents if you aren't careful.

Q. **My Macintosh IIci won't turn on via the power-on key located on the ADB keyboard. But I can turn on the unit with the on/off switch. Is the problem in my power supply or somewhere else?**

A. This problem could be several things, but it isn't your power supply. First, you could have a bad keyboard or keyboard cable. Second, you could have a bad power-on key on your keyboard. Many Mac keyboards have key switches that are easy to remove and replace. Finally, it could be a blown fuse on the motherboard. The ADB keyboard ports on the Mac II class machines are protected by a 1-amp pico fuse and an RF choke filter. Either one of these two things could have blown. You will need to test these two components by performing a continuity test with a voltmeter.

Q. **I recently performed a memory upgrade on my Mac SE, and I keep getting a Sad Mac with two sets of hex codes. I know these SIMMs are good because they were in another machine. Could this be a power problem? How should I approach it?**

A. This problem is one of two things: Either you forgot to configure the memory jumper/resistor on the logic board or your power supply is low on the 5-volt side. Start by testing the output of the power supply via the DB-19 connector. It may just need a simple adjustment.

Q. **I have an external 80 MB SCSI hard disk drive that isn't spinning. Could this be a problem with my Mac's power supply?**

A. No. The external hard disk drive motor is powered by a separate external power source inside the external drive chassis. This has nothing to do with your Mac's power supply or SCSI port. It could be the external drives power supply or source. It could also be a defective drive.

171

Q. I own a Macintosh Portable. I've had countless unexplainable problems. My screen goes blank, and when it finally comes back on the computer runs very sluggishly. I replaced my screen and my hard drive, but that didn't really helped. Could this be a power-related problem?

A. The Macintosh Portable has numerous problems similar to the ones you have described. There are several possible solutions. First, when the screen suddenly goes blank, this indicates that the computer has gone into system sleep mode to conserve battery power. Try adjusting the sleep delay function in the control panel. If that doesn't work, try connecting your power adapter to the unit.

When your Portable is acting sluggish, the machine may be trying to go into rest mode. It's possible to disable this feature. You must first open the control panel, press down the Option key, and click on Minutes until Don't Rest appears.

Q. My Portable's battery constantly needs to be recharged every week, even if I don't use it. What could be happening here?

A. This is a very common and simple problem to fix. You probably have a release of the Macintosh operating system prior to 6.0.5. When Shut Down is selected, AppleTalk can cause the serial controller to draw additional power. It's important that you either put your portable to sleep prior to Shut Down or turn AppleTalk off. It would be a good idea to upgrade to System 6.0.5 or higher.

Q. I've recently replaced the battery in my Macintosh Portable. No matter what I try I cannot get it to come back on. What should I try now?

A. Make sure that you have a good charge on the battery before you try to use the Portable. If the battery is very low, the machine won't come on until a sufficient charge has been attained. If that doesn't work, try resetting the Macintosh Power Manager. To accomplish this, you'll have to slide the lock switch to the open position and then simultaneously press the interrupt and reset switches for a second or two. Then release them. Press any key to wake up the Mac If the unit still doesn't work, verify that the protective plastic covering has been removed from the battery contacts and that the battery cover is closed. If the unit still doesn't work, it's possible that your power adapter is not charging the battery or your keyboard cable may be loose (it's used for Wake Up). The last and worst thing it could be is a logic board problem.

Q. **I have heard that there is a potential danger of PowerBook batteries causing a fire. Is this true, or is it hype? How can I protect my computer from this?**

A. The hazard about which you speak concerns the storage of the PowerBooks' rechargeable batteries. When these batteries are stored unprotected, there is a slight chance that the battery could be accidentally discharged or cause a fire. Apple is even offering free battery cases so you can safely store your extra batteries. Contact your local dealer or APDA for further details.

Q. **When I replace a battery in either a Mac Portable or a PowerBook, can I just throw the battery away or is that dangerous ?**

A. The Portable and PowerBook batteries are sealed lead acid batteries. Technically speaking, these batteries are toxic waste, as defined by the EPA. I personally wouldn't throw them in the garbage or in the river. I would return them to my local Apple dealer or to Apple directly for a proper burial.

Q. **Does the PowerBook 100 utilize the improved version of the Power Manager?**

A. No. Only the PowerBook 140, 145, and 170 utilize a new and improved Power Manager function. The PowerBook 100 uses exactly the same Power Manager as the original Macintosh Portable.

Q. **Does the Shut Down command actually turn off Macintosh Portable computers?**

A. The original Macintosh Portable and the PowerBook 100 aren't actually shut down. In both of these models, the Power Manager remains active. However, the PowerBook 140, 145, and 170 are actually turned off. This is a very nice feature that conserves battery power.

CHAPTER 7

Floppy Disk Drives

All Macintosh computers, except the PowerBook 100, can accommodate at least one internal floppy disk drive. Some models can accommodate more than one. A floppy disk drive is simply a mechanical random access device used to store and retrieve data. The disk drive itself houses magnetic read/write heads that read and write data to and from a storage medium. This storage medium is a Macintosh volume and can be either a 3.5-inch floppy disk (one volume) or a large storage device, such as a hard disk or file server (many volumes).

All new Macintosh computers use 1.44MB high-density floppy diskettes and SuperDrives. Before your computer can use a diskette, you must first initialize the diskette. During initialization, the read/write heads of the disk drive magnetically mark the media into patterns known as tracks and sectors. Tracks and sectors are like grid coordinates (or street names and house numbers) that your Macintosh uses to store information on the disk media.

The number of tracks per side on either an 800K or 1.44MB diskette is always 80. Since there are two sides to every disk, the total track count is always 160 tracks. On 1.44MB diskettes there are always 18 sectors (slices) in each track. Each sector is an area used for data storage. Each has a preallocated size of 512 bytes per sector.

Diskette capacity is determined by the following formula:

Diskette capacity = (tracks per side x number of sides) x (sectors per track
            x bytes per sector)

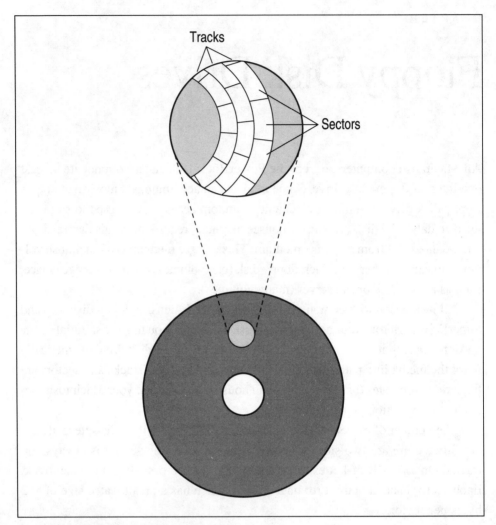

Figure 7-1. Disk tracks and sectors

The 1.44MB diskette has 80 tracks per side, two sides, 18 seconds per track, and a sector size of 512 bytes. Putting these numbers in the formula, you get

80 x 2 = 160 tracks

160 tracks x 18 sectors per track = 2880 total sectors

2880 total sectors x 512 bytes per sector = 1,474,560 bytes total storage capacity

The 800K disk has 80 tracks per side, two sides, and 512-byte sectors, just like the 1.44MB diskettes. However, the number of tracks per sector varies with the actual position on the disk. There are five regions that affect the number of sectors per track, and each is 16 tracks per side in size. The 800K diskette has from 8 to 12 sectors per track, depending on the region being used (track numbers).

This is a unique design. The purpose of varying the sector-per-track counts (as opposed to using a standard sector-per-track count) is that it enables your Macintosh computer to do two things:

1. Compensate for the physically smaller tracks as you move toward the center of the circular media.
2. Compensate for the faster rotational speeds that the Macintosh 800K disk drives have to counterbalance the physically smaller tracks, and deficiencies in the 800K recording method.

The 800K disks rotate between 394 and 590 RPM (rotations per minute), depending on the relative track position. A 1.44MB disk rotates at a constant 300 RPM. These rotational speed differences can cause serious compatibility problems between these two kinds of drives. The 1.44MB disk drive is supposed to be able to compensate for these differences. Theoretically, this is correct, but problems still can and do occur.

SWIM

The SuperDrive floppy disk drives are used on the upgraded Mac SEs and Mac IIs, as well as the Macintosh Classic, Classic II, SE/30, IIx, IIci, IIfx, LC, LC II, IIsi, and the PowerBook and Quadra families of computers.

In all current Macintosh computers that use the SuperDrive, an Apple custom IC called the SWIM (Super Woz Integrated Machine) chip provides the interface.

The SuperDrives have a number of major advantages over the earlier Apple 800K drives in that the new drives can read and write MS-DOS files in addition to standard Macintosh files.

Data Encoding Methods

A disk drive records data on a magnetic disk. The drive causes changes in the current flowing through a tiny electromagnet—the read/write head—which is held very close to the magnetic coating on the rotating disk. The changes in the current through the head cause changes in the magnetization of the disk coating. These are called magnetic transitions, and they remain on the disk until written over. When reading the disk, the magnetic transitions on the rotating disk cause changing currents in the head. Appropriate circuitry in the disk drive converts those currents to digital signals.

Digital data can be encoded as magnetic transitions on a disk in many different ways. Two different encoding methods are used with disk drives: group-code recording (GCR) and modified frequency modulation (MFM). GCR is the data format used with Macintosh files. MFM is the data format used with IBM PC (DOS) files. Other Macintoshes that have the 400K and 800K drives cannot exchange data with the IBM PC. These drives only have the ability to do group-coded recording (GCR), and are incompatible with the PC drives that encode data utilizing modified frequency modulation (MFM). However, any Macintosh computer that comes with the SuperDrive, or is upgraded to the SuperDrive, has the ability to go either way.

Floppy disk drive interface

The interface between the floppy disk drive connector and the Macintosh computer's main logic board controls four of the disk state-control lines, generates signals to select either the internal or external drive, and generates the read-data and write-data signals for the disk drives.

The older Macs with the 400K and 800K disk drives utilize an interface chip called the IWM (Integrated WOZ Machine), which is located on the logic board.

Newer Macs that have the 1.44MB Apple SuperDrive work in tandem with an interface chip called the SWIM (Super WOZ Integrated Machine). The SWIM is an upgraded version of the IWM that permits high-density recording and the ability to work with both GCR and MFM encoding. This is why SuperDrive-equipped machines can read MFM encoded diskettes form the PC.

The SWIM also converts between the NRZI serial data used to communicate with disk drives and the 8-bit parallel data used to communicate with the computer. The disk driver software converts between the data formats (GCR and MFM) used by disk drives and the normal 8-bit bytes used by the application.

The SWIM can send data to the disk drive at a maximum rate of approximately 500 kilobits (Kbits) per second. Because 4 bytes of GCR-encoded data correspond to 3 bytes of data in system RAM, the effective maximum data transmission rate in GCR mode is approximately 375 Kbits per second. However, the throughput of data to the disk depends on the amount of time spent seeking the correct location on the disk, reading RAM, and taking care of other system tasks in addition to the time spent actually transmitting data.

Troubleshooting Floppy Disk Drive Problems

The following are the most frequently encountered problems with floppy disk drives and some possible solutions.

Q. **Are the Apple 3.5-inch floppy disk drives (800K and SuperDrives) very high-failure items? What typically goes wrong with them, and why?**

A. Yes. Apple floppy drives, in general, are high-failure items, but not because of any manufacturing defects on the part of Apple. The main causes of failure are usually the following: dirt build-up, a lack of lubrication, a bent or worn head assembly, a bad motor, and broken springs or microswitches. Of these, the primary cause of disk drive failure is simply dirt build-up and user neglect. Obviously it's very important to keep your drives clean and properly lubricated.

The second most common cause of drive failure is drive usage. Floppy disk drives are mechanical devices, with lots of little springs, gears, switches, sensors, motors, and other moving parts. The chances are sooner or later these moving parts will break. It's hard to predict when they'll break, but common sense says that a floppy drive that gets heavy usage but very little tender loving care will fail before a drive that is properly maintained.

Q. **I don't understand why dirt and cleaning problems are such a big issue with Apple 3 .5-inch floppy disk drives. I have several IBM compatible computers with 3 .5-inch disk drives and don't have nearly as many problems as I do with the Apple drives. Can you explain this?**

A. It's very simple. Many of the 3.5-inch disk drives that are used in the IBM PC-compatible computers have a dust cover on the front of the drive. This keeps excessive amounts of debris from entering the "mouth" of the drive. Take a good look at your Macintosh disk drives. There is no such dust cover, which makes it very easy for dirt and other debris to get sucked into the drive mechanism. This filth can accumulate almost anywhere inside the drive, leading eventually to drive failure. The most disgusting things that I have ever seen inside an Apple 3.5-inch disk drive were hair, food particles, dead insects, and fingernail clippings. Just imagine what that stuff can do to an exposed floppy diskette inside the drive!

Q. **Is there any way I can purchase a 3.5-inch floppy disk drive with the dust cover? Is an upgrade kit available to correct this problem? If so, how much does it cost?**

A. You can perform a custom dust cover upgrade in two ways, and both are inexpensive and easy to do. The first method involves taking a 3M Post-it™ (any color will do) and placing the sticky top part directly above the entrance to your floppy disk drive. The rest of the Post-it™ blocks the entrance and acts as a dust cover. When you need to insert a floppy diskette, simply lift up the bottom of the Post-it™. The second method is similar to the first method. The only difference is that you can substitute a 3½ x 5-inch index card for the Post-it™. Take a little bit of tape to affix it to the Mac and presto, instant dust cover.

Q. **I currently use cotton swabs with a little bit of window cleaner to clean out my floppy drives. It seems to work all right. However, it's difficult to get to the back of the disk drive. I can't see back that far, and am afraid to take the drive out of the machine. Any suggestions?**

A. Yes. Stop using the window cleaner. You're very lucky that you haven't damaged those disk drives. You must never clean sensitive electronic equipment with any solvent that could leave a conductive film. Window cleaner is a very bad choice. I also don't really like the cotton swabs. While they may be good for your ears, they tend to leave fuzz balls inside the drive. If you're going to use swabs, use the foam-tipped kind.

If your drives aren't that filthy, it's best to clean them with a 3.5-inch head cleaning kit. Many different kinds of head cleaning kits are on the market. Prices range from $5 for a generic kit to $50 for one of those marketing wonders. Apple sanctions the 3M head cleaning kit as being up to their standards. I agree with that recommendation. However, I have used kits from Trackmate, Allsop, and Radio Shack without any problem. My preference is to purchase a cleaning kit that comes with a liquid cleaning solution and a cleaning diskette with what looks like a Mr. Coffee™ filter inside. I absolutely do not recommend the dry cleaning kits, which usually cost $0.50 to $1. They use a very coarse, sandpaper-like cleaning disk that in time will "file down" your heads.

Q.A great deal of controversy surrounds the frequency in which you should clean the heads in your floppy drives. I've been told to do it twice a year, and that if I do it any more than that, I will kill my heads. Is this true? Do you have a better suggestion?

A. Where did you get this information? If you use a file, sandpaper or a filthy cleaning diskette to clean your heads, then, yes, of course you'll do some damage. However, I've never seen a new Mr Coffee™-type head cleaning disk with isopropyl alcohol do any damage to a head. Keep in mind many of the actual heads are made of a titanium alloy, which is used in all sorts of military and commercial applications. The heads themselves are tough. You can bend the head assembly, which generally consists of the head, a plastic carrier, a couple of screws and a cheap little spring, by not being careful and recklessly jamming things into the drive.

How often you clean the heads of your floppy disk drives depends on two key factors: the actual usage of the drives (light, moderate, heavy, or very heavy) and the type of environment your computer is in (office, factory, on the floor, smoking/nonsmoking area). Here are the hard facts: Drives that are used frequently need more attention than those that are not. Drives used around smokers need more attention than those around nonsmokers. Computers on the floor have more crud (especially carpet and dust balls) build-up than those on a regular office desk. Computers used in dirty areas, such as a garages, factories, or other industrial areas, usually get much filthier than those in a normal office environments. Rental computers tend to be really filthy. And finally, computers that aren't properly maintained will fail.

Q.I've tried cleaning my diskette drive with an appropriate head cleaning kit, but I still have intermittent problems reading and writing to my diskettes. Should I replace the drive or try something else?

A. When the dirt condition has persisted over an extended period of time, the traditional head cleaning kit may not be enough to do the job. In these situations, start by removing the disk drive from your Macintosh. The drive mechanism itself is covered by a metal RF shield. Remove the four screws that attach the drive mech-anism to the RF shield, and then remove the drive mechanism.

With the drive mechanism now exposed, carefully inspect the drive for dirt and crud build-up. Pay very careful attention to the rear areas of the drive near the head assembly, stepper cam, motor gear, sensors, and around the eject and carrier mech-anism. Then use an air compressor or can of compressed air and blow out as much of the debris as possible. (Note: I don't use any of the TF fluorocarbon based aerosol cans. Recent scientific studies suggest that they are harmful to the ozone layer of the atmosphere.) Those of you that have allergies might want to do this outside. All of this dust in a confined area might trigger an allergic reaction.

After you blow the loose debris out, reinspect the drive and repeat the air treat-ment if necessary. If there are still areas that look dirty, carefully clean those with foam swabs and isopropyl alcohol. If it's really dirty, you may have to use a non-conductive cleaning solvent such as Blue Shower or TV tuner cleaner to directly attack those areas. Avoid spraying anything directly on the heads.

A good follow-up to any cleaning should be lubrication of the slide and eject mechanisms. Be careful not to get any of the lubricant on the heads!

Q. **What should I use to lubricate my floppy drives? I've been told to stay away from WD-40™. Is there a problem with WD-40™? If so, what should I use ?**

A. There isn't anything wrong with WD-40™. In fact, it's very slick, it doesn't clog, and can be purchased in any hardware store. Some people do have two valid complaints about WD-40™ and similar lubricants: (1) If used excessively, these lubricants attract dust like a magnet, which can cause problems, and (2) When deal-ing with any spray-type lubricant, people have a tendency to go overboard and blast every square inch of the drive. The last thing you need is lubricant on your read/write heads—and it's almost impossible to get off.

I personally have lubricated drives with just about everything available and have had the best results with the following:

1. White lithium grease
2. 3-in-1 household oil
3. Teflon™-based lubricants (expensive but very good)
4. Outers or Break Free™ gun oil

Any of the above work well when used in moderation. However, I've noticed that the grease and the household oils tend to clog up. The Teflon™ lubricants are fantastic but expensive. The Outers or Break Free™ gun oils are excellent if used sparingly. They are designed to work in the critical mechanical areas of pistols and rifles, which are frequently exposed to high pressure, temperature, and vibrations. These oils are designed not to clog and to be reliable when it counts.

Q. **I've been experiencing bad read/write problems on my Apple floppy disk drive, which is now about three years old. I tried cleaning and lubricating the drive to no avail. The drive keeps making noises as if the heads are grinding, and they look bad. Can the heads in the Apple floppy drives be replaced or aligned? Is it worth my time?**

A. Good diagnosis. The heads in your disk drive are indeed shot. You can fix almost anything in a computer if you have time, patience, money, and some luck. However, repairing floppy drives usually is not worth your time unless you have a box full of them. Head assemblies for the 800K drive cost around $60. Then you have to consider your time, which may be worth about $50 to $100 per hour (what an on-site service call would cost you). The total cost to you is $110 to $160 to repair a drive that you can purchase out of a mail-order magazine for less than $100 with a warranty. I like to work smarter, not harder. What's even worse is that there's no guarantee that you will get the drive working.

Your second option is to call an authorized Apple dealer to service your machine. This is generally the most expensive option, but they do stand behind their work. Your third option would be to trade in your drive for a rebuilt drive with a warranty. Companies like Pre-owned Electronics, Shreve Systems, and Mactronics specialize in this type of work. It'll cost you less than $80 for the 800K drive swap and less than $150 for the 1.44MB SuperDrive swap. Personally I would purchase the new 800K drive by mail-order magazine, since the purchase price of the new drive is so close to the swap/rebuild price.

I would then choose to swap the 1.44MB drives. The new price of those drives (if you can find them) is usually over $300, so the swap/rebuild makes more sense. In both situations you save the cost of a service call by performing the labor yourself.

Now let's address your question regarding head alignments. Alignments for the Apple drive are almost nonexistent. There is really not much you can do if the head assembly is out of alignment. These drives aren't like the old IBM PC drives that you could adjust with a digital alignment disk. No adjustments on the Sony drive mechanisms are used in the Apple disk drive. Even if adjustments were made, they would only prolong the agony if the head assembly was physically worn. Head adjustments are to floppy drives what front-end alignments are to automobiles. A minor adjustment here or there may be needed from time to time to keep the front end straight. But if you hit a pot hole and break off a ball joint, you can align that front end until you are blue in the face, and it will keep going back out of alignment as long as the worn or defective part is still in there. So it is with floppy disk drives that have worn head assemblies: no adjustment can compensate for a bad or worn head assembly. The heads have to come out, or the drive has to be replaced.

Q.Do you have any tips that to prevent problems with diskette ejections?

A. Yes. Just follow these simple rules to prevent disk ejection problems:

- Don't put more than two labels on a diskette.
- Before inserting a diskette into the disk drive mechanism, make sure that another diskette is not already in there.
- Insert diskettes gently into the mechanism. Don't force them!
- When installing disk drives be sure that the drives are centered and that the mounting brackets are not bent. Improper installation can cause the mechanism to bind, which will lead to ejection problems.

Q.What's the proper way to remove diskettes that won't eject?

A. The following is the best procedure for removing diskettes that won't eject:

- Don't try to forcefully pull the diskette out. You have a better chance than average of damaging the mechanism.
- If the diskette tries to eject but won't come all the way out, push the disk back in and try to eject it electronically by simultaneously pressing the <Command>, <Shift>, and 1 keys to eject an internal floppy diskette, or by simultaneously pressing the <Command>, <Shift>, and 2 keys to eject an external floppy diskette.

- If you can't eject the diskette with the key sequence, try ejecting the diskette by selecting the Eject command from the File menu of your Macintosh. I would try this four or five times. Patience sometimes pays off.
- If the diskette still doesn't come out, you must use the Macintosh tool of choice: The Golden Paper Clip. Insert the paper clip into the small pin hole that is located to the right of the disk drive opening. The diskette should pop out. If not, you must remove the drive and partially disassemble it.

To disassemble the floppy disk drive.

1. Remove the disk drive.
2. Place the drive on a flat, clean surface.
3. Remove the four screws that hold the Rf shield/shroud in place and remove the drive mechanism.
4. Try to manually work the ejection mechanism. It's located on the right hand side of the drive mechanism.
5. If that doesn't work, you must gently move a small arm with a cylindrical end. This end is located in a crescent-shaped depression. Locate this end, and carefully move the arm away from the diskette until the diskette pops forward. Then gently remove this diskette from the drive mechanism.

$Q.$ I have disk drives that keep experiencing ejection problems. I have tried cleaning and lubricating these drives and I'm still have problems with them. Is there anything that I can replace, cost effectively, or should I replace the drive?

A. Both the Apple 800K and Apple 1.44MB SuperDrives have a common failure point—the ejection motors. Omron OEM replacement motors cost about $75 each. I wouldn't waste my time replacing this motor on an 800K drive because the part plus your time is worth more than a new 800K drive. Replacing the ejection motor on the 1.44MB drive is worth your time, if you have the time to spare. However, I still think that swapping/rebuilding your drive for between $100 and $150 is your best bet. For those of you who have the time and desire, floppy disk drive parts such as ejection motors, heads, and so on can be purchased from companies like Soft Solutions in Eugene, Oregon.

Q. I have a box of bad Apple 1.44MB SuperDrives. The problem with these drives appears to be the small printed circuit board (PCB) on the bottom of the drive. Should I cannibalize the drives for the head assemblies, springs, and so on, or can I purchase these small boards from Apple or elsewhere? Is this even worth my time?

A. You could scrap the drives for the head assemblies if you wanted to, but I would recommend that you purchase a replacement circuit board instead. You're right: Apple won't sell you a replacement board. However, companies like Soft Solutions in Eugene, Oregon, have the latest Sony replacement boards in stock for about $139. If you don't feel like fixing the drive, you can still send it out for repair for between $100 and $150. A new drive from Apple will set you back at least $300 or more if they install it for you.

Q. Is there any use for the old 400K, single-sided disk drives in working condition that I took out of my original, first-generation Macintosh? Or should I just throw them away?

A. The old 400K drives are worthless in mainstream Mac Land. These drives worked with the old Macintosh filing system (MFS). Today's Macs work with the hierarchical filing system (HFS), which is supported by the 800K and 1.44MB SuperDrives. Today the drive of choice is the 1.44MB FDHD; everything else is being phased out. Now, I certainly would never tell anyone to throw out working electronic goodies, but I think you should try to find your old 400K drives a new home. Schools, churches and other charities are always looking for donations. Scrap and surplus dealers might be willing to take them off of your hands, or you can keep them as a Mac memento.

Q. I recently tried to install an internal 1.44MB SuperDrive drive in my Macintosh SE. The installation was a snap. However, when I try to format diskettes, everything goes OK until the Mac gets to verification. The machine keeps failing on verification. I installed a new SuperDrive and cable and I keep getting the same thing. What could be the problem here?

A. Mac SEs manufactured prior to September 1989 and the original Mac IIs came standard with 800K drives. These models can be upgraded now to accept an internal FDHD 1.44MB SuperDrive, but it involves more than installing the new drive. In addition to the drive, you must upgrade the Macintosh ROMs and the IWM (Integrated WOZ Machine) chip in the Mac SE and original Mac II. The ROMs contain the Mac's intelligence. The upgraded ROMs have the intelligence to work with the high-density disk drives. The IWM chip, which is a standard disk drive interface, works only with the 400K and 800K disk drives. The standard IWM must be upgraded to a SWIM (Super Woz Integrated Machine) or super floppy controller interface chip. The SuperDrive upgrade for the old SE and original Mac II requires all three elements: 1.44MB drive, upgraded ROMs, and the SWIM chip to be complete.

The following are Mac SE FDHD upgrade part numbers and locations:

Chip	Location	Apple part number
Rom Hi	D6	344-0701
Rom Lo	D7	342-0702
SWIM	D8	344-0062

These chips replace the older revision chips at the same locations to complete the SuperDrive upgrade.

The following are Mac II FDHD upgrade part numbers and locations:

Chip	Location	Apple part #
Rom Hi	Varies	661-0639
Rom Med Hi		661-0640
Rom Med Lo		661-0641
Rom Lo		661-0642

The SWIM IC is located at Mac II board reference I-10 and is Apple part number 344-50043A

These chips replace the older revision chips at the same locations to complete the SuperDrive upgrade.

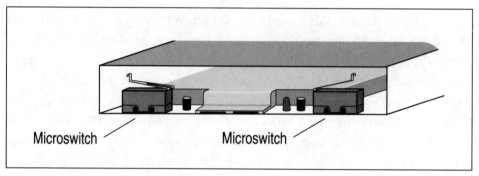

Figure 7-2. Microswitches on the SuperDrive

Q. **How much do the Apple SuperDrive upgrade kits cost, and where can I purchase them?**

A. The Apple SuperDrive upgrade retails for $449 plus labor. However, authorized Apple dealers will discount that price if you trade in your old floppy disk drive and ROMs. Rather than trade in a perfectly good 800K drive and pay approximately $400 plus labor, it might be cheaper to consider getting a third-party external 1.44MB drive, such as the Dayna File or Applied Engineering's external super drive. If you want the latest in high-density floppy drive technology, consider the new Floptical drive from Applied Engineering. The Floptical drive stores up to 20MB of data per floppy using ultra-high-density storage media. An optical servo tracks position heads with precision to attain the higher storage capacity. It's twice as fast as a standard floppy drive and is downward compatible with both the 800K and 1.44MB floppy drives.

Q. **My floppy drive operates very slowly every once in a while. Is there any diagnostic package on the market to test the rotational speed of my floppy drive and the floppy interface circuitry on the logic board?**

A. A year or two ago a package called Trackmate for Macintosh was on the market. It was a very inexpensive 3.5-inch disk drive cleaning kit with diagnostic software. The software would perform a rotational speed and head accuracy test on the suspect drive. I originally purchased it from Mactronics, located in Ft. Myers, Florida (800) 741-4366, but I have not seen it around for a while. The best package to test the floppy interface circuitry on your logic board is Mac Ekg. I don't recommend the Snooper software from Maxa.

Q. What is the best way to tell if the problem is my drive, cable, or floppy interface circuitry on the logic board?

A. The easiest way to determine whether the problem is the floppy, cable, or interface circuitry is the Easter Egg approach—the process of elimination using known good parts—which goes as follows:

1. Try another floppy drive. If the new one works, then you know where the problem was. Then you can concentrate on fixing the bad drive.
2. Replace the cable. Cables do occasionally go bad because they get stretched or accidentally cut. If the new cable does the trick, you need to go no further.
3. If the cable and the drive don't remedy the situation, then you have a problem with the circuitry on your logic board. The primary suspects would be the IWM or SWIM integrated circuit, depending on which Mac you have or the small oscillating crystal that drives the IWM and SWIM ICs. The IWM and SWIM chips are the basic floppy control circuitry of the Macintosh. This IC provides nearly all of the control signals used to communicate with the floppy disk drives. These ICs are custom made and hard to find. I would call around to chip brokers, such as Maxwell Computer Products in Los Angeles. They can either get them from various sources or point you in the right direction. They can also get the oscillating crystals in large quantities.

Q. I don't have a lot of sophisticated test equipment, but is there any easy way to tell for sure if IWM or SWIM circuitry is functioning properly?

A. Yes. If you have a good logic probe (Beckman or equivalent, with a rating of at least 25 MHz), you can take CMOS signal readings directly from the logic board. To do this, you must unplug the 20-pin floppy cable from the drive. The other end must remain plugged in the floppy connector on the logic board. You could take the readings directly from the logic board, but you could short some pins out. By using the cable you eliminate this risk. Next you must locate pin 1 on the cable. It will be on the side of the cable with the colored strip.

You'll then have to set up the logic probe by attaching the ground and power leads. Insert the logic probe into each pin of the cable, turn the machine on, record the initial reading (high, low, or pulse). Wait approximately 10 seconds, and record the second readings if they change. Turn off the machine, move the probe to the next pin, and repeat the process one at a time for all 20 pins. This is necessary because there are two sets of readings (the initial reading and the second reading within 10 seconds). You must record them both. Below are examples of readings taken from a Mac II with an standard IWM (800K) and a Macintosh IIcx with a SWIM (1.44MB). They are identical except for pins 9 and 20. I normally take the readings with just the Logic board, power supply and floppy disk drive cable installed. All of the other devices tend to get in the way and can possibly throw off your readings.

Table 7-1. Pin assignments for internal floppy disk drive connector standard IWM.

Pin	Signal at power up	Description within 10 sec.	Logic	Logic
1	GND	GROUND	LOW	LOW
2	PH0	STATE CONTROL	LOW PULSE TO HIGH	
3	GND	GROUND	LOW	LOW
4	PH1	STATE CONTROL	LOW PULSE TO HIGH	
5	GND	GROUND	LOW	LOW
6	PH2	STATE CONTROL	LOW PULSE TO HIGH	
7	GND	GROUND	LOW	LOW
8	PH3	STATE CONTROL	LOW PULSE TO HIGH	
9	NOT MEASURED FOR IWM, -12 (LOW),SIGNAL FOR SWIM			
10	WRRQ	WRITE DATA RQ	HIGH	HIGH
11	+5V	+ 5 VOLTS DC	HIGH	HIGH
12	SEL	STATE CONTROL	QUICK HIGH TO LOW	
13	+12V	+12 VOLTS DC	HIGH	HIGH
14	ENBL	DRIVE ENABLE	HIGH PULSE TO HIGH	
15	+12V	+12 VOLTS DC	HIGH	HIGH
16	RD	READ DATA	HIGH	HIGH
17	+12V	+12 VOLTS DC	HIGH	HIGH
18	WR	WRITE DATA	LOW	LOW
19	NOT MEASURED FOR IWM, PWMPU, PULL UP 5-VOLT RESISTOR IN THE SWIM CONFIGURATION			

DEFINITIONS: LOGICAL HIGH (TTL)   >2.3 + OR - 0.2 VDC
              (CMOS)   >70% VCC +/- 10%

              LOGICAL LOW (TTL)   <0.8 + OR - VDC
              (CMOS)   <30% VCC +/- 10%

Q. I have an external floppy disk drive attached to my Macintosh IIcx. Recently, I unhooked it, and when I plugged it back in, it stopped working. I have since tried another external floppy drive and it doesn't work, but my internal drive still works fine. Is this a problem with my IWM/SWIM chip?

A. No. The problem isn't with your Mac IIcx. There is a fuse located on the logic board that may be blown. When this fuse blows, it knocks out the external Db-19 floppy disk drive port. On the Mac IIcx, this fuse is located at board reference F3, which is located near the battery. On a IIci, the fuse is still located at board reference F3, only this time it is located on the logic board directly behind the external Db-19 port. In fact, all Mac models above the Mac SE, such as SE/30, IIcx, IIci, IIsi, and Quadra 700 that have an external Db-19 external floppy disk drive port also have this fuse. Occasionally these fuses have a different look. Just remember, the reference on the logic board will begin with an "F" for fuse. The rating on these fuses is 1 amp. I purchase 125-volt, 1-amp, fast blow fuses manufactured by the Little Fuse Corporation. The voltage really does not matter, as these fuses blow on current. The cost is less than $1.

Q. Is there any difference between high- and low-density diskettes other than the second hole in the case? Do you recommend converting diskettes from 800K to 1.44MB high-density floppies by using products such as the Double Disk puncher?

A. There is a very big difference between high- and low-density diskettes. The difference is in the thickness and magnetic properties of the media itself. I don't recommend that you use hole punchers such as the Double Disk puncher. True, if you punch the second hole in an 800K diskette, it will work for a while. But, if you put a whole lot of data on there and are depending on it as your backup, you may be sorry when you start developing read errors. I've been teaching data recovery techniques for over eight years and have seen countless numbers of people that think that the diskette manufacturers have somehow conspired to rip them off by selling 800K and 1.44MB disks that are really the same thing. They buy the hole puncher, and it works for awhile. But months later, when they need to restore their data from the floppies, it's gone! There really is a difference between high- and low-density media. If you're interested in understanding what is involved here, you should study up on magnetic coercivity. Additionally, 3M has an excellent diskette reference guide that superbly describes magnetic recording and media substrates in detail. The bottom line: There is no free lunch, you get what you pay for, and if it sounds too good to be true, it usually is. Spend a little bit extra to get the correct diskettes.

Q. **Is it OK to use a 1.44MB diskette in an 800K drive and format it as an 800K diskette? I haven't had any problems doing it. Have I been lucky ?**

A. Yes, you have. I too have used the 1.44MB diskettes in my 800K drives. Occasionally I lose some data, but for the most part it works in my machine. The problem occurs when I try to go to somebody else's 800K or 1.44MB drive. They seem to have trouble reading them, and this is an unreliable way to store data. It's cheaper and better to use 800K diskettes in your 800K disk drives.

Q. **Why do I have trouble taking files from an 800K disk drive and reading them on a machine with a 1.44MB SuperDrive? The SuperDrive is supposed to be able to read 400K and 800K, 1.44MB Mac and 1.44MB DOS diskettes. What's the problem?**

A. True, the Apple 1.44MB SuperDrive can read 400K and 800K diskettes as well as 1.44MB Mac and DOS diskettes. The problem is that the 400K and 800K drives use a variable rotational speed that varies between 394 and 590 RPM, depending on its relative track position. A 1.44MB disk drive rotates at a constant 300 RPM. Theoretically the 1.44MB SuperDrive can compensate when reading a 400K or 800K diskette, but still problems may occur.

Q. **Why can I read DOS files on my Macintosh with an FDHD 1.44MB SuperDrive, but not with an 800K drive ?**

A. Because the 1.44MB drive rotates at a constant 300 RPM, just like the IBM 3 .5-inch drives. The only real difference between the IBM and Mac platforms, as far as floppy encoding is concerned, is that the Mac uses GCR (group-code recording) and the IBM uses MFM (modified frequency modulation) with NRZI (non-return-to-zero, inverted). Since both the IBM and Mac 1.44MB drives rotate at 300 RPM constant, the translation software simply converts it from GCR to MFM formats. Since the 800K drives have a variable rotational speed, they can't be used for this purpose.

Q. Is there any way to tell 400K, 800K, and 1.44MB Mac floppy disk drives apart? I have a big box of them and need to sort them out.

A. It's very easy to tell these drives apart. First, you should look on the bottom of the drive. Usually you can see a label of some kind. For instance, a 1MB label would mean that this drive is an 800K disk drive. If there is no label on the bottom of your drive, you can look inside the front of the drive mechanism and count the number of small microswitches. If you are looking at the drive from the front, a 400K disk drive has one microswitch on the right, an 800K disk drive has two microswitches (one on the right and one on the left), and a 1.44MB SuperDrive has three microswitches (two on the right and one on the left). It's that simple.

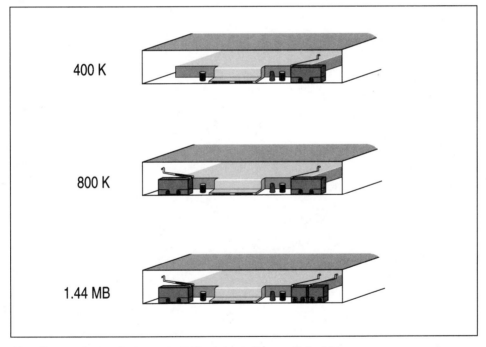

Figure 7-3. Microswitches on all Macintosh floppy disk drives

CHAPTER 8

Apple Desktop Bus (ADB)

The Apple Desktop Bus (ADB) is a single-master, multislave serial bus that's used to communicate with as many as 16 low-speed input devices, such as keyboards, mice, trackballs, and graphics tablets. The ADB is Apple's standard interface for all input devices. Even though the ADB transceiver chip is capable of addressing up to 16 different peripheral devices, daisy-chaining more than 3 devices isn't recommended by Apple, primarily because of connector resistance and signal degradation.

The ADB transceiver chip in your Macintosh works by converting the computer's TTL signals to the variable-pulse-width open-collector signal used on the bus. When the bus is idle, the transceiver performs automatic polling of the ADB device that last sent data.

Each ADB device has a default identification code known as a device handler ID, which is stored in an internal register. The ADB Manager keeps track of the device handler ID and the default address of each device on the bus, and calls the appropriate device driver when that device has data to send to the computer.

An ADB device can't initiate a data transaction. Instead, each device asserts a service request signal when it has data to send to the computer. The ADB Manager then attempts to read each device on the bus until one responds by sending data. When a device responds, the ADB Manager passes control to the appropriate device driver.

ADB Interface

The ADB interface is functionally the same on all Macintosh models except the Mac Plus and earlier models, which don't use it. In some later Macintosh computers, a custom microcontroller IC integrates ADB with other functions that were provided by individual chips. The PowerBook family of computers has its own unique ADB implementation.

Apple Standard Keyboard II

The switches in the Apple Standard Keyboard II are wired in a two-dimensional array called a keyswitch matrix. Like the keyboard in earlier Macintosh computers, the Apple Standard Keyboard II contains a microprocessor that scans the matrix to detect switch transitions as keys are pressed and released. The keyboard's microprocessor transmits the corresponding key-down and key-up events to the CPU by way of the ADB.

The major differences in the Keyboard II layout, when compared with the Apple Standard Keyboard, are in the positioning of the <Esc>, <Caps Lock>, <Ctrl>, and tilde keys.

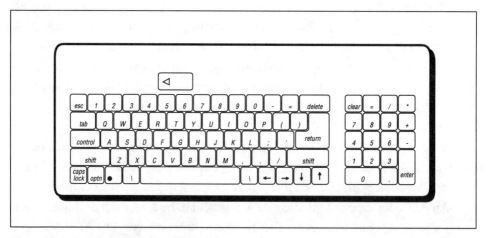

Figure 8-1. Apple standard keyboard II

PowerBook Low-Power Trackball

Instead of a mouse, the PowerBook computers use a low-power trackball that works something like an upside-down mouse. The trackball is electrically compatible with the ADB, although it uses a few pins in a large shared connector instead of the dedicated mini-circular type.

Any input devices connected to the PowerBook ADB must be low-power versions. That means keyboards and mouse devices from other models in the Macintosh family aren't usable with the PowerBook computers. If you connect such input devices to the your PowerBook ADB, it could cause an unacceptable decrease in the +5-volt supply voltage and result in improper operation.

The Power Manager IC in the PowerBook controls the power to the trackball, removing the power when it puts the computer into the sleep state and restoring it when the computer resumes normal operation.

Movement of the top of the ball's surface to the right is in the positive X direction, and movement downwards is in the positive Y direction. Movement of the top surface of the ball to the right causes the display cursor to move to the right, and movement downward causes the cursor to move down on the display. The trackball has one button, which is functionally equivalent to the mouse button.

PowerBook Low-Power Keyboard

The PowerBook family of computers has a special low-power keyboard consisting of a keyswitch matrix only, with no active electronics. The keyswitches are supported by a steel plate and electrically connected to the keyboard connector by a PC board. The keyboard processor in the PowerBooks takes care of scanning the keyswitch matrix and sending the switch codes to the CPU by way of the ADB.

Common Troubleshooting Questions on the ADB

Q. **I have an old Mac Plus and would like to purchase a new ADB keyboard. I've been told that I can't use an ADB keyboard on any Macintosh computer released before the SE. Is this true? If so, why can't I use the new keyboards on my Mac Plus?**

A. Yes, it's true. Your Plus is an older Mac that uses an RJ-11-type connector and wire for the keyboard. ADB uses a DIN 4 connector. In addition, the Plus isn't equipped with an ADB controller chip that would allow it to communicate with an ADB device.

Q. **I recently broke the keyboard cable on my Mac Plus. I went to Radio Shack and bought some standard RJ-11 telephone handset wire to replace my old cable. After replacing the old cable, my keyboard still doesn't work.**

What's the problem?

A. The Mac Plus keyboard uses the RJ-11 connector and wire that resembles the cable on your telephone headset. The connector and wire may look similar, but the wire pin-outs are reversed. You shouldn't plug the telephone headset cable into your Mac Plus keyboard. The Mac uses the straight-through-type cable, not the reversed. If you reversed the cable and turned the unit on, you most likely destroyed the keyboard's microcontroller chip and will have to replace it. This chip is typically an NEC (or equivalent) 8550 or 8728 chip located underneath the spacebar.

Q. Is it a problem to disconnect and then reconnect ADB devices while the Mac's power is on? I've been told that I shouldn't do this. What can I damage? What are the symptoms? How do you test for damage?

A. In general it's not a good idea to disconnect and reconnect ADB devices while your Mac is on. For that matter you shouldn't plug anything into the Mac while it's on. Most people inadvertently do this from time to time and get away with it. But some day, when you least expect it—pow!—the port goes dead.

If you suspect that the port is dead, you should first take a voltage reading off the ADB port before you open the machine up. Pin 3 on the ADB port carries a +5-volt DC signal that is used to power your keyboard and mouse. This is usually the source of the problem. If you're getting the +5-volt reading from the port, test the peripheral devices first. If you don't get a +5-volt reading from the port, you may have blown one of the two highest-failure items, which are the RF choke filter and the 1-amp pico fuse.

RF choke filter

The RF choke filter is a little black box located on the logic board, usually directly behind the two ADB ports. This filter is a Tokin D16-C or equivalent and has eight solder contacts that affix it to the logic board. The RF choke filter is used for RF noise suppression. It's a very high-failure item on all Macs, especially the Macintosh SE, SE/30, Mac II, and IIx. If a short occurs on your ADB port or cabling, this filter actually acts like a fuse and can blow. The ADB port then is dead and none of your ADB devices work.

The filter usually has the reference L1 or the word "Filter" stenciled near it in white lettering. You can use this as a means of identifying the component. To test this filter, you need to remove the logic board and flip it over to the solder side. Then locate the contacts for the RF choke filter and check for continuity from side to side. If you detect an open circuit, that means the RF choke filter must be replaced or temporarily bypassed with a jumper wire. The logic board is a multilayer board. You must have multilayer capable soldering equipment to perform this repair properly, unless you're really good and careful with the inexpensive stuff. I usually wire a 1-amp pico fuse across the open circuit (I put a turn or two in the lead). Pico fuses are less than one dollar and are easier to install than an RF choke filter that costs a few dollars (if you can find them). It's also safer than running a straight piece of wire (which would be like putting a penny in your home fuse box).

RF choke filter
(bottom)

```
A | o o | A
B | o o | B
C | o o | C
D | o o | D
```

Solder side of logic board

Make sure that you have continuity from A to A, B to B, C to C, and D to D. If not, replace the RF choke filter, or jump it with a wire (temporary fix) or with a 1-amp pico fuse.

If the RF choke filter tests good, you may have a problem with the second highest cause for failure, the pico fuse.

1-amp pico fuse

In addition to the RF choke filter, most Macs newer than the Mac SE are also equipped with 1-amp pico fuse, which is in the vicinity of the RF choke filter. (Note: Some Macs have a fuse that looks like a lollypop. This is a poly-blow fuse. It can be replaced with the standard 1-amp pico.) This fuse is located on the logic board around the area of the ADB ports and the RF choke filter. It usually has the designation of F1 (the letter "F" stands for fuse). The pico fuse is not your typical glass fuse. It sometimes is green or yellow in color and looks like a resistor without the color bands. Occasionally, it looks like a small piece of metal or even a lollypop. Despite its appearance, it is a fuse.

To test the fuse, you must perform a continuity test with a voltmeter or a continuity tester. You can do the test from the component side of the logic board (top). However, I prefer to take it from the solder side (bottom). The reason I take my readings from the bottom is that I know that (1) my fuse is good and (2) my solder joints that hold the fuse in place are good. The fuse is really easy to replace, but again, you have to be careful with the soldering equipment. Sometimes when I am lazy (or don't have my soldering iron), I simply attach the fuse to the leads of the old fuse (with the green or yellow picos that have leads that I can attach to). This bridges the old fuse and allows current to pass through. This is called the M.A.S.H. 4077 fix.

> **Note:** When you remove the fuse, don't physically pull it off of the
> board. Use the proper soldering equipment to remove it, or leave it in
> place and jump it with a new fuse. I've seen many people pull these
> fuses off with pliers (especially the little metal ones). You have a very
> high risk of pulling a top trace when you do this, which is a pain to fix.

Q. If the fuse goes bad in my Macintosh, will the port always be completely dead? Do you have any secret method of deducing what's wrong without opening the machine and using the voltmeter?

A. You bet. First of all, let me start off by saying that if you blow the RF choke filter on the Macintosh SE, the port will really be dead, and there is no fuse that goes on this model. Second, I can tell you my secret way of determining what's wrong. But it only applies to Macs that use the power-on key located on the ADB keyboard (for example, Mac IIs).

My secret is this: Usually when the RF choke filter goes on—let's say on a Mac II, IIx, IIcx, IIci—you won't be able to use the power-on key to turn on your Mac. It simply has no effect. This of course assumes that you have already ruled out your keyboard and cable as the culprit. When the 1-amp pico fuse blows, you usually can turn on the machine with the power-on key, but the mouse pointer is frozen in the corner of the screen, and moving the mouse has no effect. This, of course, assumes that you have already ruled out your mouse as the culprit. This method is unofficial. If you suspect one or the other as being bad, you should still test them out with a voltmeter to be sure.

Q. Does anyone make any ADB test equipment? I've noticed that hardly anybody has test equipment for the Mac. Can you recommend any vendors?

A. Yes. Mactronics of Fort Myers, Florida, sells an excellent ADB tester. It tests ADB cables, keyboards, and the port outputs, and it monitors all four ADB signal lines. I invested under $100 for this gem and it's paid dividends many times over in time and aggravation saved. Mactronics also carries SCSI testers, SIMM testers, and other valuable tools. You can fax them for a product list.

Q. What's the procedure for determining whether an ADB problem is caused by the peripheral device or in the ADB circuitry on the logic board?

A. First, try a new ADB cable, if possible. These cables are very high-failure items. They get abused a lot, so I would always keep a spare handy.

Second, try plugging your device's cable into the other ADB port (if you have it). It's possible that the connector on the current port is bent and is making poor or no contact. If it works, resolder the other connector.

Third, if you have ADB peripheral devices daisy-chained (that is, a keyboard plugged into the Mac on one side and a mouse plugged into the keyboard on the other side), try putting each into its own ADB port on the Mac. If one device works and the other doesn't, the problem is the device that doesn't work. You know this because you should already have ruled out the cable and connector.

Now let's say that you have a keyboard and mouse. The mouse is plugged into the keyboard. The keyboard works fine, but the mouse doesn't. You plug the mouse into the other ADB port, and now they both work. This is an interesting situation. Where's the problem? It's in the keyboard. The next time you take a keyboard apart, look very carefully in the corners. Many (though not all) of the keyboards have RF choke filters in both corners. It's very common for one of these filters to blow while the other stays intact. If the mouse is plugged into the keyboard, and if the side closest to the mouse blows, the mouse won't work properly. If the devices are daisy-chained together, and the filter blows on the side where the cable from the Mac to the keyboard goes in, both devices will appear to be dead.

Fourth, if your keyboard is plugged into one port and the mouse is in the other, and the keyboard appears to be dead, you must turn the machine off and then remove and visually inspect your cable for damage or bent pins on both ends. Reconnect the cable to the Mac, and attach the end to the other side of the keyboard (not the side you were using previously). You do this to rule out the possibility that an RF filter is blown inside the keyboard. The Mactronics ADB tester has a loop-back function that tests both sides of the keyboard.

Fifth, if all of your ADB devices aren't responding in either port, chances are your problem is in the ADB circuitry on the logic board. If only one of your devices has the problem, it's most likely the device itself. Rule it out by trying a known good device in its place.

Q. My ADB port is dead. I've tested both the RF choke filter and the pico fuse. Both prove to be good. Could the ADB transceiver be bad on the logic board? What should I test next?

A. Generally speaking, the ADB transceiver chip on the logic board is not a really high-failure item. Usually, it's the stuff between the port and the chip that goes.

Q. What components should you test first? Could you possibly list the Macs with the worst failure records?

A. Good questions. What should you replace first? Well, that all depends on which Macintosh you have. I have listed the highest-failure items, other than those we have mentioned already (RF choke and fuse). To test most of these, you'll need a good voltmeter and some electronics experience.

Table 8-1. Problematic Mac models and their high-failure items

Model	Location	Value	Description
Mac SE	R14	470 ohm	Resistor
	R15	1K ohm	Resistor
	Q1	2N3904	Transistor
Mac Portable		Power Manager IC	
		M50740 Keyboard	Processor IC
		Qty (2) 470 ohm	Resistors
		Qty (2) 10k ohm	Resistors
		Qty (2) 2N3904	Transistor
Mac IIs (II, IIx,		Qty (1) 470 ohm	Resistors
IIcx, IIci)		Qty (2) .01 mf	Capacitors

Q. Aside from killing the ADB port, what other problems might I encounter by disconnecting and reconnecting my ADB devices?

A. If you don't kill your port, you have a good chance of your ADB device losing its ADB ID number that was assigned to it by the Mac during startup. It reverts back to its default ID number. Sometimes, the default ID number is the same as its assigned ID number, so there's no problem. If they aren't the same, however, the device may be ignored until the Mac recognizes it.

Q. I have a situation where my both of my ADB ports get knocked out on my Macintosh SE/30. However, if I turn the machine off for 15 to 20 minutes, they work fine for awhile, but then go again. What's the problem here?

A. First, it sounds to me like you have a short in your ADB cabling somewhere. Second, you probably have the poly-blow fuse installed on your logic board (behind the ADB ports) rather than the traditional pico fuse. These fuses look like lollypops. When they blow, they usually reset themselves after 15 to 20 minutes, which is nice, but most people don't know this. I really think that you have a short somewhere that's taking this fuse out. Try another keyboard cable. If that doesn't work, check your mouse cable and the cables on your other ADB devices. If all of your cables prove to be good, check for bad or bent connectors.

Q. What's the leading cause of a keyboard dying? What things should I try when attempting to resurrect my keyboard?

A. Abuse and neglect are the leading causes of keyboard death. Open up an old, neglected keyboard sometime and look at all of the nasty things that can accumulate inside. I've found food, staples, paper clips, gum, fingernail clippings, and enough dirt to plant corn . People don't seem to understand that the ADB keyboards all have a keyboard microcontroller IC chip and some other electronic circuitry. If something really conductive shorts a couple of pins out, the keyboard will be dead.

Q. Is there a quick and dirty way of troubleshooting and repairing dead keyboards?

A. Yes. The first thing you have to do is open the keyboard, remove the assembly, and look for foreign objects. Clean the keyboard well with either a nonconductive cleaning solution or with distilled water. Yes, I said distilled water. Don't use tap water because it has trace metals that are conductive. There's no problem using distilled water. People always cringe when I recommend doing this. However, it's a known fact that most boards get cleaned in a bath of distilled water sometime during the manufacturing process (usually at the end). I also use a small cleaning brush that has antistatic bristles. Don't use a brush with plastic bristles: they pose a static hazard to the components. Make sure that you let it dry well before you power it on, or it will blow up on you.

A good cleaning cures over 80% of keyboard failures. If the keyboard is on your machine, clean it yourself, and save the cost of a service call. If you fix Macs for a living, give the customer another keyboard (preferably one you cleaned earlier). Take the dirty keyboard back to the shop, and clean a few of them at a time. It's always best not to wash keyboards in front of the customer. It tends to cause them to panic, and it may give them ideas later on when you're not around. I used to do this for a living, and I've seen customers do all kinds of strange things.

Q. Are there any other components that fail regularly inside the keyboard? If so, are they easily replaced?

A. Yes. ADB keyboards do have a common failure point: the keyboard microcontroller chip. In the standard ADB keyboard, this chip is an NEC 8048HC610, which is an 8-bit, 40-pin chip. Other keyboards, such as the enhanced ADB keyboard, typically use an NEC 80C49HC200 or equivalent microcontroller chip. These chips cost anywhere from $2 to $10, depending on which one and how many you purchase.

Q. I'm having a problem with stuck keys. Will a good cleaning help clear this up?

A. Yes. A good cleaning typically remedies most problems with stuck keys. Follow the procedures for general cleaning.

Q. I recently cleaned my keyboard and I still have one key that sticks and repeats and another that does nothing at all. What should I do? Can these keys be replaced? Is there a way to test the keys?

A. The easiest way to test the keys is with a voltmeter. First you must open up the keyboard and remove the assembly. Then you should locate the keys that are giving you a hard time. Remove the keycap that covers the keyswitch and visually inspect for damage or for any substance that might be causing them to stick (such as cola residue). Be careful when you pull of the keycap. You can use a keycap puller, chip puller, or a small screwdiver to remove the cap.

If you don't see anything obviously wrong, you'll have to test the keys by performing a continuity test with a voltmeter. To do this, locate the solder joints that are holding the switch in place. Put one of the voltmeter probes on each solder joint. Then depress the keyswitch. It should show continuity when you depress the switch. A stuck key reads continuity all of the time. A bad key reads as an open or infinity. In either case the key must be replaced. This only applies to the keyboards that use the mechanical switches, like those manufactured by ALPS for Apple. Some of the newer keyboards use a capacitive mat in lieu of individual keys. There is nothing that you can do for these keyboards. However, the ALPS-type keyboards are easy to fix. Simply take a Radio Shack desoldering tool, which costs $5 to $10 (or a soldering iron with a solder sucker), and remove the two pieces of solder holding the switch in place. Gently loosen the top retaining clip, and remove the bad switch. Then put in a new switch and solder it back in place. You can use a cheap soldering iron to accomplish this as well. You should then perform a continuity check to verify that the new key is functioning properly.

Q. **How much do the keyswitches cost, and where can I purchase them?**

A. Keyswitch prices range anywhere from 5 or 10 cents to $1 or more, depending on the quantity that you purchase. I seldom purchase new keyswitches. Instead, I call secondhand Mac companies like Shreve Systems, Pre-Owned Electronics, and Mactronics to see if I can pick up a cheap dead keyboard. I then use the dead keyboard for parts such as keycaps and switches. (Of course, I test things out to see what's good.) This is great for when the letters on my keycaps get worn. Try purchasing just the letter "A" or "B" from Apple sometime. You usually have to purchase the whole set of keys. That's why I like buying dead keyboards. I get all the keycaps and switches I need.

Q. **Trackballs and mice are inexpensive, simple devices. They can be purchased from $40 to $65 for a decent mouse and about $100 for a good trackball. What typically goes wrong with these devices? Is it smart to attempt to repair the trackball and mouse, or should I just replace them when they fail?**

A. Certain repairs on these devices can be cost effective. They are quick and easy. For instance, trackballs and mice have problems with frequent dirt build-up on the bottom rollers and around the light sources (LEDs) and interrupter wheels. It takes a few minutes to open up the mouse, blow it out well with compressed air (no CFCs) and then scrub the rollers with cleaning swabs and isopropyl alcohol. Some manufacturers sell cleaning pads that you roll the mouse across, but I prefer to use swabs because I can get into all the nooks and crannies.

Broken mice are another common problem with a quick fix. For whatever reason, users seem to pull on those cables until they break. It takes five minutes to solder a new mouse cable in place.

Finally, the only other repair that I would spend any time on would be replacing the mouse or trackball switch. This switch is used every time you click and drag with the trackball or mouse. They get a lot of wear and tear, and they tend to be high-failure items that take less than three minutes for the average technician to replace. You can test these switches by performing a continuity test, just like testing the keyswitches.

Q. **Where can I purchase mouse and trackball switches? Who manufactures them? Are they expensive?**

A. Trackball and mouse switches are very inexpensive, usually less than $1. Two manufacturers of these switches are Cherry and Omron. Any large electronics distributor that carries these brand names should be able to get them for you. But you will have to buy quantity. Make certain that you get either the exact replacement switch or one that is a very close match.

Q. **I don't know if a mouse cable is worth replacing. Every vendor I have seen in the trade magazines wants $15 to $20 for these cables, plus my time. Is there any place that I can purchase a mouse cable cheaper to make the repair worth my while?**

A. Yes. It's easier than you think. You can purchase two mouse cables for less than $6. This is a neat trick. Purchase a straight keyboard cable for $6 and cut it in half. You now have two mouse cables. If you recall, the mouse and keyboard are both ADB devices. All ADB devices use the standard four-wire cable. The mouse just has the connector on one end. The other end is wired directly to the mouse. Don't purchase a coiled keyboard cable (it will look like a little pigtail on your mouse). One thing that the standard mouse cables have is a strain relief near the end of the cable inside the mouse. You can make your own strain relief by tying a knot in the end. Strain reliefs prevent the cable from getting broken by pulling and tugging.

Q. **Are the ADB chips inside the mice and trackballs worth replacing? If so, how much do they cost?**

A. No, the ADB transceiver chips inside the trackballs and mice aren't worth replacing. They are custom ICs, and you'll spend a great deal of time trying to track them down. Time is money; work smarter, not harder. Buy a new trackball or mouse.

Q. Are the Kensington Trackballs a good brand of trackball to purchase? I heard that they have had problems in the past. Is this true?

A. Yes. Kensington has had some problems in the past, especially with dirt build-up under the right and rear rollers on their Turbo Mouse ADB trackball. These two rollers actually have an adhesive label covering a small opening beneath each of these two rollers. This label is on the bottom of the trackball and contains the part number and serial number. I've had one of these trackballs and was constantly getting crud buildup in these two spots as well as around my LEDs. Because of the dirt, the trackball has trouble going left to right or up and down. You have to clean it, which takes about five minutes, every few months or so. However, I've been very satisfied with my Kensington products over the years. They're a good company, and they stand behind their products.

CHAPTER 9

Video Displays

A computer video display operates much like a television without a tuner or an IF (intermediate frequency) section. Instead of receiving an RF (radio frequency) signal, converting it to an IF signal, and detecting the signal to produce video, a display receives the video information straight from the computer through red, green, and blue (RGB) video lines. Horizontal and vertical synchronizing pulses supplied from the computer lock the picture. There are several types of computer monitors, but each monitor receives an input signal from the computer and converts the signal into a graphic image.

To understand the operation of video displays, you must know the monitor types and understand the methods of supplying horizontal and vertical synchronization and monitor resolution. We'll review each of these elements in detail.

Monitor Types

There are two common types of monitors: digital and analog. A digital computer monitor receives TTL (transistor-to-transistor logic) signal levels and produces colors through combinations of 1s and 0s. Monochrome digital monitors have one or two video inputs and display one or two shades of amber, green, or white and black.

Three, four, or six video input lines may be used for color digital computer monitors: red, green, blue, red intensity, green intensity, or blue intensity. The intensity lines are used in digital monitors to vary color saturation. Color digital monitors can display 8, 16, or 64 colors, depending on the number of video inputs. Using TTL signal levels limits the number of colors displayed by the color digital monitor.

Three video input lines are used for color analog computer monitors: red, green, and blue. A single input line in an analog monochrome computer monitors produces shades of gray. Colors or shades of gray are created by varying a voltage between 0.0 and 0.7 volts peak-to-peak. An infinite number of colors or shades of gray are possible.

Because of the low resolution of early computer monitors, picture quality and clarity were extremely poor. The development of high-resolution monitors meant faster scanning frequencies and more displayed pixels. More pixels displayed in less time increases the monitor's bandwidth and vastly improves picture quality. For example, the NTSC (National Television Standards Committee) television system uses a scanning frequency of 15.7 kHz and produces a bandwidth of 4.2 MHz. A typical Mac II high-resolution computer monitor uses a scanning frequency of over 35 kHz and produces a bandwidth of over 25 MHz.

Sync Input Methods

To display an image, a monitor requires two synchronizing signals for the scan circuits: horizontal sync and vertical sync. Computers operate at different scan frequencies for each format.

A multiscan monitor, like the NEC Multisync, can receive and lock to a range of scanning frequencies within its specifications. The monitor automatically locks to the frequency applied to the input. For example, one multiscan monitor model can sync to horizontal frequencies between 15 kHz and 35 kHz. If this monitor receives an MDA format the horizontal circuits automatically sync to 18.5 kHz, and the vertical circuits sync to 50 Hz.

Computer monitors use three different sync input schemes. The first method uses separate vertical and horizontal sync inputs. The second method uses a vertical and horizontal composite sync input. The third method uses vertical and horizontal composite sync on a video line (usually green); for example, Apple Macintosh monitors use a composite sync signal on the green video input line.

Monitor Resolution

Resolution refers to the maximum number of light-to-dark transitions a monitor is able to produce. Resolution is measured in pixels (picture elements) or lines. Horizontal resolution is almost always defined by pixels, whereas vertical resolution may be specified in vertical lines or pixels.

A pixel is the smallest area of light or dark the monitor can produce. The number of pixels displayed from the top to the bottom of the screen is vertical resolution, or vertical lines. The number of pixels displayed across the screen is horizontal resolution.

Good resolution is needed to produce a crisp picture. Four factors contribute to good resolution:

1. Bandwidth
2. Dot pitch
3. Refresh rate
4. Scanning method (progressive or interlaced)

Bandwidth

The bandwidth of a monitor is the maximum frequency that the video circuits can pass. Bandwidth determines the fine detail of the picture. If the frequency response of the video circuit decreases, the small images and fast transitions appear to be out of focus or blurry.

Dot pitch

Dot pitch is the distance between like colors in the shadow mask; for example, the distance between the center of one red hole and the next red hole, as shown in Figure 3. Dot pitch determines the smallest-size pixel a color CRT can produce. The smaller the dot pitch, the sharper the image. Typical values of dot pitch are between 0.26 and 0.31 millimeters.

Dot pitch is the distance between like colors. The red pixels in this example might be 0.28 millimeters apart.

```
DOT PITCH
 |—>•R        •G     •B     •R              <—|
           •B     •R    •G
         •R    •G     •B     •R
```

Refresh rate

Refresh rate refers to the time it takes to display a full frame of video information. If the refresh rate of a monitor is 60 Hz, it takes 1/60 of a second to display a full picture.

Scanning Methods

Two methods may be used for vertical scan: progressive scan or interlace scan. Progressive scan sweeps the picture tube once to produce a full frame of video. Interlaced scan uses two fields of sweep (even and odd) to produce a full frame of video.

A disadvantage of the interlaced scan is the half-line jitter, which causes the picture to flicker. Interlaced monitors enable high resolutions while keeping the bandwidth lower than that required by a noninterlaced monitor with the same resolution and vertical scan frequency.

Cathode Ray Tube (CRT)

The concept behind a CRT is actually very simple: an electron beam from the cathode strikes the screen which gives off light. Circuits external to the CRT define a grid, forming a thin stream of electrons.

The screen grid has a positive voltage on it to pull the electrons through the control grid. Only the electrons that pass through the hole in the control grid form the true beam current or the current that eventually strikes the face of the CRT. The screen grid is shaped like the control grid and also has a hole through which the electron beam passes.

One or more accelerating grids follow the screen grid (each of which has increasing levels of positive bias) to increase the speed of the electron beam. In addition, one or more focus grids form the electron beam into a fine hairlike thread that hits the phosphor screen, resulting in a very tiny spot of light.

The final group of CRT elements is responsible for producing the visual image. These elements include the phosphor screen and a structure called the second anode. The second anode is quite similar in shape to the other grids, but it has a very high positive potential on it. A special coating lines the inside of the CRT between the second anode and the phosphor screen. This is at the same potential as the second anode and keeps the beam from straying off course.

The second anode speeds the electron beam to an extremely high rate. The beam suddenly collides with the phosphor screen, causing light to be emitted by the phosphor. A color CRT has a phosphor screen with three colors of phosphor (red, blue, and green) that are very close to each other. Each one is struck by electrons from the corresponding beam from one of three identical electron gun assemblies.

For an image to be produced on the screen, the electron beam must be made to vary in intensity by changing the bias between the cathode and the control grid.

The CRT beam is cut off with the normal DC bias, which is applied to the control grid. This results in a black level being displayed on the screen, since no beam current reaches the screen. Video information is applied to the cathode, the control grid, or both, which reduces the amount of G1 bias and enables more of the electron beam to strike the phosphor screen. Reducing the bias to zero allows maximum beam current and maximum CRT brightness. Varying the bias produces brightness levels between cut-off and full brightness.

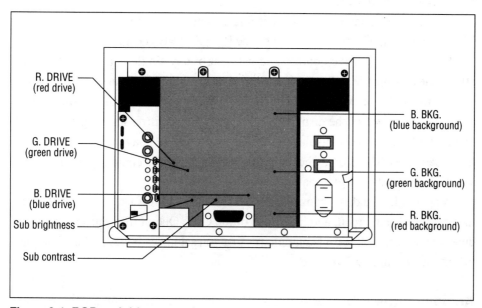

Figure 9-1. RGB and drive controls

RGB Drive Controls

The computer sends the three color signals to the monitor. The signals enter the monitor at the video connector. Transistors amplify each RGB signal, depending on the setting of the corresponding drive control.

For example, if the G-DRIVE is turned up, two things occur. First the display appears more green. Second, the display also increases in overall luminance (that is, it increases the amount of light emitted, reflected, or transmitted from

213

the surface of the screen). But if the G-DRIVE control is turned down, the opposite occurs: The display appears less green and luminance decreases. It is important to remember that the adjustment of a particular drive control affects both the color and luminance of the display. When adjusting a color monitor, you must accurately set these controls.

The drive controls have a greater effect on the brighter areas of the display than on the darker areas. For this reason, when adjusting any drive control, you always focus your attention on the brightest bars on the gray-bar display.

RGB Background Controls

The red, green, and blue signals are further amplified by the background (RGB, BKG) amplifiers, which are adjusted by the R-BKG, G-BKG, and B-BKG controls.

Just as with the drive controls, adjustment of any single background control affects the appropriate color on the screen and the overall luminance of the screen.

Although the background and drive controls work in a similar fashion, they affect different parts of the display. Whereas the drive controls have a greater effect on the bright areas of the display, the background controls have a greater effect on the darker areas. Therefore, when adjusting any background control, you focus your attention on the darker gray bars of the gray-bar display.

Also, unlike the drive controls, the background controls set the DC voltage to the individual red, green, and blue guns of the CRT. One of the adjustment procedures, which you will learn later, requires that you set the cathodes in the color guns to a predetermined DC voltage.

Achieving the White Balance

Achieving the white balance can be difficult because each of the three color guns conduct and pass electrons at different levels. You cannot simply set all the controls to mid-range or some other predetermined setting and expect to achieve the desired balance, as indicated by the white balance test display. But when mixed in the proper proportions, red, green, and blue light produce white light.

The table to the right illustrates a few of the possible color combinations that can occur as a result of combining different levels of red, green, and blue pixel elements. It also suggests what you can do if a particular color needs to be adjusted out of your picture.

RGB COLOR MIXING CHART

Combined RGB Pixel Elements	Perceived Colors

1. R   G   B   WHITE
    •   •   •

White light is produced by the proper levels of red, green, and blue.

2. R   G   B   RED
    •

An excessive amount of red in your picture can be eliminated by either decreasing your red level or by raising your green and blue levels.

3. R   G   B   GREEN
        •

An excessive amount of green in your picture can be eliminated by reducing your green level or by increasing the red and blue levels.

4. R   G   B   BLUE
            •

An excessive amount of blue in your picture can be eliminated by reducing the blue levels or by increasing the green and red levels.

5. R   G   B   YELLOW
    •   •

An excessive amount of yellow in your picture can be eliminated by increasing the blue levels or by reducing the red and green levels.

6. R   G   B   CYAN
        •   •

An excessive amount of cyan in your picture can be eliminated by reducing the blue and green levels or by increasing the red level.

7. R   G   B   MAGENTA
    •   •

An excessive amount of magenta in your picture can be eliminated by reducing the red and blue levels or by slightly increasing the green level.

Compact Macintosh Computers with Built-in Video Circuitry

The Macintosh Plus, SE, SE/30, Classic, and Classic II have built-in monitor and video circuitry. These models, which are the compact Macintosh computers, are sometimes referred to as all-in-ones. Due to their designs, they have an above-average failure history. The item that fails most with compact models is the power/video sweep board.

The older Macs, such as the 128, 512, 512KE, and Plus, have the highest failure history of computers manufactured by Apple. Failure in these models usually occurs for one of the following reasons:

1. The board doubles as a power supply and analog video board, making it a critical module.
2. Many of the components are underrated and and prone to failure.
3. These units have no cooling fan to remove the excessive heat that builds up inside. Heat is a major factor in component failure.

With the Macintosh SE and SE/30 models, Apple got smart and made the power supply and analog board two separate units. Although the power supply is much better than on the old models, the DC output is still borderline at best. The power supply bolts onto the analog video board. The analog video board is the largest board inside the Mac SE and SE/30 and is interchangeable between these SE models. Apple even added a cooling fan to prolong the units life. Unfortunately, this board is still a very cheap design with numerous underrated components that usually develop problems within two years.

The components that fail the most frequently are

- Flyback transformer
- Power transistor
- Cooling fan
- Underrated capacitors
- Resistors

The symptoms vary, depending on how and which components fail. However, the end result is the same: the quality of the video is affected.

The Macintosh Classic and Classic II have the fewest video-related problems of the compact Macintosh family. These models have gone back to the old-fashioned design of integrating the power supply and video into the same circuit board, as in the Mac Plus. Fortunately these boards are smaller and use fewer components. The Classic and Classic II also have a decent cooling fan. The high-failure components are similar to those that go bad in the SE and SE/30, with the exception of the cooling fan.

A Word of Caution

If you have problems with the built-in internal video circuitry and are in any way unsure about your ability to repair the Macintosh, you should not attempt it. If you don't know what you're doing, there is a very real possibility that either you or the computer will get hurt in the process, especially when you are dealing with power supplies and high-voltage video circuitry. If the unit is under warranty, return it to the Apple dealer for service. Otherwise, send the defective board to a third-party maintenance company such as Micromat Computer Systems of Novato, California. Micromat is usually less expensive than going to an Apple dealer because they actually do component level repair, where Apple dealers do a swap. There is absolutely nothing wrong with doing a swap, as long as they don't gouge you on the price for parts and labor. However, if you're in a big hurry, you may have to bite the bullet and go to your local Apple dealer.

If you have a problem with your Macintosh Classic video display, most likely it's the power/video sweep board. This is a combination power supply and analog video board. There are two different flavors of the power/sweep board: one for the Mac Plus and earlier models, and the other for the Classic and Classic II. Both types are very high-failure items. This board has many components and performs several functions. Many of the components are underrated, and some fail within less than 1000 hours of use.

About 50% of component failures can be found through visual inspection. Other failures require that you remove several components from the circuit and test them properly. Of course this means you need some test equipment. In many cases the failure of one component causes others to fail as well. Locating all of the failed components can be tricky and may require a schematic diagram to show the relationship and values of components in the circuit. This can be time-consuming and difficult for the average user.

Repairing Analog Video Circuitry

If you have a fair amount of electronics experience and want to properly repair the analog video circuitry in compact Macintosh computers, at a minimum you should have the following tools.

1. A CRT discharge tool to eliminate high-voltage safety hazards.

2. A good digital or analog voltmeter. Fluke, Beckman, and Simpson voltmeters are the best, but Radio Shack also sells some decent ones. A good voltmeter costs about $50. Top-of-the-line meters start at $100 and go on up to as high as $900 for the very best. My preference is the Fluke 8x (80, 83, and so on) series meters. I got mine for less than $250, and it gets the job done.

3. A bag of alligator wires.

4. A decent 25-watt, pencil-tip soldering iron and desoldering tools (iron or pump). I get most of my stuff from a large mail-order house called Techni Tool. They have reasonable prices and excellent customer service. In a pinch, I go to Radio Shack. Their tools are of average quality, but they do the job. While you are at it, pick up a spool of thin 60/40 or 67/33 solder.

5. A can of electronic contact cleaner.

6. Antistatic video alignment tools.

If you're going to repair compact Macs for a living, put together a grab-bag of electronic parts, such as resistors (1/4- and 1/2-watt), potentiometers, high-frequency capacitors, connectors, wire harnesses, TDA (deflection) ICs, 74LS38N ICs, diodes, and flyback transformers.

How many of each of these components you purchase depends on the number and type of Macintosh computers you plan to work on. A small investment of $100 to $200 is more than enough to get you the parts necessary to get started. If you can afford it, try to find someone (like Shreve, Pre-owned, or Mactronics) who can sell you used or dead analog boards to practice on. You also might want to check the classified listings in your local paper for dead Macs.

Techniques for Repairing Compact Macs

Before you open up a compact Mac, always turn the unit on and listen for unusual sounds and smell for burning or other odors. Then feel the case to see if the unit is overheating. Sometimes the cooling fans go bad or are non-existent and cause an undesirable overheating condition. Next, take power supply readings to rule this module out as a suspect. Then and only then can you open up the Mac.

After you have opened it up, remove the analog board and inspect for obvious signs of component failure, such as charred resistors, bulging or burnt capacitors, melted wires, burnt connectors, or signs of overheating around power transistors.

If you can't find anything that looks bad, carefully inspect all of the solder joints for cracks. Due to the very high frequency of the horizontal sweep circuitry, cracked solder joints are a very common problem, especially in the top half of the analog board near the flyback transformer, capacitors, and connectors.

Another common problem with compact Macs may be a bad flyback transformer. The most common symptoms of the problem are

- A distinct buzzing or ringing noise coming from the unit. This is often a sign of cracked epoxy seals on the flyback.
- A terrible burning or car exhaust smell.
- A jittering or wiggling screen.
- The screen snaps and crackles at you.
- The picture fades in and out. This could also be a problem with a power transistor located in the flyback circuitry. When the power transistor fails, it often takes the flyback with it, and vice versa.
- No high voltage to the CRT. You get no picture whatsoever.

Troubleshooting Video Displays

Q. **Recently I accidentally dropped my Macintosh Classic on the floor. My video display screen is now slightly tilted down and to the right. Is there any adjustment that I can make?**

A. Yes. It's called a yoke adjustment. The yoke is a large wire coil that surrounds the neck of the CRT. To adjust the yoke, you first need to turn off the unit and remove the back cover. You then have to loosen a single Philips screw that holds the yoke in place. Turn the unit on and be very careful not to touch anything other than the white plastic wheel that surrounds the yoke (I call this the captain's wheel). Have somebody sit in front of the unit while you move the wheel and adjust the picture. This saves you the hassle of leaning over exposed areas during the adjustment process. If you don't have anybody around, use a mirror or be very, very careful. After you get rid of the tilt, tighten the retaining screw until it's snug. Don't force it too hard or you may break the thin, glass neck of the CRT. Turn the unit off, unplug it, and re-install the rear cover.

Q. I have a Mac SE/30 analog board with an unusual problem. At first, my machine bonged and appeared to start up fine. However, I never got a Desktop or any icons. Instead I got a glowing white screen. Then the screen went completely black. What's the problem?

A. An all-white or all-black raster is often the sign of a failed IC (chip) on the analog board. This chip is usually a 74LS38N (quad input, NAND), which costs less than $1. However, before you replace this chip, inspect all of the cable connections on the analog board for the possibility of a burnt connector. It's not a bad idea to take a quick peek for cracked solder joints as well.

Q. The display on my compact Mac has collapsed to a horizontal line. Where is the problem, and why is this happening?

A. When a display collapses to a horizontal line, it indicates that you have lost your vertical sweep. As always, you should check for a burnt connector wire or cracked solder joints on the analog board. The various resistors (especially the 1/4-watt) and the transistors in the vertical circuit also are suspect. But keep in mind that this isn't a very high-frequency circuit, nor is it especially failure-prone. The most frequent cause of the screen collapsing to a horizontal line is insufficient power from the power supply to the video circuitry. But you would have caught this if you had taken power supply and voltage readings before you opened up the machine.

If you don't have a voltmeter handy, listen for the bong, the fan (if you have one), and the hard drive spinning up. These are all good indicators that you have power and that the problem actually is in your video. Remember, it's all in the process of elimination!

Q. I have a display that collapses to a vertical line. Does this indicate a problem in my horizontal sweep circuitry? If so, what are the most likely suspects in this case?

A. You're absolutely right. When the screen collapses to a vertical line it signifies there is a problem with the horizontal sweep. The horizontal circuitry controls the left-to-right motion of the electron beam. Absence of the horizontal sweep results in a single vertical line. This is one of the biggest problem areas in the compact Macintosh video circuitry. The reason that this is such a failure-prone area is in part because the horizontal sweep is at a high frequency of 22.5 kHz (22,500 sweeps per second). High-frequency circuits are very prone to cracked solder joints. I would look for these first (especially in the top half of the analog board around the capacitors, connectors, and other chips).

If you can't locate any cracked solder joints, it's possible that you have blown a horizontal deflection capacitor or a bad TDA (deflection) chip. The location of these components varies from machine to machine. Do a visual inspection of the capacitors across the top of the analog board, looking for bulging and discoloration, for example. Apple is notorious for using underrated components in these areas. If you find bad capacitors, upgrade them from 25 to 35 volts, 85 degrees to 75 to 100 volts, 85 to 100 degrees. Go with a 100-volt, high-frequency, nonpolarized capacitor rated at 105 degrees, and you'll never have to worry about it again.

Q. **I recently performed an upgrade on my Macintosh. After reassembling the unit, I get only a single illuminated pixel in the middle of my screen. The upgrade that I performed had nothing to do with the analog video board. The machine bongs, and I hear the fan turning. What is wrong here?**

A. A single illuminated pixel in the middle of your screen indicates the absence of both the horizontal and vertical sweeps. Three things could be wrong:

1. You may have accidentally bumped the wire that goes from the yoke to the analog board. It's very possible that this wire is either loose or disconnected.
2. The yoke wire may be plugged into the connector on the analog board, but the connector itself may have been pulled physically out of the board. The connector may also be very loose and may need to be resoldered back in place. Perform a thorough visual inspection. See if you can wiggle the connector around.
3. You may have a bad yoke, although this is indeed rare. I've seen bad yoke assemblies in the past, but they aren't high-failure items and don't frequently produce the single illuminated pixel problem. If it does happen, however, you must replace the yoke.

Q. The video on my compact Mac is badly out of focus. I've tried adjusting it as best I can, but I can't get the picture to come in clearly. What is the problem?

A. There are two likely culprits in this situation. First, the resistors in the focusing circuitry have a tendency to burn out. Unfortunately these resistors often don't show any visible signs of a problem. Second, you may have corroded pins on the rear of your CRT. I see this problem frequently in older Macs. To clean these pins, turn off the machine, discharge the CRT, carefully remove the CRT socket board, and clean the pins with contact cleaner and a cloth.

Q. I recently replaced an analog board in my compact Mac. The original problem was no video. The replacement board fixed that, except I now have bright, horizontal scan lines across my screen. What is the proper way get rid of these lines?

A. Your cut-off and brightness settings may be too high. To adjust these scan lines out, you need to

1. Turn both the brightness and cut-off adjustments to their maximum positions. Don't force the adjustment; gently move the potentiometer until the stopper catches. At the maximum setting, those scan lines are really glowing.
2. Lower the cut-off adjustment very slowly until the scan lines disappear.
3. Use your brightness controls to adjust the picture to your personal liking.

Q. What are the symptoms of a bad CRT?

A. A bad CRT produces several common symptoms that are easily observed on the video display. However, the same symptoms that are produced by a bad CRT may also be the result of a problem that is external to the CRT. Here are some examples:

1. Dark or dim picture. This could result from a CRT with weak emission, a shorted gun element, or an open cathode. Other possibilities include wrong bias, insufficient second anode voltage, low or missing filament voltage, or a problem in the video circuits.

2. Dark blacks and overdriven whites. A weak CRT gun (or all three guns in a color CRT) could result in nonlinear light output from the tube (frequently called bad gamma). The same symptoms also are caused by problems in the video amps or by wrong bias voltages to the tube.

3. Bad color tracking or gray-scale. A tri-color CRT that has a weak gun produces a picture that cannot be color balanced. Instead of pure whites and shades of gray, the picture may look slightly red or green. Misadjusted background or bias controls, or a defective chroma demodulator also produces these symptoms.

4. Overly intense color. Another symptom possibly caused by a defective CRT is a bright-colored raster that cannot be adjusted. This may result from a short inside the CRT or an open control grid. An external defect, such as a shorted driver, may also cause the symptom.

Q. Is there any way to repair a bad CRT? Is there any good CRT test equipment available? How much does it cost?

A. Whenever I have a problem with a bad CRT, I simply replace it. However, if you repair quite a few monitors, it may be worth your while to check into a CRT tester or restoration unit, such as the Sencore CR-70. These units eliminate CRT shorts and other common problems. However, these units are expensive ($1500 to $2000) and require a bit of training to use. Repair depots are more likely to have these than the average Mac owner.

Q. What is a white balance test, and why would I perform such a test?

A. You can determine if the colors are properly balanced by looking at a white raster (a lit portion of the monitor screen). If the monitor is properly adjusted, the white raster does appear white. If the monitor is out of adjustment, the white raster appears colored, if only slightly. For example, it may appear slightly green or perhaps blue.

The procedure used to balance the three colors on Apple monitors is called a white balance adjustment. You adjust the various color controls located in the rear of the monitor (some monitors need to be opened to access these) until a video signal designated as white is in fact displayed as white.

Q. Are monitor adjustments common problems in servicing computer monitors? How many color adjustments does a typical color monitor have? What are they used to adjust? Do I need to use any special test patterns during the adjustment process?

A. Monitor adjustments are about the only thing the average Mac user can hope to do with a color monitor (except possibly replace a CRT tube). These monitors are very complex, and it's extremely dangerous for a novice to attempt component-level repair. But color problems and adjustments are very common. These too can be tricky if you don't know what you are doing. This chapter should give you a better understanding of how color convergence works and what the various adjustments control.

Usually a color monitor has five or six controls (adjustment ports) that work together to control the output of the three color guns: two or three drive controls (one each for red and blue, and sometimes one for green) and three background/bias controls (one for red, blue, and green).

When adjusting these controls, you need to display a specific pattern on the monitor. On the AppleColor HiRes RGB Monitor, you use a gray-bar test pattern, which displays a range of gray shades rather than color. Some gray-bar tests display 8 bars, others have 16 bars.

Q. What adjustments should the average user be concerned with?

A. The only adjustments that the average user really needs to worry about are brightness and contrast. These controls are located on the outside of the monitor.

Q. Can I make any external adjustments on a typical Macintosh HiRes RGB monitor (other than brightness and contrast) without opening up the monitor?

A. Yes. There are eight external adjustments on the Apple Macintosh HiRes RGB monitor: cut-off, focus, horizontal shift and size, vertical shift and size, vertical static convergence, and horizontal static convergence. Both the horizontal and vertical shift controls are preset at the factory and usually don't need to be adjusted.

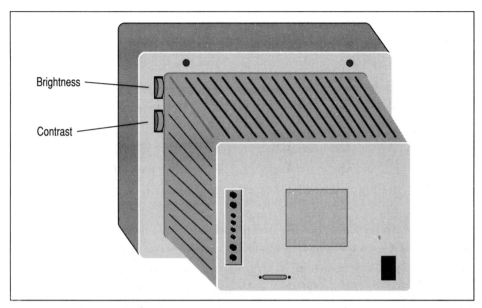

Figure 9-2. Brightness and contrast controls

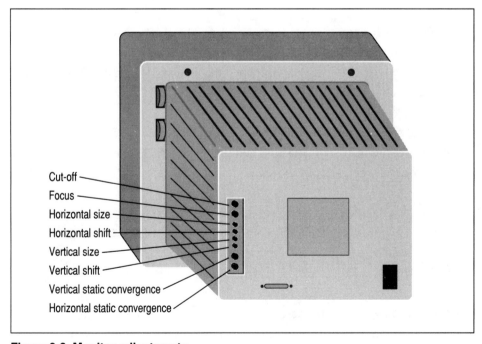

Figure 9-3. Monitor adjustments

225

Q. Do I need any test pattern software to properly perform these adjustments?

A. Yes. To properly perform these adjustments, you need test pattern software. Apple has some good test patterns on their IIcx and IIci diagnostic diskettes. Unfortunately this software is available only to authorized Apple dealers. An excellent alternative to Apple's software is Test Pattern Generator (TPG), a utility program by fellow author and Mac guru, Larry Pina. TPG works with all kinds of different monitors, from Plus up through third-party equipment.

Q. I understand that the horizontal and vertical shift adjustments are preset at the factory. However, when do I perform the other adjustments on the Mac HiRes RGB monitor? Which test patterns do I use with them?

A. External adjustments affect many different aspects of the video picture. The table below best illustrates when you should perform a specific and which test pattern you should select from either Larry Pina's TPG or Apple's diagnostic utilities.

External Adjustment   **Use This Test Pattern**

Horizontal size ....Cross-hatch
Adjust the horizontal size control when the display is too narrow or lacks the proper width.

Vertical size ....Cross-hatch
Adjust the vertical size control when the display lacks the proper height; in other words, when it looks too short.

Focus ....Focus screen
Obviously you adjust the focus control when the display is out of focus.

Cut-off ....None required

You may have to perform a cut-off adjustment when the CRT or one of the internal circuit boards is replaced. This adjustment must be made prior to per forming the white balance test. The following are symptoms of a poor monitor cut-off adjustment setting:

- The display is very bright and out of focus.
- The display is either very dark or very light.
- The monitor keeps shutting itself down (an overvoltage condition).

White balance Gray-bar scale

Perform the white balance test immediately following a cut-off adjustment. Like the cut-off adjustment, you should perform this test after "major surgery" on your monitor. The symptoms of poor white balance are

- The display is still too dark or light.
- When the gray-bar scale patterns are displayed, one color is predominant, perhaps too much green or red. It's not always necessary to adjust all of the red, green and blue controls to achieve the correct white balance. Normally, you have to do a very slight adjustment to the RED-BKD and R-DRIVE controls to neutralize color predominance.

External Adjustment   **Use This Test Pattern**

Horizontal and vertical convergence ....Cross-hatch on black background
Adjust the horizontal and vertical convergence controls if the screen images are still out of focus or appear to be shadowed. This often indicates that the red, green, and blue electron beams are not properly aligned.

Q. Do you recommend the use of an isolation transformer when servicing monitors? If so, why? And where can I purchase one?

A. I strongly recommend the use of an isolation transformer for anyone doing frequent monitor repairs. Isolation transformers isolate the circuitry of the monitor from the AC line source (wall outlet). This reduces the chances of your being killed if you accidentally and simultaneously come in contact with high voltage and something with earth ground. The Sencore Powerite is an excellent isolation transformer and safety analyzer. It retails for $495 and is well worth it if you work on monitors for a living. Remember, these things are not toys; you can be killed.

Q. Do monitor cables ever go bad? If so, what signs should I be looking for?

A. Yes. Monitor cables go bad all of the time. People are always pulling on them, tripping on them, and forcing them into the video ports. The first things I look for are bent or broken pins. I have gotten some real strange colors on my screen with bents pins. If the pins look OK, I'll perform a continuity test on the cable.

Q. I want to make my own cable for the my Apple Macintosh HiRes RGB and monochrome monitors. What type of connector do I need, and what are the pin assignments?

A. You need 15-pin D-sub connectors. The pin assignments are as follows:

Macintosh HiRes RGB	
Pin	**Signal Description**
1	Red video ground
2	Red video
3	Composite sync
4	Composite sync ground
5	Green video
6	Green video ground
7	N/C
8	N/C
9	Blue video
10	N/C
11	N/C
12	N/C
13	Blue video ground
14	N/C
15	N/C
Connector shell	Shield ground

Apple High Resolution Monochrome	
Pin	Signal Description
1	N/C
2	N/C
3	Composite sync
4	Composite sync ground
5	Black/white video
6	Black/white video ground
7	N/C
8	N/C
9	N/C
10	N/C
11	N/C
12	N/C
13	N/C
14	N/C
15	N/C
Connector shell	Shield ground

Q. The 15-pin connector used on the high-resolution monitors appears to be the same as used on the Apple IIc and IIgs computers. Can I take my Mac monitor and attach it to these units?

A. You could physically attach it to the Apple IIc and IIgs computers, but you would damage either the monitor or the computers. The 15-pin port is also found on some Ethernet connections. You must not attach these monitors to the Apple IIc or GS or accidentally connect a 15-pin Ethernet cable. It may fit, but it won't work.

Q. What are the advantages and disadvantages of the built-in color video circuitry in, for example, the Macintosh IIci?

A. The IIci's built-in video circuitry has both pros and cons. The pros are you don't have to purchase a card, this circuitry does not occupy one of your expansion slots, and since it is located on the motherboard, it's very fast.

229

The cons are the built-in video steals memory from Bank A of your primary RAM to create the frame buffer, which leaves less memory for your programs to use, the larger the monitor that you attach to this port, the more memory it steals, and you can only attach certain monitors to this port, which limits you in monitor selection.

Q. **My screen recently went from very nice colors to black and white. I tried another monitor in its place but I get the same thing: black and white. What's happened? What should I check?**

A. The first thing you should do is go into the control panel and verify that your color monitor settings haven't been blown away. This is the usual cause. However, the color setting is also stored in parameter RAM on your main logic board. It's maintained by a small lithium battery (approximately 3.5 volts DC). It's possible that this battery has gone bad and your settings are not being kept. A sign of this would be that your settings keep reverting back to a default of black and white. Check your battery with a voltmeter. Finally, if you have a Macintosh II-class machine equipped with its own video board, you may have a loose or bad video RAM chip on the board. Remove the board, and gently push down on the chips to reseat them.

CHAPTER 10

SCSI and Hard Disk Drives

SCSI (pronounced "skuzzy") stands for the Small Computer Systems Interface. SCSI was adopted by the American National Standards Institute in 1986 as a standard specification for computer and peripheral communication. SCSI isn't a printer interface or a hard drive interface. It's an input/output interface. Almost any peripheral device can be manufactured to work in a SCSI environment. Some examples include hard disk drives, scanners, tape backups, CD-ROMs, and laser printers.

Since SCSI is defined as a standard, theoretically all SCSI devices in the Macintosh and IBM PC world should be interchangeable. In practice, however, SCSI is like the RS-232 standard. It's a standard, yes, but many manufacturers have their own derivative of it. What happens is that some devices work on both platforms, Mac and PC, while others do not.

Apple first started using the SCSI interface in 1986 with the Macintosh Plus. Any Macintosh computer manufactured before the Mac Plus doesn't support a SCSI interface; any Macintosh built after that date does.

Apple's SCSI implementation permits a total of eight devices, including one host and seven targets. The host (initiator) is your Macintosh, while the targets are your peripheral devices. In a basic SCSI chain, there are eight SCSI ID numbers (addresses) from 0 through 7. You must never configure a device to SCSI ID number 7, because 7 is the highest priority and is always reserved for the Macintosh. You're free, however, to use any of the ID numbers 0 through 6, if you follow one simple rule: Each SCSI peripheral must have its own ID number, 0 being the lowest priority and 6 the highest priority that you can assign a device. Typically, internal hard disk drives are set for 0. This isn't mandatory (I have mine on 5, and it seems to boot a bit faster). If you have a scanner, it's advisable to put it on ID number 6. I can't explain why, but scanners are notorious for causing problems on the

SCSI bus (cabling system). Somehow, they don't always seem to follow the rules, so I start with my scanners on ID number 6.

Macintosh computers rely on the NCR family of SCSI controller chips. Older Macs such as the Plus and SE use the 5380 chip. Mac II family members use the 53C80 chip, which is the low-power, CMOS version of this chip. The Mac LC and IIsi utilize a special hybrid chip called the 85C80, which is a dual serial/SCSI chip, and the IIfx uses a custom version of the 53C80 that includes a DMA (direct memory access) controller. These chips occasionally fail but are relatively easy to purchase and replace.

Common Troubleshooting Questions on SCSI

Q. **I recently plugged my external hard disk drive into the external DB-25 port of my Mac II while it was on. Now my drive won't work on this machine but it works on another machine. Did I kill my SCSI chip? Is there any way to test this port?**

A. You should never plug anything into any port while the Mac is on, no matter how tempting it is. You have a good chance of blowing something up. I don't think that you killed the chip. The Macintosh SE/30, Mac II family, and newer computers have a 1-amp pico fuse protecting the +5-volt line (term power) on that port. Test the fuse with a voltmeter. If it reads "open," replace it. The company Little Fuse makes these fuses, and they can be purchased at any electronics store. Just ask for 125-volt, 1-amp , pico fuses from Little Fuse. The voltage doesn't really matter since this fuse blows on current. These fuses cost less than $1 each. The fuse in the Mac II is located at board reference F2. On other Macs, it's usually located on the logic board directly behind the DB-25 port and close to the internal SCSI port.

Mactronics sells a small, hand-held SCSI port tester that tells you which ID numbers are occupied and communicating. It also tells you if the port is powered and being initialized. It also tells you if the fuse is good.

Q. **I have a strange problem with an external hard drive. Whenever I attach my hard drive to the DB-25 SCSI port, the drive doesn't work until I turn the machine off and wait for 15 to 20 minutes. What's going on?**

A. Some Macs that have a fuse protecting the SCSI port use a different kind of fuse called a poly-blow fuse. When this fuse blows, it resets after 15 to 20 minutes. You are either shorting out the fuse by plugging in the drive while the Mac is on, or you have a short in your SCSI cable. Try replacing the cable.

Q. **Do I have to assign my SCSI ID numbers in any specific order? For example, if I have a device on ID numbers 0 and 1, do I need to put the next device on ID number 2?**

A. No. You can use 2, 3, 4, 5, or 6, provided that they are not being used by any other device. The Mac doesn't care.

Q. **I have multiple hard drives attached to my Mac. If I want to start from one of my other drives instead of the internal, how do I do this?**

A. Very simple. Go into the control panel and select Start-up device. You'll be allowed to change the startup order of your disk drives.

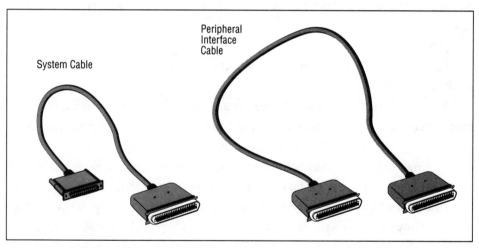

Figure 10-1. SCSI cables

Q. **Should I buy shielded or unshielded SCSI cables? Are the shielded really worth the extra money?**

A. I always purchase double-shielded cables. These cables have extra shielding that cuts down on electrical interference on the SCSI bus. Electrical interference is a frequent cause of data errors. These cables might cost twice as much as unshielded cables, but they are worth it, especially if you have long SCSI chains. A double-shielded cable shouldn't cost you more than $25 to $45 for up to 10 feet with molded ends.

Q. I work in an environment where there are many Macintosh users. Some of these have problems with their SCSI devices not being recognized by their Macs. But when I attach these devices to my Mac, they work fine. I think the problem may be that they have too many devices plugged into a power strip. What do you think?

A. Make sure that the users are turning their external SCSI devices on before they turn on their Macs. In addition, turn on all of your SCSI devices, even if you aren't planning to use them. I don't like it when users plug everything into those power strips. They get into the bad habit of turning everything on at once. If you do that with external SCSI devices, you run the risk of the Mac initializing it's SCSI port before the external device powers up. This can cause the external device to be ignored.

Q. What are some good utilities and tools for working with the SCSI devices?

A. As I said earlier, I really like the Mactronics SCSI port tester as a hardware-based test device. Now, I currently use three software packages for SCSI diagnostics:

1. Mac Ekg performs a component-level diagnostic on my SCSI controller circuitry on my logic board and does performance tests on my disk drive.
2. SCSI probe, by Robert Pollic, is an excellent SCSI utility. It's available through the bulletin boards and is excellent for displaying SCSI ID information and lets you access a device that you powered on before the Mac.
3. Disk Manager for Macintosh by Ontrack is an excellent overall SCSI hard disk drive diagnostic package. It's far superior to Apple's hard drive utilities and works with tons of third-party drives. It's also very easy to use and is inexpensive. I strongly recommend getting a copy of this utility.

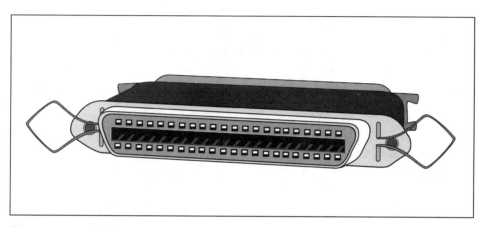

Figure 10-2. A SCSI cable terminator

Q. What is SCSI termination and why is it important? And why is it, at times, such a problem?

A. Yes, SCSI termination is a real problem for some people. Termination is defined as closing off the ends of an electrical circuit in order to absorb the signals at each end of the chain (cable). This reduces electronic echoing and resonance. It also creates sufficient differences between high and low signals for the various devices on the bus, which allows the bus to determine which devices are communicating. Proper termination is necessary for effective communication.

Termination is accomplished through the proper placement of terminating resistors. Simply put, these terminators tell the Mac where the SCSI bus begins and ends, and match the impedance of your cabling. The importance of termination increases as you daisy-chain more devices over longer distances. Improper termination can lead to failures, such as startup problems, intermittent problems, drives that don't spin up right away, drives that crash when copying several files, and other difficulties.

Rule #1 for termination: On all Macs except the IIfx, terminate the first device in the SCSI chain and the last device in the SCSI chain. Any other terminators must be removed. Think of them as book ends, one at the beginning, and one at the end. The first device is not necessarily SCSI ID number 0 or 1. Those are logical ID numbers. I'm talking about physical devices. Normally an internal hard drive is at the beginning, so it's physically the closest to the Mac. The last device is physically farthest away from the Mac on the SCSI chain (the last device on the daisy-chained

235

cable). It too gets a terminator. Any terminators in between must be removed. If you have only a hard drive installed, it should be (and usually is) terminated. For example, if you had a Mac with an internal hard drive, a scanner, a CD-ROM, and a laser printer, the terminators would be placed as shown below (devices are listed in order of decreasing proximity to the computer):

Mac w/internal drive*   scanner   CD-ROM   laser printer *
(terminator here)   (terminator here)

The internal hard drive and laser printer get terminated. Most people forget that the internal hard drive usually is terminated internally. That is, it has a terminating resistor pack already attached to it. This counts as the one at the beginning. Next, you terminate the laser printer, which is the one at the end. Then remove any remaining terminators. What many people do is terminate the scanner and the laser printer. Then they wonder why the internal hard drive and scanner work OK, while the CD-ROM and laser printer do not.

Rule #2 for termination: Never have less than one nor more than two terminators. Of course, this depends on how many devices you have.

Keep in mind that these rules are the textbook guidelines. I've had to use three and four terminators to get some devices working, but this is very abnormal. Always try the textbook approach first. If that doesn't work, you may have run into an exception to the rules. Try different combinations of things.

Q. Why is the SCSI termination different in the Macintosh IIfx? How is it accomplished?

A. Apple had to modify the SCSI termination scheme on the IIfx because of the increased data transfer rate. There are three items that you should be familiar with: the SCSI terminator II, the internal SCSI termination block, and the internal SCSI filter. Here's a brief explanation of each:

1. The SCSI terminator II (also called the glitch eater) is a black terminator pack that always must be installed when you have one or more external SCSI devices attached to the Macintosh IIfx. One and only one of these should be installed at the end of the SCSI chain. The internal hard drive

or SCSI termination block acts as the first terminator. Remove other terminators on the external devices. Under no circumstances should you use more than one of the glitch eaters on the SCSI chain. It could damage the IIfx SCSI circuitry.

2. The internal SCSI termination block must be installed in the 50-pin internal connector to provide internal SCSI termination in Mac IIfx systems without internal SCSI hard drives installed. Any IIfx shipped without an internal hard disk drive has this termination block installed. It must be removed when you install an internal hard disk drive.

3. The internal SCSI filter was provided with IIfx systems shipped prior to March 1990. This filter was designed to provide filtering of the SCSI signal lines. When a SCSI drive is attached to a IIfx with no SCSI drive installed, this filter must be removed from the IIfx logic board and attached to the hard drive.

Q. I get multiple icons appearing on my Desktop for the same hard disk drive. What could the problem be?

A. This problem really sounds like a SCSI ID problem. You should make sure that no two devices have the same ID number and that no device is using ID number 7, which is reserved for the Mac. Also check the cabling and termination.

Q. I recently installed a removeable hard disk drive, but I can't get the drive to mount. What things should I check first?

A. When troubleshooting SCSI problems, you should always start by checking the SCSI ID numbers, the cabling, and termination, and verify that the removable cartridge is formatted for use in the Macintosh.

Hard Disk Drives

The hard disk drive is one of the most important devices inside your Macintosh. This is where important application programs and data are stored. Hard drives get their name from their storage medium, which typically is a thin, hard metal platter that has a magnetic coating. This platter is housed inside the drive mechanism where the data is stored, accessed, and retrieved.

You can compare the operation of a hard disk drive to that of a record player.

A record player uses a needle to detect the impressions on the record surface. Disk drives use electromagnetic heads to read, write, and locate magnetic information on the disk platters. The heads actually are small magnets mounted on an armature assembly—the equivalent to a record player's needle and stylus.

Disk drives have one or more platters mounted on a spindle assembly. Record players can have one or more records on a turntable. The difference here is that the record player can only play one record at a time, where the hard disk drive platters rotate at the same time. However, in contrast to the record player, the hard drive heads—the needles—never touch the surface of the platters. Some users believe that the heads fly inside the hard drive. They do not have wings and a tail, nor do they fly. The heads actually float on a very thin cushion of air that is formed by the very fast rotation (3600+ RPM) of the platters. This very much like a Hover-Craft.

Furthermore, the read/write heads don't follow one continuous physical track as do the record needles. Instead, tracks on the disk media are actually concentric (circular), magnetic areas, where data is stored. Remember, heads never actually touch the platter. If they do, it's called a head crash and is very bad news! Information is transmitted from the Mac to the hard drive in the form of electrical pulses. The pulses pass through the control circuitry of the disk drive assembly to the read/write heads. The read/write heads then magnetically alter (magnetize and demagnetize) the appropriate track areas on the platter. These alterations are sometimes referred to as flux changes, which are simply binary on/off (1/0) bit patterns. Bit patterns are the foundation of digital computer information. After the media has been magnetized, these magnetic impressions stay put, even if the machine is off.

All hard drives basically do the same thing: store information. They all have the same basic parts, such as heads, platters, motors, and head actuators. Some hard drives cost more than others for the same reason that some cars are more expensive. You have economy, sport, and luxury models in hard drives, just as in cars.

The most important thing to keep in mind when purchasing a hard drive is to avoid going overboard. Only purchase what you can afford and what your system can fully utilize. For example, many people rush right out and buy the fastest drive that money can buy: 5-millisecond access time, linear voice coil, 1:1 interleave ratio, synchronous data transfer capability, 10MB per second transfer rate, SCSI 1 and 2 compatible, mag wheels, and air shocks all for their Mac Plus.

These people forgot that the Mac Plus isn't one of the faster Macs out there. In fact, you would be lucky if the Mac Plus could handle a 500 or 600K per second asynchronous data transfer mode at a 3:1 interleave ratio. In addition, the Mac Plus can't even take advantage of a SCSI 2-class drive. In other words, these people have wasted their money. This is a Quadra-class hard drive. An average Mac Plus machine can only take advantage of an average hard drive. You're fine with a nice 15- to 20-millisecond, 3:1 interleave, 40MB Conner or Quantum hard drive, which costs only about $200.

Q. What is sector interleaving, and how does it affect the performance of my hard disk drive. Should I always purchase hard drives with fast access times and a 1:1 interleaves?

A. Too many people get hung up on this high-speed access time and 1:1 interleave business. Just remember, a faster hard drive access time doesn't mean that your computer can digest the information any quicker. You are basically hurrying up to wait. If you get a drive that is preformatted with the wrong (not optimum) interleave factor, the performance of your hard disk drive could be reduced anywhere from 2 to 17 times what it effectively could be. Interleaving is determined during the low-level format process that hard drives go through. A hard drive interleave factor determines the order in which sectors (pie slices) of information (typically units of 512 bytes) are read. It's common for the disk tracks to be divided into 17 sectors of information. A 1:1 interleave, which is really no interleave, means that all of the sectors on one track are read consecutively, one after the other—1, 2, 3, 4, 5, up to 17—in one revolution. The computer gets hit with all of the information at once. This is fine if you have a Mac II or Quadra-class machine, which can handle a 1:1 ratio. The Mac Plus and Macintosh SE are machines that cannot digest all of that information at once. Because they process data slower, they can't read each sector in consecutive order. They need time to chew and swallow. Sector interleaving is really sector numbering. Rather than number the sectors 1 through 17 in consecutive order, which is a 1:1 interleave, the slower computers number the sectors around 3:1, that is, three revolutions to read one track of information. A 3:1 ratio would look something like 1, 7, 13, 2, 8, 14, 3, 9, 15, 4, 10, 16, 5, 11, 17, 6, 12. To read the sectors in order, the machine would have to go 1, wait, wait, 2 wait, wait, 3, and so on. By renumbering the sectors the machine has sufficient time to digest and process the information. Three revolutions to read the track isn't as good as the 1:1 single revolution, but it's better than setting the wrong ratio, which could cause the machine to wait as many as 17 revolutions to read all of the sectors on a single track. When in doubt about recommended interleave ratios, call Apple or your hard drive vendor first. You may have to low-level format your hard disk again to work with your machine.

Here are some examples of Mac interleave factors:

Mac Plus	3:1
Mac SE and Classic	2:1
Mac II and Quadras families	1:1

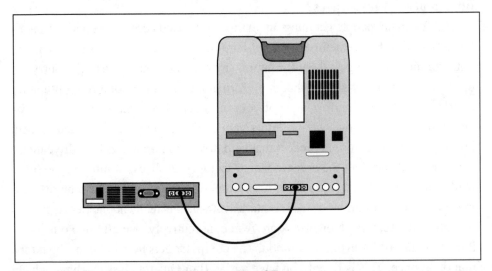

Figure 10-3. Hard drives connected to a Mac SE

Q. I recently took a hard drive out of my Macintosh SE and put it into a Mac IIci. Even though it's in a faster machine, it still seems to run very slow. I checked with the manufacturer, and they said that this drive is a high-performance that works in either machine without problems. They further went on to tell me that it should work better in the IIci, not worse. My machine now locks up on me, and when it does work, it's very slow. I give up. What should I do?

A. If you just took this hard drive out of the SE and put it into the IIci, you definitely have a problem. First, the IIci supports a 1:1 interleave ratio, while the SE works with a 2:1 ratio. If the drive had been originally formatted in the SE, the 2:1 ratio has been set. You were still working with the 2:1 when you took it over to the IIci, which can handle 1:1. You lost some performance there. Second, did you reinstall the operating system on the hard drive? If not, you should have. The IIci uses different operating system resources than does the SE. This could be causing some of your problems. I suggest you back up your valuable data and reformat the drive with either the Apple Hard Drive Set-up utility or some other utility like Disk Manager by Ontrack. Then reinstall your Macintosh system so it is set for a IIci. That should clear up the problem.

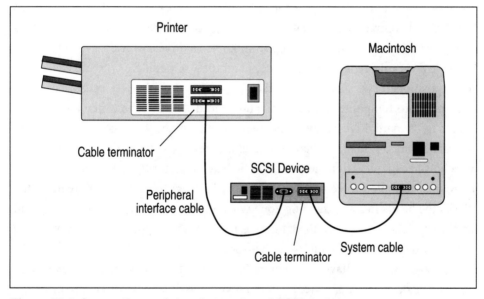

Figure 10-4. Connecting peripherals to external SCSI devices

Q. My hard drive has trouble booting. When I first turn it on in the morning, I get a blinking question mark icon. If I wait a little while and turn the machine off and then back on, the drive boots and works like a champ. The strange thing is, it'll do this all the time for a month or two, then it'll work fine for the rest of the year. I would hate to throw a working drive out, but this is kind of annoying. Why am I having this problem and what, if anything, can I do about it? Should I leave the machine on all of the time ?

A. This problem is a classic one. What you're experiencing is a temperature-related problem. I get these all of the time in Maryland, but only during the winter months when it's cold outside. My computer is in the basement, which isn't well heated. The problem is the platters inside the hard disk are usually made of metal (very few are glass). When you heat and cool metal, it expands and contracts. Even the slightest contraction (just a micron or two), could throw off a disk read. This is a very common occurrence with stepper motor hard drives, which are found in most of the low- to mid-range Macs. A stepper motor is a mediocre type of head actuator or positioner. I personally don't like stepper motor hard drives because they are very prone to temperature problems and head drift. However, they are also the "ketchup" of hard drives: they're inexpensive and get the job done. And that's why manufacturers use them in their computers. I prefer a voice coil/servo hard drive, which utilizes a precision electromagnetic head actuator to make it very fast and extremely reliable. Voice coil drives usually have an "auto-parking" feature that places the heads in a safe landing zone when there's a power loss to avoid a head crash. They also cost two to three times as much as the stepper motor drives, which many people and manufacturers can't afford.

It sounds like you have a stepper motor drive in a cold machine (approximately 45 degrees or less). There's really nothing you can do about this situation, except try a voice coil mechanism. Personally I would leave it the way it is. There's no need to leave it on all of the time. Just come in, turn the machine on, and let it warm up. First thing in the morning, you need to warm up too. Go get a cup of coffee. Turn the machine off and then back on again, and wait for spring. Like you said, it's annoying, but the machine will work like a champ.

Q. I recently purchased a new hard drive. I installed it, formatted it, and loaded the Macintosh operating system. The drive works fine when it's cold, but after an hour or so of continuous operation, it starts acting strange. I get all kinds of read errors. I have run every diagnostic package imaginable, from surface analysis to controller testing, and they all say the drive is good. What should I check?

A. First, let the machine warm up, and then test it, unless you have already done so. Run multiple-pass tests overnight if necessary. If the drive bombs out, you had a latent defect and must replace the drive. But if the drive proves to be good, chances are you low-level formatted the drive while it was cold. Low-level formatting lays down track and sector patterns on the disk drive and sets the interleave. If you did this while the drive was cold, you may be experiencing a thermal expansion problem, which is somewhat rare. Try reformatting the drive after it has warmed up (10 minutes), and then reinstall the operating system. If that doesn't work, send the drive back to your vendor (if it's still under warranty).

Q. What's file fragmentation? Do you recommend the use of defragmentation software? Will it help the performance of my hard disk drive ?

A. When you store data on the hard disk drive, the computer writes the information to the first available location that it can. It always tries to store the files in a contiguous manner as best it can. However, over time when the drive gets full and you copy and delete many files, the drive isn't as organized as it once was. Often there isn't sufficient room to store the file in one contiguous group of clusters, so the machine stores what it can in the first available area and then moves to the next available free space to finish the job. This spreading of files across multiple tracks is called file fragmentation. Fragmentation is a natural occurrence with hard disk drives. The Mac can handle minimal fragmentation without a problem. However, if your Mac hard drive gets a lot of use, then you may eventually develop fragmentation problems. Symptoms of these problems are (1) application programs and files gradually start taking longer to load and (2) the status light of the hard drive blinks on and off rather than staying on continuously. In addition, excessive fragmentation causes excessive wear and tear on the read/write head actuator.

I recommend periodic defragmentation (optimization) of the hard disk drive as part of regular your preventative maintenance routine. If you use the machine a lot, optimize the drive more frequently (every couple of weeks or so). Some people have special utilities that defragment their drives every time they turn their machines on. This is overkill. It also is unwise because the defragmentation process finds all the pieces of your files and moves other files around in order to form a contiguous hard drive. It moves and squeezes pieces wherever it can. After your drive is defragmented, you may not be able to recover deleted information that was on your drive prior to the defragmentation. It usually gets overwritten, and that's something to think about. What if you want to recover a file you threw out? You can't if that optimizer kicks in during startup. A few words to the wise:

1. Use optimizers manually, not automatically at startup
2. Back up your work before you start moving things around on your hard disk drive. I use Speed Disk from the Norton Utilities.

$Q.$ I'm going to purchase a hard disk drive for my Macintosh SE. Should I purchase an internal or external drive? What are the benefits and the trade-offs?

A. In general I prefer external hard disk drives for several reasons:

1. They can be moved between machines.
3. Little installation is involved.
3. External disk drives have their own power supply, which means the power supply inside your Mac doesn't have to work as hard. This isn't a big deal if you have a Mac II or Quadra. But if you have a Mac SE, SE/30, Classic, or Classic II, it might make a difference. These units have marginal power supplies to begin with, so I don't like to push them. In addition, if you have a Macintosh SE with two internal floppies, you'll have to give one up, unless you purchase a custom adapter.

External units, however, have two major drawbacks:

1. They're easy to steal
2. Since the external drives are self-contained (with cabinet and power supply), they usually cost more than internal drives

Q. **I recently had my Macintosh attempt to boot and then hang up. The first time I got a Happy Mac icon briefly, then it disappeared and I got the question mark icon. I turned the machine off and then back on. After I did this, I got the happy Mac and the machine froze. How should I try to fix this?**

A. Well, the happy Mac is a good sign. However, I think you may have damaged boot blocks on the hard disk drive or corrupted operating system files. The first thing you should try to do is run either Norton Utilities Emergency Disk or Mac Tools Rescue to remedy the situation. If that doesn't work, try to reinstall the Macintosh operating system. Finally, update the driver on the hard disk with the Macintosh utilities or Disk Manager for Macintosh. This clears up most problems.

Q. **My hard drive doesn't do anything. I don't get any lights, nor does it spin. It's dead. Is there any hope for it?**

A. First, I'd verify that your power wire is properly attached. Second, I'd verify that you have adequate power, meaning output from the power supply to the hard drive. Finally, check the bottom of your hard drive for a small fuse. It might have blown. The fuse is usually located on the bottom of the drive's circuit board near the corner where the power connector is. Fuses usually have the designation "F" near them (that is, F1). Check the fuse with a voltmeter or continuity tester. These fuses cost only a few pennies. Many hard drives get thrown out and the only problem is that little fuse.

CHAPTER 11

Networking

AppleTalk is a network system that supports networks ranging in size from local area networks (LANs) with two devices to internets capable of supporting thousands of devices. LocalTalk is a low-cost cabling system used in conjunction with AppleTalk networks but not as a substitute for AppleTalk. One way to look at it is to think of AppleTalk as the network protocol (providing the "rules of the road") and LocalTalk as the cabling method.

In real terms, LocalTalk is a low-speed RF (radio frequency) transmission method used to link and communicate with devices on AppleTalk networks. A typical LocalTalk network can attain transmission speeds of up to 230.4 kilobits per second with a maximum cable length of 300 meters. This is slow, although there are companies that sell LocalTalk accelerators.

Still, I prefer standard LocalTalk. It's inexpensive, simple to install, and easy to support. Although accelerators can double or triple the transmission speeds of LocalTalk, it's important to keep in mind that the serial (RS-232/422) port of the Macintosh can only go so fast. Many times people spend a substantial amount of money on acceleration boards and are disappointed by the bottleneck that occurs. If you need high speed, you should consider something other than LocalTalk, such as EtherTalk (Ethernet).

A LocalTalk cabling system consists of cables, cable extenders, and connectors. LocalTalk devices and cables are configured to work in a bus-type network topology. Bus networks are connected in a direct line from node to node. Standard LocalTalk cables utilize shielded twisted-pair construction. The typical color code used is blue and white. Pin 1 is typically blue, while pin 2 is typically white. These wires are connected to a mini-DIN-3-type connector. The third pin is the shield. The impedance (electrical opposition) of the LocalTalk cables is 78 ohms, which must be observed in all cable segments.

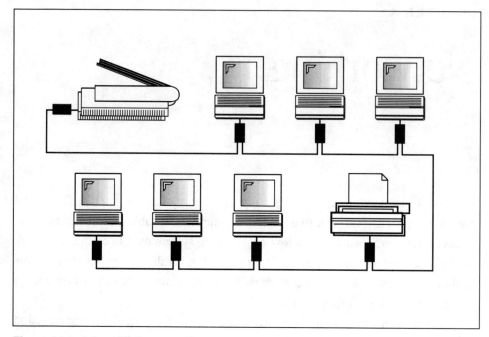

Figure 11-1. A LocalTalk network

Configuring LocalTalk Cables

You must follow specific rules in configuring LocalTalk cables. Obviously you must make sure that all of your connections are solid and complete. In addition, you must be sure that

1. All nodes are attached in a bus topology (line). They can't be in a circle.
2. LocalTalk connectors used at the end of the LocalTalk system have only one cable plugged into them. There should be no dangling wires hanging off of this end connector.
3. LocalTalk connectors, other than the end connectors, have two cables plugged into them.
4. If a device (node) on a LocalTalk network must be disconnected, it's acceptable to simply unplug the cable from the device and leave it plugged into

the LocalTalk connector box. Under no circumstances should the other network cables attached to the connector box be disturbed, unless you're replacing the LocalTalk connector box with a cable extender. The LocalTalk bus (cabling) must always form a line, without breaks.

Terminating resistors are located in the end LocalTalk connector boxes. The impedance of these resistors is 100 ohms. If you recall, the end connector boxes should have only one cable plugged into them. When one cable is attached to this box, a switch inside the box opens. When this switch is open, the terminating resistor inside is connected. For this reason, you must not plug more than one cable into the end connector boxes, as this would disconnect the terminating resistor. Terminating resistors are used to absorb electrical signals when they reach the end of the network. If these signals are not absorbed by the terminating resistors, they can reflect back to the other end of the network, causing network transmission problems.

Troubleshooting LocalTalk Cabling

The most common mistakes and problems that are encountered when configuring LocalTalk cabling are

1. Circular/loop network or improper termination
2. Bad connections or disconnected segments
3. Network cabling exceeds the 300-meter maximum
4. EMI/RF noise problems

The following sections offer some examples, symptoms, and solutions to each of these problems.

Circular/loop network or improper termination

A circular or loop network occurs when the LocalTalk cabling is not in a bus topology (straight line). This condition produces symptoms that interfere with proper network operation, such as

1. Noticeable decrease in data transfer times

2. Failures during and after data transfers

3. Nodes on the network are unable to see other nodes or certain shared devices

The specific problem in the circular/loop dilemma is a lack of termination. Since the cabling is in a loop, both terminating switches are open, which disables the terminating resistor, thereby creating an impedance and reflection problem. In other words, there is no end to the bus network nor active terminators to absorb the stray signals. These signals then rotate around the network and can cause collisions with other signals that affect and decrease network performance. Unfortunately, it's hard to predict exactly when and where the network problems will take place. These collisions can be felt anywhere and everywhere on the network.

Bad connections or disconnected segments

Bad connections and disconnected segments are the most frequent cause of network aggravation. For the network to function properly, the cabling (transmission line) must be continuous from beginning to end as well as terminated at both ends. Any break or loose connection can disrupt the smooth operation of the network (I can't stress this enough). There are several causes for bad connections and disconnected cable segments:

1. *Oversight during installation.*

   We're only human, we make mistakes. It's possible that a cable or connector was omitted or that the rules for LocalTalk cabling were not followed. You should backtrack your steps, inspect your work, and rule out the obvious. You may have a cable or cable extender that popped loose.

2. *End users stepping, pulling or tripping over the cables, connector boxes and cable extenders.*

   In a perfect world, all of the network cables would be out of the end user's way. However, this usually isn't the case. It's very common for people to break or otherwise damage cables by stepping on them or running them over with their chairs. Needless to say, these breaks knock out connections on your network. Whenever possible, try to keep the cables, extenders, and connector boxes out of heavily trafficked areas.

3. *Stretched cables.*

LocalTalk cables typically come from Apple in three flavors: 2-, 10-, and 25-meter segment lengths. When installing a node (workstation) to the network—it never seems to fail—the 2-meter cable always comes up a few inches short. Rather than use the 10-meter cable, you simply move things around and pull hard to stretch the cable just enough to make the connection. Pulling and stretching is not good for the cable. It can cause wire breaks and/or intermittent connections. You should either use a longer cable, such as the 10- or 25-meter, or make one up yourself. Be sure to leave some extra cable at each drop, just in case the user wants to move things around later on. Remember, it's easier to grow into than out of.

4. *Defective cables, connector boxes, and extenders.*

From time to time you will encounter defective cables, connector boxes, and extenders that need to be replaced. When these items go bad, they cause breaks in your network cabling that can leave certain nodes disconnected and/or cause a termination/impedance problem. Some things that I look for are

- Obvious physical damage to the cable, connector box, or extender
- Dirt and debris built up inside the cable connections
- Incorrect pin-out, bad solder joints or connections, or the wrong type of cable used when making homemade cables

Bad connections and disconnected segments can produce a variety of intermittent or constant data transmission errors. These errors are often produced by improper termination, as in the loop network. To recap, those errors were:

1. Noticeable decrease in data transfer times
2. Failures during and after data transfers
3. Nodes on the network are unable to see other nodes or certain shared devices

The reason that termination becomes a problem with disconnected segments is simple: When a break occurs in the transmission line of a bus network, two separate networks are formed that can't see each other. Additionally, these two new networks have a termination problem at one end, which will generate the errors I've talked about.

Network cabling exceeds the 300-meter maximum

The cabling for a standard LocalTalk network should not exceed 300 meters (about 1000 feet) in length. If the cabling exceeds 300 meters, the impedance of the line is affected and the strength of the signal deteriorates, producing network problems. When calculating total cable length, I add up the actual length of my cables and add 10% to that total. I then count the number of connector boxes I have on the network and assign them a value of 3 meters (10 feet) and add this number to the total. Many people overlook the fact that the connector boxes affect the impedance of the line and don't factor them into their total. I simply count them as 3 meters, just to be on the safe side.

Usually problems with exceeding the maximum cabling occur when someone extends the network without the network administrator knowing. It's a good idea to check the end connector boxes to make sure that nobody has tapped in. If you are at or near the maximum of your network cabling, you can extend this network to accommodate several more users by doing the following:

1. Set up a second network and use a bridge to connect this network to the first. Bridging is an excellent way of connecting two LocalTalk networks, but it does require some planning and can be rather costly. I recommend it for adding many users or another network, but not for a node or two.

2. Purchase a LocalTalk repeater, which boosts and strengthens the network signals and lets you to attach more nodes. Farallon sells this type of repeater for use with their PhoneNet LocalTalk system. The retail price of this repeater is $495, but the street price is around $300. I like using repeaters for quick and dirty network extensions. They work very well. However, I wouldn't go overboard and make massive LocalTalk networks using dozens and dozens of repeaters within the single network. This could get confusing from a network management perspective.

EMI/RF noise problems

One final problem that many people encounter in setting up their network is EMI (electromagnetic interference) and RF (radio frequency) noise. EMI/RF noise is generated by electromagnetic and radio frequency sources, respectively. This type of noise (not Jimi Hendrix) can cause electrical disturbances with the network signals, which usually result in intermittent network problems. EMI/RF noise can be found in many different locations, such as near large motors or fluorescent lighting fixtures. Although Apple's LocalTalk cables are shielded to help prevent this, it's still best not to run your cables too close to these areas. If you don't use Apple's LocalTalk cables, it's a good idea to check with the manufacturer of your cables regarding noise susceptibility.

Troubleshooting on Your Network

Q. **What LocalTalk diagnostic utilities are available to help me troubleshoot and assess the condition of my network? Where can I purchase them?**

A. Three good LocalTalk utilities come to mind immediately: InterPoll, NetMinder LocalTalk, and LocalPeek.

InterPoll is an excellent software package by Apple Computer that assists in network monitoring and problem diagnosis. InterPoll is especially good for testing your network when it is first set up in order to identify when two or more devices (such as a Macintosh and a laser printer) are not communicating properly. InterPoll is also useful in determining whether or not devices (such as file-servers and printers) are attached to the network. What I like most about InterPoll is its ability to examine individual workstations on the network for potential problems.

NetMinder LocalTalk is a LocalTalk network analyzer written by Neon Software that retails for $395. NetMinder LocalTalk allows the network administrator to monitor and capture data packets that are traveling across the LocalTalk network (in other words, network traffic). This product is excellent for network traffic monitoring and for performing high-speed data capture and analysis. These features make NetMinder LocalTalk ideal for troubleshooting performance degradation situations. This software analyzer works on your existing Mac CPU and so is much less expensive than a pricey hardware-based analyzer.

LocalPeek is an interesting LocalTalk analyzer written by the A.G. Group. It retails for $495. LocalPeek performs many network diagnostic functions. First, it provides the network administrator with information that is necessary to plan, manage, monitor and troubleshoot the LocalTalk network. LocalPeek uses extensive audiovisual (graphs, sound, and color) capabilities to present the information to the network administrator. Second, LocalPeek can perform very sophisticated network, hardware and software diagnostics. Finally, this package also reports on the network load. I find LocalPeek a very user-friendly LocalTalk analysis package.

All three of these packages usually can be purchased from the larger authorized Apple dealers. NetMinder and LocalPeek can also be purchased through the mail order channel or directly from the manufacturer. When in doubt you can always call APDA. If they don't have it, they can usually help you find it. If you can afford it, having all three of the packages is useful. However, if you can afford only one package, start with LocalPeek; it's easy to get and is very user friendly. Next, I recommend purchasing InterPoll and then NetMinder. Don't get me wrong, NetMinder is an excellent package. However, due to the complexity of packet capture and traffic analysis, it may be overkill for the administrator with a typical network. It's really meant for the power network administrator.

> **Note:** Chooser, which comes standard with all Macs at no extra charge, is one of the best diagnostic tools out there for testing shared devices. However, the devices must be turned on, with AppleTalk active and physically attached to the LocalTalk system, before Chooser can see them. Remember, Chooser can see only shared devices; it cannot recognize these devices unless the software for that device is installed at the workstation that you're using. If no shared devices are installed in the network segment you're testing, you should use InteroPoll or LocalPeek instead of Chooser.

Q. My Apple dealer has a network diagnostic package called **NodeCheck. Is this something worth having?**

A. Not really. NodeCheck is a software package that lets you look for nodes and node addresses. It's a package that has been made obsolete by InterPoll. InterPoll is an enhanced replacement for NodeCheck and should be used instead.

Q. What is the best way to approach problems on LocalTalk networks? What questions should be asked? Where should I begin?

A. The best strategy for troubleshooting any network problems always begins with asking the right questions, such as

• **Have there been any recent moves, adds or changes to the network?**

If the network had been working well previously, and something has recently been changed on the network, chances are the change has something to do with the problem.

• **How many nodes on the network are affected by this problem?**

This is very important. If only one workstation is experiencing these problems, chances are you either have a bad connection or a software problem (such as an old version of Finder or System or a bad device driver) at the workstation itself. However, if more than one workstation is having a problem communicating with a shared device, such as a printer, then the problem is most likely in the cabling or at the shared device itself.

• **Are the problems continuous or intermittent ?**

Continuous problems (such as being unable to see Printer A) are often cause by shared device and/or workstation malfunctions or by a cable break at the device or workstation itself. The problem usually is not in the primary network cabling. If you recall, a break in the primary network cabling (bus) results in two unterminated networks, which would generate intermittent problems. If you're experiencing intermittent problems check for

1. Cable breaks in the primary network cabling
2. Improper termination at the end connector box
3. A bad connector box
4. A loop/circular network

• **Has the 300-meter (1000-foot) cabling limit been exceeded?**

As previously discussed, exceeding the 300-meter limit can cause problems.

Please keep in mind that 300 meters is a recommendation, not an edict. You usually have some sort of fudge factor on your side, but I wouldn't push it too far. Problems associated with exceeding the limit can be either immediate or delayed, depending on the network size and traffic. However, there is one very common symptom of this situation: The problem devices are at opposite ends of the network. The solution is to try to move the devices closer together, reducing the cable length or installing a LocalTalk repeater to boost the signal. If the network had been working fine previously, and if the problem devices are close together in a continuous section, then chances are the cable length is OK. Look for cable breaks, bad connector boxes, or loose connections near the affected devices.

- **Is the total number of nodes on this LocalTalk network equal to or less than 32?**

Many people forget that a network node can be either a workstation or a shared device. The total number of nodes (nodes=shared devices + workstations) on a single LocalTalk network must not exceed 32. If you exceed this total, you'll have problems.

Q. What's the best approach in troubleshooting those hard to find problems on the LocalTalk network?

A. There are two basic approaches to troubleshooting difficult LocalTalk problems. The first approach is for networks of less than 10 nodes, the second for networks of more than 10 nodes. Both approaches assume that you have ruled out the obvious and have ensured that the rules of LocalTalk have been followed up to this point (for example, there are no loops or breaks).

The first approach is for LocalTalk networks of less than 10 nodes. First, disconnect, inspect, and reconnect all cable and connector box connections one at a time. This helps eliminate bad or loose connections as the culprit. Be vigilant for breaks, loose connections, bent connectors and stretched cables. Additionally, you want to verify that two cables are plugged into each connector boxes that is not on the end of the bus.

Now try bypassing suspect nodes, cables, and connector boxes. Commonly referred to as the "Easter egg" approach, this is effective. To bypass a suspect node, simply disconnect the cable from the node to see if the problem goes away. Do not remove any of the cables from the connector box. If the problem goes away, you have your culprit. If not, bypass this node's connector box and cable by redoing them and installing a cable extender in its place. If the problem goes away, then either the connector box or the cable was the problem. You can go back and test these individually. If neither the node, node cable, nor connector box was the problem, chances are you have a problem on a primary cable segment. Bypassing these can be tricky, especially with the longer cable segments. These segments often run under desks or through the walls over the ceiling. Rather than go through the aggravation of replacing one of these cables before you know for a fact that it is bad, test it first by simply disconnecting it from the connector box and installing a known good cable in its place. You may have to temporarily run a known good cable down the hall and up the stairs to bypass a cable in the wall or ceiling. (Note: Be conscious of the 300-meter total cable limit.) However, I do not recommend replacing the original cable until you know for sure that it is bad. This method can help you determine whether or not it's the cable segment.

Finally, use InterPoll and/or LocalPeek network diagnostic software to look at your network's vital signs. You may just have too much traffic on this network.

The second approach to troubleshooting difficult LocalTalk problems is for LocalTalk networks of more than 10 nodes. Again, make sure that all rules of LocalTalk have been followed up to this point. Count the number of nodes on the network. Remember, nodes are workstations and shared devices, and their total cannot exceed 32.

Locate the approximate center of the network cabling and remove the centermost network cable segment from the connector boxes. You have now created two separate network halves. You should then run InterPoll or LocalPeek on either of the halves to locate the problem. This method is called the split search method. The idea here is that by splitting the large network into separate networks, it's easier to isolate which network or side has the problem. Once you have determined which side the problem is on, you can concentrate on that side, which is much easier than going through the entire network. You can even take the suspect side and split it again to narrow it down further.

Once you have the problem narrowed down to a smaller area of less than 10 nodes (preferably 4 or 5), you can follow the steps outlined in the first approach for smaller networks, which you have now effectively created.

Q. I've been told that I should set up an AppleTalk network. Is that the same as a LocalTalk network? What is an AppleTalk network? What should I purchase?

A. An AppleTalk network consists of two things: The AppleTalk protocol architecture and the network components themselves. The protocol architecture dictates how the various hardware, software, and connectivity components of the network will function together to provide the network services to the users. Protocols, in other words, are the "rules of the road."

AppleTalk is a network protocol used in an AppleTalk network system. Since 1984, all Macs have built-in AppleTalk support. The components of an AppleTalk network system are the computers, wires, connectors, shared devices, and software that comprise the network itself. AppleTalk simply dictates how these items will work together.

In its simplest form an AppleTalk network consists of a Mac, a laser printer, and LocalTalk cables. This type of system meets the most fundamental definition of a network, which is "two or more devices that are connected to and communicate with each other." LocalTalk is just a cabling method or network type. The rules of the road are still AppleTalk, which simply defines the process of sending and receiving information from one device to another. The AppleTalk protocols can operate on many different network types, such as LocalTalk, IBMs Token Ring, and Ethernet.

LocalTalk is the inexpensive network type most familiar to Macintosh users. It's ideally suited for individual and smaller work groups. All Macintosh computers have a serial LocalTalk port built into them, as do most Apple peripheral devices, such as laser printers.

Token Ring is another network type commonly used for networking IBM PCs and for communicating with mainframe computers. Macs can connect to and communicate within a token ring network with the appropriate hardware and cable. The performance of a token ring network is about four to five times that of LocalTalk.

Ethernet is the de facto standard for high-performance networking in the computer world. Ethernet is designed to accommodate many users, cover long distances, and work with many different computer platforms at a considerable speed. Macintosh computers can attach to Ethernet networks, provided that they have the appropriate Ethernet interface, EtherTalk software, and the correct cabling. The new

Macintosh Quadras are coming standard with a built-in Ethernet designed around the Sonic chip set, which is excellent. The performance of an Ethernet network is approximately six to eight times that of LocalTalk.

Which network type is right for you? It all depends on factors such as

- How many users and devices do you need to connect?
- How much money do you have to spend?
- Do you already have an existing network? If so, what kind is it? Or will this network be replacing or communicating with that network?
- What type of computers and peripherals do you currently have? How many shared devices will you have?
- Do you need to share files and/or data with other users?
- Does this network need to talk with other computer platforms, such as IBM PCs, mini-computers, or mainframes?
- What's the projected usage and growth estimate for this network?

The list goes on and on. Network administrators make their living by answering these questions and many more. If you're new to networks, do your homework or find a good network consultant who will work with you.

Q. **I have my Macs networked using the Farallon PhoneNet LocalTalk network system. I've been having a lot of problems with performance degradation and intermittent problems with network services such as printing. Many of my users complain that shared devices are available in the Chooser only sporadically, not all of the time as they should be. What could be going on here? Should I replace my PhoneNet with Apple's LocalTalk cabling?**

A. Farallon PhoneNet is just another way of doing LocalTalk. Therefore, all the rules of LocalTalk still apply. The problem you describe is commonly referred to as ghosting. Ghosting is defined as the appearance and disappearance of shared devices or network services. Ghosting in any network environment such as LocalTalk or Ethernet can be caused by

1. Exceeding the cabling limitations. Remember, each network type has its own cable limitations. The standard LocalTalk limitation is 300 meters

259

(1000 feet) when using Apple's shielded twisted pair wire. Farallon PhoneNet can vary depending on whether you have the network configured as a bus, a passive star, or an active star. The limitations for those topologies would be from 2000 feet on up to 4000 feet (the sum of all branches). Unshielded twisted pair Ethernet has a limitation of 330 feet from the hub to the device, thin Ethernet (thin coaxial cable) has a standard limitation of 3300 feet.

2. Too many devices. Standard LocalTalk has a limit of 32 nodes total using shielded twisted pair. Using Farallon PhoneNet LocalTalk with unshielded twisted pair, you can use 20 to 40 nodes in the bus topology and up to 254 using an active start topology. Using thin Ethernet you have a limitation of 40 nodes per segment and 1024 nodes for the entire network.

3. Improper termination. All bus type networks must be terminated. Standard LocalTalk bus networks self-terminate at the end connector boxes when properly installed. Farallon PhoneNet systems do not self-terminate. You must terminate them manually by physically adding the terminator. Apple thin ethernet cables and transceivers are self-terminating where some of the generic Ehernet products are not. These are things you need to know before you purchase and install them.

4. Bad cable connection. Check your cables, connectors, and extenders.

Performance degradation typically is caused by

1. Too many devices.
2. Not enough shared resources to accommodate all of the users on the network.
3. Excessive traffic. If everybody is working on a large network, things tend to slow down. If you're working with LocalTalk and it's too slow for your company, you may need to upgrade to an Ethernet or token ring network. If you already have an Ethernet network and it's too slow, you may have to redesign it altogether. You should use a network traffic monitoring tool such as LocalPeek, EtherPeek, or Traffic Watch, depending on the network type you have.
4. Software conflicts. You could have a corrupt or old version of System or Finder installed on the workstation. Viruses can be another cause of soft-

ware corruption and conflicts. Additionally, you could be experiencing a device driver compatibility problem. Many network service devices require that the appropriate device driver program be installed on each workstation that uses the device. In fact, I recommend that the device driver be the same version on each workstation. When shared devices are slow to respond (such as a LaserWriter printer), the culprit is often an incompatibility between device drivers.

5. Excessive network services. For example, if you're running printer, E-mail, and modem network services on a decent-sized network, you should put these services on their own file server rather than have them bog down a single file server. Therefore, you would need to set up a print server, mail server, and a modem server, in addition to the file server.

$Q.$ What are some of the most common problems on Mac-based Ethernet networks? Describe a few situations, symptoms, and solutions.

A. Most of your basic failures are related to one of two things. The first is user error, which is self-explanatory: The user did something wrong. The second is a problem with the start-up disk of the Macintosh. Many times these problems occur because the machine was started with the wrong version of the system software. On other occasions the EtherTalk software, which is necessary to allow the Mac to communicate, is installed improperly or is missing from the start-up disk altogether. When in doubt, I always verify which version of the operating system I am running and reinstall the EtherTalk software. I recommend to all of my clients that they upgrade their EtherTalk software to Phase 2. In any case, the EtherTalk versions must always match to ensure proper communication. If you're still having a problem, you may need to reinstall the system, check your cables and connections, or possibly reseat your Ethernet communications board.

Problem:

The EtherTalk icon is missing at start-up.

Solutions:

1. Your Ethernet card may not be properly seated. Reseat the card.
2. EtherTalk software isn't properly installed on the start-up disk. Reinstall EtherTalk properly.

3. The system software on your Mac may be damaged. Check for viruses, then reinstall the system software.

4. Your Ethernet card may not be working properly. Try a known good card.

Problem:

More than one EtherTalk icon appears in the network extension section of your control panel.

Solution:

- 99.9% of the time this error occur because older versions of EtherTalk are on your start-up disk. Remove the older versions of EtherTalk from your start-up disk.

Problem:

The EtherTalk icon is missing from the network extensions section of your control panel.

Solutions:

1. Your Ethernet card may not be properly seated. Reseat the card.

2. EtherTalk software is not properly installed on the start-up disk. Reinstall EtherTalk properly.

3. Your Ethernet card may not be working properly. Try a known good card.

Problem: Network services, such as print servers, modem servers, or mail servers, are missing.

Solutions:

1. Check your cables, connections and termination.

2. Check your network service zones.

3. It's possible that the version of EtherTalk installed on your system doesn't match the version installed on the network. They must match to work properly. As of the printing of this book, I recommend that EtherTalk on both the system and network be upgraded to at least Phase 2.

Q. Is there an easy way to tell whether or not a problem is related to the network or to something else? Do networking problems have specific symptoms?

A. Yes, networking problems do have specific symptoms. Whether or not a networking problem is simple or complex, the end result is still the same: One or more devices will have difficulty or will not be able to transfer data to other devices on the network. These problems typically are found in the cabling, shared device, workstation, or some combination of the three. For example, User A comes into work on Monday, turns on the Mac, and plays a quick game of Tetris. But the machine locks up before User A attempts to log into the network. Since no network transfers were taking place at that time, the problem usually is found in that workstation (its memory, power, or bad software) and not the network.

Q. Is there any sort of checklist out there for troubleshooting common Ethernet and EtherTalk problems.

A. I can't think of any off the top of my head, but we can make our own.

1. Do you have EtherTalk selected in the control panel?
2. Are all of your cables and connections good?
3. Is your Ethernet transceiver attached to the correct port?
4. Are the devices you want to communicate with powered up, ready, and attached to the same network?
5. Is your network properly terminated? If you're using self-terminating equipment, this is not really an issue. However, unterminated cables must be terminated using a 50-ohm resistor. Many people erroneously use a 75-ohm resistor, which is not the correct impedance.
6. Is your Ethernet card working? Try to reseat your card first, and if that doesn't work, try a known good card.
7. Is it possible that your system software, device drive revisions, or application programs are the culprit? Have you added a new application package lately? Have you been having trouble with viruses on the network?
8. Could the problem be in the network design itself? It's possible that you're pushing too much traffic through a particular segment. It is also possible that there are too many network services being run off of one machine.

Re-evaluate your network configuration. You may need to change the topology or move certain network services (such as printing and E-mail) to their own servers.

Q. **My company has many different models of Macintosh computers. We are going to be setting up a small departmental network. Should we use a Macintosh SE or SE/30 as the AppleTalk, or should we dedicate a Macintosh IIci to the cause?**

A. Most small networks can get along fine with an SE or SE/30, depending on the application. I am partial to the SE/30 because it runs System 7 and virtual memory well. However, if this network is being used for heavy database applications, you should consider using your IIci instead. Database applications can really bring down a servers performance.

Q. **What is your opinion on print spoolers and print servers. What is the best way to utilize them?**

A. Print spoolers and print servers are devices used to store information and communicate with printers. Normally in a network environment the shared server directs printer traffic. If a big job or graphic is printing, network performance suffers or comes to a standstill. For this reason many people set up print servers, which are servers dedicated to network printing services. They allow the burden of printer traffic to be taken off the file server. The best way to implement the print server is to put it on its own network, out of the way of the other network traffic. This is easily accomplished through the use of a simple routing package such as Apple's Internet Router or Liason. The router packages retail for less than $400, which is money well spent. It's also a good idea to load up your printers with as much memory as they can take (or as much as you can afford).

Q. **In your opinion, what is the best way to soup up a file server?**

A. The best way to soup up a file server is to select the right one to begin with. I mean seriously, you can't expect to upgrade a Mac Plus to a Macintosh IIcx or IIci horsepower. Select the right server for the job. If you have selected the right server and you want to maximize its performance, there are two basic things you should look at:

1. *Hard drives.*

The most important element here is selecting a good-quality, high-speed hard drive. Lately I have been partial to Mass Microsystems Diamond Drives. These drives are manufactured by Maxtor and come in capacities from 120 to 510MB (at this time). These drives support data buffering and caching and have excellent access times (10 to 15 milliseconds). I also like the high-speed MacinStor drives from Storage Dimensions. I would not recommend any drive using the older Quantum or Sony mechanisms, as they have some bad problems. In any case most of the work done on the file server is at the hard drive (disk accesses and so on). This makes hard drive selection critical. Remember the old saying, "A chain is only as strong as its weakest link"? Well, this applies to networks.

2. *CPU power and expandability.*

When evaluating Macs for suitability as AppleTalk, I always start by looking at their memory and CPU capabilities. First, I usually won't select a Mac with a CPU less than a Motorola 68030 for a medium to large network. The older Macs are OK for small, low-traffic networks, but I want to be able to grow into my network over the next two or three years, not grow out of it immediately. The 68030 and 68040 processors give me the power I need to grow. If you are going to use the Mac either for E-mail or as a print server, consider purchasing a Mac with 4 to 8MB of memory. If you are simply going to use the Mac as a basic file server, you need not go above 8MB, as Mac servers generally don't benefit much beyond this point.

Expandability is very important in selecting a Mac as a file server. The file server is often loaded with disk drives as well as network and communication cards. I always look for a machine with more than one slot, preferably three to six. This way I have the room I need to grow if I have to. It's easier to grow into something than out of it. I really like the Mac II (despite the lack of the 030 chip), IIx, IIfx, IIcx, IIci, and Quadra family as file servers, especially the monstrous Quadra 900/950 machines.

CHAPTER 12

File Transfers

Transferring files from your Macintosh computer to a DOS machine or other computer platform involves the translation and conversion of your data from one file format to another. On the surface it looks easy enough until you encounter your first set of problems. File transfers, for some reason, can be unbelievably time-consuming and frustrating.

A number of software companies offer packages that let you transfer files from Mac to DOS and back in a variety of formats. Choosing the right package for your needs is, in part, what this chapter is about. But before you go off and buy one of these file transfer programs, it's important first to develop a systematic plan for making the conversion. In other words, you need a good game plan. The plan can be written down or kept in your head, but it must be well thought out in advance. I find it best to jot things down. You need to ask yourself the following questions:

1. What computer platforms and operating environments will you be exchanging data with—DOS, UNIX, Windows, Sun, NeXT, minis, mainframes, or others?
2. Specifically, which application programs are currently being used or will be used on these platforms? Are any of these packages multiplatform capable, that is, file-compatible on both ends? (Examples of these include Microsoft Word for Mac and Microsoft Word for IBM.)
3. Are your computers stand-alone or networked? And what hardware and software are already installed on these computers? You also need to determine what budget you're working with and how much you want to spend.

4. How critical is the information being transferred? Will you lose your job or just pull out your hair if the transfer and conversion are less than 100% perfect?

How are you going to move data from one platform to another? Getting there, of course, is half the fun and half the battle. You really need to know where you're going and what you plan to do (or not to do) when you arrive. There are two routes you can take to move data from one computer to another. The first route is simply disk drive to disk drive. An example of this would be taking a 3.5-inch DOS floppy and reading it on the Mac, and vice versa. The second route is by means of a cable, such as a serial hook-up, modem link, or network transfers. Your plan must include how you're going to get there. With the right plan and software, and some common sense, the file transfer process is a breeze. Without it you'll suffer permanent hair loss.

Let's take a look at one common file transfer situation. You want to exchange data between your IBM 386 clone in the office and the new Macintosh PowerBooks that your staff use in the field. Your data is stored on 5.25-inch disks. The Power-Books have the 3.5-inch SuperDrives but no 5.25-inch drive support. What's the best way to accomplish the transfer?

The Macintosh PowerBooks can be equipped with an external disk drive that can work with the 5.25-inch disks. The drive is called the DaynaFile II by Dayna Communications. It retails for around $600, which is expensive, but it does work. A better alternative would be to equip your IBM clone computer with a 1.44 MB floppy disk drive that uses the same size media that your Macintosh PowerBooks and all new Macintosh models use. Likewise, many of the newer PCs are currently being shipped with 3.5-inch floppy drives.

Since your Macintosh computers already have the 1.44MB SuperDrive, you only need to use the proper software (such as the Apple File Exchange (AFE) utility program, which now comes with your Mac system software) to read either of the IBM 3.5-inch disk formats (720K and 1.44MB).

No software is really the best for all file transfer and conversion situations. The AFE software utility, however, does a very good job of allowing any Macintosh equipped with a SuperDrive floppy disk drive to recognize DOS disks and copy (exchange) files back and forth between the two platforms.

The two criticisms that I have of AFE are minor, but I do feel that they should be mentioned: First, the program and documentation are not overly user friendly and are a bit cumbersome to deal with. Second, AFE does not perform automatic DOS disk recognition. You have to load the program first. This can be a major inconvenience. They really should have made it automatic. However, AFE comes with your Macintosh operating system software, which means that it is one less thing to purchase.

The three best packages that automate the DOS disk recognition process are AccessPC from Insignia Solutions, DOS Mounter from Dayna, and Macintosh PC Exchange from Apple Computer. These packages load automatically during startup and recognize a 3.5-inch DOS disk when it's inserted into the Apple SuperDrive. All three packages can be purchased for less than $100. It's difficult to choose which one of these programs is best. It never fails: each of the packages has some neat feature that the other does not.

For instance, AccessPC recognizes 3.5-inch DOS disks on a Mac like the others, but it also lets you work with other manufacturers' external 5.25-inch drives attached to the Mac. This gives you the flexibility of working with either format. In addition, AccessPC lets your Mac work with DOS-formatted removable media, such as the Bernoulli and Syquest cartridges. It also works with either System 6.0.x or 7.0.x of the Mac operating system. Macintosh PC Exchange works only under System 7, but it automatically recognizes DOS disks like the other packages, only without any of the cool utilities AccessPC has. It also lets you format DOS disks on your Mac and exchange documents between DOS or Windows-based computers that use DOS formatted disks. Basically it's a cut-and-dry application. Somehow I get the feeling that Apple left this program out of the System 7 software. It really should come included with System 7, because it does a nice job.

Do you need to use products like AFE, DOS Mounter, AccessPC, and Macintosh PC Exchange to move files between Macs and IBM PCs that are networked? That's a good question. I use those utilities only for disk-based file transfers. These programs aren't necessary when you're dealing with a network environment. Most networking operating systems offer similar disk mounting/recognition features that let you see network server files directly on your desktop.

Two utility programs will let DOS-based machines read and write to Macintosh formatted disks. These programs are Mac to DOS from P.L.I. and Mac In DOS from Pacific Micro. You can even format a diskette on your IBM for use in a Macintosh with these programs. Both programs work with the Macintosh 1.44MB high-density format but not the 800K format.

Files created on the DOS and Mac platforms are significantly different. Their respective operating systems each work with data differently. There are four major (and other minor) differences between the two platform files. A good file exchange program will have an appropriate method for dealing with these incompatibilities. The four major differences are

1. The Macintosh file names can be up to 32 characters in length. The file names used in the DOS environments are limited to a maximum of 8 characters, plus an optional 3-character file extension separated from the file name by a period.
2. Macintosh file names can contain special characters, such as ®, ©, and spaces, which are invalid characters under DOS.
3. Macintosh files have icons, creator information, and special information about the file. DOS applications have a three-letter extension that can be used to identify their creator and other information about the file.
4. Many Macintosh application programs and files are stored in two pieces called the data and resource forks. DOS files consist of only one part. A good file transfer utility normally allows you to store the two Macintosh forks that comprise the single Macintosh file as two separate DOS files. Then, when you move this file back to the Mac side, the two pieces once again combine to form the single Mac file.

File Transfer Troubleshooting

Q. I don't have a 1.44MB SuperDrive in my Macintosh SE. Is there any way to read DOS disks in my 800K drive? My Apple dealer wants $349 plus labor and my old parts back for a new SuperDrive. Can I keep my 800K drive and read the DOS disks?

A. You're in luck. There is a way for the 800K Macintosh drives to read and write to the IBM 3.5-inch 720K disks only. Kennect has a product called the Rapport floppy drive interface and software that allows you to do this.

Incidentally, with the Rapport product you also can attach an external 3.5-inch Kennect Drive 2.4 (SuperDrive equivalent) or an external 5.25-inch drive (Kennect Drive 1200 or 360) to its floppy interface on Macintosh units that cant normally be upgraded to SuperDrive (such as the Mac Plus) through the Apple sanctioned channel. It also works on Macs that don't have the Apple SuperDrive but could be upgraded through the Apple channel, such as the older revisions of the Mac II and SE. The Kennect solution is a bit expensive (around $400 to $500 for everything), but for users who have no other choice, it works. Dayna also has similar drives (Dayna File II 1.44) that attach to the Mac SCSI port, but they are a bit expensive.

Q. **What are multiplatform applications, and how do they figure into the file transfer equation? Which multiplatform packages are the easiest to use for exchanging files between the DOS and Mac platforms? What kind of problems can I expect? What alternatives do I have?**

A. Multiplatform applications are application programs that have file-compatible counterparts on both the DOS and Mac sides. In essence the only thing you should have to do is move the data from one program to the other using the disk route with AccessPC, Macintosh PC Exchange, and AFE utilities, or by network or modem.

The easiest kinds of files to move from the DOS to the Mac platform are created by the following packages: Excel, WordPerfect, Microsoft Word, Aldus PageMaker, Ventura Publisher, and Fox Base+. I've never had a problem going from the DOS versions of these programs to the Mac versions. Going from the Mac versions back to the DOS versions is not as easy as going from DOS to Mac. Getting it to go both ways without some weirdness is difficult, but not impossible. I occasionally get bizarre-looking characters in my files or lose something in the conversion. But when I try the conversion again, it works. Twilight Zone? You bet!

One alternative to using multiplatform programs is the use of multilingual programs. Multilingual programs are application programs that let you open a file in one format and save it in another. This comes in handy when you're working with graphic file formats such as EPS, PICT, and TIFF. These file formats are standards that graphics programs on both platforms use. Application programs such as Adobe Photoshop let you open all kinds of graphic file formats and save them as a TIFF, EPS, and so on.

Unfortunately this route can cause problems. Some DOS graphics programs compress TIFF files when they save them, while other DOS and Macs usually do not. The end result is that another graphics package may have trouble interpreting where this file came from and what it really is.

Another problem is that EPS files created by one graphics program may not be fully compatible or understood by other graphic programs. This happens all the time when exporting between an older revision of one package and a newer revision of the other. It always happens to me with Aldus Freehand. Somebody needs to come out with an up-to-date compatibility database.

Q. **I have all kinds of application programs on my DOS-based machines, such as spreadsheet, word processing, and graphics packages, but we don't have a corresponding program on the Mac to exchange with them? Could I use the Apple File Exchange utility to perform file transfers, or is there something better?**

A. If your DOS-based programs don't have a corresponding Mac partner, you'll need to use a special type of program called a file translator. Technically speaking, the Apple File Exchange utility is a translator, but it only comes standard with one translation option: Mac Write to DCA-RTF (oh boy!). However, there are ways to beef up the Apple File Exchange utility with all of the translators you may ever need. Data Viz has one of the most versatile translation packages around called Mac Link Plus. It allows you to do file translation between IBM, Mac, NeXT, and Sun platforms, which is incredible! Mac Link Plus can translate dBASE, EPS, Excel, binary, TIFF, PICT, PageMaker, text, and many other formats with ease.

If you work with a variety of word processing programs that the Data Viz product doesn't support, consider purchasing another product called Word-for-Word from Mastersoft, Inc. Word-for-Word has a very nice conversion interface and is loaded with every word processing translator you can think of.

My personal favorite is a relatively new package called Software Bridge from Argosy Software. This package has all kinds of interesting translators and an excellent file recognition capability that makes the translation process go very quickly.

The translation packages that I have mentioned all retail for less than $175.

$Q_\bullet$ My company uses both Macs and IBM computers as well as a DEC VAX mini and IBM mainframes. This is a very graphics-intensive environment. Most of our files are stored in the CGM format, but our Macs store graphic images using PICT formats. Is there any software package out there that will let us painlessly translate from our IBM and other CGM files to the PICT format used on our Macs? Why is CGM such a problem to work with?

A. CGM, which stands for Computer Graphics Metafile, is an ANSI/ISO standard format for interchanging and storing pictures. It's not widely used in the Macintosh world, although many other hardware platforms (such as IBM PCs, minis, and mainframes) and software platforms (such as Lotus FreeLance, Harvard Graphics, and SAS) do support it. Working with CGMs in the PC, mini, and mainframe world is easy. There is an abundance of software to support it. Unfortunately, it's not popular in the Mac community, which uses PICT and PICT2, among other formats. The best package for this job would be MetaPICT by GSC Associates. The program is extremely powerful and does an excellent job of translating between CGM and PICT or PICT2. This package has gained wide acceptance, especially in the government and scientific graphics communities. An additional excellent feature of MetaPICT and other GSC Associates products is their ability to work with the different subsets of CGM that different vendors sometimes use. This package sells for around $180.

$Q_\bullet$ Are there any good file conversion utilities that will let me take PICT graphic files generated on my Macintosh and export them to other platforms using CGM formats?

A. The problem you describe is exactly the reverse of going from CGM to PICT. This is a frequent translation path for users trying to move data from the Mac to a program on an IBM or other platform such as Harvard Graphics, FreeLance, or Ventura Publisher, and to create files that can be imaged by Genigraphics and Autographics service bureaus. GSC Associates has a very interesting package called GraphPorter that can accomplish this. It's interesting to note that this program is actually a printer driver. Instead of immediately printing your document, Graph-Porter saves a description of the file to disk in a CGM exchange format, which many other platforms can read. In other words, this package is really a CGM file generator. I believe it is the only commercial package of its kind for the Macintosh. Another nice feature is that you can also translate and transfer these files from a Mac to other platforms via modem, using the Kermit file transfer protocol, without leaving your application. The cost of this program is $169.

Q. **I do a great deal of CAD work on an IBM system using the Auto-CAD software. These systems typically output the graphics files in the HPGL (Hewlett Packard Graphics Language) format. I'd like to take these files from the IBM and use them on the Mac. What's the best process for moving CAD graphics images from a CAD station to a Mac? Is there any software that can do this?**

A. The best way to move a graphics image from a CAD station to a Macintosh is to first create an HPGL plot file of the desired image from the CAD program. This is accomplished by redirecting the plotter output to the hard disk. If both the CAD station and the Mac are on the same network, then the Mac can up-load the file with the appropriate translation software. Another method to use is a serial data transfer between the two computers using a null modem cable and data capture software. Floppy transfers are rarely, if ever used. The HPGL plot file tends to be massive in size.

An excellent choice in this situation is CAD to Mac, by Celect Software. It only costs $195 and can do almost anything with CAD output being exported to a Mac. CAD to Mac actually translates the plot file into vector-based PICT files that can be edited. You can then simply use a Mac drawing program like MacDraw, FreeHand, or PageMaker and work with it. It's that easy. Most of the CAD translators that I have seen before do not do this. Instead they create bit-mapped output that is time-consuming to edit.

CAD to Mac also lets you view the CAD file without having to be on the CAD station or having the expensive drafting software. I also like the fact that it comes with serial cable and data transfer software. At $195 it's a bargain. One last side note: Celect software is owned by a company called Cincinnati Electronics, which is a large defense contractor that does a great deal of CAD work. They actually developed this product for their own in-house use, because there was nothing else out there for them. It was designed by the engineer for the engineer.

Q. How do packages such as Mac Link Plus/PC and Laplink Mac compare to the other generic translation packages on the market? How do they differ?

A. Mac Link Plus/PC and LapLink Mac III are translation packages that are bundled with a serial cable and software to manage the wire transfers. Mac Link Plus/PC uses the superb and popular Data Viz translators and comes with software for both the Mac and the DOS machine. LapLink III does the same thing, except the software and translators work on the DOS side. LapLink III is awkward to work with. Mac Link Plus/PC is better. These bundled packages are ideally used when you are seeking an inexpensive file exchange solution between Macs and DOS machines that don't have their respective 1.44MB floppy disk drives.

Q. I recently attempted to translate a simple document from Microsoft Word on the Mac side to WordPerfect on the IBM side. The attempt was unsuccessful. I believe that something is seriously wrong. I can no longer open the document. The machine keeps telling me that the application that created the document is missing or busy. Microsoft Word is still on my Mac, and it works fine. How can I open this file that was damaged during translation? Unfortunately I do not have a backup. Is there any way that I can copy the important data out of this file?

A. Shame on you. The best way to avoid a data recovery situation is by having a good backup of your data. You are absolutely right, something went wrong during the file conversion process. I believe that your problem is with the file creator code or similar data structure. You could attempt to rebuild these structures, but that would take too much time and you may come up empty. The best way to open a stubborn file is with a piece of software called CanOpener by Abbott Systems. It's excellent and costs less than $100.

Q. I've been having trouble importing EPS files on my Mac that were created on an IBM. I thought EPS on IBM is the same as EPS is on the Mac? What type of problems are common to EPS transfers?

A. EPS (Encapsulated PostScript) files are text-only files that contain instructions on how to create the desired text and graphic images, rather than the images

275

themselves. When you move this file from an IBM to the Mac, the Mac thinks that this file is a simple text file, and it tags it as a text file (like a document) rather than treating it as an EPS file. The Mac applications trying to import the EPS file will then ignore the EPS file tagged as text-only. The only way to change this is by using a utility program like Fedit or ResEdit to change the file type (which resides in the file header) from TEXT to EPSF. The application then recognizes this file as EPS.

A second common problem is that the bit-map image approximations created on the Mac side are different from those on the PC side. This difference can cause a problem when you attempt to import the EPS file that was created on the other platform. The only solution is to go back into the application program that created the EPS file, open the file, activate any bit-map suppress preview, and then save the file again.

Q. I have a Mac but would like to run IBM software. Should I purchase a second computer (such as an IBM clone), or should I consider purchasing DOS emulation software or a DOS processor board for my Mac?

A. I use both the Mac and the IBM very heavily so I have several of each of these computers. If you're going to use both platforms heavily (and can afford it), consider purchasing an IBM clone. Typically, you can pick up a decent 386SX clone with VGA color graphics for about $1000.

You can emulate DOS on a Mac by using programs like Soft PC and Soft AT from Insignia Solutions. These programs are software interpreters that change commands from the DOS applications into Macintosh processor equivalents. When Soft PC or AT is running, DOS programs are executed exactly as if you were working on an IBM PC. I even got MS Windows to come up under Soft AT. It was slow as a turtle, but it still came up. Some of the most serious Mac zealots would consider using this package as grounds for excommunication from the Mac community. I don't buy into that; computers are tools not, religious icons. Anyhow, there is too much prejudice in this world, and people sometimes forget that both DOS machines and Macs each have their own unique place.

I think that Soft PC and Soft AT are very clever and useful, but I only recommend it for casual DOS users. IBM power hitters will find it too slow for heavy DOS usage. If you need a PC, get a PC. If you need a Mac, get a Mac. If want to do a little DOS on your Mac, get Soft PC or Soft AT.

CHAPTER 13

Problems and Solutions

This guide to common Macintosh problems and how to solve them has been compiled from my own personal experiences with these models and from failure histories compiled by several service companies. This chapter is designed to be used as a companion with the other chapters in this book. For instance, if a reference is made to testing, repairing, or replacing a power supply, it's assumed that you have read the power supply chapter, which would have more specific strategies for dealing with the problem at hand. Please keep in mind this is a listing of the most common symptoms and solutions that service companies see every day. It is by no means a complete listing of every Mac failure for every model.

The Compact Mac Family: Macintosh Plus and Later Models

Problems related to video
Problem 1
Screen is bright, unit bongs (passes P.O.S.T.), but no video information is displayed.

Suspects:
- Bad capacitors or resistors in the video section or the 74LS38N IC.
- The PAL chips on the logic board, especially those at board references D1 and E1, which are part of the composite video and sync circuitry.

Solutions:
- Test the power/sweep board and repair or replace if necessary.
- Test, repair, or replace the logic board.

Problem 2

No video, machine bongs (passes P.O.S.T.), and the drives operate.

Suspects:
- Bad capacitors or resistors in the video section or the 74LS38N IC.
- The PAL chips on the logic board, especially those at board references D1 and E1, which are part of the composite video and sync circuitry.

Solutions:
- Turn the brightness knob fully clockwise.
- Inspect all video cables for burnt wires.
- Verify all cable connections are good.
- Try replacing the CRT socket cable.
- Test the power/sweep board and replace if necessary.
- Test, repair, or replace the logic board.

Problems related to peripheral devices
Problem 1

Moving mouse doesn't move the cursor.

Suspects:
- Possible suspects on the logic board are R41, R42, R43, R44 and CR2 and CR3.

Solutions:
- Reconnect the mouse.
- Test mouse and repair or replace if necessary.
- Test the logic board repair or replace if necessary.

Problem 2

Cursor moves but clicking the mouse produces no response.

Suspects:
- There is a 99% chance that the problem is with the mouse.

Solutions:
- Test the mouse and check the mouse connector on the logic board.
- Repair or replace the mouse if necessary.

Problem 3

No response to any key on the keyboard.

Suspects:
- Possible suspects could be a loose connector on the logic board or possible failure of one or more of the following components: R43, R44,CR2 & CR3. Long shot would be a possible failure of the SCC IC at board reference D9.

Solutions:
- Test the keyboard cable and replace if necessary.
- Test and repair or replace the keyboard.
- Repair or replace the logic board.

Problem 4

No response from a particular key on the keyboard.

Suspects:
- There is a 90% chance that a keyswitch on the keyboard has failed.

Solutions:
- Replace the keyswitch.
- Replace the keyboard.

Problem 5

Known good printer won't print from the Mac.

Suspects:
- Possible suspects on the logic board would be a printer port connector or a failure of one of the following chips: MC3488 and 26LS30 or SCC 8530.

Solutions:
- Make sure the printer is plugged in and turned on.
- Make sure that you have a good printer cable that is properly connected.
- Make sure the Chooser and the control panel are set correctly.
- Reinstall the Macintosh System Software.
- Reinstall the application program that you are trying to print from.
- Repair or replace the logic board.

Problems related to floppy disk drives
Problem 1
Unable to insert the diskette entirely into the floppy drive.

Solutions:
- Turn the power off and hold the mouse button down while switching the power back on to ensure the eject cycle has been completed.
- Replace the disk drive.

Problem 2
Drive won't eject the disk.

Solutions:
- Simultaneously press <Shift>, <Command>, and either 1 (for the internal drive) or 2 (for the external drive).
- Pull down the File menu option and select Eject. Try this a few times.
- Eject the disk manually by inserting an open paper clip into the hole near the drive slot.
- Replace the disk drive.

Problem 3
Disk ejects and the display shows disk icon with the X.

Solutions:
- Possible bad diskette. Replace diskette with a known good one.
- Clean the disk drive with head cleaning kit.

- Replace the disk drive cable.
- Repair or replace the disk drive.

Problem 4

Computer won't read the diskettes on either the internal or the external disk drives.

Solutions:
- Try a known good diskette.
- Clean the disk drive.
- Replace the disk drive cable.
- Replace the RFI shield.
- Replace the disk drive.

Problem 5

Machine passes P.O.S.T., but the diskette drive doesn't operate.

Suspects:
- IWM IC
- The two ROM ICs

Solutions:
- Clean the diskette drive.
- Replace the disk drive cable.
- Repair or replace the disk drive.
- Repair or replace the logic board.

Problem 6

Drive continually ejects the disk.

Solutions:
- Check the disk drive cable.
- Replace the disk drive.

Problem 7

Disk drive runs continuously.

Solutions:
- Replace the bad disk.
- Replace the disk drive cable.
- Replace the disk drive.
- Repair or replace the logic board (very rarely happens).

Problem 8

400K drive won't boot.

Solutions:
- If the logic board has Rev. A ROM chips and the diskette drive (actuator motor) has a serial number of F518 or higher, upgrade to Rev. B ROM chips.
- Replace the disk drive.

Other problems
Problem 1

When turned on, the Macintosh Plus continuously beeps and tries to power up.

Solutions:
- Check the DC output from the power supply and adjust if necessary.
- Repair or replace the power/video sweep board.

Problem 2

Thumping or clicking noise.

Solutions:
- Verify that the logic board cable is connected.
- Test DC output from power supply and adjust if necessary.
- Repair or replace the power/video sweep board.

Problem 3

Bad odor, almost like an exhaust smell, emanates from unit.

Suspects:
- There is a 95% chance that you have a failure on the power/video sweep board in the video circuitry. The most common failure point is the flyback transformer and the power transistor.

Solutions:
- Inspect flyback transformer and power transistor.
- Inspect for burnt connectors and capacitors.

Problem 4

Machine doesn't do anything. It appears to be dead.

Solutions:
- Verify that the power cord is good and that it is plugged in.
- Turn the power on.
- Check the fuse on the power/video sweep board.
- Verify that all cables are properly connected.
- Repair or replace the power/video sweep board.

Problem 5

Macintosh Plus is operating much slower than usual during start up.

Solutions:
- Verify the ROM revisions. If the ROM 342-0341A or B (ROM HI) and 342-0342A (ROM LO) are installed on the logic board and an external device is connected to the SCSI port, turn the external device on before turning on the computer.

Problem 6

When the developers switch is installed, the Macintosh Plus resets intermittently.

Solution:
- The switch may be getting hung up. Remove the switch and file the end a little bit.

Macintosh SE, SE/30, Classic, and Classic II

Problems related to video
Problem 1

Screen is dark, but the machine passes P.O.S.T.

Suspects:
- A likely suspect would the 74LS38N IC.

Solutions:
- Adjust the brightness knob.
- Adjust the cut-off potentiometer (on the Macintosh Classic only).
- Inspect the yoke wire for damage. Verify that the yoke cable connection is good.
- Repair or replace the power/video sweep board (Macintosh Classic) or the analog board (Macintosh SE and SE/30).
- Test CRT socket board.
- Test CRT (see if filament glows) and replace if necessary.

Problem 2

Screen is bright and the audio is present, but no video information is visible.

Suspects:
- Once again, the likely suspect would the 74LS38N IC.

Solutions:
- Repair or replace the power/video sweep board (Macintosh Classic) or the analog board (Macintosh SE and SE/30).

Problem 3

Screen is completely dark, and the cooling fan is not operating.

Solutions:

- Immediately test the DC output from your power supply. Replace the power supply if voltage readings are low (Macintosh SE and SE/30) or the power/video sweep board (Classic and Classic II).
- Test video section of analog video board (Macintosh SE and SE/30) or the power/video sweep board (Macintosh Classic and Classic II).

Problem 4

Screen collapses to a horizontal line.

Solutions:

- This indicates an absence of a vertical sweep. Check the DC output from your power supply, the 12-volt side may be low. Adjust the power supply (power/video sweep board for Classic and Classic II) if possible, otherwise replace. Test the TDA 1170N chip.
- Repair or replace the power/video sweep board (Macintosh Classic) or the analog board (Macintosh SE and SE/30).
- Look for burnt connectors and resistors, cracked solder joints, and burnt capacitors on the board.

Problem 5

Screen collapses to a single vertical line.

Suspects:

- This indicates that there is an absence of a horizontal sweep. This problem is very common. The most likely suspects would be burnt capacitors and resistors (especially the horizontal deflection capacitor).

Solution:

- Repair or replace the power/video sweep board (Macintosh Classic) or the analog board (Macintosh SE and SE/30).

Problem 6

Single illuminated pixel appears on the screen.

Suspects:
- The yoke wire is loose or not connected.
- A burnt connector or cracked solder joint at the connector where the yoke wire connects to the analog video board.

Solutions:
- Check yoke wire and connect if necessary.
- Repair/replace the power/video sweep board (Macintosh Classic) or the analog board (Macintosh SE and SE/30).

Problem 7

Vertical or horizontal bars or stripes are displayed.

Solutions:
- Repair or replace the power/sweep board (Macintosh Classic) or the analog board (Macintosh SE and SE/30).
- Possible electrical short in primary RAM. All compact Macs use primary memory to create the video frame buffer. Test SIMMs and replace if necessary. On the Classic and Classic II, test memory expansion card as well.

Problem 8

Screen jitters.

Solutions:
- Make sure no electrical equipment is in the vicinity that could be causing electrical interference (such as a fan or space heater). If there is, then move the computer.
- Possible component failure on the analog board. Repair or replace the power/sweep board (Macintosh Classic) or the analog board (Macintosh SE and SE/30).

   The most likely component failure on the analog board is the flyback transformer and/or the power transistor that is tied into the same circuit. This transistor is heat sinked and usually knocks out the flyback.

Problems related to peripheral devices
Problem 1
Cursor doesn't move when the mouse is moved.

Solutions:
- Verify the mouse connection.
- If the mouse was connected to a keyboard, connect it directly to the rear ADB port while the machine is off. Then turn the machine on. If the mouse works, replace the keyboard.
- If the mouse doesn't work in either of the ADB ports, try another mouse. If a new mouse works, then the old one was bad. If you don't have another mouse, use the Mactronics ADB port tester to verify the port; otherwise test the ADB port with a voltmeter looking for +5 volts DC.
- If the new mouse doesn't work, or you don't get +5 volts DC, the most likely failure is the RF choke filter on the logic board. This filter looks like a small black box and sits behind the ADB ports. To test this port you must perform a continuity test across the four sides of the filter. If you are dealing with an SE/30, Classic, or Classic II, then you should also test the ADB fuse in that same area. These fuses are often disguised, but all have a board designation with the letter "F," as in F1. Also check the fuses by performing a continuity check. If the fuse reads open, replace it.

Problem 2
Cursor moves, but clicking the mouse button has no effect.

Solutions:
- Repair or replace the mouse.

Problem 3

No response to any key on the keyboard.

Solutions:
- Check the keyboard connection to the rear ADB port.
- Replace the keyboard cable.
- Repair or replace the keyboard.
- Repair or replace the main logic board.
- Don't forget to check the RF choke filter located on the logic board. This filter is currently found on all desktop Macintosh models that use ADB. On all models above the SE, check the ADB fuse on the logic board.

Problem 4

Cannot double-click to open a disk or application.

Solutions:
- It is possible that you have too many System Folders and system files on your hard disk. Remove them and reinstall the system software.
- If you are using version 6.0.x of the system software, then zap parameter RAM by simultaneously holding down the <Shift>, <Option>, and <Command> keys and at the same time selecting Control Panel from the Apple menu. Then go back into the control panel and reset the mouse controls. Turn the machine off and then back on.
- Repair/replace the mouse.

Problem 5

Known-good printer won't print.

Solutions:
- Make sure the printer is plugged in and turned on.
- Make sure that you have a good printer cable that is properly connected.
- Make sure the Chooser and the control panel are set correctly.
- Reinstall the Macintosh system software.
- Reinstall the application program that you are trying to print from.

- Repair or replace the logic board. Possible suspects on the logic board would be a bad printer port connector or an IC failure in the serial circuitry, such as the MC3488 and 26LS30 or the SCC 8530 ICs.

Problems related to floppy disk drives
Problem 1
Machine passes P.O.S.T., but one internal drive doesn't operate.

Solutions:
- Try a known good floppy diskette.
- Verify that the internal disk drive cable is properly connected and that it is good. Replace if necessary.
- Check for bent pins on the internal drive connector.
- Replace the internal disk drive.

Problem 2
Machine passes P.O.S.T., but neither internal drive operates.

Solutions:
- Try a known good floppy diskette.
- If you have recently been in the machine, verify that the disk drive cables are connected. Look for bent pins on the internal drive connector.
- Repair or replace the logic board.

    The IC most likely to be giving you a problem is the IWM/SWIM IC, which functions as the floppy drive controller interface. The Mac SE could have either an IWM or SWIM, depending on the version. The SE/30, Classic, and Classic II all utilize the SWIM IC. Another possible failure point on the SE is an ASIC chip called the BBU, which controls rotational speed. Take signal readings with a logic probe.

Problem 3

External drive doesn't operate.

Solutions:
- Try a known good diskette.
- Make sure the external drive is on the right side of the Macintosh away from any magnetic fields.
- Check the cable connections and external DB-19 connector.
- Take a DC output reading from the connector, looking for 5 and 12 volts. This would indicate whether or not your power supply output was weak. Adjust the power supply if necessary. If the machine appears to be working, except for the external drive, and you have an SE/30, Classic, or Classic II, look for a 1-amp pico fuse on the logic board near the port. Perform a continuity test on the fuse and replace if blown.
- If your power outputs are OK, it's possible that the external floppy disk drive is bad.

Problem 4

Diskette won't eject.

Solutions:
- Simultaneously press <Shift>, <Command>, and 1 (for the internal drive) or 2 (for the external drive).
- Pull down the File menu option and select Eject. Try this a few times.
- Eject the disk manually by inserting an open paper clip into the hole near the drive slot.
- Replace the disk drive.

Problem 5

Unable to insert the disk entirely into the floppy drive.

Solutions:
- Eject the disk manually by inserting an opened paper clip into the hole beside the drive.

- Switch off the power and hold the mouse button down while switching the power back on (to complete eject cycle).
- Replace the disk drive.

Problem 6

Disk ejects; the display shows disk icon with the X.

Solutions:
- Possible bad diskette. Replace diskette with a known good one.
- Clean the disk drive with head cleaning kit.
- Replace the disk drive cable.
- Repair or replace the disk drive.

Problem 7

Disk drive runs continuously.

Solutions:
- Replace the bad disk.
- Replace the disk drive cable.
- Replace the disk drive.
- Repair/replace the logic board (very rarely happens).

Problem 8

Disk initialization fails.

Solutions:
- Verify that proper media is being used.
- Try another disk.
- Clean the floppy disk drive.
- Repair or replace the floppy disk drive.

Problems related to SCSI
Problem 1

Mac works with the internal or external SCSI device but won't operate with both of them.

Solutions:
- Check all of your SCSI connections. Make sure you turn on external SCSI devices before you turn on the Mac. Make sure all of your cables are good.
- Make sure that the SCSI device ID switch setting on the external SCSI device is unique. It must not duplicate any ID switch/jumper setting on any other attached SCSI device.
- Check termination on the external SCSI device.
- Check termination on the internal SCSI device.

Problem 2

Internal hard disk won't operate.

Solutions:
- Make sure that your power supply is providing the proper DC outputs. If not, replace the power supply.
- Verify that the hard disk drive cable is good and properly attached.
- Make sure that there are no bent pins on the internal SCSI connector.
- Reinitialize, repair, or replace the hard disk drive.
- You may be experiencing a stiction problem with the drive, the drive may have a blown fuse on its circuit board, or the drive may be bad. Try another known good drive.
- Repair or replace the main logic board. The likely suspect is the 5380 SCSI controller IC on the logic board.

Problem 3

External hard disk won't operate, but the internal hard disk works fine.

Solutions:
- Check all of your SCSI connections. Make sure you turn on external SCSI devices before you turn on the Mac. Make sure all of your cables are good.
- Make sure that the SCSI device ID switch setting on the external SCSI device is unique. It must not duplicate any ID switch/jumper setting on any other attached SCSI device.
- Check termination on the external SCSI device.
- Check termination on the internal SCSI device.
- If you have a Mac SE/30, Classic, or Classic II, you may have a blown SCSI port fuse on the logic board. This fuse is a 1-amp pico fuse and is usually designated with the letter "F." Its location is usually directly behind or in the vicinity of the DB-25 SCSI port connector.

Other problems
Problem 1
Thumping or clicking noise.

Solutions:
- Verify that the logic board cable is connected.
- Test DC output from the power supply and adjust if necessary.
- Repair or replace the power supply (the power/video sweep board on the Mac Classic and Classic II).

Problem 2
Machine doesn't do anything. It appears to be dead.

Solutions:
- Verify that the power cord is good and that it is plugged in.
- Turn the power on.
- Check the fuse on the power/video sweep board in the Classic and Classic II. Test the fuse inside the power supply on the SE and SE/30.
- Verify that all cables are properly connected.
- Repair or replace the power/video sweep board (Classic and Classic II).
- Repair or replace the power supply (SE and SE/30).

Problem 3

Bad odor, almost like an exhaust smell, emanates from unit.

Solutions:

- There is a 95% chance that you have a failure on the power/video sweep board (Classic and Classic II) or the analog video board (SE and SE/30) in the video circuitry. The most common failure point is the flyback transformer and the power transistor. Also inspect for burnt connectors and capacitors.

Problem 4

Mac displays Sad Macintosh icon.

Solutions:

- See Chapter 4 on P.O.S.T. to learn how to interpret the Sad Mac error.
- Verify that your power supply is providing the correct power levels.
- Verify that the three-pin jumper or RAM-size resistor on the logic board is configured correctly for system RAM (Macintosh SE only).
- Verify that jumper on memory expansion board is configured correctly for SIMMs or No SIMMs (Macintosh Classic).
- This could be a SIMM-related failure or dead short on one of the SIMMs. Remove the SIMMs and test them. Replace if necessary.

Problem 5

Sad Mac icon and black lines are displayed, and you hear a screeching sound.

Solutions:

- See Chapter 4 on P.O.S.T to learn how to interpret the Sad Mac error.
- Verify that your power supply is providing the correct power levels.
- Verify that the three-pin jumper or RAM-size resistor on the logic board is configured correctly for system RAM (Macintosh SE only).
- Verify that the jumper on the memory expansion board is configured correctly for SIMMs or No SIMMs (Macintosh Classic).
- This could be a SIMM-related failure or dead short on one of the SIMMs. Remove the SIMMs and test them. Replace if necessary.

Macintosh Portable

Problems related to power
Problem 1

Screen is blank and the Portable is not responding.

Solutions:
- If the computer is new, verify that the plastic sheet has been removed from between battery and contacts.
- Reset the power manager by unlocking the interrupt and reset switches and then depressing and releasing both switches simultaneously.
- Reconnect the power adapter and try again after 5 minutes.
- Try a known good, fully charged battery. If the computer works, replace the main battery.

Problem 2

Power adapter is plugged in and connected, but the battery indicator desk accessory doesn't indicate that the charger is connected.

Solutions:
- Verify that the charger is connected properly.
- Try another battery. If the battery now charges, replace the main battery.
- Replace the power adapter.

Problem 3

After main battery removal, some control panel settings are different.

Solutions:
- If the battery cover was replaced when the main battery was removed, the power to the computer was interrupted and the different settings are normal. Go into the control panel and restore them.
- Replace the backup (9-volt) battery.

Problem 4

Low-power warning is displayed soon after startup.

Solutions:
- The battery needs to be recharged. Connect the power adapter.
- Minimize the use of the hard disk drive, floppy disk drive, modem, and other power consuming devices, or attach the Portable to the power adapter and plug into the wall outlet.

Problem 5

Battery needs recharging after the computer is unused for four or more days.

Solution:
- If your Portable has system software version 6.0.4 or earlier and AppleTalk is active, you may experience the power drain when the machine is powered off using the Shut Down command. When Shut Down is executed, the SCC chip and associated circuitry will continue to draw power. To prevent this, you must select the Sleep option from the Special menu or deactivate the AppleTalk setting using Chooser prior to Shutdown. Then upgrade the system software to version 6.0.5 or higher.

Problems related to video display
Problem 1

Some screen pixels never come on.

Solution:
- Four or five pixels that are permanently off or void are considered acceptable. If your display contains more than five off or voided pixels, you must replace the LCD display.

Problem 2

A row of pixels is always darkened with black streaks.

Solutions:
- Check the LCD display cable.
- Replace the LCD display.

Problem 3

Some pixels are always on.

Solutions:
- If any pixel remains on constantly when its not supposed to be on, replace the LCD display.

Problem 4

Portable appears to be working (it passes P.O.S.T.), but there is no display.

Solutions:
- Verify that the display cable is securely connected.
- Replace the display cable.
- Replace the LCD display.

Problem 5

Display is very blurry.

Solutions:
- Adjust the angle of display screen.
- Adjust the screen contrast with the control panel until it is acceptable.

Problem 6

Nonbacklit display looks excessively dark.

Solutions:
- This could be a lighting problem. Move the unit closer to a better light source or move light source closer to the unit.
- Adjust the screen contrast with the control panel until it is acceptable.
- Replace the LCD display.

Problem 7

Nonbacklit display is too bright (light).

Solutions:
- Adjust the angle of the display screen.
- Adjust the screen contrast with the control panel until it is acceptable.
- Replace the LCD display.

Problem 8

Back-light doesn't operate.

Solutions:
- Verify that version 1.3 or higher of the Portable CDEV is installed. The earlier versions of this CDEV don't support the back-lighting feature. To verify the version of this CDEV, select the file Portable in the System Folder and then Get Info from the File menu. The version will be displayed.
- Check all inverter connections.
- Replace the inverter PCA.
- Replace the LCD display.

Problem 9

Back-light level cannot be changed.

Solution:
- Verify that version 1.3 or higher of the Portable CDEV is installed. The earlier versions of this CDEV don't support the back-lighting feature. To verify the version of this CDEV, select the file Portable in System Folder and then Get Info from the File menu. The version will be displayed.

Problems related to floppy disk drives
Problem 1

Computer passes P.O.S.T., but the internal drive doesn't operate.

Solutions:
- Try a known good floppy diskette.
- Verify that the internal disk drive cable is properly connected and that it is good. Replace if necessary.
- Check for bent pins on the internal drive connector.
- Replace the internal disk drive.

Problem 2

Diskette won't eject.

Solutions:
- Simultaneously press <Shift>, <Command>, and 1 (for the internal drive).
- Pull down the File menu option and select Eject. Try this a few times.
- Eject the disk manually by inserting an open paper clip into the hole near the drive slot.
- Replace the disk drive.

Problem 3

Unable to insert the disk entirely into the floppy drive.

Solutions:
- Eject the disk manually by inserting an opened paper clip into hole beside the drive.
- Switch off the power and hold the mouse button down while switching the power back on (to complete eject cycle).
- Replace the disk drive.

Problem 4

Disk ejects; the display shows disk icon with the X.

Solutions:
- Possible bad diskette. Replace diskette with a known good one.
- Clean the disk drive with head cleaning kit.
- Replace the disk drive cable.
- Repair/replace the disk drive.

SCSI-related problems
Problem 1

Mac works with the internal or external SCSI device but won't operate with both of them.

Solutions:
- Check all of your SCSI connections. Make sure you turn on external SCSI devices before you turn on the Mac. Make sure all of your cables are good.
- Make sure that the SCSI device ID switch setting on the external SCSI device is unique. It must not duplicate any ID switch or jumper setting on any other attached SCSI device.
- Check termination on the external SCSI device.
- Check termination on the internal SCSI device.

Problem 2

Internal hard disk won't operate.

Solutions:
- Make sure that your power supply is providing the proper DC outputs. If not, replace the power supply module.
- Verify that the hard disk drive cable is good and properly attached.
- Make sure that there are no bent pins on the internal SCSI connector.
- Reinitialize, repair, or replace the hard disk drive You may be experiencing a stiction problem with the drive, the drive may have a blown fuse on its circuit board, or the drive may be bad. Try another known good drive.

- Repair or replace the main logic board. The likely suspect is the SCSI circuitry on the logic board.

Problem 3

External hard disk won't operate, but the internal one works fine.

Solutions:
- Check all of your SCSI connections. Make sure you turn on external SCSI devices before you turn on the Mac. Make sure all of your cables are good.
- Make sure that the SCSI device ID switch setting on the external SCSI device is unique. It must not duplicate any ID switch or jumper setting on any other attached SCSI device.
- Check termination on the external SCSI device.
- Check termination on the internal SCSI device.

Problem 4

After connecting an external SCSI device, the computer no longer boots.

Solutions:
- Turn on the external SCSI device before starting up the computer.
- Verify that the SCSI cable is good and that proper cable termination is provided.
- Verify that no two SCSI devices have the same address.

Problems related to peripherals
Problem 1

Cursor doesn't move when you are using a trackball.

Solutions:
- Clean the trackball.
- Check the cable connections between the trackball and the logic board.
- Replace the trackball cable.
- Replace the trackball.
- Reset the power manager.

Problem 2

Cursor doesn't move when you are using a mouse.

Solutions:
- Check the mouse connection to the ADB port.
- Reset the power manager.
- Clean the mouse ball and inside of the mouse case.
- Replace the mouse.
- This could be a blown ADB port on logic board. Check the ADB port on the logic board.

Problem 3

Cursor occasionally doesn't move or it moves erratically.

Solutions:
- Clean the trackball and its internal rollers.
- Replace the trackball assembly.

Problem 4

Device that is connected to the modem port doesn't work properly.

Solutions:
- Verify that the External Modem option is selected from the Portable CDEV.
- If you are using System 6.0.4, upgrade to 6.0.5 or higher.
- This could be a sign of serial circuitry failure on the logic board. Repair or replace the logic board.

Problem 5

No response to any key on the keyboard.

Solutions:
- If the screen is blank and you are trying to wake the Portable from system sleep, then reset the power manager.

- Check the keyboard connection to the logic board.
- Replace the keyboard.

Problem 6

Known good printer won't print from the Mac.

Solutions:
- Make sure the printer is plugged in and turned on.
- Make sure you have a good printer cable that is properly connected.
- Make sure the Chooser and the control panel are set correctly.
- Reinstall the Macintosh System Software.
- Reinstall the application program that you are trying to print from.
- Repair or replace the logic board. Possible suspects on the logic board would be a printer port connector or a failure of the serial circuitry on the logic board.

Problems related to modems and serial devices
Problem 1

Portable doesn't recognize serial devices.

Solution:
- Upgrade to the System 6.0.5 or higher.

Problem 2

Internal modem options don't appear in the Portable CDEV when modem is installed.

Solutions:
- Remove and reseat the modem card.
- Replace the modem card.

Problem 3

External modem causes the Portable to lock up after coming out of sleep.

Solution:
- If System 6.0.4 is being used, upgrade to System 6.0.5 or higher.

Problem 4

Modem doesn't respond to incoming calls.

Solutions:
- If the system doesn't respond to incoming calls while it is in sleep mode, verify that the When Phone Rings option in the Automatic Wake-Up option of the Portable CDEV is active.
- Replace the modem card.

Other problems
Problem 1

Screen goes blank and the computer itself goes down after a few minutes.

Solution:
- The computer is going into sleep mode in order to conserve battery power. Adjust the sleep delays in the control panel, or connect the power adapter and operate the unit off of the wall outlet.

Problem 2

Hard disk acts very sluggish, and the screen keeps going blank.

Solution:
- The computer is powering down hard disk and/or going into sleep mode to conserve battery power. Adjust the sleep delays in the control panel, or connect the power adapter and operate the unit off of the wall outlet.

Problem 3

Some applications run slower after the machine has been on for just a short time.

Solution:

- The Portable is switching to system rest. To disable system rest, you must open the control panel, hold down the <Option> key, and then select Minutes Until Automatic Sleep. When the dialog box appears, select Don't Rest.

Problem 4

Screen suddenly goes blank.

Solution:

- The Portable has gone into sleep mode to conserve battery power.

The Modular Macintosh II Family: Macintosh LC and LC II

Problem 1

Computer doesn't power on, screen is black, fan is not running, and LED is not lit.

Solutions:

- Check cables.
- Plug the monitor directly into the wall socket to verify that the monitor has power.
- Test the power cord and replace if necessary.
- Test and replace the power supply. The LC and LC II have terrible power supplies. They are seriously underrated and very prone to failure. If you have to replace this, get a replacement power supply from a third party that has a higher output rating than Apple's.

Problem 2

Unit intermittently shuts itself down.

Solutions:

- Make sure that all air vents are clear so that air can cool the unit properly.
- Check the power cable and replace if necessary.
- Test the power supply and replace if necessary.

Problem 3

Computer keeps locking up or crashing.

Solutions:

- Make sure you are running version 6.0.7 or higher of the system software.
- Reinstall the system software.
- If the machine keeps crashing on certain applications, reinstall those applications.
- Remove all INITs from the System Folder or system extension.
- Test the power supply and replace if necessary.
- Test the SIMMs and replace if necessary.

Problem 4

System intermittently doesn't power on.

Solutions:

- Check call cables and connections.
- Verify that you are getting power from the wall outlet
- Test the power supply and replace if necessary.

Problem 5

Computer seems to boot, but then you see the message "Finder is old version" displayed on the screen.

Solution:

- Zap parameter RAM by depressing the <Command>, <Option>, P, and R keys and holding them down while the system is restarted. You should hear the normal startup chords, and then about 3 seconds later you will hear an additional chord. This means that parameter RAM has been zapped. This is a different key sequence than is used on the older Macs.

Problems related to video
Problem 1

Machine passes P.O.S.T., but strange vertical and/or horizontal lines appear on screen, or the screen is completely dark.

Solutions:
- Replace video cable.
- Test the monitor replace if necessary.
- Test and replace the video RAM SIMM if necessary.
- Failure on the built in video circuitry on the logic board. Repair and replace if necessary.

Problem 2

Machine passes P.O.S.T., but the monitor is very bright.

Solutions:
- Make sure that the video cable is hooked up and there are no bent pins. Also verify that this video cable is the correct video cable for your monitor configuration. Replace the video cable if necessary.
- Test the monitor and repair or replace if necessary.

Problem 3

Machine passes P.O.S.T. (it bongs), but the video screen is dark and the front LED is lit.

Solutions:
- Adjust brightness on monitor.
- Replace monitor.
- Replace video cable.
- Test SIMMs on the logic board.

Problem 4

Screen is completely dark, fan is not running, and LED is not lit.

Solutions:

- Verify that the power cord is good and that it is plugged in.
- Verify that you have wall power and try to turn the machine on.
- Check the fuse inside the power supply and replace if necessary.
- Verify that all internal cables are properly connected.
- Remove the expansion card, if installed.
- Remove any external peripherals, if connected.
- Repair or replace the power supply.

Problems related to floppy disk drives

Problem 1

Computer passes P.O.S.T., but the internal floppy drive doesn't operate.

Solutions:

- Try a known good floppy diskette.
- Verify that the internal disk drive cable is properly connected and that it is good. Replace if necessary.
- Check for bent pins on the internal drive connector.
- Replace the internal disk drive.
- Possible failure of the SWIM floppy controller IC on the logic board. Repair or replace the logic board.

Problem 2

Diskette won't eject.

Solutions:

- Simultaneously hold down <Shift>, <Command>, and 1 (for the internal drive).
- Pull down the File menu option and select Eject. Try this a few times.
- Eject the disk manually by inserting an open paper clip into the hole near the drive slot.
- Replace the disk drive.

Problem 3

Unable to insert the disk entirely into the floppy drive.

Solutions:

- Eject the disk manually by inserting an opened paper clip into hole beside the drive
- Switch off the power and hold the mouse button down while switching the power back on (to complete eject cycle).
- Replace the disk drive.

Problem 4

Disk ejects and the display shows disk icon with the X.

Solutions:

- Possible bad diskette. Replace diskette with a known good one.
- Clean the disk drive with head cleaning kit.
- Replace the disk drive cable.
- Repair or replace the disk drive.

Problem 5

Disk drive runs continuously.

Solutions:

- Replace the bad disk.
- Replace the disk drive cable.
- Replace the disk drive.
- Repair or replace the logic board (very rarely happens).

Problem 6

Disk initialization fails.

Solutions:
- Verify that proper media is being used.
- Try another disk.
- Clean the floppy disk drive.
- Repair or replace the floppy disk drive.

Problem 7

System attempts to eject disk but cannot.

Solutions:
- Try pushing disk completely back in.
- Eject disk manually by pushing opened paper clip into hole beside the drive slot.
- Remove and disassemble the disk drive to extract your diskette.

SCSI-related problems

Problem 1

Internal hard drive runs continuously.

Solutions:
- Replace the hard drive cable with a known good cable.
- Replace hard drive.

Problem 2

Mac works with internal or external SCSI device but won't operate with both of them.

Solutions:
- Check all of your SCSI connections. Make sure you turn on external SCSI devices before you turn on the Mac. Make sure all of your cables are good.

- Make sure that the SCSI device ID switch setting on the external SCSI device is unique. It must not duplicate any ID switch or jumper setting on any other attached SCSI device
- Check termination on the external SCSI device.
- Check termination on the internal SCSI device.

Problem 3

Internal hard disk won't operate.

Solutions:
- Make sure that your power supply is providing the proper DC outputs. If not, replace the power supply.
- Verify that the hard disk drive cable is good and properly attached.
- Make sure that there are no bent pins on the internal SCSI connector.
- Reinitialize, repair, or replace the hard disk drive. You may be experiencing a stiction problem with the drive, the drive may have a blown fuse on its circuit board, or the drive may be bad. Try another known good drive.
- Repair or replace the main logic board. The likely suspect is the SCSI controller IC on the logic board.

Problem 4

External hard disk won't operate, but the internal one works fine.

Solutions:
- Check all of your SCSI connections. Make sure you turn on external SCSI devices before you turn on the Mac. Make sure all of your cables are good.
- Make sure that the SCSI device ID switch setting on the external SCSI device is unique. It must not duplicate any ID switch or jumper setting on any other attached SCSI device.
- Check termination on the external SCSI device.
- Check termination on the internal SCSI device.
- You may have a blown SCSI port fuse on the logic board. This fuse is a 1-amp pico fuse and is usually designated with the letter "F." Its location is usually directly behind or in the vicinity of the DB-25 SCSI port connector.

Problems related to peripheral devices

Problem 1

Cursor doesn't move when the mouse is moved.

Solutions:
- Verify the mouse connection.
- If the mouse was connected to a keyboard, connect it directly to the rear ADB port while the machine is off. Then turn the machine on. If the mouse works, replace the keyboard.
- If the mouse doesn't work in either of the ADB ports, try another mouse. If a new mouse works then the old one was bad. If you don't have another mouse, use the Mactronics ADB port tester to verify the port; otherwise, test the ADB port with a voltmeter looking for +5 volts DC.
- If the new mouse doesn't work, or you don't get +5 volts DC, the most likely failure is the RF choke filter on the logic board. This filter looks like a small black box and sits behind the ADB ports. To test this port you would perform a continuity test across the four sides of the filter. You should also test the ADB fuse in that same area. These fuses are often disguised, but all have a board designation with the letter "F," as in F1. Also check the fuses by performing a continuity check. If the fuse reads open, replace it.

Problem 2

Cursor moves, but clicking the mouse button has no effect.

Solution:
Repair or replace the mouse

Problem 3

No response to any key on the keyboard.

Solutions:
- Make sure that version System 6.0.7 or higher of the system software is being used.
- Check the keyboard connection to the rear ADB port.

- Replace the keyboard cable.
- Repair or replace the keyboard.
- Repair or replace the main logic board.
- Don't forget to check the RF choke filter located on the logic board. This filter is currently found on all newer Macintosh models.

Problem 4

Cannot double-click to open a disk or application.

Solutions:
- It is possible that you have too many System Folders and system files on your hard disk. Remove them and reinstall the system software.
- Make sure that version System 6.0.7 or higher of the system software is being used.
- Repair or replace the mouse.

Problem 5

Known good printer won't print from the Mac.

Solutions:
- Make sure the printer is plugged in and turned on.
- Make sure that you have a good printer cable that is properly connected.
- Make sure the Chooser and the control panel are set correctly.
- Reinstall the Macintosh system software.
- Reinstall the application program that you are trying to print from.
- Repair or replace the logic board. Possible suspects on the logic board would be a printer port connector or a failure of the serial circuitry on the logic board.

Other problems
Problem 1

Real-time clock is not operating. Time is not being properly kept.

Solutions:
- Make sure that version System 6.0.7 or higher of the system software is being used.
- Test the battery on the logic board in circuit. You should read at least 2.75 to 3.25 volts, which is marginal. It is best if you read above 3.25 to 3.75 volts.
- Repair RTC circuit on the logic board or replace the logic board.

Problem 2

No sound coming from the speaker.

Solutions:
- Verify that volume setting in the control panel is above 1.
- Replace the speaker.

Macintosh IIcx, IIci, IIsi, and Quadra 700

Problems related to the system
Problem 1

Computer doesn't power on, screen is black, fan is not running, and LED is not lit.

Solutions:
- Check cables.
- Plug monitor directly into wall socket, and verify that monitor has power. This tells you that the wall power is most likely good.
- Replace power cord.

- Check the battery on the logic board. Replace the battery within or below the range of 2.75 to 3.25 volts. The recommended range is 3.25 to 3.75 volts.
- Test and replace power supply if necessary.

Problem 2

System intermittently crashes or locks up.

Solutions:
- Make sure system software is correct version.
- Make sure all software is known good.
- If the unit has Macintosh a IIci cache card with a serial number that begins with CF, remove and return this card to Apple.
- Make sure SIMMs meet or exceed the specification for the specific unit. Test all SIMMs and replace if necessary.
- Test the power supply and adjust or replace if necessary.
- Check the power cord and replace if necessary.
- Test power supply and replace if necessary.

Problem 3

Computer seems to boot, but then you see the message "Finder is old version" displayed on the screen.

Solution:
- Zap parameter RAM by depressing the <Command>, <Option>, P, and R keys and holding them down while the system is restarted. You should hear the normal startup chords, and then about 3 seconds later you will hear an additional chord. This means that parameter RAM has been zapped. This is a different key sequence than is used on the older Macs.

Problem 4

Mac IIsi keeps restarting itself.

Solution:
- Set the locking power switch on the rear of the computer to the unlocked (horizontal) position.

Problems related to video
Problem 1

Screen is dark, you can't tell if the machine has passed P.O.S.T, or not, but the power supply fan is running and the front LED is lit.

Solutions:
- Test the power supply outputs. Replace if the readings are too low.
- Test the video cable and replace if necessary.
- Test monitor and replace if necessary.
- Move video card (if one is installed) to a another slot.
- Replace video card (if one is installed).
- Remove all NuBus expansion cards (if any are installed).
- Disconnect any external peripherals (except the monitor).
- Test SIMMs and replace if necessary.
- If computer is a Mac IIsi with an installed ROM SIMM, then replace the ROM SIMM.
- It may be an internal video circuitry failure (IIci and IIsi). Repair or replace the logic board.

Problem 2

Unit passes P.O.S.T., but the display is still dark.

Solutions:
- Try to adjust the brightness on monitor.
- Test monitor and replace if necessary.
- Inspect video cable. Look for bent pins and make sure that it is the proper cable for your video configuration. Replace the video cable if necessary.

- Move video card (if one is installed) to another slot.
- Replace video card with a known good one (if one is installed).
- Test RAM SIMMs and replace them if necessary.
- If computer is a Mac IIsi with an installed ROM SIMM, replace ROM SIMM.
- It may be an internal video circuitry failure (IIci and IIsi). Repair or replace logic board.

Problem 3

Machine passes P.O.S.T., but the screen is bright and no video information is visible.

Solutions:
- Replace the video cable.
- Test the monitor and replace if necessary.
- Move the video card (if one is installed) to another slot.
- Replace video card (if one is installed).
- Verify that you have a small ROM jumper installed over the shunts on the logic board. On most revisions, this jumper is almost dead center.

Problem 4

Screen is completely dark, the power supply fan is not running, and the front LED is not lit.

Solutions:
- Check power cord and replace if necessary.
- Check power coming from the wall outlet.
- Test the outputs from the power supply. Reseat or replace if the readings are too low or nonexistent. If you get nothing, then check the fuse inside.
- Remove NuBus cards.
- Disconnect any external peripheral devices.
- Check for a possible dead short on the logic board.

Problems related to floppy disk drives

Problem 1

Machine passes P.O.S.T., but the internal drive doesn't operate.

Solutions:
- Try a known good floppy diskette.
- If you have recently been in the machine, verify that the disk drive cables are connected. Look for bent pins on the internal drive connector.
- Repair or replace the logic board. The chip most likely to be giving you a problem is the SWIM IC, which functions as the floppy drive controller interface. Take signal readings with a logic probe.

Problem 2

External drive doesn't operate.

Solutions:
- Try a known good diskette.
- Make sure the external drive is on the right side of the Macintosh away from any magnetic fields.
- Check the cable connections and external DB-19 connector.
- Take a DC output reading from the connector, looking for 5 and 12 volts. This indicates whether or not your power supply output is weak. Adjust power supply if necessary. If the machine appears to be working, other than the external drive, look for a 1-amp pico fuse on the logic board near the port and perform a continuity test on it. Replace it if it is blown.

  Note: The fuse is always designated with the letter "F" on the logic board. On some of these models, the fuse is not always in the vicinity of the DB-19 external port. They occasionally hide this fuse back near the battery compartment on the logic board.

- If your power outputs are OK, it's possible that the external floppy disk drive is bad.

Problem 3

Diskette won't eject.

Solutions:
- Simultaneously hold down <Shift>, <Command>, and 1 (for the internal drive) or 2 (for the external drive).
- Pull down the File menu option and select Eject. Try this a few times.
- Eject the disk manually by inserting an open paper clip into the hole near the drive slot.
- Replace the disk drive.

Problem 4

Unable to insert the disk entirely into the floppy drive.

Solutions:
- Eject the disk manually by inserting an opened paper clip into hole beside the drive.
- Switch off the power and hold the mouse button down while switching the power back on (to complete eject cycle).
- Replace the disk drive.

Problem 5

Disk ejects, and the display shows disk icon with the X.

Solutions:
- Possible bad diskette. Replace diskette with a known good one.
- Clean the disk drive with head cleaning kit.
- Replace the disk drive cable.
- Repair or replace the disk drive.

Problem 6

Disk drive runs continuously.

Solutions:
- Replace the bad disk.
- Replace the disk drive cable.
- Replace the disk drive.

Problem 7

Disk initialization fails.

Solutions:
- Verify that proper media is being used.
- Try another disk.
- Clean the floppy disk drive.
- Repair or replace the floppy disk drive.

Problems related to SCSI devices
Problem 1

Internal hard drive runs continuously.

Solutions:
- Replace the hard drive cable with a known good cable.
- Replace hard drive.

Problem 2

Mac works with internal or external SCSI device but won't operate with both of them.

Solutions:
- Check all of your SCSI connections. Make sure you turn on external SCSI devices before you turn on the Mac. Make sure all of your cables are good.

- Make sure that the SCSI device ID switch setting on the external SCSI device is unique. It must not duplicate any ID switch or jumper setting on any other attached SCSI device.
- Check termination on the external SCSI device.
- Check termination on the internal SCSI device.

Problem 3

Internal hard disk won't operate.

Solutions:

- Make sure that your power supply is providing the proper DC outputs. If not, replace the power supply.
- Verify that the hard disk drive cable is good and properly attached.
- Make sure that there are no bent pins on the internal SCSI connector.
- Reinitialize, repair, or replace the hard disk drive. You may be experiencing a stiction problem with the drive, the drive may have a blown fuse on its circuit board, or the drive may be bad. Try another known good drive.
- Repair or replace the main logic board. The likely suspect is the SCSI controller chip on the logic board.

Problem 4

External hard disk won't operate, but the internal one works fine.

Solutions:

- Check all of your SCSI connections. Make sure you turn on external SCSI devices before you turn on the Mac. Make sure all of your cables are good.
- Make sure that the SCSI device ID switch setting on the external SCSI device is unique. It must not duplicate any ID switch or jumper setting on any other attached SCSI device.
- Check termination on the external SCSI device.
- Check termination on the internal SCSI device.
- You may have a blown SCSI port fuse on the logic board. This fuse is a 1-amp pico fuse and is usually designated with the letter "F." Its location is usually directly behind or in the vicinity of the DB-25 SCSI port connector.

Problems related to peripheral devices
Problem 1

Cursor doesn't move when mouse is moved.

Solutions:
- Verify the mouse connection.
- If the mouse was connected to a keyboard, connect it directly to the rear ADB port while the machine is off. Then turn the machine on. If the mouse works, replace the keyboard.
- If the mouse doesn't work in either of the ADB ports, try another mouse. If a new mouse works, then the old one was bad. If you don't have another mouse, use the Mactronics ADB port tester to verify the port; otherwise test the ADB port with a voltmeter looking for +5 volts DC.
- If the new mouse doesn't work, or you don't get +5 volts DC, the most likely failure is the RF choke filter on the logic board. This filter looks like a small black box and sits behind the ADB ports. To test this port you perform a continuity test across the four sides of the filter. Also test the ADB fuse in that same area. These fuses are often disguised, but all have a board designation with the letter "F," as in F1. Also check the fuses by performing a continuity check. If the fuse reads open, replace it.

Problem 2

Cursor moves, but clicking the mouse button has no effect.

Solution:
- Repair or replace the mouse.

Problem 3

No response to any key on the keyboard.

Solutions:
- Check the keyboard connection to the rear ADB port.
- Replace the keyboard cable.

- Repair or replace the keyboard.
- Repair or replace the main logic board.
- Don't forget to check the RF choke filter located on the logic board. This filter is currently found on all newer Macintosh models. It is also possible that the ADB circuitry has failed.

Problem 4

Cannot double-click to open a disk or application.

Solutions:
- It is possible that you have too many System Folders and system files on your hard disk. Remove them and reinstall the system software.
- Repair or replace the mouse.

Problem 5

Known good printer won't print from the Mac.

Solutions:
- Make sure the printer is plugged in and turned on.
- Make sure that you have a good printer cable that is properly connected.
- Make sure the Chooser and the control panel are set correctly.
- Reinstall the Macintosh system software.
- Reinstall the application program that you are trying to print from.
- Repair or replace the logic board. Possible suspects on the logic board would be a printer port connector or a failure of the serial circuitry on the logic board.

Other problems

Problem 1

Real-time clock is not operating. Time is not being properly kept.

Solutions:

- Test the battery in circuit. You should read at least 2.75 to 3.25 volts, which is marginal. It is best if it reads above 3.25 to 3.75 volts.
- Repair RTC circuit on the logic board, or replace the logic board.

Problem 2

No sound coming from the speaker.

Solutions:

- Verify that volume setting in the control panel is above 1.
- Replace the speaker.

Macintosh II, IIx, and IIfx

Problems related to the system

Problem 1

Computer doesn't power on, screen is black, fan is not running, and LED is not lit.

Solutions:

- Check cables.
- Plug monitor directly into wall socket, and verify that monitor has power.
- Replace power cord.
- Check the batteries on the logic board. Replace both of them if either battery is within or below the range of 2.75 to 3.25 volts. The recommended range is 3.25 to 3.75 volts.
- Test or replace power supply.

Problem 2

System intermittently crashes or locks up.

Solutions:
- Make sure system software is correct version.
- Make sure all software is known good.
- Make sure SIMMs meet or exceed the specification for the specific unit. Test all SIMMs and replace if necessary.
- Test the power supply and adjust or replace if necessary.

Problem 3

System shuts down intermittently.

Solutions:
- Make sure that air vents on sides and top of main unit are not covered up. The units are equipped with a thermal protection switch that can shut the system down. Let the machine cool off for 15 to 20 minutes. It should then be OK. If for some reason it doesn't come back on, replace the thermal switch on the logic board (TS#1 on II and IIx).
- Check the power cord and replace if necessary.
- Test power supply and replace if necessary.

Problem 4

Mac IIfx sounds the error chords (death march) during power-up.

Solutions:
- Make sure that your power supply is functioning properly. Test the outputs.
- Open up the unit and look for original Apple SIMMs manufactured by NEC. Replace any NEC SIMMs that have a date code of 9052 or earlier. Apple has a recall on these SIMMs and should take them back.
- If you are not using NEC SIMMs, test the installed SIMMs and replace any that fail.

Problem 5

Macintosh IIfx doesn't boot.

Solutions:
- Make sure that your power supply is functioning properly. Test the outputs.
- Open up the unit and look for original Apple SIMMs manufactured by NEC. Replace any NEC SIMMs that have a date code of 9052 or earlier. Apple has a recall on these SIMMs and should take them back.
- If you are not using NEC SIMMs, test the SIMMs and replace any that fail.

Problems related to video

Problem 1

Machine passes P.O.S.T., but strange vertical or horizontal lines appear on the screen, or the screen is completely dark.

Solutions:
- Replace video cable.
- Move video card to another slot.
- Test the monitor and replace if necessary.
- Replace the video card.
- Test SIMMs.

Problem 2

Machine passes P.O.S.T., but the monitor is very bright.

Solutions:
- Make sure that the video cable is hooked up and there are no bent pins. Also verify that this video cable is the correct video cable for your monitor configuration. Replace the video cable if necessary.
- Test the monitor and repair or replace if necessary.

Problem 3

Machine passes P.O.S.T. (it bongs), but the video screen is dark. The front LED is lit.

Solutions:

- Adjust brightness on monitor.
- Replace the video cable.
- Move the video card to another slot.
- Replace the video card.
- Replace the monitor.
- Test SIMMs on the logic board.

Problem 4

Machine doesn't do anything. It just appears to be dead.

Solutions:

- Verify that the power cord is good and that it is plugged in.
- Verify that you have wall power and try to turn the machine on.
- Check the batteries.
- Check the fuse inside the power supply and replace if necessary.
- Verify that all internal cables are properly connected.
- Remove the expansion cards, if installed.
- Remove any external peripherals, if connected.
- Repair or replace the power supply.

Problem 5

Video display has a "ghosting" problem, or the machine boots and then loses video.

Solutions:

- Open up the unit and look for original Apple SIMMs manufactured by NEC. Replace any NEC SIMMs that have a date code of 9052 or earlier. Apple has a recall on these SIMMs and should take them back.
- If you are not using NEC SIMMs, test the installed SIMMs and replace any that fail.

Problems related to floppy disk drives
Problem 1

Machine passes P.O.S.T., but one internal drive doesn't operate.

Solutions:
- Try a known good floppy diskette.
- Verify that the internal disk drive cable is properly connected and that it is good. Replace if necessary.
- Check for bent pins on the internal drive connector.
- Replace the internal disk drive.

Problem 2

Machine passes P.O.S.T., but neither internal drive operates.

Solutions:
- Try a known good floppy diskette.
- If you have recently been in the machine, verify that the disk drive cables are connected. Look for bent pins on the internal drive connector.
- Repair or replace the logic board. The chip most likely to be giving you a problem is the SWIM IC, which functions as the floppy drive controller interface. Take signal readings with a logic probe.

Problem 3

Diskette won't eject.

Solutions:
- Simultaneously hold down <Shift>, <Command>, and 1 (for the internal drive) or 2 (for the external drive).
- Pull down the File menu option and select Eject. Try this a few times.
- Eject the disk manually by inserting an open paper clip into the hole near the drive slot.
- Replace the disk drive.

Problem 4

Unable to insert the disk entirely into the floppy drive.

Solutions:
- Eject the disk manually by inserting an opened paper clip into hole beside the drive.
- Switch off the power and hold the mouse button down while switching the power back on (to complete eject cycle).
- Replace the disk drive.

Problem 5

Disk ejects; the display shows disk icon with the X.

Solutions:
- Possible bad diskette. Replace diskette with a known good one.
- Clean the disk drive with head cleaning kit.
- Replace the disk drive cable.
- Repair or replace the disk drive.

Problem 6

Disk drive runs continuously.

Solutions:
- Replace the bad disk.
- Replace the disk drive cable.
- Replace the disk drive.

Problem 7

Disk initialization fails.

Solutions:
- Verify that proper media is being used.
- Try another disk.
- Clean the floppy disk drive.
- Repair or replace the floppy disk drive.

SCSI-related problems
Problem 1

Internal hard drive runs continuously.

Solutions:
- Replace the hard drive cable with a known good cable.
- Replace hard drive.

Problem 2

Mac works with internal or external SCSI device but won't operate with both of them.

Solutions:
- Check all of your SCSI connections. Make sure you turn on external SCSI devices before you turn on the Mac. Make sure all of your cables are good.
- Make sure that the SCSI device ID switch setting on the external SCSI device is unique. It must not duplicate any ID switch or jumper setting on any other attached SCSI device.
- Check termination on the external SCSI device.
- Check termination on the internal SCSI device.

> **Note:** If you have a IIfx, please refer to Chapter 10 for specific information on the IIfx SCSI.

Problem 3

Internal hard disk won't operate.

Solutions:
- Make sure that your power supply is providing the proper DC outputs. If not, replace the power supply.
- Verify that the hard disk drive cable is good and properly attached.
- Make sure that there are no bent pins on the internal SCSI connector.

- Reinitialize, repair, or replace the hard disk drive. You may be experiencing a stiction problem with the drive, the drive may have a blown fuse on its circuit board, or the drive may be bad. Try another known good drive.
- Repair or replace the main logic board. The likely suspect is the SCSI controller chip on the logic board.

Problem 4

External hard disk won't operate, but the internal one works fine.

Solutions:

- Check all of your SCSI connections. Make sure you turn on external SCSI devices before you turn on the Mac. Make sure all of your cables are good.
- Make sure that the SCSI device ID switch setting on the external SCSI device is unique. It must not duplicate any ID switch or jumper setting on any other attached SCSI device.
- Check termination on the external SCSI device.
- Check termination on the internal SCSI device.
- You may have a blown SCSI port fuse on the logic board. This fuse is a 1-amp pico fuse and is usually designated with the letter "F." Its location is usually directly behind or in the vicinity of the DB-25 SCSI port connector.

    Note: If you have a IIfx, please refer to Chapter 10 for specific information on the IIfx SCSI.

Problem 5

External SCSI drive attached to a IIfx doesn't appear on the Desktop.

Solution:

- The problem is most likely termination related. Please refer to Chapter 10 for specific information on the IIfx SCSI.

Problems related to peripheral devices
Problem 1

Cursor doesn't move when mouse is moved.

Solutions:
- Verify the mouse connection.
- If the mouse was connected to a keyboard, connect it directly to the rear ADB port while the machine is off. Then turn the machine on. If the mouse works, replace the keyboard.
- If the mouse doesn't work in either of the ADB ports, try another mouse. If a new mouse works, then the old one was bad. If you don't have another mouse, use the Mactronics ADB port tester to verify the port; otherwise test ADB port with a voltmeter looking for +5 volts DC.
- If the new mouse doesn't work, or you don't get +5 volts DC, the most likely failure is the RF choke filter on the logic board. This filter looks like a small black box and sits behind the ADB ports. To test this port you perform a continuity test across the four sides of the filter. Also test the ADB fuse in that same area. These fuses are often disguised, but all have a board designation with the letter "F," as in F1. Also check the fuses by performing a continuity check. If the fuse reads open, replace it.

Problem 2

Cursor moves, but clicking the mouse button has no effect.

Solution:
- Repair or replace the mouse.

Problem 3

No response to any key on the keyboard.

Solutions:
- Check the keyboard connection to the rear ADB port.
- Replace the keyboard cable.
- Repair or replace the keyboard.

- Repair or replace the main logic board.
- Don't forget to check the RF choke filter located on the logic board. This filter is currently found on all newer Macintosh models. It is also possible that the ADB circuitry has failed.

Problem 4

Cannot double-click to open a disk or application.

Solutions:

- It is possible that you have too many System Folders and system files on your hard disk. Remove them and reinstall the system software.
- Repair or replace the mouse.

Problem 5

Known good printer won't print from the Mac.

Solutions:

- Make sure the printer is plugged in and turned on.
- Make sure that you have a good printer cable that is properly connected.
- Make sure the Chooser and the control panel are set correctly.
- Reinstall the Macintosh system software.
- Reinstall the application program that you are trying to print from.
- Repair or replace the logic board. Possible suspects on the logic board would be a printer port connector or a failure of the serial circuitry on the logic board.

Other problems

Problem 1

Real-time clock is not operating. Time is not being properly kept.

Solutions:

- Test the battery in circuit. You should read at least 2.75 to 3.25 volts, which is marginal. It is best if it reads above 3.25 to 3.75 volts.
- Repair RTC circuit on the logic board, or replace the logic board.

Problem 2

No sound coming from the speaker.

Solutions:
- Verify that volume setting in the control panel is set above 1.
- Replace the speaker.

Problem 3

IIfx locks up or displays an error code when the first application is launched.

Solutions:
- Make sure that your power supply is functioning properly. Test the outputs.
- Open up the unit and look for original Apple SIMMs manufactured by NEC. Replace any NEC SIMMs that have a date code of 9052 or earlier. Apple has a recall on these SIMMs and should take them back.
- If you are not using NEC SIMM, test the SIMMs and replace any that fail.

PowerBooks 100, 140, 145, and 170

Before attempting to repair any Macintosh PowerBook computer, you should first perform the five basic service checks summarized below. By doing so you rule out the possibility that there isn't some underlying cause of the perceived failure. Many simple problems often give the illusion that the failure is more serious than it really is.

1. Check the AC power adapter and the battery.

   A bad battery, a low battery, or a bad AC power adapter often causes the PowerBook to exhibit symptoms of a more serious failure. To perform these tests, you'll need to use an inexpensive digital voltmeter.

   For the AC power adapter test, follow these steps:

   a. Plug the AC power adapter into the wall outlet.
   b. Turn your voltmeter on and set it on the DC voltage scale. If your voltmeter isn't autoranging, place it on the first scale above 10 volts DC.

c. Touch and hold the positive (red) lead of the voltmeter to the inside of the adapter plug, which is positive. Then touch and hold the negative (black) lead of the voltmeter to the outside of the adapter plug, which is negative (-). Hold both leads firmly in place and watch your voltmeter for a DC voltage reading. Mentally note this number.

d. The nominal DC range for a good AC power adapter is between 7.5 and 8.0 volts DC. If your adapter's voltages are not within this specification, then you must replace it. Under no circumstances should you attempt to use the AC power adapter from the older Macintosh portables. The older adapters are not interchangeable with the PowerBooks and may result in serious damage to the computer

For the battery test follow these steps:

a. If you have any information stored in a RAM disk, save this information before moving on to the next step, or this information will be lost.

b. Disconnect the PowerBook from the AC adapter

c. Remove the battery. Be very careful not to short the positive and negative battery terminals together. Such a short could cause a battery discharge, a condition that could pose a safety and/or fire hazard to you. You should store this battery in an Apple-approved battery storage case, which is available at no charge from Apple computer. Call Apple at (800) 377-4127 for additional information.

d. Turn your voltmeter on and set it on the DC voltage scale. If your voltmeter is not autoranging, then place it on the first scale above 10 volts DC.

e. Touch and hold the positive (red) lead of the voltmeter to the battery contact marked (+), which is positive. Then touch and hold the negative (black) lead of the voltmeter to the battery contact marked (-), which is negative. Hold both leads firmly in place and watch your voltmeter for a DC voltage reading. Mentally note this number.

    f. The nominal reading for the battery is 5.75 volts DC. If your reading is less than that, you should attempt to recharge the battery. If the battery can not be recharged, then it must be replaced.

2. Verify that version 7.0.1 or later of the Macintosh system software is installed.

Strange problems with peripheral devices, such as printers, modems, and other serial devices or hard disk drive mounting and Desktop problems are often caused when the proper version of the system is not present. All PowerBooks must have at least System 7.0.1 or later to function properly.

3. Check all internal and external cable connections.

Poor cable connections internally and externally can often give the impression that a device or major component is not working properly. Rule out the obvious!

4. Verify that any installed add-in cards are configured and seated properly in their expansion sockets.

A poorly seated or misconfigured add-in card can cause both the card and the PowerBook to malfunction.

5. If all else fails, disconnect all external peripherals and remove any add-in cards (if installed).

When in doubt, always disconnect all external devices such as printers, scanners, ADB devices, disk drives, other SCSI devices, and internal add-in cards (such as modems). Many times if one of these devices fails, it can appear that the Power-Book is having the failure. If the PowerBook works properly after disconnecting the external devices, you have ruled out the PowerBook as the source of the problem. Once you have the bare bones PowerBook operational, you may then install each of the removed devices one at a time until you locate the culprit. This process of elimination is the key!

Problems related to power supply
Problem 1

Machine appears to be dead. The screen is blank.

Solutions:
- If the unit is a PowerBook 100, verify that the storage switch is in the on position and reset the unit. If the unit is either a model 140 or 170, reset the Power Manager.
- Connect the unit to the AC power adapter, plug the adapter in, and let the unit charge for 5 to 10 minutes. Then try to restart the unit.
- Test the AC power adapter and battery. Replace if necessary.
- Verify that all board and internal cable connections are good.
- Test and replace the keyboard assembly if necessary.
- Return the unit to Apple for service.

Problem 2

AC power adapter is plugged in and connected to the PowerBook, yet the battery DA does not show that the charger is attached.

Solutions:
- Make sure that the adapter is properly attached to the PowerBook.
- Test the wall outlet to ensure that you have line power. You can use a voltmeter or plug a lamp into that outlet to verify the outlet is functioning properly.
- Test the AC power adapter and the battery. If the AC power adapter is good and the battery still will not charge, then replace the battery.
- Make sure that the battery thermistor cable is making a good connection (140/170 only).
- Return the unit to Apple for service.

Problem 3

When first starting the computer, you are greeted with a low power warning.

Solutions:
- This is a sign that the battery needs to be recharged. Attach the AC power adapter.

- If you are using any peripheral devices, they must conform to the low power rating established by Apple.
- When operating the PowerBook solely on battery power, minimize the use of power-consuming devices such as disk drives and backlighting. If you need to make extensive use of these devices, attach the AC power adapter.
- Test the battery and replace if necessary. If operating while the unit is attached to the AC power adapter, test the adapter and replace if necessary.

Problem 4

Settings on control panel change after removing or replacing the battery.

Solutions:
- If you have a PowerBook 100 and have removed or replaced the primary battery only, you'll need to replace your back-up batteries. However, if you removed or replaced the backup as well, this is a very normal occurrence. When all sources of power are removed from the model 100, the contents of PRAM are lost. They can be reset through the control panel.
- If the unit was a 140 or 170 machine, you should verify that all connections to the interconnect board are good.
- Replace the interconnect board (140, 145, 170 only).

Video-related problems
Problem 1

Screen suddenly goes blank or the unit periodically shuts itself down every few minutes.

Solutions:
- No service action is required. The PowerBook has gone to sleep to save battery power. If the unit continues to shut itself down too frequently, then adjust the sleep delay time in the control panel. If you have access to an AC outlet, then connect the AC power adapter to save battery power.

Problem 2

Backlighting feature does not operate.

Solutions:

- If the unit is a model 100, 140, or 145, adjust the screen brightness. This does not apply to the 170, as this setting is preset at the factory.
- If the unit is a model 100, check all of the internal connections to the main logic board. If the model is a 140, 145, or 170, check the following connections: display, daughterboard, interconnect board, and the inverter board. It's very common for these cables to be accidentally cut or badly pinched. Replace bad cables if necessary.
- Repair or replace the inverter board (140, 145, or 170 only).
- Repair or replace the interconnect board (140, 145, or 170 only).
- Replace the logic board on the unit if it is defective.

Problem 3

Pixel problems, such as more than five pixels or a row of pixels do not come on, or a single pixel or row of pixels always stay on when they should be off.

Solutions:

It's acceptable and common to have five or less pixels that never come on. If you have more than five pixels or any of the aforementioned symptoms, follow these procedures:

- Verify that the display (all models) and interconnect board (140 and 170 only) connections are good and that cables are not pinched or otherwise torn.
- Try a known good display.
- Replace the interconnect board (models 140 and 170 only).

Problem 4

A very fine white line always appears in the middle of the screen.

Solution:

- No service action required. This symptom is typical for the PowerBook 100, 140, and 145 and any future PowerBook models that use a Film-compensated Supertwist Nematic (FSTN) display. It should never happen on a Power-

Book 170 or any future models that use a transmissive active matrix display. If you have a PowerBook 170 that exhibits this symptom, the unit is defective and should be returned to Apple.

Problem 5

Image on the display of a PowerBook model 100, 140, or 145 doesn't appear to be uniform.

Solution:
- No service action is required. This symptom is typical for the PowerBook 100, 140, and 145 and any future PowerBook models that use a Film-compensated Supertwist Nematic (FSTN) display. You can minimize the effect by adjusting the brightness and contrast controls. This should never happen on a PowerBook 170 or any future models that use a transmissive active matrix display. If you have a PowerBook 170 that exhibits this symptom, the unit is defective and should be returned to Apple.

Problem 6

Rainbow colors can be seen when looking at the PowerBook 100, 140, or 145 display from a sharp angle.

Solution:
- No service action required. This symptom is typical for the PowerBook 100, 140, and 145 and any future PowerBook models that use a Film-compensated Supertwist Nematic (FSTN) display. It won't happen on a PowerBook 170.

Problem 7

Machine passes P.O.S.T. and appears to be functioning properly, but there is nothing on the display.

Solutions:
- Adjust the brightness and contrast controls (models 100, 140, and 145 only).
- Check all internal connections. Make sure none of the cables are pinched or torn.

- Replace the invert board (140, 145, and 170 only).
- Replace the interconnect board (140, 145, and 170 only).
- Replace the display assembly.

Problem 8

Display of a PowerBook 100, 140, or 145 gets very dim or stops working.

Solution:

- No service action required. This symptom is usually caused when the unit has been exposed to temperatures outside Apple's acceptable operating range of 5 to 40 degrees Celsius. This symptom is typical for the PowerBook 100, 140, and 145 and any future PowerBook models that use a Film-compensated Supertwist Nematic (FSTN) display.

Problem 9

Fuzzy after-image (ghost) is apparent on the display of a PowerBook 100, 140, or 145.

Solution:

- No service action required. This symptom is typical for the PowerBook 100, 140, and 145 and any future PowerBook models that use a Film-compensated Supertwist Nematic (FSTN) display.

> **Note:** The SCSI, printing, peripheral device, and floppy disk drive problems on the PowerBooks are the same as those on other Macintosh computers.

Free fix: Apple has acknowledged that some of the floppy disk drives on the PowerBook 140, 145, and 170 exhibit numerous problems with formatting media and data transfer. Owners of models 140, 145, and 170 that have been experiencing these problems should call Apple directly at (800) 767-2775 to get the problem corrected.

Apple has also acknowledged that some of the trackball assemblies on the PowerBook 140, 145, and 170 are defective. The defective trackballs appear to malfunction when other ADB devices are connected to them. The problem has been corrected in newer models of the 140, 145, and 170. Apple will replace defective trackballs under warranty.

Other problems
Problem 1
Certain applications appear to be running slower after a few seconds.

Solution:
* This indicates that the unit is going into system rest. Attach the unit to the AC power adapter.

Problem 2
PowerBook 100 generates error chords (the death march) during the startup process.

Solutions:
* The error chords are generated as a result of a hardware failure during the startup process. The PowerBook 100 error chords have three parts: the standard startup tone, the error chord, and the test chord. If this unit generates these chords, you should

1. Turn the machine off and reconnect it to the AC power adapter for 5 to 10 minutes. Then restart the machine.
2. Disconnect all peripheral cables and devices from the unit, and remove the internal memory expansion card if present. Then try to restart the unit. If the problem persists, the failure is on the logic board. If not, one of the peripheral devices or cables is defective and was causing the system to malfunction. The primary suspect in this situation is the memory expansion card, if one is installed.

Problem 3

PowerBook 140, 145, or 170 generates error chords (the death march) during the startup process.

Solutions:

- The error chords are generated as a result of a hardware failure during the startup process. The PowerBook 140, 145, and 170 have two different sets of error chords generated when a failure occurs during start-up: a two-part, eight-tone error chord and a simple four-tone error chord. If the unit generates either of these error chord sets, you should

  1. Turn the machine off and reconnect it to the AC power adapter for 5 to 10 minutes. Then restart the machine.
  2. Disconnect all peripheral cables and devices from the unit. Restart the machine. Remove the internal modem if one is installed. Restart the machine. If the error chords do not recur, the problem was with one of the removed cables or devices.

- A two-part, eight-tone, error chord indicates that a memory failure has occurred. The most likely cause is a defective memory expansion card. You should first replace this card. If the error persists, you have a chip failure on the logic board. The logic board must be replaced.

- A simple four-tone error chord during startup indicates that a failure other than memory has occurred. This error chord is somewhat vague. You need to determine which module has failed by the following process of elimination:

  1. Turn the machine off. Disconnect the internal SCSI hard disk cable. Restart the machine. If the error chords do not recur, the hard disk drive or the SCSI cable is defective.
  2. Turn the machine off. Disconnect the floppy disk drive cable. Restart the machine. If the error chords do not recur, either the floppy disk drive or the cable is defective.
  3. If the error chords still persist, then the problem is a failure on the logic board.

CHAPTER 14

Printers and Printing Problems

Printers do one basic thing: produce hard copy from the computer, such as text and graphics. Some can even produce high-resolution color. A great variety of printers are available, and prices can range from under $100 to over $100,000, depending on the speed, quality, and precision of the output desired. Printers can be grouped into two basic categories: impact and nonimpact printers. These names refer to the methods used to produce the printed image.

Impact Printers

Impact printers use a striking device to transfer ink from a ribbon to the paper, forming the character. This striking device is either a daisy wheel, thimble, or dot matrix print head. The daisy wheel and thimble units are often referred to as a fully formed character printers, similar to a typewriter but with some extra features such as paper sheet feeders and bold print. In fact, the original microcomputer printers were based in part on the design of the IBM Selectric typewriter. These printers produce entire characters—such as A, B, C, 1, 2, 3—one at a time. Optional type fonts are easily obtained by replacing the existing print element with another element of the desired font.

Daisy Wheel Printers
Pros
- Excellent for forms (that is, multipart)
- High-quality text- or correspondence-grade print
- Very reliable
- Relatively inexpensive

Cons
- Very slow, typically less than 100 characters per second (cps)
- Single print wheel with single typefaces make integrating different typefaces clumsy
- Graphics capability is almost nonexistent
- Very noisy

Dot-matrix printers

Dot matrix printers form characters from the patterns of dots. These patterns are created by a moving print head. The print head contains several tiny needles, typically 9, 18, or 24. These needles strike the ribbon against the paper in the appropriate pattern necessary to produce the necessary characters. As the print head moves back and forth, a matrix of dots is placed on the paper, creating the text, graphics, or both. The higher the pin count in the print head, the better the print quality. For example, a 24-pin print head produces more dots per inch than a 9-pin head, making the print look fuller and more defined. This type of print technology offers increased speed and flexibility over the daisy wheel printers. The Apple ImageWriter printers are examples of printers that utilize this technology.

Pros
- Very flexible. The printer can print in draft, with near-letter-quality and letter-quality modes. Dot matrix printers can also print many type sizes without replacing the print element.
- Fast. Most dot matrix printers can deliver print speeds from 120 cps to over 600 cps.
- Works well with standard and multipart forms.
- Average graphics capability.
- Prices vary from low to high. However, many affordable models are available

Cons
- Even though the print is very good, dots and jagged edges are still visible. This problem gets worse as the type gets larger.
- Very loud. Many people find the noise offensive and purchase expensive soundproof cabinets

Nonimpact Printers

Even though dot matrix printers have been called the printers of the 1980s, they aren't well suited for all environments. The very nature of their impact print technology makes them noisy and places substantial limitations on print quality and speed. These limitations have made nonimpact printers very appealing to consumers. Nonimpact printers can produce both graphics and text with dots in a way similar to dot matrix printers. However, there are no print heads that strike the paper. Nonimpact printers typically fall into one of three categories: thermal, inkjet, and laser. The names refer to the method used to transfer the patterns of dots to the paper.

Thermal printers

Printing by a thermal printer is accomplished by heating the pins in a thermal print head, which causes a reaction on the chemically treated paper it uses. Even though the paper is special, this method of printing is fairly inexpensive. However, the print quality is often very poor, and these units are very slow. Thermal printers have never really caught on in the business community, but their low price has given them limited acceptance in the home and portable printer market.

Pros
- Quiet
- Inexpensive
- Most are very small in size and are portable

Cons
- Poor print quality
- Uses special paper
- Very slow
- Not widely accepted
- Not good with multipart forms

Inkjet printers

Inkjet printers have gained increasing popularity over the past several years. Inkjets utilize a print head equipped with a nozzle. As the print head travels across the page, ink is sprayed onto the paper line-by-line, forming the appropriate text and graphics. Instead of using a ribbon or thermal paper, these units house a small replaceable ink cartridge that feeds ink to the nozzle. Many inkjet printers come equipped with a paper bin that can accept standard 8 1/2 x 11" sheets of paper, rather than the fan-fold or thermal papers. One example of a popular inkjet printer is the Hewlett Packard DeskJet.

Pros
- Very quiet
- Excellent resolution, typically around 300 dots per inch
- Modestly priced (from $450 up to $1500+)
- Very Popular for people who want quality print at a reasonable price

Cons
- Slow, typically 1 to 2 pages per minute
- Ink cartridges tend to be expensive and don't last long
- On some of the less-expensive models, the pages smear easily and are often wet when "hot off the press," but the technology is constantly getting better
- Limited upgradability, and not good with multipart forms.

Laser printers

The laser printer has become the printer of the 1990s. This technology was introduced in 1983 by Canon USA and is an offshoot of the photocopying process. In both the laser printer and the photocopier, output is presentation-quality and is produced at high speeds—from 4 to over 17 pages per minute (ppm). The most popular laser printers, such as the HP Laserjet Series II and III, Apple LaserWriters, Canon, and Wang, are based on the Canon LBP-CX engine design and typically produce a resolution of 300 dpi x 300 dpi (dots per inch) at an average speed of about 8 pages per minute. Other companies, such as AST and Quadram, have based their laser printer designs around the Ricoh engine design. Although comparable in speed, consumables, maintenance, and upgrade options, the retail prices of these models tend to be higher than the Canon-based designs.

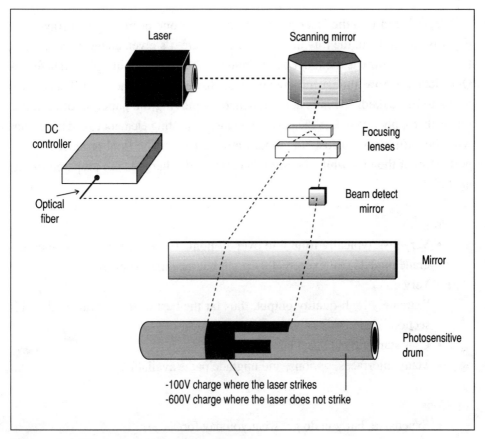

Figure 14-1. The laser printing process

Basic Theory of Operation

The laser printing process is very straightforward. Basically, your computer takes a picture of each page that you're working on and sends it to your laser printer to be "developed." This is accomplished through a series of complex operations. First, a pulsing laser beam is reflected off the internal optics (mirror). Second, this beam is adjusted by the focusing lenses. The beam then produces the picture dot-by-dot and line-by-line on the drum. The drum is a special photoconductive cylinder that holds an electrical charge. Toner, a colored powder-like material, is also charged. The toner is attracted to areas that have opposite charges and is repelled by areas that have like charges. The drum acts as a "negative" of sorts in order to transfer the image to the paper.

349

Paper is fed into the laser printer by means of one or more paper trays. The paper is moved from the tray into the printer where it's given an electrical charge; the paper then attracts the toner away from the drum and the image is transferred. Our picture is now almost fully developed. However, the toner is still "raw" and needs to be "baked." This is accomplished by moving the paper across internal rollers that apply pressure to the paper and toner. A heating element called the corona wire then affixes or "bakes" the toner onto the paper. The final product is transported out of the unit while the drum is cleaned, discharged, and prepared for the next picture.

Pros
- Very fast, typically from 4 to over 17 ppm. There are several commercial-grade models that exceed 100+ ppm, but they are expensive
- Very quiet
- Extremely high-quality output, thus far the best of those evaluated in this section
- Uses standard cut sheet paper
- Many interfaces, options, and upgrade paths available.

Cons
- Expensive, but you do get what you pay for
- Not good with multipart forms
- Laser printers are rather large and heavy

Summary

In conclusion, this section has examined various features of microcomputer printers including the pros and cons of both impact and nonimpact class printers as well as the advantages and basic theory behind laser printer technology. Next we focus on such details as print quality, fonts, and upgrade paths that you need to consider when evaluating or purchasing a laser printer.

Print Quality, Resolution, and Fonts

Because laser printers come in many shapes, sizes, and configurations, you must consider many factors and ask many questions before you can determine whether or not a particular printer will be appropriate for your needs. Here are some of the issues that you should address:

1. What is the resolution of the printer? A resolution of 300 dpi or better is desirable. This number is an indicator of the quality of the printed image. A rating of 300 dpi indicates that the density of the dots that form the image is 300 x 300 dots per square inch. Higher density equals a sharper image.

2. How much internal RAM (random access memory) does this printer come with? What can it be expanded to? Many fonts and page description languages (PDLs) that are available require substantial amounts of RAM to be properly loaded and utilized (such as Postscript). At a minimum you should have 1MB installed in your laser printer, but 2 to 4MB is preferable. Memory upgrades usually enable the printer to operate at an optimum level of performance.

3. How often do I have to replace consumable items such as toner cartridges, ozone filters, OPC belts, and so on? Consumable items cost money, and these expenses can add up quickly. Some printers such as the Ricoh and Ast are higher maintenance than the Canon and HP.

4. Standard versus optional features. Extra font cartridges, some paper trays, and PDLs (such as Postscript) are not factory equipment and tend to be pricey options. Always ask which fonts, trays, and PDLs are standard and which are optional.

5. Which interfaces does the printer support: RS-232, RS-422, Centronics, SCSI, or Appletalk? Any combination of the above? This is very important, as it has a direct bearing on which computer(s) you can attach the printer to. For instance, the basic HP Laserjet printers come standard with RS-232 and Centronics interfaces. You can also order a special HP with an Appletalk interface. But if you wanted to attach a standard HP to an Apple Macintosh right out of the box, you couldn't, unless you purchased the special HP with an Appletalk interface. You must either get another printer or purchase a special package called Macprint by Insight Development for about $125. This package includes the appropriate cables and software drivers necessary to attach the printer. These are things that you need to know up front!

Fonts

A font is best described as a complete set of letters, numbers, symbols, and punctuation marks in one size of a particular typeface, such as 12-point Times Roman Bold or 14-point Times Roman (the fonts used throughout this manual).

Fonts typically fall into one of two basic categories:

1. Display fonts, which are large fonts of 18 points (18/72 inch) or more
2. Book fonts, which are 14 points (14/72 inch) or less

Hundreds of fonts are available to you. It's very important that you're aware of which fonts come standard and which fonts are optional. Not all laser printers are capable of supporting every font on the market. Some printers can work with only bit-mapped fonts, while other printers work with scalable fonts. Some printers can work with both but require special upgrades. We'll discuss these issues next.

Bit-mapped fonts

No matter how good or solid your printer-generated output may appear, it's important to understand that these printed images are really made of tiny dots. Curves, circles, numbers, letters, and lines are all made up of dots. The tighter the dots are packed or placed, the better or more solid the output will be. There are two basic methods of placing the dots: bit-mapped screen fonts or scalable printer fonts.

A bit-mapped font is a detailed map made up of bits (corresponding dots) that are used to form an approximation of the desired character (kind of like connecting dots to form the character). Bit-mapped fonts produce well-formed characters, especially in point sizes less than 20. The larger the point size, the more noticeable the jagged dot patterns become, which is not desirable when you want to produce high-grade print. If you look very closely at the large type size below, you'll notice the difference.

36-pt printer font

36-pt scaled bit map

This example was generated on a Macintosh computer using both bit-mapped and scalable fonts. Unfortunately, the HP laser printers that I use don't have the Adobe Postscript option, which would allow me to print both the scalable fonts as well as the bit-mapped fonts. The end result is that I have to settle for an all bit-mapped manuscript for now (which is OK for me). The scalable fonts would have been smoother, but I still think the bit-mapped looks pretty decent. However, hard-core desktop publishing folks would be having a fit with my bit- mapped example.

Scalable fonts

Scalable fonts are very different from their bit-mapped brothers and sisters. Rather than using a bit map to form an approximation of the character, scalable fonts use a mathematical model or an algorithm to produce the characters—basically a mold or outline of where the dots are to be placed or "poured," kind of like cement. This mold doesn't say "This is a Times Roman 12-point character or a Courier 10-point character." Instead it determines placement and distance relationships and ratios of the various locations of the character such as top, bottom, curves, and so on. So, in effect, you only need the basic outline of a particular font such as Generic Courier or Times Roman rather than Courier 10, 12, 14, or 20 and Times Roman 12, 14, or 24. Theoretically the outline can be increased or decreased (scaled) to almost any size, as long as the distance ratios are proportionally balanced (meaning you don't go overboard, like a Times Roman 95000 point). In general, scalable fonts have a much smoother and cleaner look to them. Most high-grade publications utilize the scalable fonts.

What fonts do you have built into your printer? Most printers have a built-in test routine that you can execute to see which fonts are "native" or built into your printer. Most manufacturers mention this test in their operation guides or user manuals. For example, it's very easy to generate a font printout on the very popular HP Laserjet III by following the procedure given below. Both standard built-in fonts and optional cartridge fonts (if any) are listed.

Font determination procedure

To list the fonts built into your printer, complete the following procedures:

1. Make sure that the printer is turned on and has warmed up.
2. Take the printer off line by pressing the <On-line> button once. The yellow light will go off.
3. Depress the <Print Fonts / Test> button one time, and a listing of your fonts will be printed. This listing should be several pages long. The following pages are examples of a typical HP Laserjet III listing.

It's even easier to perform this on the Apple LaserWriter printers. The only thing you have to do is power on the LaserWriter. If it's in working condition, a test print page is generated automatically for you.

Internal fonts

Several internal fonts come standard with the laser printer from the factory. Typically, these fonts are your average fonts, nothing fancy or sophisticated. However, manufacturers usually have a large assortment of optional font cartridges or soft fonts that you can purchase.

Font cartridges

Font cartridges are a decent way of expanding your font collection (if your printer permits it). Additional fonts give you a great deal of variety and options when composing documents and graphics. The only drawback to optional font cartridges is that they are somewhat expensive and you may not get everything you want on one cartridge. This means you might have to buy several cartridges, which can add up to a small fortune.

The cartridges themselves are about the size of fat cassette tapes and are easily inserted into a slot on the printer. For instance, the HP III supports two optional font cartridges, left and right. Font cartridges are always resident (available) on the printer, and they do not occupy any memory or disk space on the computer. However, it isn't a bad idea to upgrade your printer's memory to 1 or 2MB or more.

Pros

- Easy to install
- Many to choose from
- When installed, they reside in the printer and are readily available
- Cartridge fonts load very quickly

Cons

- Very expensive
- You have to buy several cartridges to get all of the good fonts
- Hard to mix fonts in your document that reside on several cartridges

Soft fonts

Soft fonts are software-based fonts that reside on the computer, not on the printer. Since these fonts aren't printer-resident, they need to be downloaded or "sent down" to the printer. This can be a very slow process. Additionally, soft fonts take up memory and disk space on the computer.

Pros

- Inexpensive and abundant. Many user- and special-interest groups have extensive font collections that are shareware (free or almost free).
- Flexible. You can integrate many different fonts easily, and you can eliminate fonts that you don't want.

Cons

- The downloading process to the printer is very slow.
- Soft fonts occupy disk space and memory on the computer.
- Soft fonts are software that reside on the disk drive. They can become corrupt very easily, which can cause severe printing problems and miscues.

Page Description Languages (PDLs)

When people want to effectively communicate with one another, they speak in a manner that is easily understood. A failure to communicate would, of course, result in a misunderstanding or other problems. When we create documents and presentations on the computer and output them to the printer, these two pieces of hardware need to communicate. The language spoken here is commonly referred to as a page description language or PDL.

Examples of PDLs are
- HPPCL5 and HPPCL for Hewlett Packard printers
- Truetype and Quickdraw for Apple LaserWriter printers
- Adobe Postscript, an industry accepted standard language for the higher-end laser printers

Adobe Postscript

The Adobe Postscript PDL has become the de facto standard for page languages in the desktop publishing world. High-quality printers come standard with Postscript. Postscript is also a very popular option that most manufacturers offer as an upgrade for non-Postscript models. It's an expensive but worthwhile option if you can afford it.

Postscript supports scalable fonts that result in improved output. However, the real beauty of Postscript is that it can be used on many different computer systems and laser printers. This is especially handy when different platforms need to be compatible and work with one another's text and graphics. Postscript provides the common ground needed to bring everybody together.

Summary

In this section we have reviewed how to properly select and evaluate the various laser printers in the marketplace. Fonts and page description languages were discussed as well. The next section covers several printer interfaces, such as RS-232 and Centronics, as well as important configuration information.

Laser Printer Interfaces and Configurations

In the previous section we talked about PDLs that the computer and printer use to talk to one another. To take that discussion one step further, these devices cannot talk unless there is some physical connection between them. This connection is obtained through cables and a suitable interface on both the printer and computer. Interfaces are the focus of this section.

Printer interfaces can be broken down into two basic categories, serial and parallel. Let's take a closer look at each of these.

Serial interfaces

The most common type of serial interface is RS-232, which is a communications standard promoted by the Electronic Industries Association (EIA). This standard defines a 25-pin cable and establishes the rule by which data is transmitted serially. Most computers today have an RS-232 (serial) port. Many printers are also RS-232-compatible as well. The problem is that RS-232 is a very loose standard. Some manufacturers don't follow the rules and only use 8 or 9 of the 25 pins, which makes things pretty confusing for the layperson.

For instance, an IBM PC/XT uses a 25-pin connector, an IBM AT uses a 9-pin connector, and an Apple Macintosh uses a round 8-pin connector. All of these computers are RS-232 compatible, but they are still somewhat unique. Special port adapters are sometimes required to attach standard RS-232 printers (which typically have either 9 or 25-pin connectors) to these machines.

Pros
- Although a little confusing, RS-232 is a well-defined standard that has been around a long time. Many computer and printer manufacturers support this standard.
- RS-232 cables are very easy to make.

Cons
- Getting over the initial confusion is a bit frustrating, and port adapters are clumsy to work with.
- Cables generally should not exceed 50 feet.
- Serial data transmission is done one bit at a time, which is slow.

The common speed for serial data transmission between IBM PCs and compatibles and laser printers is approximately 9600 baud. Typical speeds between the Apple Macintosh computers and laser printers is approximately 19,200 baud. Generally speaking, baud refers to the transmission speed of a communications channel. Baud rates are commonly used to represent bits per second. In a typical PC serial (asynchronous) data transmission, 10 bits are used to represent one character, such as the letter A. Roughly calculated 9600 baud would equal approximately 960 characters or bytes of data transmitted per second. It is necessary to match the baud rate of the computer and the printer to ensure that data is transmitted properly.

Serial printing and the Macintosh

If you are attempting to attach a Hewlett Packard Laser Printer to your Macintosh computer, you'll need a special software and cable package called MacPrint by Insight. This package is necessary because the Macintosh operating system doesn't directly support the HP printers. Specifically, the print drivers (also known as resources) aren't there. Mac Print is less than $125 and provides these drivers and the special cable (25- to 8-pin) to connect the DB-25 HP serial port to the Din 8-pin Mac serial port. This package is easily installed. After you install MacPrint, simply use the mouse pointer to pull down the Apple command menu (upper left), go into the Chooser, and click on the icon that represents the printer you want to use. The corresponding software (printer) drivers will be loaded for you. If you don't want to use MacPrint, you can always purchase the HP printer with the built-in Appletalk interface.

If both your Mac and the printer have Appletalk interfaces, configuration is a snap. You simply need the 8-pin round din cable (on both ends) and the appropriate driver. Go into the Chooser, select the icon, and the Mac will do the rest.

Note that the appropriate print driver must be properly installed in the System Folder for it to be recognized under the Chooser.

Centronics parallel printer interface

The most common printer interface in the PC world is the parallel interface, which is frequently referred to as the Centronics interface. It is named after Centronics Corp., the company that developed it.

As the name implies, a parallel interface provides enough lines (wires) to transmit 8 bits (1 byte) at once rather than one bit at a time like the serial interface. The parallel interface is much faster than the serial interface, and it's a lot easier to work with. The parallel interface on the laser printer is a 36-pin connector: 16 pins are data lines (8 bits each way), and several of the remaining lines are dedicated to handshaking and control. Handshaking signals permit the computer and printer to inform each other of their status and conditions.

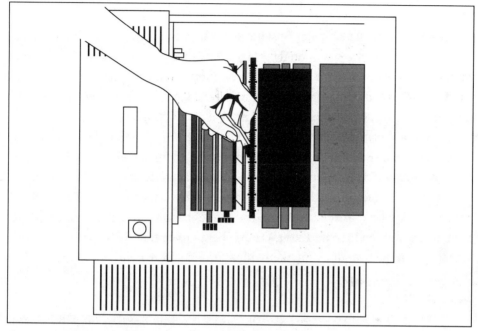

Figure 14-2. Cleaning the discharge rollers

Pros

- Widely accepted printer interface and very easy to work with.
- Very fast (8 bits at a time as opposed to 1 at a time).

Cons

- Most, but not all, of the manufacturers follow the rules for the parallel Centronics interface standard. This makes for an occasional incompatibility.
- Cables cannot usually exceed between 6 to 30 feet without some sort of line booster.

It's possible to purchase an adapter to connect a Centronics-type printer to a Macintosh computer via the SCSI port on the Macintosh. Hewlett Packard is one of several companies that makes this device (referred to as a Centronics-to-SCSI adapter). The advantage is you can take an inexpensive parallel printer from the PC world (that you might have lying around in a pile) and quickly and inexpensively adapt it to work in Mac Land. Don't forget you still need the corresponding print driver.

SCSI Interface

The SCSI (Small Computer Systems Interface), is an ANSI standard interface. This interface is very popular on the Macintosh as well as on the newer computers coming out. It's not really a printer or drive interface, it's a systems or intelligent interface. In fact, monitors, printers, hard drives, tape units, scanners, and practically anything can be designed to work around the SCSI interface.

SCSI is a versatile, high-speed parallel interface widely used in Macintosh computers and some IBM PS/2 machines. The Macintosh implementation of SCSI utilizes either 25 or 50 pins, depending on the device attached and its cabling scheme. Fortunately, all Macs, from the Mac Plus on up, come standard with a DB-25 SCSI port. There are several excellent printers on the market today that support SCSI, such as the high-end Apple LaserWriters. I anticipate that SCSI will gain wider acceptance in the overall PC market within the next 18 months.

Summary

In this section we've covered the various configuration considerations that you should know when dealing with laser printers. We also took a look at the various printer interfaces that are available. Some printers still only come with one interface (serial or parallel). Other printers, such as HP and Canon, give you two interfaces (serial and parallel), and an optional third interface such as Appletalk. Other manufacturers, like Texas Instruments and QMS, give you all three or multiple interfaces. This allows both your PCs and Macs to talk to the same printer without the need for a network. I believe that the multiple interface (3+) laser printers are the way to go if you have different types of computers (Mac, IBM, and so on) all over the place and if you can afford it. If you only have Macs, get an Apple LaserWriter or compatible with an Appletalk interface.

ImageWriters and Other Dot Matrix Printers

Q. Can I use the same cable to attach both a standard ImageWriter printer or an ImageWriter II to my Macintosh IIcx?

A. No, you can't. The original ImageWriter and 15-inch ImageWriter use a DB-25 connector. The ImageWriter II, II-L, and II-LQ use the DIN 8 connector, which is the same connector found on the back of any Mac from the Plus on up. Therefore, the cables required to attach a standard ImageWriter and an ImageWriter II will be different.

Q. What resolution and print speed does an ImageWriter II support?

A. An ImageWriter II supports three different levels of print quality: near-letter-quality (NLQ), standard, and draft print. NLQ is the highest quality print supported. While in this mode the ImageWriter II can produce output at a rate of 45 characters per second (cps). The second mode supported by the ImageWriter II is called standard print. In this mode the ImageWriter can generate output of average quality at a rate of 180 cps. The last mode supported is draft mode. This mode is the fastest of the three modes at 250 cps. However, the quality of the print is the lowest. Draft mode is commonly used when you need a "quick and dirty" printout as opposed to something that is correspondence quality.

Q. Can my ImageWriter II support color printing? If so, how can this be accomplished?

A. The ImageWriter II can support color printing provided that you have a color ribbon installed and a software package that can support color printing.

Q. How many colors can the ImageWriter II support in color printing mode?

A. The ImageWriter can support printing in seven colors. Actually it's six colors plus black.

Q. Every time I try to print a document of over 20 pages on my ImageWriter printer, my Mac hangs up until the print job is near completion. Is there anyway that I can free up my Mac so I can work while the document is printing ?

A. Yes, Apple sells an inexpensive 32K memory option card for the ImageWriter. The memory on this card allows your printer to hold a document up to approximately 20 pages long, which frees up your Mac to print extra-long documents.

Q. Does the ImageWriter II family of printers have a built-in diagnostic routine that the user can perform? If so, how can this be accomplished and when should it be performed?

A. Yes, the ImageWriter II has a built-in diagnostic. You should run it whenever you set up an ImageWriter for the first time or when you suspect that there might be a problem. I also run it every time I install a color ribbon to test the various colors.

To execute this test, you must perform the following steps:

1. Make sure the printer is off.
2. Hold down the form feed button while you turn on the printer.
3. Immediately release the form feed button.
4. The test printout will begin and continue until you turn off the printer. I always run this test for at least 60 seconds.
5. Turn off the printer when you are finished.

Q. What exactly is printed on the test printout page, and how does this help me?

A. Several important things are printed on the test printout. First, the ROM revision and dip switch settings are displayed, and then the actual character set is generated. The repeated printing of the character set is well worth examining closely. It's important for you to make sure that all of the characters are complete and well formed. In addition, it's important to examine the spacing between the characters and lines to make sure that the characters are of equally dark print (no light spots). This test also can be used to tell you quickly if the problem is really with the printer. Chances are if this test comes out OK, your printer is probably alright and you may have either a cable problem or some other problem with your Mac (such as Chooser not being set and so on).

Q. If my characters aren't well formed or if I have light print on my ImageWriter, what should I check first?

A. As a rule of thumb for any dot matrix printer, the first thing you should always check in this situation is the ribbon. The ribbon shouldn't be loose, and it should be positioned between the paper and ribbon guides. Also, make sure that your paper is straight and that your ribbon isn't old or dried out. Another good idea is to inspect the print head for debris or signs of head damage.

Q. **Do you recommend doing a screen print as a quasi-diagnostic test? If so, how is this accomplished?**

A. The screen dump or print is a very useful tool to verify that the ImageWriter, Macintosh Chooser settings, and cable configuration are all good and working as a team. If one of these players isn't working, the screen print won't happen.

To perform a screen print you must

1. Make sure ImageWriter is on and the cables are properly connected.
2. Depress the <Caps Lock> key into its on position.
3. Depress and hold down the <Command> and <Shift> keys. While these keys are being held down, type the number 4.
4. If the ImageWriter configuration is correct, then the contents of your screen will be displayed.

If the test doesn't execute, repeat the test. It's possible you didn't hold down the proper keys. If that still doesn't work, verify the following:

1. Make sure that the printer cable is securely attached to the Mac and the printer.
2. Verify that you've select the correct printer driver (resource) in the Chooser. For instance, if you have an ImageWriter attached, it would not be acceptable to choose the LaserWriter print driver. Make sure that the appropriate icon is selected and that you've chosen the appropriate port. The appropriate port would be the port that your printer is plugged into. Your choices are the modem port or the printer port.
3. Verify that the AppleTalk active/inactive setting is set to inactive.
4. Repeat the test again.

Q. What are the standard dip switch settings for the ImageWriter II printer, and what would that configuration be?

A. The dip switch settings for a default or standard configuration are:

Switch 1 (SW1)	1	2	3	4	5	6	7	8
	Off	Off	Off	Off	Off	On	Off	Off

Switch 2 (SW2)	1	2	3	4
	On	On	Off	Off

These settings configure your ImageWriter II to the following:

- American character set
- No line feed on carriage return
- 9600 baud transmission speed
- 11-inch forms
- Disable perforation skip
- 12 cpi (characters per inch)
- DTR serial handshake
- No option cards installed

Q. Recently we had a bad electrical storm. The surge suppressor that my ImageWriter was plugged into was damaged. I replaced the surge suppressor. However, my ImageWriter still refuses to come on. Where do I begin to look for a solution to my problem?

A. The first thing that you should do is try another wall outlet, or test the one you are plugged into. It's possible that the circuit breaker for that outlet tripped during the storm. If the breaker is OK, then try another power cord. If that doesn't work, the problem is most likely on your ImageWriter drive PCB board.

The drive PCB board is located on the bottom of the ImageWriter. This module contains the power supply, print head and motor circuitry. It's protected by two fuses. Fuse 1 has an electrical current rating of 1 amp. Fuse 2 is rated at 5 amps. It's possible that one or even both of these fuses took a shot. You'll need to perform a fuse continuity test on them with your voltmeter. However, it's been my experience that if these fuses took a hit, you have a 50/50 chance that this board will work when you replace the fuses. The third thing that could have been damaged is the 120-volt AC transformer, which is also mounted on the drive PCB board. This transformer converts the incoming 110/115 AC line current into 28 volts DC that the ImageWriter uses. If you have a decent knowledge of electronics, transformer replacement is simple. However, it's much easier (and more expensive) to exchange your dead drive PCB for a rebuilt one or send the dead one out to a board repair shop.

Q. **What preventive maintenance should I do on my ImageWriter printer?**

A. You should always keep your printer clean and free of loose debris by routinely vacuuming or blowing it out with a can of air. If debris and grease start to build up on the moving parts, it may be necessary to clean and lubricate the printer. Only use nonconductive cleaning solvents inside the printer. If you have to lubricate the printer, go easy on the application of the lubricant. I always use a silicon-based lubricant or a lithium-based grease. It's also a good idea to clean any contacts that look corroded and to reseat any cables that may have wiggled loose.

Q. **My print head is misfiring and causing very erratic print quality. Can I fix or rebuild the print head, or should I purchase a brand new one?**

A.Unless you're very, very experienced at print head repair, I wouldn't attempt it. There are many tiny wires inside the print head that must be properly placed. It really isn't worth your while to try this on your own. However, several companies specialize in print head repair at less than one half the price of a new one with a full warranty. One of the best companies is Impact Print Heads, located in Texas. Often I can get a rebuilt print head from them faster than I can get a new one from my local Apple dealer. I also get it much cheaper. If you're really in a pinch, you should buy the new print head if the dealer has it. But if you aren't in a big hurry, go for the rebuilt print head and save some money. Before you replace your print head, try cleaning it with isopropyl alcohol and a fine, clean cloth.

Q. **What's your opinion of using inexpensive re-inked printer ribbons?**

A. I've seen very few re-inked printer ribbons that I would consider as even close to the same overall quality as new ribbons. New ribbons give you crisp, fresh characters and last a fairly long time. Most re-inks are OK for a little while, but then the quality really drops off. You get what you pay for.

Q. **What's the function of the main PCB board in my ImageWriter printer? What are the symptoms if this module fails?**

A. The ImageWriter main PCB board is essentially the brain of the printer. This board receives and interprets all data coming from the computer and processes it. In addition, it provides the drive PCB with control signals. This board also monitors all of the dip switches, sensors and ribbon type, home switch, and cover open switches. Finally, the main PCB synchronizes the printing process. If this board was to fail outright, the printer usually powers on but doesn't pass the self test.

Q. **What are the most common problems that users experience when working with the Apple ImageWriter printers ?**

A. It's my experience that most problems with printers in general are caused by user error or oversight. Examples would be improper cabling or configuration, wrong dip switch settings, loose ribbon, incorrect control panel settings, no paper, not plugged in, or wrong print mode.

However, the ImageWriter does have two very common failures:

1 Worn out print heads. When the print head becomes worn out or defective, the print quality decreases rapidly. Common output problems are no print, half printed characters, gibberish, or light print. It's usually necessary to replace the print head or have it rebuilt. However, it isn't a bad idea to try cleaning the print head first. Make sure the print head is lined up properly when you replace it. Take your time, and don't force it.

2. Loose ribbon wire. When the ribbon wire becomes loose, the quality of the print will sporadically go from light to dark. The ribbon wire actuates or moves the gear down the ribbon assembly. When the ribbon wire is loose,

it tends to slip, which prevents the ribbon cartridge from advancing. It's important to make sure that your cables aren't loose.

LaserWriter Troubleshooting

Q. **I recently purchased an Apple LaserWriter. I plan to connect it to my Macintosh at home. What things do I need to consider in selecting an appropriate location?**

A. First, it's advisable to place your LaserWriter on a level surface. Second, the room temperature should be between 50 and 90 degrees Fahrenheit, with a humidity level between 20 and 80 percent. Third, there should be adequate room around the laser printer for air to circulate freely. Finally, your LaserWriter shouldn't be exposed to open flames, noxious fumes, or direct sunlight.

Q. **Is it OK to move my LaserWriter around with the toner cartridge installed?**

A. It's OK to move your LaserWriter very short distances without removing the toner cartridge. However, if you plan to transport your LaserWriter, the toner cartridge should be removed before transport.

Q. **Is there any real difference between an HP series II or III Laserjet printer and the Apple LaserWriter IINT? Which is better ?**

A. Both the HP and LaserWriter II are built around the same Canon engine design. Internally, many of the components are identical. However, there are some subtle cosmetic differences. The Apple LaserWriter IINT comes standard with Postscript version 47, the HP does not. Therefore, the main interface board is different in these machines. To answer the second part of your question, it's very difficult to say which is better without knowing your budget or needs. What's best for you is what works for you. I happen to like them both. If I were looking for a decent, economical laser printer, I would go with the HP III with the third-party Mac Print package. If I wanted to do some decent graphics work, I would go with the Apple LaserWriter. It's really a matter of choice and application.

Q. Are laser printers easy for the average user to service ?

A. No. Laser printers are very complex pieces of equipment. There are many screws, wires, modules and other pieces that must be replaced exactly as they were removed. In addition, to perform many of the service tests, you have to be properly trained because there are areas inside the laser printer where a high-voltage hazard exists. However, there are some routine procedures that you can perform.

Q. What routine procedures? And is it worth it, or should I just take my laser printer to the dealer for all of my service needs?

A. The laser printer is very heavy. It would be unwise (from a hernia standpoint) to lug the beast down to the dealer for T.L.C. It's also very expensive to have the dealer come to your site. The average user should have no problem performing routine preventative maintenance (PM) procedures. These procedures are very important and are frequently overlooked.

PM is useful for preventing problems before they happen. If more people would take better care of their laser printers, they would not have to worry so much about the repair aspect. I know of several laser printers that have been running problem-free for five or six years, with the only repair being basic PM. An ounce of prevention is worth a pound of cure. There are six routine things that you can do to prolong the life of your laser printer:

1. Replacing the toner cartridge when necessary. The toner cartridge is a very important component of the laser printer. It does much more than hold toner. It's a key player in the image-formation and developing system of your laser printer. Not only is toner stored inside the cartridge, but also there is a photosensitive drum, developing cylinder, cleaning blade, and a primary corona grid. When a malfunction occurs in this unit, you may experience problems, such as fuzzy lines, toner stains, thin vertical white lines or stripes, fuzzy vertical lines, all black or all white sheets of paper, and very dark or light print. To replace the toner cartridge you must

    a. Turn the printer off, open the top cover and remove the old toner cartridge.

b. Unpack the new cartridge from its box, then rock the cartridge from side to side to evenly distribute the toner.

c. Install the new toner cartridge.

e. Remove the sealing tab and tape.

f. Close the top cover and then replace the cleaning pad.

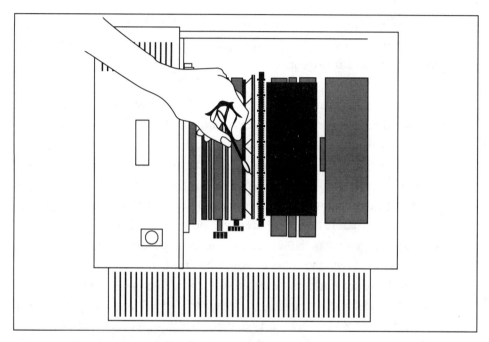

Figure 14-3. Cleaning the transfer wire corona

2. Cleaning the transfer corona wire when necessary. The transfer corona wire is very thin piece of wire located inside the center area of the laser printer. It's almost transparent and is directly under a mesh of very thin crisscross wires. The purpose of the transfer corona wire is to place an electrical charge on the paper, which attracts the toner from the drum to the paper. When there is a problem with the transfer corona, you may experience problems such as light print, gray images, or thin lines or stripes. The normal solution to this problem is cleaning of the transfer corona wire. Occasionally these wires break and must be replaced. To clean the transfer corona wire, use the steps listed on the following page.

a. Turn the unit off and open the top cover.

b. Locate the transfer corona wire and perform a visual inspection.

c. Gently clean the wire using a Q-tip and alcohol.

d. Inspect the area again, making sure you didn't break the wire or leave any debris.

If you're still having problems after you clean the transfer corona wire, it's possible that the problem is the primary cartridge corona wire located inside the toner cartridge, or the toner cartridge itself.

3. Clean the primary cartridge corona wire. The primary corona wire, located inside the toner cartridge, applies a uniform layer of negative electrical charge across the photosensitive drum surface. This prepares the drum to receive the laser beam. Where the laser beam strikes the drum, the negative charge is removed. The negatively charged toner then is attracted to the areas on the drum hit by the laser and form the page image. The reason they attract is that these areas are now more positive than the negatively charged areas. Now the paper is more positively charged than the drum areas. When the paper contacts the drum, the toner is attracted away from the drum to the more positively charged paper (opposite charges attract). This process transfers the image from the drum to the paper. When the primary corona wire is dirty or defective, this process is affected. Often the symptom are either vertical stripes, foggy stripes, or a completely black image. To clean the primary corona wire you must

a. Turn the laser printer off and open the top cover.

b. Clean the cartridge wire by using the small cleaning tool that comes with the printer. This tool fits into a groove on the cartridge. You simply have to slide it back and forth to clean the primary corona wire.

c. Replace the toner cartridge and close the top lid. If the cleaning doesn't clear up this problem, try another toner cartridge.

4. Clean the separation belt. The separation belt is located to the rear left of the LaserWriter. It basically peels the left side of the paper away from the drum

in the toner cartridge. This belt often becomes dirty, and stains frequently appear on the paper. These stains are often irregular-shaped vertical lines. If a proper cleaning does not remedy the stains, it's possible that the rollers inside the laser are dirty. If the rollers aren't dirty, the problem is most likely inside the toner cartridge. To clean the separation belt you must

    a. Open the top cover and locate the separation belt.

    b. Using a clean cotton swab dipped in alcohol, carefully clean the separation belt. If you visually see any other debris in the unit, it must be wiped or vacuumed out.

5. Replace the cleaning pad as necessary. Whenever you replace the toner cartridge, it's also a good idea to replace the fuser assembly cleaning pad as well. The purpose of this felt pad is to clean the upper fuser pressure roller. When the pad gets dirty, the upper roller passes contaminants to the lower pressure roller, which then transfers streaks or lines to the paper. To replace the cleaning pad you must

    a. Turn the printer off and open the top cover.

    b. Locate the top lid of the fuser assembly. It should be green in color.

    c. Open this lid and remove the old cleaning pad.

    d. Install the new cleaning pad/felt

    e. Close the fuser lid and top cover.

6. Clean the interior of your laser printer. Obviously, a clean laser printer is a happy laser printer. Unfortunately, loose toner and other debris build up over time. Therefore, a thorough cleaning is necessary. I always clean out my laser using a special 3M vacuum designed for laser printers. Since toner is actually lighter than dust, it catches these particles using a micron filter. Then I wipe down the inside using a fine, clean cloth with a little bit of alcohol. I pay special attention to the transfer guides, transfer rollers, bottom of the toner cartridge, and the feeder guide. I don't use WD-40 or any other lubricating sprays to grease up the printer. It's not a good idea to spray these things inside the laser printer. If you have a squeaky gear or

something, you can apply a very small amount of lithium grease to that area. That way you don't have lubricant being shot all over the place.

Q. **I keep getting paper jams and curls on my LaserWriter after I load it with paper. What should I do ?**

A. The first thing you should do is open the unit and clear any paper that is obstructing the paper path, which is giving you the paper jam. The paper curls are usually caused by the use of improper paper. The proper paper is 16- to 20-pound bond (standard copier paper).

Q. **I get frequent paper jams after continuous use. But when I open up the LaserWriter, there are no jams to be found. If I turn off the unit for a half hour or so, it works fine for several hours. What is going on here?**

A. The main cause of the "paperless" jams is timing. Almost every stage of the printing process is timed. The first thing you should check is the wiring from the display to the DC controller module. Look very carefully for any loose wire connections. If everything looks in order, then the likely culprit is the DC controller. One of the functions of the DC controller is to command and monitor sensors to report on a paper jam condition. The other suspect would include either the pickup or delivery sensor that communicates with the DC controller. However, since your problem went away after the unit was off for awhile, I believe that you have an intermittent failure on the DC controller module. This module is apparently heating up and then cutting out.

Q. **The Ready/Wait indicator on my LaserWriter doesn't stop flashing. I even waited for over an hour and it just kept flashing and refused to come online. Could the problem be my cables or my Mac?**

A. No. Unfortunately a Ready/Wait indicator that flashes for more than a few minutes is stuck in an infinite loop. The most likely cause for this situation is a main I/O board failure. The main PCB is trying to communicate to the engine via the DC controller, it's getting hung up, and the light never stops flashing. One way of positively verifying this would be to check the green test LED on the back of the laser unit. If it's on, the main I/O board is your culprit.

$Q_\bullet$ I have an old LaserWriter printer. I need to know what all of the status lights indicate. Sometimes they flash and other times they remain steady. Why?

A. Below is a chart that explains the various status lights and their meanings on an old LaserWriter:

Table 14-1.

	Flashing	Steady
Green	Warming up	Ready to print
Yellow	The unit is getting ready to print something.	Paper tray is empty
Red	N/A	Paper jam alert
Test LED on back of LaserWriter	Bad news, main I/O board failure or other serious problem	

$Q_\bullet$ The Ready/Wait indicator on my LaserWriter doesn't stop flashing. I even waited for over an hour and it just kept flashing and refused to come online. Could the problem be my cables or my Mac?

A. No. Unfortunately a Ready/Wait indicator that flashes for more than a few minutes is stuck in an infinite loop. The most likely cause for this situation is a main I/O board failure. The main PCB is trying to communicate to the engine via the DC controller, it's getting hung up, and the light never stops flashing. One way of positively verifying this would be to check the green test LED on the back of the laser unit. If it's on, the main I/O board is your culprit.

$Q_\bullet$ Is there an easier way for me to test the functionality of my Laser-Writer IINT printer other than turning it off and on to generate the user test page?

A. Yes. You can perform a very easy test called an engine test. The engine test switch is located on the right side of the laser printer behind a small removeable panel. The button itself is down a 4- or 5-inch hole. If you press this button, a test page is printed with "zebra stripes," which is normal. Try to use something nonmetalic when you push this button in such as the bottom of a Bic pen. On the older LaserWriters, you'll have to manually jump pins 1 and 2 on J-205 to perform this test.

Q. I did an engine test and the striped pages kept on printing and wouldn't stop. Now every time I turn my LaserWriter on, I get zebra stripes. How do I make them stop?

A. When you perform the engine test, you only need to hold the button down momentarily. If you have an older LaserWriter, you quickly short jumper pins 1 and 2. If for any reason you hold it down more than one or two seconds, the unit will keep spewing pages until it runs out of paper, or until you turn it off. Now, if you've turned off the printer and then turned it back on, and you still get the striped pages, that would tell me that the button is stuck. Try working the button (off and on) several times to unstick it.

Q. What are the symptoms of a bad engine in my laser printer?

A. A bad engine (sometimes called a motor) does one very simple thing: It rotates the gears that drive the paper-feeding system. In addition, it rotates the gears used by the drum. Most engine failures result in a paper jam condition. However, the engine (motor) is pretty sturdy, and one of the last things that you can expect to go bad. Normally I only get motor-related paper jams when I've been working inside the Laser-Writer and forget to hook up the engine wire. (Also see paper jam questions.)

Q. How do you feel about refilled toner cartridges?

A. I don't like them for the simple reason that there is no free lunch. You can get a refill or two out of a cartridge, but not much more. The refill/recharge companies recycle hundreds of cartridges, and there is no way for you to know how many times a particular cartridge has been around. The drum and other components inside the cartridge have a limited life—why push it? The toner cartridge is one of the most critical components in the image-formation process. Additionally, many companies "drill and fill" the cartridges without replacing the drum and other worn parts, which is just asking for trouble. The quality of the toner is another place that some (not all) of these companies skimp. Do yourself a favor: Buy a new cartridge and save yourself the potential headache.

Q. I have a LaserWriter IINT. A replacement toner cartridge for this model is more expensive than the cartridge for an HP Series III or Canon. Can I use the Canon or HP III cartridge in my IINT?

A. Yes, it'll work fine. In fact, I save a lot of money by doing this. Internally these printers are almost identical and are based on the same Canon design. The only real differences are in the main I/O board, front display, and some cosmetics. Go for it!

Q. What's a fuser assembly? Where is it located, and what does it do? And how do I know when I have a problem with it?

A. The fuser assembly is an important module that basically consists of two pressure rollers and a heating element (bulb). Using heat and pressure, this assembly fuses, or affixes, the toner onto the paper. Think of it this way: The electrically charged paper attracts the toner into specific patterns that form the image. The toner is held in place, then the fuser unit applies heat and pressure to "melt" the toner, thus making it permanent on the paper. The fuser unit also houses the thermistor and thermoprotector sensors that regulate the temperature of the rollers. Without the fusing stage, you would be able to wipe or smear the toner on the printed page.

The symptoms of a fuser problem are poor fixing (fusing) of the toner to the paper, which would eventually lead to smearing. Additionally, when the fuser unit becomes contaminated with dirt, it causes streaks and lines in the print. You can always try replacing the fuser cleaning pad first. If that does not work, then the fuser unit must come out.

To replace the fuser unit you must first locate the fuser unit. The fuser unit is the module inside the printer that has a green top. It looks almost like a put-put golf surface. The fuser unit is located toward the front of the laser unit and usually has a high temperature warning. That's a hint. Don't attempt to remove this unit until it has cooled down (about five minutes). Remove the screws holding this unit in place as well as any wires attached to it. The unit can then be lifted out. You can either install a new fuser unit or send yours out to be rebuilt. A quality rebuild job involves a complete overhaul, rollers and all. There are many companies that provide this service inexpensively and provide a full warranty. Sunflower Repair Services in Overland Park Kansas is excellent at fuser repair and as a laser printer parts source. Ask for Richard (the owner) and tell him Doug sent you. He may give you a better deal.

Q. **Is there any way for me actually to test the laser itself? Can the laser be adjusted? When would the laser be adjusted ?**

A. The laser can be both tested and adjusted. However, this should only be performed by someone with a considerable amount of laser repair training. The adjustments require a high-precision multimeter and a laser power tester, which are expensive tools. I very rarely adjust the laser output. The only time I can recall doing it was when I replaced a DC controller and afterwards my print was either too light or too dark, and the print density adjustment had no effect. But this was a very rare case. Please keep in mind this adjustment requires extreme precision, and you must have the technical specs on the laser printer to properly test and adjust the laser. You shouldn't attempt to guess at it.

Q. **Can you recommend a specific troubleshooting methodology for me to approach general Macintosh-related printing problems?**

A. I use the following procedures to troubleshoot printing problems:

First, I rule out the obvious. I verify that the printer-to-Mac configuration is good, and I also ask questions: Is the printer plugged in? Is the Mac plugged in? Do I have a good cable going from the Mac to the printer? If I have installed a new cable, I make sure that it really is a printer cable. Does the printer have paper? If the printer is a dot matrix, I make sure it has a good ribbon. With laser printers, I make sure that the toner cartridge is good.

Second, I ascertain whether or not the laser printer has power going to it. I ask more questions: Is the laser printer the only thing plugged into this outlet? If not do the other devices work? If all devices are out, I go for the fusebox in my basement. If the laser is the only device in this outlet, I'll plug something else into the outlet to make sure the outlet is dead. If my voltmeter is handy, I'll use that instead.

Third is software. I always check the version of the operating system. I always have bizarre printing problems with two versions, especially on my network: System 6.0.7 and any version prior to 6.0.5 (6.0.4 and earlier). My personal favorites are 6.0.5 for older Macs and 7.x for the newer ones (make sure you get System 7 tuned up and any new patches for it). When in doubt, I reload the operating system.

You would be surprised how many different types of problems this clears up. The operating system can become easily corrupted. The same thing goes for fonts, CDEVs, DAs, and INITs. When in doubt, I reload them all from scratch. I have had numerous run-ins with corrupt fonts and print drivers. In one case on a Mac IIfx, I kept getting a math coprocessor error and I couldn't print with that font. This was the dead give away. Another good question to ask yourself is, Does this only happen in one particular application program? If so, perhaps you should reload that package.

Fourth, I make sure that the Chooser is set correctly and that AppleTalk is set to inactive (unless you're on a network).

Fifth, I look at the hardware. I will immediately load a special diagnostic program called Mac Ekg to test all of the hardware on my Mac. If this checks out, then I am 99.9% sure that the problem is with the printer itself.

Q. **How often does the printer port go out on the Mac? If it does go out, is it easy to repair?**

A. There are two ways to print on the Macintosh. The first is via SCSI port, which requires that you have a printer with a SCSI interface. The second is via the 8-pin DIN port, which is RS-232. There are actually two of these ports on most Macs (one is Printer, one is modem). These ports are not very high failure items. The main cause of failure is plugging devices into the Mac while it is on. The SCSI port on all Macs newer than the SE-30 have the SCSI port fused with a 1-amp pico fuse. I use 125-volt, 1-amp. Since the fuse blows on current, the voltage rating is not that important. It's designed to protect the port. This fuse does not look like a normal glass fuse that you probably are used to. A fuse is always designated on the motherboard with an F (for example, F2 is fuse 2). To test the fuse, you need to perform a continuity test using a voltmeter. When replacing the fuse you must be careful. While the fuse costs about 50 cents, the motherboard is very expensive and very easy to damage with a soldering iron (which you need to properly replace the fuse). When this fuse blows, it will take out all external SCSI devices attached to that Mac. These fuses normally are not available at Radio Shack, so try an electronics shop. The manufacturer is a company called Little Fuse Company.

The two 8-pin DIN RS-232 ports are not fused. Therefore, if you get a bad short, you will damage the chip that controls the serial functions. The chip that performs these functions in most Macs is called the SCC, or Serial Communications Controller. The SCC is usually a Zilog 8530 or equivalent and supports both RS-232 and 422 communications. Mac Ekg performs a complete diagnostic on this chip. The most common thing that happens with these ports is that people always seem to try to force the cable into the hole, which screws up the connector. Sometimes the connector becomes loose and needs to be soldered. Other times the connector needs to be replaced. You can get these connectors for $1 or $2 at any decent electronics store.

Q. Can either my modem or printer port be used for printing?

A. Yes, both of these ports are RS-232 or 422 serial ports that are tied into the same SCC circuit. Either one can be used for printing provided that your Chooser settings match the port you want to use.

Q. Which of the two 8-pin serial ports has a higher priority? Where should I connect my printer for best results?

A. The printer port (channel A or 1) has a slightly higher priority than the modem port (channel B or 2). Keep in mind that both ports have the same pin out (signal assignments) and are tied into the same circuit, so it really does not matter which one your printer is attached to (unless you're on a network).

CHAPTER 15

Preventive Maintenance and Warranty Service

In this chapter, we'll discuss the steps you need to take to ensure the proper operation and longevity of your Macintosh computer. The key to keeping your Mac happy and healthy is simple enough: preventive maintenance. We'll look at the procedures involved in a good maintenance program and how often they should be performed. We'll also look at the pros and cons of the Apple Limited Warranty as well as AppleCare—Apple's extended warranty program (service contract). In many cases, service contracts can save you the expense and aggravation of trying to repair serious problems that may occur with the more advanced Macs, such as the Quadra and PowerBook families. Should you get one when you purchase your Macintosh? And what do these service contracts cover?

Implementing a Smart Preventive Maintenance Program

Preventive maintenance takes effort, but it's by far the best way to reduce costly failures and data loss, and ultimately to extend the life of your Macintosh computer. A large number of computers brought in for service end up being repaired by simply performing some routine preventive maintenance. Maybe the circuit boards needed cleaning or the socketed chips reseating. This is obviously terrific for the service company owner or technician who charges you $40, $50, or $100 per hour even more to perform the repair. With a smart preventive maintenance program, however, you can save this money as well as a trip to the service center.

Developing and implementing a preventive maintenance program is important to everyone who uses or is responsible for Macintosh and other computer systems.

Among the key issues you need to consider when developing this program are:

1. Frequency of preventive maintenance procedures
2. House cleaning
3. Dealing with corrosion

The following sections detail each of these considerations.

Frequency of preventive maintenance procedures

This largely depends on your computer operating environment. Each environment is going to be different. If your Mac is located in a dirty or dusty environment, such as a construction site or a basement, you may need to clean the unit at least two or three times per year. In most clean office environments, you'll need to clean your computer only once every 12 to 18 months. It's a well-known fact that computers in a typical office full of nonsmokers require less frequent preventive maintenance procedures than their counterparts in an office full of people who smoke. Machines that are vertically placed on the floor tend to pick up carpet and dust balls more than machines that are placed on your desk in the traditional horizontal position. Remember this simple, common sense rule: If you open a computer system and discover enough dirt inside to plant corn, you need to increase the frequency of your cleanings.

House cleaning

The most important part of an effective preventive maintenance program is a routine and thorough cleaning of your whole computer system. Dirt and debris, for example, can build up on the internal components of your Macintosh, which can lead to several problems. The dirt and debris may act as insulators and prevent proper system cooling, which can shorten the life expectancy of your computer. Excessive heat build-up also can impact the thermal expansion and contraction of the metal inside the machine, which can lead, for example, to cracked solder joints.

Another factor to consider is that the dirt and debris can be conductive and corrosive. The conductive particles can easily cause a short or partial short to occur on an electronic component (such as a chip or capacitor). The particles with corrosive elements can cause electrical contacts to tarnish, resulting in bad electrical connections.

Dealing with corrosion

The three components most affected by corrosion are socketed chip legs, expansion board contacts, and cable connections.

The main reason I discourage cigarette smoking around a computer is that the smoke particles have chemical properties that are both conductive and corrosive. Even worse, these smoke particles can accumulate on the read/write heads inside your floppy disk drive or on the surface of your diskette media. This situation can result in permanent data loss.

Macintosh floppy disk drives have high failure rates because they don't have dust covers to prevent dirt and debris from entering and quickly accumulating inside the drives. This is one hole you should plug before it becomes a problem. Previously I suggested something as simple as covering this hole with either a 3M Post-It or a 3 x 5 index card and a piece of tape.

The other main entry points for debris are the cooling vents. Dirt and debris literally get sucked into the unit. You shouldn't attempt to block these cooling vents because it would cause the unit to overheat and possibly shut down.

Cleaning Tools and Supplies

To properly perform a general cleaning on your Macintosh and all of its internal components, you must have certain basic tools and supplies. At a minimum, you need to have the following:

- Tools to open up the Macintosh unit. (Be careful!)
- Canned air or a small air compressor. (Please, no TF fluorocarbon-based products that can harm the ozone layer.)
- A small cleaning brush (preferably with the bristles made of an antistatic or static-reduced material).
- A nonconductive, nonresidue cleaning solution for circuit boards (for example, Blue Shower, Tech Spray, contact cleaner, or TV tuner cleaner).
- Isopropyl alcohol and lint-free, foam-tipped cleaning swabs (for those hard to reach places).
- An antistatic wrist strap (so you don't kill any electronic components with static electricity).

- A box of Gold-wipes distributed by Mactronics. (Gold-wipes, by the way, are excellent for cleaning contacts on any gold, tin, silver, and other metallic contacts that can be found on expansion boards, especially SIMMs.)

To properly clean and lubricate the floppy disk drives, you need the following:

- A 3M, Trackmate, or other nonabrasive 3.5-inch floppy disk drive head cleaning kit.
- A small bottle or can of high-grade, nonclogging lubricant with a pin-point applicator (silicon-, lithium-, or Teflon-based).
- Clean rags or tech wipes to mop up any excess lubricant or grime.

Another item you may want to consider is a small vacuum cleaner with an antistatic nozzle tip. If you plan to clean computers and laser printers, you should consider getting a vacuum cleaner with a micron particle filter (like the 3M model). Toner and smaller dust particles are difficult for traditional vacuum cleaners to contain.

Some people prefer to use a vacuum cleaner rather than the canned air for cleaning out equipment, but canned air is superior for directing concentrated blasts in small areas. The vacuum cleaner is more useful when you don't want to remove the main logic board completely from the system unit. You can use the vacuum cleaner to suck out the debris rather than blast it on other components, which occasionally happens when you use canned air. For service calls in the field, canned air is much easier to pack in a tool kit than most of the portable vacuum cleaners on the market.

A new trend in the market is the sale of so-called computer-grade air to consumers. There really is no such thing as computer-grade air—it's just a gimmick. Think about it: The air that circulates through your computer is regular air. You can use regular air to clean the machine, as long as it's moisture and residue free. There is nothing wrong with using a small air compressor like the Black and Decker Power Pump to blast the dust out. You can also inflate your car tires with it. Another interesting thing to consider is rechargeable air cans that you can refill with the air compressor. Many mail-order companies sell these cans. When ordering this product, make sure that it has some sort of particle filter and a moisture trap.

When purchasing a vacuum cleaner for computer maintenance, make sure that the tip is made of an ESD-safe (antistatic) material and that the motor has a low EMI (electromagnetic) rating. Remember, ESD can kill or damage electronic circuits. EMI and other magnetic fields can wreak havoc on disk drive media, which have magnetic properties. Older home and Dustbuster-type vacuums can be sources of these problems and should be avoided. Under no circumstances should you ever reverse the thrust on a wet/dry vacuum to blast out the computer. You may end up blasting all kinds of nasty things out of the wet/dry into your computer.

If you suffer from allergies triggered by dirt and dust, then cleaning debris out of your computer might cause some discomfort. As a fellow allergy sufferer, I sympathize with you. Don't clean your computer in your office. Go to somebody else's office, have a friend blast it out for you (you can blame them later for the mess), or take the machine outside where it's not so confined. Another thing to keep in mind is that if you blast out the debris in the same confined office space where the computer resides, there is a good chance that the same junk will get sucked back into the machine sooner or later.

To do a more effective job of removing the dirt with either canned air or a vacuum, you should first use a small antistatic cleaning brush to go over the dirty surfaces. This loosens the debris and makes it easier to remove. Lint-free, foam-tipped cleaning swabs are excellent for getting to the hard-to-reach places inside the floppy disk drives. You can also use swabs for scrubbing electrical contacts and connectors. I like the lint-free, foam-tipped swabs better than cotton-tip swabs (Q-tips) because they seldom leave any residue. Q-tips tend to leave cotton fuzz everywhere, which isn't good. Foam-tipped swabs are more expensive than Q-tips, and you purchase them at any electronics supply store.

Cleaning Procedures

Before you disassemble and clean any Mac, you should first visually inspect the unit for visible external damage. Then power up the Mac and make notes on any obvious problems that may exist.

Run the Mac Ekg diagnostic program to locate any latent problems that might be hiding in the Mac. I always like to know what I am getting myself into. If you service computers for a living, you must be very careful when working on other people's machines. Some users may experience a temporary memory loss when you locate a problem other than the one they called you in to fix. They could then point the finger and say, You broke it. In a court of law they would win. That's why I always run Mac Ekg before I open the machine, review the results with the customer, and then make the customer sign off that any condition I found was actually there before I started. Better safe than sorry.

To properly clean your system, first disassemble most of it. You can take out every single piece or just go down to the main logic board; either way is acceptable. It depends on how much time you have and which Mac you are working on. I usually remove every single piece except the main logic board, unless I am working on one of the compact Macs, such as the Mac Plus, or a Mac SE. You have to remove the logic board in these models to get at everything. I still remove every piece (boards and disk drives), except the picture tube. I don't like opening the Macintosh Portable. The Portables can be a real nightmare to get back together again. In any case, please be certain that you heed all the static and safety issues outlined in Chapter 3 of this book.

Cleaning Circuit Boards, Connectors, and Contacts

After you remove the circuit boards, you clean them using canned air or a vacuum, nonconductive cleaning solution, Gold-wipes or foam-tipped swabs, and an antistatic brush.

First, loosen the debris on the board in and around contacts and connectors with the small brush. Second, remove the debris with the vacuum or by blasting it with the canned air. Third, clean the contacts and connectors, which promotes reliable connections between boards and other devices. On the main logic board you'll want to remove the SIMMs, inspect them (for bent pins), and clean the sockets thoroughly. Then clean the contacts on the bottom of each SIMM with Gold-wipes or swabs and cleaner.

The fourth step in the cleaning procedure is to inspect and clean all of the connectors on the logic board, especially the power supply connector. You can also spray the contact pins on any cards you may have had installed in the expansion slots (if your particular Mac has slots). Be careful not to bend any of the pins on the card connector. Try to handle the boards by their outer edges. Your skin secretes oil that can be left in the form of a fingerprint on the chips. These oils can contribute to a condition known as galvanic corrosion. Handle the chips as little as possible.

Finally, clean the ends of all of the cables and other connectors inside your computer. Don't forget the connectors on the floppy and hard disk drives. Hard disk drives are sealed units that you should not open. Therefore, limit your cleaning job to the small circuit board and connectors.

In the old days technicians used pencil erasers to clean contacts on edge connectors such as those found on SIMMs. This is no longer recommended because the eraser removes some of the metal on the contact. If you do this too much, you can remove the contact completely. Use Gold-wipes or swabs with contact cleaner instead.

Reseating Socketed Chips

Chip walking is the process by which chips that are installed in a socket work themselves loose. When chips walk they no longer make proper contact with the rest of the computers circuitry, and this can cause immediate or intermittent failures on your machine. To correct this situation, you must locate all of the socketed chips and ensure that they are properly reseated. This a very simple and key procedure in preventive maintenance. Fortunately the newer Macs use very few socketed integrated circuits (chips), which gives them an edge on reliability. The older machines, such as the Mac Plus and Mac SE, are very prone to this condition, however.

To properly reseat your chips, you must do the following:

1. Locate all of the socketed chips in your machine.
2. Make sure that you observe all safety and static precautions.
3. Take a clean, lint-free (preferably antistatic) cloth and cover your index and middle fingers with it. This reduces the possibility of galvanic corrosion.
4. Go from socketed chip to socketed chip and gently push the chip back into its socket. You may not feel some of the chips move at all (which is fine), while you may feel others drop back into the socket. Under no circumstances should you use the palm of your hand and body weight to mash the chips down. You may exert too much force on the board and crack it (which is extremely hard, if not impossible, to fix).

Warranties and Service Contracts

Your Macintosh was designed to be a reliable, high-performance computing machine. After all, nobody would purchase a Mac if it failed all the time. Over the years, however, Apple computers have had their share of problems. Older Macs, such as the Mac 128K, 512K, 512KE, and the Mac Plus, were often plagued with numerous problems: no cooling fans, the power supplies were underrated, some components were very marginal, and other serious design flaws. That's why you only got a 90-day limited warranty back then. Today, however, all Macs come with a one-year carry-in warranty. Apple still has its problems with Macintosh computers problems such as recalled batches of SIMMs, flaky hard disk drives, and some very bad PowerBook 100 batteries—but Apple has gotten much better in the area of customer service. For instance, a colleague of mine purchased a PowerBook 170 that developed a problem the first month he had the machine. He called Apple immediately, reported the problem, and within 48 hours had a new PowerBook replacement.

This example brings up an important point to remember: If your machine is broken and still under warranty, do not attempt to fix it yourself. Take it straight to an authorized Apple service provider and make an immediate warranty claim. It's best to take it back to the dealer you purchased it from. If that isn't an option, go to the nearest authorized Apple service provider in your area. If you aren't sure of your nearest dealer, call Apple directly at (408) 996-1010 and they'll help you. Make sure you take all of your receipts and paperwork with you.

What the Apple warranty covers

Every product that has the Apple logo is covered by a limited warranty against defects in workmanship. The warranty begins on the day of initial retail purchase. Currently the length of this warranty is one year. Here are five major provisions excerpted from the Apple limited warranty that you should be familiar with:

1. *Warranty*
   The warranty will be honored by any authorized Apple dealer in the country of original purchase, regardless of where in that country the product was originally purchased.

2. *Products Repaired*

   All products repaired under warranty are done so at no cost to the customer.

3. *Burden of Proof*

   The burden of proof to establish that a product is under warranty lies with the customer. It is the customer's responsibility to provide proof of purchase that contains the date of purchase and serial numbers of the equipment purchased.

4. *Modifications*

   Unapproved modifications and damage caused by misuse or accident will void the warranty unless it is very clear that there is not a relation between the modification and the product failure. (This is a discretionary catch-all that gives the dealer great latitude in deciding whether or not your repair is covered under the warranty.)

5. *System Software*

   System software, media, and documentation will be replaced upon request if Apple releases an update during the warranty period.

Exclusions to the Apple limited warranty

The Apple limited warranty was designed to cover only defects in material and workmanship in hardware and software. Seven basic items are not covered under the warranty, and authorized Apple service providers are taught to look for and enforce them:

1. *Expired Warranty*

   Obviously you can't expect them to warranty something that is out of warranty.

2. *No Trouble Found*

   This situation occurs when you say there is a problem and they don't find one. Apple considers a system functional if it passes their diagnostics and can run known good software. I recommend bringing Mac Ekg with you and insist that they keep and run diagnostics all night. If they don't find a problem, they will suggest you check your line power at home (which you should have checked first).

3. *Unauthorized Modifications*

   Rewiring your Mac, rebuilding your logic board, and installing an accelerator are all considered examples of unauthorized modifications. Realistically they could consider almost any upgrade unauthorized if they wanted to. However, Apple does have a list (a short one) of modifications that it deems acceptable.

4. *Misuse and Abuse*

   Apple immediately voids your warranty if the product has been damaged by accident, misuse, abuse, or misapplication. This is another catch-all. The point Apple is trying to get across here is that these machines should be handled properly. If the dealer notices any excessive wear and tear on the product or foreign substances in the unit (such as coffee in the keyboard), he or she voids your warranty. The dealer is taught to look for obvious signs of neglect.

5. *User Error*

   User error is not covered under your Apple warranty. You would be surprised how many people go in for warranty service because they have too many INITs or a virus on their system.

6. *Damaged or Missing Chips*

   If the dealer opens up your Mac and discovers that you have a physically damaged chip (that is, a bent leg or a cracked or burnt chip), he or she voids your warranty under the misuse provision. These problems are usually caused by improper installation of chips, cables, or boards. It's often a sign that the customer was trying to perform an upgrade of some kind and botched it.

   Apple does not accept any unit for warranty service that has missing chips. Your warranty is voided.

7. *Non-Apple Peripherals*

   Your Apple limited warranty does not cover problems with non-Apple peripherals, cables, and connectors. If a non-Apple product is the cause of your Macintosh failure, your warranty is voided.

The Apple limited warranty may seem harsh, but in my view it's fair. Plain and simple, Apple covers defects in material and workmanship; they should not have to warranty things that people have destroyed. Making such repairs would cost Apple a great deal of money in time and material, and somebody would have to pay. If Apple were to lose money on every repair, they would have to raise the prices on their computers so high that nobody could afford them.

A good way to augment your warranty and protect your investment is with the AppleCare program.

What is AppleCare?

AppleCare is an extended maintenance agreement between an authorized Apple service provider and the Apple computer equipment owner. AppleCare was designed to give customers a way of protecting their investment at an annual cost that is less than one typical repair charge. AppleCare covers both parts and labor on all Apple computers and Apple manufactured peripherals and cables. Apple Computer, Inc., fully backs any equipment covered under AppleCare.

AppleCare is insurance. The minimum term for which you can purchase this insurance is 2 months, and the maximum is 36 months. Apple dealers always try to push AppleCare at the time of purchase of your system for several reasons. First, they make at least 50% profit on each AppleCare program they sell. If you pay for it at the time of the computer purchase, they get their money sooner. Second, the dealers are free to set their own retail price for AppleCare. Apple only suggests what prices should be. Finally, dealers get a generous reimbursement for any repairs made under an AppleCare customer. So it's in their best interest to sell it.

There is only one advantage to signing up for AppleCare when you purchase your Macintosh computer: convenience. You get everything out of the way at once. However, AppleCare does absolutely nothing for you until the day after your Apple limited warranty expires. AppleCare picks up where the limited warranty leaves off, without a lapse in coverage. Personally I would keep my money until I was ready to buy a service that I can immediately use. Why let someone else use your money for a year? What if you decide that you don't like this Mac after a few months and want to get rid of it? Well, you're in luck; the AppleCare coverage transfers with it, but you still have to fill out forms and so forth. Your better off waiting to buy AppleCare when you need it.

With AppleCare you can cover not only new Macs but also older Macintosh equipment. I recently took an old Mac Plus to the authorized Apple service provider in my area and told them I wanted an estimate on an AppleCare policy for it. I was expecting them to laugh at me, but each dealer performed exactly the same ritual. They went over that unit with a fine-tooth comb before giving me an estimate. The problem is that one dealer quoted me $162 per year, the other $200. Heck, I can buy a used Mac Plus for around $200 or $300. What were they thinking? Now if the pricing were in this ballpark for a Mac IIsi, IIci, IIfx, Quadra 900 or 950, or a PowerBook 170, I would definitely go for it. These machines use a number of custom chips that are hard to find, complex, expensive, and worth protecting.

If you have an older or less expensive Mac, such as a Mac Plus, SE, SE/30, Classic, Classic II, or Mac II, diagnose the failure yourself. You can replace anything in a Mac machine on your own. Replacement parts such as power supplies, hard drives, and video cards are all very easy to come by. You can get new or refurbished equipment from many of the vendors listed in the appendix of this book. The only thing that is hard to come by is the logic board. You can get one through the gray market, but at a price. Your better off sending the logic board out to a company like Micromat to get the module reworked. Apple, of course, frowns on this practice.

AppleCare has two main drawbacks:

1. AppleCare contract prices can vary from dealer to dealer. Some dealers follow Apples confidential list of suggested retail prices, which are reasonable. Other dealers feel the need to gouge people. Shop around.
2. AppleCare does not cover any non-Apple products. This can pose a real headache to anyone who doesn't have a pure Apple environment. Most folks want the total package, that is, both their Mac and non-Mac equipment covered under a single service contract. Some Apple dealers are large enough to write their own custom versions of AppleCare contracts. Apple sanctions this but only supports them with respect to the Apple goods. Once again, shop around and check out their references.

Glossary

AC (alternating current)—When the flow of electric current within a circuit reverses direction at regular intervals, causing electrons to surge backward and forward along the path. In the U.S. this occurs 60 times per second.

ADB (Apple Desktop Bus)—Refers to compatible input/output devices, such as keyboards, mice, and monitors. Low-speed serial bus.

ADB transceiver—A 4-bit microprocessor that assists the main processor to control the ADB system.

address—The specific location of a byte in memory.

address bus—Communications link between the microprocessor and the system RAM. Transmitted by a group of wires. The number of wires determines how many addresses can be accessed directly by the main processor.

address map—Parts of the address space of the Macintosh assigned to specific devices.

address register—The part of the microprocessor which determines addressing.

address translation—Occurs when one set of addresses is converted into another corresponding set.

alert box—A warning that appears on the screen to report an error message.

ampere—A unit of measure pertaining to the strength of flow of an electric current.

AMU (Address Management Unit)—The IC in the Macintosh II that does 24- to 32-bit address mapping. Also called Hochsprung memory.

analog—A physical system that performs operations such as actual measurements (of electricity, for example) and converts this data into a specific class of mathematical problems. Also refers to voltage controlled, as opposed to digital.

analog board—The combination power supply, power distribution, and video board found in the Macintosh Plus, Macintosh Classic, and Classic II computers. In the Macintosh SE and SE/30 models, it acts only as a video/power distribution board. It does not function as a power supply.

anode—The positive pole of an electrical device.

anode well—A receptacle on the CRT that receives the high-voltage lead from the flyback transformer.

Apple menu—The pull-down menu on the far left in the menu bar. It is denoted by an apple.

AppleTalk network—The hardware and software that links computers and peripherals together in a network. This capability is built into every Macintosh.

application program—A software tool used to manipulate information. An example would be MacWrite or MacPaint.

ASC (Apple sound chip)—The IC that generates a stereo audio signal that works with other sound circuits to drive the internal speaker. There is no ASC in the Macintosh SE.

aspect ratio—The proportional appearance of text and graphics on a monitor as a function of horizontal and vertical resolution.

asynchronous—Refers to events that take place which are not synchronized one after the other by any mutual timing signal or clock.

audio jack—Used to attach headphones and other similar devices. It is located on the back panel of the Macintosh.

back panel—Located on the back of the computer and includes various connectors and ports for peripheral devices.

back up—To make an additional copy of any application or program stored on disk.

bit—A single digit in a binary number. The smallest amount of information the computer can process.

bitmap display—Display in which the image is a representation of bits in an area of RAM called the screen buffer. Each pixel on the screen is mapped to a bit in the screen buffer.

block—A group of data or memory that is moved and stored as a unit.

block device—It reads and writes blocks of bytes at a time. A hard disk drive is a good example.

blooming—Occurs when the display size increases irregularly as the brightness is increased. Usually indicates a problem on the analog board.

board—Refers to the circuit board.

bong—A noise made by the Macintosh during power-up.

boxer fan—A small rotating fan (standard on the Macintosh SE) with a boxlike mounting frame. Used to cool the inside of the unit.

buckling—Display linearity distorts as the brightness is increased. Usually indicates a problem on the analog board.

buffer—Area of memory set aside to store frequently used information and instructions.

bus—Circuits (wires) inside the computer that transmit information internally from one part of the system to another or externally to monitors and communications equipment.

button—A buttonlike image in a dialog box that allows you to initiate an action. Also, a mechanical switch on a mouse.

byte—A unit of measurement for computer memory and storage. Consists of a fixed number of bits.

cache—A portion of RAM or ROM set aside for storing frequently accessed portions of programs or files.

cache RAM—High-speed RAM used as a buffer so as to make instructions more quickly available to the main processor.

cache slot—A slot in the Macintosh IIci in which a cache card may be installed.

capacitor—An electronic component capable of storage an electric charge. Basically consists of two conductors separated by an insulator.

card—A plug-in circuit board.

case cracker—A special tool used to separate the case of the compact Macintosh computers.

cathode—The negative pole of an electrical device.

character—A symbol that conveys information, such as letters, numbers, punctuation marks, and pictures.

character device—Reads or writes a stream of characters one at a time, such as a printer.

chooser—A desk accessory that allows you to specify the devices your Macintosh will use. For example, use it to indicate to the machine what type of printer is being used.

circuit board—An epoxy-impregnated, thin, insulated board with tracklike metal wiring paths on which electrical currents travel.

click—To select an application or option by positioning the pointer on the desired application and then pressing the mouse button to activate that option.

clock—A crystal that oscillates at a certain frequency and governs the cycle speed of a chip.

clock battery—Maintains the time and data and provides power to an area of memory where the volume setting and other control panel information is stored. Can be located above the power switch or soldered to the logic board, depending on the model of Mac.

closed—Refers to a closed circuit in which current flows normally at a controlled rate.

CLUT DAC—The IC in an expansion video card or in a Macintosh IIci. It converts digital video data to analog signals.

command—An instruction that causes the computer to perform some action.

configuration—A general term that refers to the way hardware, software, or networks are set up.

continuity—A closed circuit that allows the flow of electricity in a continuous path.

control lines—Wires that control signals.

control panel—A desk acessory that lets you make various speaker, keyboard, mouse, and Desktop adjustments.

co-processor—An auxiliary processor designed to relieve the demand on the main microprocessor. Usually performs specific tasks such as mathematical calculations. This allows the computer to process data at a faster speed.

CPU (central processing unit)—An integrated circuit that acts as the brain of the computer.

CPU GLU—General logic unit in the Macintosh Portable that selects devices and performs control functions.

cross-hatch—A grid of regularly spaced squares used to align a CRT.

crowbar circuit—Overvoltage protection circuit used to prevent fires. It shuts down the power supply under dangerous conditions.

CRT (cathode ray tube)—A vacuum tube in which electrons are accelerated and deflected under the influence of electronic fields, producing a visible image.

current—The passage of electricity from one pole of an apparatus to another.

current startup disk—Contains the System Folder the computer is currently using. The startup disk appears in the upper-right corner of the Finder Desktop.

cut-off adjustment—A coarse brightness control that affects horizontal blanking.

data bus—An internal pathway (wires) in which data is transferred within the computer. The wider the bus, the more information can be transmitted at one time. MC68000 has a 16-bit data bus, MC 68020 and MC 68030 have 32-bit data buses.

data disk—A disk that houses your work product.

DB-9F connector—Female connector that has holes or sockets.

DB-9M connector—Male connector, has plugs or pins.

DB-9 shell—Metal or plastic housing for a DB-9 connector.

DC (direct current)—The opposite of alternating current. Electricity flows continuously or in pulses but travels only in one direction.

default—The automatic action or setting a computer takes unless given a different instruction.

declaration ROM—A ROM on the NuBus expansion card.

desk accessory—A mini application available from the Apple menu regardless of the application being used at the time. The Calculator and Notepad features are examples.

Desktop—The Macintosh working environment with its menu bar.

digital—A type of output signal that represents the size of a stimulus or input signal in the form of a series of discrete quantities coded to represent digits in a system of numerical notation.

digital board—Refers to the logic board.

DIP (dual in-line package)—Refers to integrated circuits with two lines of pins.

directory—A listing of the contents of a disk or folder.

discharge—When a capacitor or CRT releases its electrical charge.

discharge tool—A specific piece of equipment used to discharge electricity from the Macintosh CRT.

disk—Direct access storage devices that record data on a magnetic surface.

disk caching—Using a portion of RAM to store recently used information from the hard disk. This allows for faster access.

disk capacity—The maximum amount of information a disk can hold, usually measured in kilobytes for floppys and megabytes for hard disk drives.

disk drive—A drive that utilizes a 3.5-inch disk that can be built in or external.

disk drive port—A port used to attach external disk drives to Macintosh Plus, SE, and SE/30 models.

diskette—A 3 5-inch microfloppy disk.

display—That which is shown on the screen; does not refer to the screen itself.

DMA (direct memory access)—A way to get data into or out of memory without using the CPU.

document—A file created by an application that contains information generated or manipulated by that application.

dots—The painted area on the screen that includes the pixel and the black area that surrounds it.

double-click—Done by positioning the pointer on the desired application and then rapidly clicking the mouse button twice. Used to open an application.

DPI (dots per inch)—In the compact Macintosh computers, the display is 72 dots per inch, both horizontally and vertically.

drag—To move an object to a new location by positioning the pointer on the object to be moved, depressing the mouse button, repositioning the object with the mouse, and then releasing the mouse button to secure the object in place.

DRAM—Dynamic random access memory.

drive capacity—The maximum storage capacity of the data disks that can be used in a disk drive.

driver—A software program that sets up the parameters from which the microprocessor can direct the operation of a peripheral device.

error message—A display that tells you of an error in the execution of a program or in your input to the computer.

ESD (electrostatic discharge)—A direct current discharge that can damage certain computer components.

expansion card—A circuit board designed to plug into an expansion slot.

expansion slot—An internal connector designed to accept expansion cards. The Macintosh SE and SE/30 have one, while the Macintosh Plus computer does not.

Finder—An application that creates the Macintosh Desktop. It is used to manage documents and applications and to gain access to the disk drives.

floppy disk—A removable, flexible plastic piece of magnetic media used for data storage.

FPU (Floating Point Unit)—The IC that provides support for extended math processing operations.

flupping—Occurs when the overvoltage protection circuit crowbars the power supply in response to an overvoltage condition. Usually caused by a shorted rectifier, failed electrolytic capacitor, or the TSM chip on the logic board.

flyback transformer—A part that transforms low voltage into the high voltage needed to drive the CRT.

Folder—A holder of documents, applications, and other folders on the Desktop.

foldover—When the display folds back on itself. Indicates a problem on the analog board.

font—A set of characters with a particular design and style. The Macintosh has a variety of font options.

Font/DA Mover—A utility program that lets you add or delete fonts from a disk's system file.

format—To prepare a disk for use by partitioning out sectors or blocks to which information will be stored.

GCR (group-code recording)—A method of formatting data. three bytes are written as four 8-bit patterns so that no pattern contains more than two consecutive 0's. It is used to help NRZI to write data on 3.5-inch floppy disks and Apple Hard Disk 20 hard disks.

ghosting—An afterimage on the CRT that fades slowly enough to be seen.

GLU (general logic unit)—The IC used to perform control functions.

GLUE chip—The IC that selects devices and performs other control functions in the Mac II, Mac IIx, and Mac IIcx.

hard disk—Random access drive that stores large amounts of information on non-removable magnetic disk platters.

hard disk interleave—How sectors are numbered on a hard drive. Placing consecutive sectors in various locations on the disk alternating with other sectors.

head—The device that reads information from the hard disk and also writes information to it.

HFS (hierarchical file system)—Allows a root directory and a hierarchy of multiple subdirectories.

high address—Ending address of a block or code.

H-size—Horizontal width control.

IC—Integrated circuit.

icon—A small picture that represents an application, file, collection of files, or message to the user.

IC puller—A set of tongs used for pulling ICs from their sockets.

initialize—Same as format.

input—Information transferred into a computer via keyboard, mouse, modem, or disk drive.

installer—A program that automates the installation process of the Macintosh operating system.

integrated circuit—A collection of several electronic components housed in one chip.

interface—Connection between two devices.

interrupt—A hardware feature that signals the CPU that an input or an output is required.

interrupt handler—Routine that takes control in the event of an interrupt.

interrupt priority level—A number assigned to an interrupt based on the importance of the function. If an interrupt is of higher priority, then the current processor function the exception processing sequence is started.

interrupt vector—Exception vector for an interrupt.

invisible files—Files specified to remain invisible to the user. There is an invisible file named Desktop File created by the finder that contains the names of folders and icons.

I/O connector—Refers to the mouse, disk drive, modem, and audio connectors at the back of the logic board.

I/O processor—The IC in the Macintosh IIfx. One IOP controls the SCC. Another IOP controls the SWIM and ADB interfaces.

IWM (Integrated Woz Machine)—The IC that controls the floppy drives in the

Macintosh II and Macintosh SE computers manufactured before September 1989.

jumper—A piece of metal or wire used to short two connectors.

K (kilobyte)—A measure of computer memory equal to 1024 bytes.

LED (light emitting diode)—Most hard drives and some external drives use LEDs for lights to indicate its functioning.

logical address—Address used by software.

logic board—The largest flat printed circuit board in the Macintosh. Also called motherboard or systemboard.

main memory—Memory directly addressable by the CPU. The computer's primary working storage.

manager—Routine found in the operating system or Toolbox. Some managers are used to control the information flow between a Macintosh and its peripheral devices.

MB (megabyte)—A measure of computer memory equal to 1,048,576 bytes.

MC 68030—Main processor in the Macintosh SE/30, IIx, IIcx, IIci, IIsi, IIfx, and PowerBook 140 and 145 computers.

MC 68030 PDS—Processor-direct or slot in the Macintosh SE/30, IIci, IIsi, and Macintosh IIfx.

MC68881—Optional paged memory management unit in the Macintosh II.

MC68882—Floating point unit in the Macintosh IIx, IIcx, IIci, and IIfx computers.

MDU (memory decode unit)—Selects devices and performs other control functions in the Macintosh IIci.

memory—Computer's working storage. Can store information to be retrieved later.

menu bar—A row of words at the top of the screen. Each word is a title for the menu of options revealed when the word is selected with the cursor.

MFM (modified frequency modulation)—A way of recording data onto magnetic media.

MFS (Macintosh File System)—An original Macintosh file system in which all files are kept in the root directory. It does not allow for subdirectories.

MMU (memory management unit)—The component that performs address mapping in the Macintosh computer.

modem port—A serial communication port on the back panel of the computer. There are two of these ports.

Motorola 68000—The microprocessor in the Macintosh Plus, SE, and Classic computers.

Motorola 68020—The microprocessor in the Macintosh II that can be added to the Macintosh SE by means of an accelerator card.

mouse—Small mechanical device whose movement by the user corresponds to pointer movements on the screen.

mouse button—The bottom or top of the mouse that, when pressed, initiates some action on whatever is under the pointer. Releasing the button confirms the action.

MS DOS—A microcomputer operating system widely used by IBM-class microcomputers. It is also knows as DOS, or disk operating system.

MultiFinder—A multitasking application that permits concurrent programs and background activities to run on a Macintosh.

multitasking—Refers to procedures in which several separate but interrelated tasks operate under a single program identity.

multitester—A meter that can measure at least voltage, current, and resistance.

nanosecond—One billionth of one second.

NCR 5380—The IC used to implement the SCSI interface in the Macintosh.

NuBus—A 32-bit synchronous bus used for expansion cards in the Macintosh II family.

NuBus controller—The IC that controls the NuBus interface.

NuBus expansion slot—A connector attached to the NuBus where an expansion card can be installed.

NuChip—The IC that controls the NuBus interface in the Macintosh II, IIx, and IIcx.

NuChip 30—The IC that controls the NuBus interface in the Macintosh IIci.

OEM—Original equipment manufacturer.

ohm—A unit of measure for resistance.

operating system—A special program or group of programs that control basic tasks for operating the computer.

OVPC—Overvoltage protection circuit.

PAL—The IC that implements programmable array logic.

parameter RAM—RAM in which system parameters and control panel settings are sorted.

parity—A way to detect memory errors using an extra bit for each byte stored in RAM. This is read in such a way as to check that the value read is the same as the value stored.

parity bit—Refers to the extra bit that is attached to the byte of memory.

PC board—Printed circuit board.

PC mount—A component that has wire-like leads that can be soldered to a PC board.

picture tube—Large vacuum tube display used in televisions and computer monitors.

piezoelectric fan—A small fan that vibrates at a desired radio frequency and flexes twin mylar blades. The blades move back and forth like a fan.

pin straightener—A tool used to straighten bent pins on integrated circuits.

pitch—The fixed distance between objects, such as characters on a page.

pixel—A picture element. A small rectangular division of the video screen. The smaller the rectangle the sharper the picture.

PMMU (paged memory management unit)—The IC in the Macintosh II that performs logical-to-physical address translation from 24-bit to 32-bit addressing.

port—Interface between the computer and its environment. Usually connects the Macintosh to its peripheral devices.

pot—Short for potentiometer, which is used to measure EMF (electromotive force), a variable resistor that limits electrical current flow.

powering on—Turning on the Macintosh computer.

processor-director slot (PDS)—Expansion slot that provides unbuffered access to the main processor.

programmer's switch—Refers to a user-installed button that resets the computer.

PROM (programmable read-only memory)—Any type that is not recorded during its fabrication but that requires physical operation to program it.

purity tabs—Magnetic rings on the neck of the CRT used to control screen centering.

RAM—Random access memory.

RAM cache—RAM you can designate to store certain information an application uses repeatedly. This helps to speed up work, but it is not wise to use it with applications that use a lot of memory.

raster—The part of the screen that lights up.

RBV (ram based video controller)—The IC in the Macintosh IIci that reads and formats video data and controls the video CLUT DAC.

RCA plug—RCA standard shielded plug.
resistor—A component that limits the flow of electricity.

resolution—The number of pixels across the screen and the number of pixels from top to bottom. Resolution on the compact Macintosh is 512 x 342.

RFI—Radio frequency interface.

ROM (read-only memory)—A device where information is stored permanently or semi-permanently and can be read out but not altered in any way.

RTC (real-time clock)—Battery-powered IC or clock chip that keeps track of the time and date, also contains parameter RAM.

scan lines—Diagonal lines caused by the horizontal retrace.

schematic—A circuit drawing.

Schottky diode—A rectifier with a low forward voltage drop and fast reverse recovery time. Designed to meet the requirements of switching power supplies.

screen—The face of the picture tube.

SCSI (Small Computer System Interface)—A fast communications standard for attachment of devices such as hard disk to small systems.

SCSI chip—NCR 53C80 or NCR 5380 chip used to implement the SCSI.

SCSI devices—Devices that use SCSI.

SCSI port—The port on the back panel of the computer where SCSI devices are connected.

SE bus—A direct data path to the microprocessor, implemented through a 96-pin expansion connector inside the Macintosh SE.

sector—A part of a track on the surface of a disk. Tracks and sectors are used to organize information on the disk.

semiconductor—A material with conductive properties halfway between a metal and an insulator.

serial communications controller—The IC that handles serial I/O through the modem and printer ports.

short—An abbreviation for short circuit, which is the opposite of an open circuit. In a short circuit electricity flows uncontrollably.

SIMM (single inline memory modules)—The logic board of any model from the Macintosh Plus on is equipped with SIMM sockets. RAM chips are indirectly soldered to the logic board.

SIP (single inline package)—Integrated circuits and other parts with one single line of pins.

slot—A space in which to install a card.

slot space—Address space for NuBus slots in Macintosh II-family computers. In the Macintosh SE/30 and Macintosh IIfx, it is used for cards that emulate NuBus cards.

Sony sound chip—Drives the internal speaker or external sound jack.

sound—Auditory perception of vibrations.

sound buffer—Part of the memory where sound circuitry reads data to create the sound signal.

spring clamp—Another name for the Macintosh case cracker.

SRAM (static random access memory)—RAM that keeps the data as long as the power is on, without refreshing.

startup disk—Disk that contains the system files needed to get the computer started. A startup disk must have at least the Finder and a system file. It may also contain other files.

SWIM (Super Woz Integrated Machine)—The IC that controls the FDHD drives. It is synchronous when the data transmissions or operations are controlled by a mutual timing clock or signal.

System Folder—A collection of files that are necessary to run the Macintosh system.

system startup information—Read at system startup. Configured parameters that are stored in the first two logical blocks of a volume.

terminator—A device used in a SCSI chain to eliminate echoes passing along the chain. A SCSI chain should never have more than two terminators one at the beginning and the other at the end.

thermal resistance—The ability to conduct heat. Resistance is defined as the ratio of the potential difference across the conductor to the current.

trace—Interpretive diagnostic technique that provides an analysis of each executed instruction and writes it on an output device as the instruction is executed.

transistor—Consists of a semiconductive material with a very narrow N (negative charge) region sandwiched between two P (positive) regions. The outer regions are called the emitter and collector, with the center region being called the base.

trimmer pot—A variable potentiometer.

TTL—Transistor-to-transistor logic, the most common form of integrated circuit logic.

user interface—The boundary where the user and computer communicate with one another.

vertical blanking interrupt—Equivalent to the 60.15 Hz interrupt in the Macintosh II family.

vertical blanking interval—Time between the display of the last pixel on the right of the last line of the screen and the first pixel on the left of the first line of the screen.

VIA (versatile interface adapter)—The IC that controls most of the Macintosh's I/O interrupts. The Macintosh SE/30, II, IIx, and IIcx each have two VIAs.

vinyl jacket—Insulating jacket for the analog board.

voltage—Electromotive force, measured in volts.

VOM—Volt ohmmeter. An inexpensive pocket meter.

VRAM (video RAM)—Used in most video expansion cards. Dual-port RAM that reads and writes and has built-in shift registers that allow bit-stream output.

virtual memory—Simulates more memory than the machine contains. This allows the computer to run many programs at the same time.

V-size—Refers to a monitors vertical size control.

yoke—A wiring harness mounted around the neck of the CRT. It controls the horizontal and vertical sweep.

Macintosh Resources

Locating good suppliers of Macintosh hardware, software, replacement parts, components, diagnostic test equipment, and other services can often be frustrating. Many times just trying to get a simple Mac-related question answered can be equally frustrating. Throughout this book, I have mentioned several vendors and other organizations that I believe are excellent resources for products, services, and help. The following is a listing of these and other resources that can make your Mac life easier.

Apple Computer, Inc.
20525 Mariani Ave.
Cupertino, CA 95014
408-996-1010
Manufactures of Apple Macintosh computers, peripherals, and software.

**Apple Programmer's and
Developer's Association (APDA)**
20525 Mariani Ave.
Cupertino, CA 95014
408-562-3910
APDA offers a broad range of programming products and resources for developers using Apple platforms.

Apple User Group Connection
20525 Mariani Ave., M/S 36AA
Cupertino, CA 95014
800-538-9696, extension 500
The Apple User Group Connection provides information on how to locate the Apple User Groups nearest you.

Arrow Graphics
8986 Watchlight Court
Columbia, MD 21045
410-715-1339
Arrow Graphics is a full service Macintosh graphics and printing firm. It specializes in quality custom graphic designs, line art, logos, color separations, corporate presentations, brochures, catalogs, letterheads, and much more.

Asanté Technologies, Inc.
821 Fox Lane
San Jose, CA 95131
408-752-8388
Asanté is a manufacturer of high quality Macintosh Ethernet cards, hubs, and other networking products.

Berkeley Macintosh User Group (BMUG)
1442-A Walnut St., #62
Berkeley, CA 94709
510-549-BMUG
BMUG is one of the largest and most established Macintosh user groups in the country. It consists of user interest groups willing to share information with members.

Boston Computer Society (BCS)
One Center Plaza
Boston, MA 02108
617-367-8080
BCS is another well established Macintosh User Group.

Byte
One Phoenix Mill Lane
Peterborough, NH 03458
603-924-7681
Byte is an excellent high-technical monthly magazine that covers many different computer platforms and products.

Celect Software
7400 Innovation Way
Mason, OH 45040-9699
513-573-6800
This company makes superb, high-end graphics importer and exchange software for CADs and Macs.

Central Point Software
15220 N.W. Greenbrier Pkwy., #220
Beaverton, OR 97006
503-690-8090
Manufactures outstanding Macintosh utility programs, such as Mac Tools Deluxe.

Dataviz, Inc.
35 Corporate Dr.
Trumbull, CT 06611
203-768-0030
Manufactures the Maclink Plus file exchange program as well as a full line of Macintosh translators.

Dayna Communications, Inc.
50 South Main St., 5th Fl.
Salt Lake City, UT 84144
801-531-0203
Manufactures some very fine software and hardware products, such as Dayna-File, DaynaDrive, and DOS Mounter.

Daystar Digital
5556 Atlanta Highway
Flowery Branch, GA 30542
Manufactures accelerator boards and other hardware products for the Macintosh.

Farallon Computing, Inc.
2000 Powell Street
Emeryville, CA 94608
510-596-9023
Farallon manufactures high quality Macintosh networking products.

GSC Associates, Inc.
2304 Artesia Blvd., Ste. 201
Redondo Beach, CA 90278
213-379-2113
GSC Associates manufactures Graph-Porter and MetaPICT, which are powerful CGM to PICT translators for the Mac and other platforms.

High Tech Training International
1429 Colonial Boulevard, Ste. 103
Fort Myers, FL 33907
800/741-4366 (U.S. only)
813/939-2944 (International)
410/783-8274 (24-hour message service)
CompuServe ID 71302,360
High Tech Training International is a recognized world-wide pioneer and leader of hands-on Macintosh training seminars.

Jameco Computer Products
1355 Shoreway Rd.
Belmont, CA 94002
415-592-8097
Mail-order supplier of miscellaneous electronic components.

JDR Microdevices
2233 Branham Lane
San Jose, CA 95124
408-559-1200
Another good mail-order supplier of miscellaneous electronic components.

Jensen Tools
7815 S. 46th St.
Phoenix, AZ 85044
602-968-6231
Jensen Tools manufactures and supplies high quality computer tool kits and test equipment.

Kennect Technology
271 E. Hacienda Ave.
Campbell, CA 95008
408-370-2866
800-552-1232
Kennect manufactures excellent Macintosh disk drive products, such as Rapport and Drive 2.4.

Kensington Microware
251 Park Ave., South
New York, NY 10010
212-475-5200
800-535-4242
Manufactures and supplies computer accessories such as trackballs and system saver.

Kingston Technology Corp.
17600 Newhope St.
Fountain Valley, CA 92708
714-435-2600
Kensington is an excellent supplier of high grade memory products.

Mactronics of South Florida
1429 Colonial Blvd., Unit #103
North Ft. Myers, FL 33907
813-939-2944
Mactronics designs, manufactures, and distributes diagnostic and test devices, such as Simm Testers, SCSI Testers, and ADB Testers. The company also sells hard-to-get items, such as Macintosh parts and schematics, in quantity.

MacUser
950 Tower Lane, 18th Fl.
Foster City, CA 94404
415-378-5600
MacUser is an excellent Macintosh-oriented magazine.

MacWarehouse
1690 Oak St.
P.O. Box 3031
Lakewood, NJ 08701
908-367-0440
800-ALL-MACS
MacWarehouse is one of the largest and best mail-order suppliers of Macintosh hardware and software products. The company has exceptional customer service and its technical staff is very knowledgeable.

MacWeek
310 Howard St.
San Francisco, CA 94105
415-243-3500
MacWeek is a very informative weekly magazine.

Macworld
501 Second Street
San Francisco, CA 94107
415-243-0505
800-234-1038
Macworld is another high quality Macintosh-oriented magazine that is published monthly.

Mac Zone

18005 NE 68th St., Ste. A-110
Redmond, WA 98052-9904
206-883-3088
800-248-0800
Mac Zone is another fine mail-order supplier of Macintosh hardware and software products.

Maxwell Computer Products

23432 Victory Blvd.
Woodland Hills, CA 91376
818-347-1800
Maxwell Computer Products is a highly specialized chip (IC) brokerage firm that specializes in the location and volume sale of hard-to-get integrated circuits for Compaq, IBM and compatibles, and Macintosh computers. They supply many third-party maintenance organizations with components needed to service these computers.

MicroMat Computer Systems

7075 Redwood Blvd.
Novato, CA 94945
415-898-6227
800-829-6227
MicroMat Computer Systems is a first-rate, Macintosh service organization that sells parts and performs expert, component-level repairs.

OnTrack Computer Systems

6321 Bury Dr., #15
Eden Prairie, MN 55346
612-937-1107
800-752-1333
This company manufactures an excellent hard disk formatting and diagnostic package called Disk Manager Mac.

PartsPort, Ltd.

1801 Walthall Creek Dr.
Colonial Heights, Virginia 23834
804-530-1128
800-253-5640
PartsPort, Ltd. specializes in hard-to-get computer and printer parts, especially high resolution monitor repair parts.

Power Plus Systems

3458 West 1987 South
Salt Lake City, UT 84104
801-973-8489
800-722-0602
Power Plus Systems manufactures quality replacement power supplies for Macintosh and other computers. The company's supplies are heavy duty, made in the United States, and very reasonably priced.

Pre-Owned Electronics
205 Burlington Rd.
Bedford, MA 01730
617-275-4600
800-274-5343
Pre-Owned Electronics is a supplier of hard-to-get new, used, and rebuilt Macintosh parts.

SCS Corp.
3804 Victoria Park Ave.
Toronto, Canada
416-502-3090
SCS is an excellent Canadian-based company that supplies many of the parts, prints, and semiconductors to repair Apple Macintosh computers and printers.

Sencore
3200 Sencore Dr.
Sioux Falls, SD 57107
800-SENCORE
Sencore manufactures quality electronic test equipment, especially video.

Shreve Systems
3804 Karen Lane
Bossier City, LA
318-742-0546
800-227-3971
Shreve Systems is a very interesting "Mac Chop-Shop." You'll find excellent deals on new and used Mac logic boards, upgrades, and parts.

Shiva Corp.
155 Second St.
Cambridge, MA 02141
617-864-8500
Shiva manufactures high quality networking products such as NetModem.

Sunflower Repair
Overland Park, KS
913-681-3388
800-373-0611
Sunflower repair is a first rate service company that specializes in laser printer repair. It also sells repair parts for laser printers.

Symantec Corp.
10201 Torre Ave.
Cupertino, CA 95014
408-253-9600
800-441-7234
Symantec manufactures and distributes excellent Macintosh utilities, including the Norton Utilities.

Techni-Tool
5 Apollo Rd.
P.O. Box 368
Plymouth Meeting, PA 19462
215-941-2400
Techni-Tool is an excellent supplier of quality tools, test instruments, computer cleaning, and maintenance supplies.

Traveling Software
18702 N. Creek Pkwy.
Bothwell, WA 98011
206-483-8088
800-662-2652
Traveling Software manufactures an excellent product called LapLink Mac.

Soft Solutions
907 River Road, #98
Eugene, OR 97404
503-461-1136
Soft Solutions carries a variety of hard-to-get items, such as 800K and 1.44 MB Superdrive repair parts. The company also stocks Macintosh components.

Sound Technology
1020 S. E. Everett Mall Way
Everett, WA 98208
206-348-9322
Sound Technology is a component level repair company that specializes in Mac logic boards and other difficult repairs.

Macintosh Error Codes

The following pages contain a detailed list of the most current Macintosh System Error Codes. You may be familiar with many of these. Your best bet in dealing with these codes is to write down the error that you get and use the techniques described in Chapter 2 to troubleshoot the problem. System Errors, General System Errors, and many of the codes are preceded with an "Id=XXX" syntax, where "XXX" is one of the codes listed herein. Other error codes not preceded by "ID=XXX," which are less common, have been included as well.

Code	System Errors
1	Bus error
2	Address error
3	Illegal instruction error
4	A zero divide error
5	Check trap error
6	Overflow trap error
7	Privilege violation error
8	Trace mode error
9	Line 1010 trap error
10	Line 1111 trap error
11	A misc. hardware exception error
12	Unimplemented core routine error
13	Uninstalled interrupt error
14	I/O core error
15	Segment load error
16	Floating point error

17	Package 0 not present (List Manager)
18	Package 1 not present (Reserved for Apple)
19	Package 2 not present (Disk INIT)
20	Package 3 not present (Standard File)
21	Package 4 not present (Floating Point)
22	Package 5 not present (Transcendental Function)
23	Package 6 not present (International Utilities)
24	Package 7 not present (Binary-Decimal Conversion)
25	Out of memory
26	Cannot launch a file
27	File system map trashed
28	Stack had moved into application heap
30	Reinsert off-line volume
31	Incorrect disk
33	ZCBFree has gone negative
40	Welcome to Macintosh greeting
41	Can't load the Finder
42	Handled like a shutdown error
43	Can't find system file to open
51	Unserviceable slot interrupt
81	Bad opcode given to sane pack 4
84	Happens when a menu is purged
85	System error - Can't find MBDF
86	System error - Recursively defined HMenus
87	Can't load WDEF
88	Can't load CDEF
89	Can't load MDEF
98	Can't patch for particular model Mac
99	Can't load patch resource
101	Memory parity error
102	System is too old for current ROM
103	Booting in 32-bit on a 24-bit machine

20000	User choice Shut Down/Restart
20001	User choice Switch Off/Restart
20002	Allow user to exit-to-shell, return if cancel
32767	General system error

General System Errors

0	No error *or*
0	No truncation necessary
-1	Queue element not found during deletion *or*
-1	Truncation indicator is wider than specified width
-2	Invalid queue element
-3	Core routine number out of range
-4	Unimplemented core routine
-5	Invalid queue element
-8	No debugger installed to handle debugger command

Color Manager Errors

-9	From Color2Index/I Tabmatch
-10	From Color2Index/I Tabmatch
-11	From Make I table
-12	From Make I table
-13	From Make I table
-14	From Make I table
-15	From set entry
-16	From set entry
-17	From set entry
-18	From set entry
-19	From set entry
-20	From set entry
-21	From set entry

Code	I/O System Errors
-17	Driver can't respond to control call
-18	Driver can't respond to status call
-19	Driver can't respond to read call
-20	Driver can't respond to write call
-21	Driver reference number doesn't match unit table
-22	Driver reference number specifies nil handle in unit table
-23	Requested read/write permission doesn't match driver's open permission, *or*
-23	Attempt to open RAM serial driver failed
-24	Close failed; permission to close MPP drive denied
-25	Tried to remove an open driver
-26	DRVRInstall couldn't find driver in resources
-27	Bad I/O call
-28	Couldn't RD/WR/CNTRL/STS - Driver not opened
-29	Unit table has no more entries
-30	DCE extension error

Code	File System Errors
-33	Directory full
-34	Disk full
-35	No such volume; volume not found
-36	I/O error
-37	Bad file name
-38	File not open
-39	End of file, no additional data in the format
-40	Tried to position before start of file (R/W)
-41	Memory full (Open) or file won't fit (Load)

-42	Too many files open
-43	File not found; folder not found; edition container not found; target not found
-44	Disk is write protected; volume is locked through hardware; file is locked
-45	Publisher writing to an edition
-46	Volume is locked through software
-47	File is busy (delete); section doing I/O
-48	Duplicate filename (rename); file found instead of folder
-49	File already open with write permission
-50	Error in user parameter list
-51	Reference number invalid
-52	Get file position error
-53	Volume is off line
-54	Software lock in on file, not a subscriber (permissions error on file open)
-55	Drive volume already on-line at MOUNTVOL
-56	No such drive (tried to mount a bad drive #)
-57	Not a Mac disk
-58	External file system (file identifier is non-zero)
-59	File system internal error; during rename the old entry was deleted but could not be restored
-60	Bad master directory block
-61	Write permissions error; not a publisher

Code	Font Manager Errors
-64	Error during font declaration
-65	Font not declared
-66	Font substitution occurred

Code	Disk, Serial Ports, Clock Specific Errors
-64	Drive not installed
-65	R/W requested for an off-line drive
-66	Couldn't find 5 nibbles in 200 tries
-67	Couldn't find valid address mark
-68	Read verify compare failed
-69	Address mark CHECKSUM didn't check
-70	Bad address mark bit slip nibbles
-71	Couldn't find a data mark header
-72	Bad data mark CHECKSUM
-73	Bad data mark bit slip nibbles
-74	Write underrun occurred
-75	Step handshake failed
-76	Track 0 detect doesn't change
-77	Unable to initialize IWM
-78	Tried to read 2nd side on a one-sided drive
-79	Unable to correctly adjust disk speed
-80	Track number wrong on address mark
-81	Sector number never found on a track
-82	Can't find track 0 after track format
-83	Improper sync
-84	Track failed to verify
-85	Unable to read same clock value twice
-86	Time written did not verify
-87	Parameter RAM did not read verify
-88	INITUTIL found the parameter RAM uninitialized
-89	SCC receiver error (framing, parity, OR)
-90	Break Received (SCC)

Code	Appletalk Errors
-91	Error opening socket *or*
-91	Invalid address *or*
-91	Table is full
-92	Date length too big *or*

-92	Packet too large *or*
-92	First entry of the WriteData structure did not contain the full 14-byte header
-93	No router available (for noon-local send)
-94	Error in attaching detaching protocol, *or*
-94	Protocol handler is already attached, node's protocol table is full, protocol not attached, *or*
-94	Protocol handler pointer was not 0
-95	Hardware error (excessive collisions on write)
-97	Driver open error code (port is in use)
-98	Driver open error code (parameter RAM not configured for this connection)
-99	Hard error in ROZ
-99	Soft error in ROZ

Code	**Scrap Manager Errors**
-100	No scrap exists error
-102	Format not available (no object of that type in scrap)

Code	**Storage Allocator Errors**
-108	Ran out of memory (not enough room in heap zone)
-109	Get-Handle-Size fails on BaseText or SubstitutionText; nil Master Pointer (handle was nil in HandleZone or other)
-110	Address was odd, or out of range
-111	Attempted to operate on a free blick, Get-Handle-Size fails on BaseText or SubstitutionText ((which zone failed (applied to free block))
-112	Trying to purge a locked or non-purgeable block
-113	Address in zone check failed

-114	Pointer check failed
-115	Block check failed
-116	Size check failed
-117	Trying to move a locked block (MOVEHHI)

Code	**HFS Errors**
-120	Directory not found
-121	No free WDCB available
-122	Move into offspring error
-123	Not an HFS volume
-124	Server volume has been disconnected
-125	Insufficient memory to update a PIXMAP
-127	Internal file system error

Code	**Menu Manager Errors**
-126	System error code for MBDF not found
-127	Could not find HMENU's parent in MENUKEY
-128	User cancelled an operation

Code	**HFS File ID Errors**
-130	No file thread exists
-131	Directory specified
-132	File ID already exists

Code	**Color QuickDraw and Color Manager Errors**
-147	Region too big or complex
-148	Pixel map record is deeper than 1 bit per pixel
-149	Not enough stock space for the necessary buffers *or*
—149	Insufficient stock
-150	Color2Index failed to find an index
-151	Failed to allocate memory for temporary structures
-152	Failed to allocate memory for structure
-153	Range error on ColorTable request

-154	ColorTable entry protection violation
-155	Invalid type of graphics device
-156	Invalid resolution for MAKE I table
-157	Invalid pixel depth
-158	Invalid parameter

Code	Resource Manager Errors (Other Than I/O)
-185	Extended resource has bad format
-186	Resource bent can't decompress a compressed resource
-188	Resource already in memory
-189	Writing past end of file
-190	Offset or count out of bounds
-192	Resource not found
-193	Resource file not found
-194	AddResource failed
-195	AddReference failed
-196	RMVEResource failed
-197	RMVEReference failed
-198	Attribute inconsistent with operation
-199	Map inconsistent with operation

Code	Sound Manager Errors
-200	Required sound hardware not available (no hardware support for the specified synthesizer)
-201	Insufficient hardware available (no more channels for the specified synthesizer)
-203	No room in the queue
-204	Problem loading the resource
-205	Channel is corrupt or unstable (invalid channel queue length)
-206	Resource is corrupt or unstable
-207	Insufficient memory available
-208	The file is corrupt or unusable; or not AIFF or AIFF-C

-209	The channel is busy
-210	The buffer is too small
-211	The channel is not currently being used
-212	Not enough CPU time is available
-213	A parameter is not correct
-220	No sound input hardware is present or available
-221	Invalid sound input device
-222	No buffer has been specified
-223	Invalid compression type
-224	The hard drive is too slow to record
-225	Invalid sampling rate
-226	Invalid sampling size
-227	The sound input defice is busy
-228	An invalid device name
-229	An invalid reference number
-230	Aninput device hardware failure
-231	An unknown type of information
-232	An unknown quality

Code	**MIDI Manager Errors**
-250	No client with that ID has been found
-251	No port withthat ID has been found
-252	Too many ports are currently installed in the system
-253	Too many connections have been made
-254	Pending virtual connection created
-255	Pending virtualconnection resolved
-256	Pending virtual connection removed
-257	No connection exists between the specified ports
-258	Could not write to all of the specified ports
-259	The name supplied is longer than 31 characters
-260	A duplicate client ID
-261	Command not supported for the port type

Code	Notification Manager Error
-299	Invalid (Q)Type must be OR'D (NMType)

Code	Start Manager Errors
-290	SDM could not be initialized
-291	The slot resource table could not be initialized
-292	The slot resource table could not be initialized
-293	Expansion cards could not be initialized
-300	No expansion card present in slot
-301	CRC check failed for slot declaration data
-302	FHeader format is not a valid Apple format
-303	Incorrect revision level
-304	Directory offset = nil
-305	The long word test field <> $5A932BC7
-306	No (S) info array; memory manager error
-307	A fatal reserved error; the reserved field <>0
-308	An unexpected Bus error
-309	The byte lanes field was bad
-310	An error occurred during (S)Get-F-FHeader
-311	An error occurred during (S)Dispose-PTR (dispose of the F-Header block)
-312	Dispose pointer error
-313	No board (S) resources
-314	An error occurred during (S)Get-Pram-Rec (See SIM-status)
-315	No board ID located
-316	The INIT-Status-V field was negative after the primary or secondary INIT
-317	An error occurred while attempting the slot resource table
-318	A SDM table could not be created

-319	The board ID was wrong; re-initialize the Pram Record
-320	Bus error time-out
-330	Reference ID was not found in the list
-331	Bad (S)Resource S-List; structure bad ID1<ID2<ID3 type format is not being followed
-332	Reserved field was not zero
-333	The code revision is wrong
-334	The code revision is wrong
-335	The L-Pointer is = Nil (from (S)Offset-Data) If this error has occurred, check (S)Info record for additional info
-336	(S) BLock = Nil error (Do not attempt to allocate and use an (S) Block = Nil
-337	The slot is out of bounds
-338	The selector is out of bounds; this function is not implemented
-339	New-PTR error
-340	Block-move error
-341	Status of the slot has failed
-342	An error has occurred during (S)Get-DRVR-Name
-343	An error has occurred during (S)Dis-DRVR-Name
-344	No additional resources or the specified (S)Resource data structures were not found
-345	An error occurred during (S)Get-Driver
-346	Bad pointer had been passed to (S)Cald-S-Pointer function
-347	The Byte-lanes field in the expansion cards format block was determined to be zero
-348	The offset was too big
-349	No opens were successful in the loop

-350	SRT over-flow
-351	The record was not found in the SRT
	Device manager slot-support errors
-360	Invalid slot number error
-400	A GCR format on high density media error

Code	**Edition Manager Errors**
-450	The manager was not initialized package, could not be loaded
-451	Not a valid section type
-452	Not registered
-454	A bad edition container spec or invalid edition container
-460	Multiple publishers; already a publisher
-461	Container not found; the alias was not resolved
-463	Not the publisher

	SCSI Manager Errors
-470	Invalid field in SCSI parameter block
-471	Over-run error; an attempt was made to transfer too many bytes
-472	Transfer error; a write flag conflicts with data transfer phase
-473	SCSI Bus error during transfer
-474	Selection failed; SCSI Sel-to-Err exceeded
-475	ACSI time-out error; SCSI Req-To exceeded
-476	SCSI Bus was reset, the request was aborted
-477	A non-zero (SCSI Bad) status was returned
-478	The device did not go through the status phase
-479	The SCSI link command was never executed
-489	An unimplemented routine was called

Code	SYS-ERR's That Are Used Instead of Inline $A9FF & $ABFF
-490	A user debugger break
-491	A user debugger break; display string on stack
-492	User debugger break; execute the commands on the stack

Code	Quick-Draw Error
-500	The bit-map would convert and occupy a region greater than 64KB

Code	Text Edit Error
-501	The scrap item is too big for the text edit record

Code	Misc. O/S Error
-502	Selector for the HW-Priv-Bad

Code	Misc. Process Errors
-600	Not found; there is no eligible process with a specified process serial number
-601	Memory fragmentation error; there is not enough room to launch an application
-602	Application mode error; the memory mode is 32-bit, however, the application is not 32-bit clean
-603	Protocol error; an application made calls in an improper order
-604	Hardware configuration error
-605	Application memory full error; partition size specified in resource not big enough to launch the application
-606	Application is background only
-607	The buffer is too small
-608	No outstanding high level event

| -609 | The connection is invalid |
| -610 | No user interaction allowed; an attempt at a post-high-level-event from background was made without an established session |

Code	**Memory Dispatch Errors**
-620	Not enough physical memory
-621	The specified range of memory is not held
-622	Cannot make the specified range of memory contiguous
-623	The specified range of memory is not locked
-624	A call was made while interrupts were masked
-625	Cannot defer additional user instructions

Code	**Pack 13 - Database Access Errors**
-800	Data item was = Null
-801	The data is received/available
-802	Error while executing a function
-803	Bad type; the next data item is not the requested data type
-804	The function has timed out
-805	The query is currently executing
-806	The session ID is invalid
-807	Invalid session number
-808	Specified database extension not found and/or an error occurred while opening the database
-809	Asynchronous calls are not supported by this database
-810	An invalid asynchronous parameter block has been specified
-811	No handler for this data type installed for the current application

| -812 | Wrong version number |
| -813 | The DB-Pack function has not been called/initiated |

Code	**Help Manager (HM) Errors**
-850	Help balloons are disabled
-851	HM resource not found
-852	HM memory full error
-853	HM balloon aborted; due to cursor movement the help balloon was not displayed
-854	Current menu and item are the same as the previous menu and item
-855	The help manager has not been set up
-856	HM bad selector
-857	HM skipped balloon; no balloon contents to fill in
-858	The wrong version of a HM resource
-859	The help message record contained an unknown help type
-860	HM could not load the package
-861	This operation is not supported; bad parameter
-862	No balloon up (displayed)
-863	Close view will not permit the user to remove the balloon

Code	**Appletalk (PPC Toolbox) Errors**
-900	The PPC Toolbox has not been initialized
-902	Invalid location-kind-selector in the location name
-903	No port; invalid port name; bad port preference
-904	The system is unable to allocate memory
-905	Network activity disabled
-906	Destination port does not exist
-907	The PPC Toolbox unable to create a session

-908	Invalid session reference number
-909	Bad request; bad parameter for this operation
-910	This port name already exists
-911	No user name (unknown) at destination
-912	Session request rejected at destination
-915	No response from application
-916	Port closed
-917	Session closed
-919	PPC Port record invalid
-922	Ownername not specified during sharing setup
-923	Default user reference number does not exist
-924	Unable to create a new user reference number
-925	Network error
-926	No information error; PPC start failed
-927	Incorrect password
-928	Invalid user reference number
-930	Bad service method; not a PPC real time service method
-931	The location name is bad or invalid
-932	Guests not allowed; destination port requires user authentication

Code	**Appletalk (NBP Errors)**
-1024	Buffer overflow in the Look-Up-Name
-1025	Name has not been confirmed for Confirm-Name
-1026	The name has been confirmed at a different socket
-1027	Duplicate name
-1028	Name not found
-1029	NIS open error

ASP Errors (XPP Drivers)

-1066	The server does not support this version of ASP
-1067	The buffer is too small
-1068	No more server sessions
-1069	No servers at this address
-1070	Parameter error
-1071	The server is busy and cannot open another session
-1072	Session closed
-1073	Size error; the command block is too big
-1074	Server error; too many clients
-1075	Server error; no acknowledgement to an attention request

Code	Appletalk (ATP Errors)
-1096	Router request failed; retry count exceeded
-1097	Too many concurrent requests
-1098	Too many concurrent sockets responding
-1099	Bad ATP responding socket
-1100	Bad response buffer specified
-1101	Release not received
-1102	Control block not found
-1103	Add-Response issued without Send-Response
-1104	No data error for request to MPP

Code	Data Stream Protocol (DSP Driver Errors)
-1273	Open request denied
-1274	Send/Receive queue size is too small
-1275	A read has been terminated by forward reset
-1276	Attention message too long
-1277	Error while attempting to open a connection
-1278	State error for this connection

-1279	Request aborted by either DSP-Remove or DSP-Close function
-1280	Reference for this connection is bad

Code	HFS Errors
-1300	File thread does not exist; file ID not found
-1301	File ID exists
-1302	File error; specified file is a directory not a file
-1303	The files are on different volumes
-1304	The catalog has been changed and the CAT-position might be invalid
-1305	The desktop has been damaged or corrupted

Code	Apple-Event Errors
-1700	Data coercion has failed; data could not be coerced to requested descriptor type
-1701	Descriptor record not found
-1702	Apple event data could not be found
-1703	Incorrect descriptor type
-1704	Invalid descriptor record
-1705	Bad list item; operation failed
-1706	Version of Apple Event Manager is out-dated; replace with newer version
-1707	Not an Apple Event
-1708	Event not handled by an Apple Event Handler
-1709	The AE-Reset-Timer was passed an invalid reply
-1710	Invalid send mode was passed
-1711	Wait loop for reply cancelled
-1712	Apple event timed out
-1713	No user interaction permitted
-1714	Not a special function; incorrect keyword
-1715	Handler missed parameters

-1716	Unknown Apple address type
-1717	Handler not found for an Apple Event
-1718	A reply has not arrived
-1719	Illegal list index

Code	**Appletalk (ATP Errors)**
-3101	Packet too large for buffer; partial data returned
-3102	No MPP error
-3103	Check-Sum error
-3104	Extraction error
-3105	Read queue error
-3106	ATP length record
-3107	ATP bad response record
-3108	Record not found
-3109	Closed socket error

Code	**Print Manager with Apple Laserwriter Errors**
-4096	No free connect control blocks available
-4097	Bad connection reference number
-4098	Request already active
-4099	Write request too big
-4100	Connection closed
-4101	Printer could not be found or closed
-5000	Access denied for this file
-5006	Permission and Deny Mode conflicts for the mode in which the current fork has been opened
-5015	No more locks; byte range locking failure from the server
-5020	An attempt has been made to unlock an already locked range
-5021	An attempt has been made to lock an already locked range

APPENDIX B: MACINTOSH ERROR CODES

Code	AFP Errors (XPP Drivers)
-5000	AFP access denied
-5001	AFP authorization continued
-5002	AFP bad UAM
-5003	AFP bad version number
-5004	AFP bit map error
-5005	AFP can't move error
-5006	AFP deny conflict
-5007	AFP directory not empty
-5008	AFP disk full
-5009	AFP end of file error
-5010	AFP file busy
-5011	AFP flat volume
-5012	AFP information not found
-5013	AFP lock error
-5014	AFP miscellaneous error
-5015	AFP no more locks
-5016	AFP no server
-5017	AFP object already exists
-5018	AFP object not found
-5019	AFP parameter error
-5020	AFP range not locked
-5021	AFP range overlap
-5022	AFP session closed
-5023	AFP user not authorized
-5024	AFP call not supported
-5025	AFP object type error
-5026	AFP too many files open
-5027	AFP server going down
-5028	AFP cannot rename
-5029	AFP directory not found
-5030	New icon size/type error
-5031	Volume is read-only
-5032	An object is M/R/D/W locked

Code	Sys-Environs Errors
-5500	SYS-Environs Trap is not present
-5501	Bad version
-5502	The version is larger than the call handle

Code	Gestalt Errors
-5550	Unknown error; no response
-5551	Undefined selector
-5552	Selector already exists
-5553	Gestalt location error; laserwriter driver errors; function not loaded in system heap
-8132	Manual feed time out error
-8133	General Postscript error
-8150	No Laserwriter selected
-8151	Laser-prep dictionary error; version mismatch
-8150	No Laser-Prep dictionary installed
-8160	The zoom scale is out of range

Code	Power Manager Errors
-13000	The Power Manager is stuck busy
-13001	Time out while waiting to begin a reply handshake
-13002	The Power Manager did not start a handshake
-13003	During a send, the Power Manager did not handshake
-13004	During a receive, the Power Manager did not initiate a handshake
-13005	During a receive, the Power Manager did not complete a handshake

Code	Mac TCP Errors
-23000	Bad network configuration
-23001	Bad IP configuration error
-23002	Missing IP or LAP configuration
-23003	Error in Mac-TCP load
-23004	Error in getting an address
-23005	A connection is closing
-23006	Invalid length
-23007	Connection already exists; request conflicts
-23008	Connection does not exist
-23009	Insufficient resources to perform the request
-23010	Invalid stream
-23011	Stream already open
-23012	Invalid BUF-PTR
-23014	Invalid RDS
-23014	Invalid WDS
-23015	Open failed
-23016	Command time-out
-23017	Duplicate socket exists
-23030	Cannot open new protocol
-23031	Cannot locate protocol to close
-23032	Packet too large to send without fragmentation
-23033	The destination is not responding
-23034	Error in WDS format
-23035	ICMP echo time-out
-23036	No memory to send fragmented packet
-23037	Cannot route the packet off the network
-23041	Name syntax error
-23042	Cache fault error
-23043	No result
-23044	No name server
-23045	Auth-name error
-23046	No answer error

-23047	DNR error
-23048	Out of memory

Code	**Primary or Secondary INIT Code Errors**
-32768	Temporarily disable the card but run the primary INIT
-32640	Errors -32640 to -32768 are reserved for future internal file system errors
1	No available cache buffers
2	Requested block in use
3	Requested block not found
4	The block being released was not in use
16	The file position was beyond the mapped range
17	Extents file overflow
32	Record was not found
33	Record already exists
34	No available space
35	Record does not fit the node
36	Bad node detected
37	Bad B-Tree header encountered
48	C-Node not found
49	C-Node already exists
50	Directory C-Node not empty
51	Invalid reference to the root
52	Bad news on catalog structure
53	Thread to directory error
54	File thread does not exist
64	Bad B-tree rotate

Code	**Slot Declaration (SDM) ROM Manager Errors**
1	Slot dispatch table could not be initialized
2	VBL queues for all slots could not be initialized

3	Slot priority table could not be initialized
10	SDM jump table could not be initialized
11	SDM could not be intialized
12	Slot resource table not initialized
13	Slot PRAM could not be initialized
14	Expansion cards could not be initialized

Code	HD-20 Driver Errors
16	Handshake went low before starting
17	Timeout waiting for the handshake to go low
19	Timeout waiting for the handshake to go high
32	Handshake went high before starting
33	Timeout waiting for sync bytes
34	Timeout waiting for group
36	Timeout waiting for sync buffer hold-off
37	Timeout waiting for the handshake to go high
38	Check-Sum error on response packet
48	The first byte in the response packet is wrong
49	Sequence number in the response packet is wrong
50	Drive number in the response packet is wrong
64	No response packet was received

Code	SCSI Manager Errors
2	Communications error; timeout
3	Bus busy; arbitration failed druing a SCSI "Get" operation
4	Bad parameter
5	SCSI Bus not in correct phase for operation

6	SCSI Manager is busy; SCSI-Get was called
7	SCSI Manager was busy when SCSI-Get was called
8	SCSI sequence error
9	SCSI Bus timeout error before data was ready
10	Complete phase error; SCSI Bus not in status phase

Code	Serial Driver Errors
1	Serial overrun error
16	Serial parity error
32	Serial hardware overrun
64	Serial framing error

Code	Miscellaneous Result Code
1	Event not enabled at Post-Event

Code	CDEV Errors
0	Memory error
1	Resource missing error
3	CDEV value is unset
-1	General CDEV error

Code	Script Manager (SM) Errors
0	SM not truncated error
1	Truncation was performed
-1	SM general error

Code	Communication Toolbox Errors
0	No error
-1	General communcation toolbox error

Code	Communication Resource Manager Errors
0	No error
-1	CRM generic error

APPENDIX B: MACINTOSH ERROR CODES

Code	Communication Manager (CM) Errors
0	No error
1	CM rejected
2	CM failed
3	CM timeout
4	CM not open
5	CM not closed
6	No request pending
7	CM not supported
8	No CM tools
9	User cancelled request
11	Unknown error
-1	Generic error

Code	File Transfer (FT) Manager Errors
0	No error
1	FT rejected
2	FT failed
3	FT timeout error
4	Too many retries
5	Not enough space
6	Remote cancel
7	Wrong format
8	No FT tools
9	User cancelled request
10	Not supported
11	Unknown error
-1	Generic error

Code	MIDI Manager & Packet Errors
1	MIDI overflow error
2	MIDI SCC error
3	MIDI packet error
255	MIDI-MAX error

Code	Terminal Manager Errors
0	No error
1	Not sent
2	Environ(s) has changed
7	Not supported
8	No tools
11	Unknown error
-1	Generic error

Code	Additional Appletalk Errors
-1	Overrun error ReadRest routines)
-2	CRC error
-3	Underrun error
-4	Length error

Index